York in the Great War

1914 to 1918

A. J. Peacock

YORK SETTLEMENT TRUST

YORK IN THE GREAT WAR : 1914-18
VOLUME TWO OF A
HISTORY OF YORK
FROM 1900 TO 1918

Keyed in by	PIP STEVENS
Cover design and drawing by	BRIAN KESTEVEN
Photographs by	ALAN GEBBIE
Index compiled by	NICKY CUNNIFF

ISBN 0 9519229 1 2

Published (1993) by	The York Settlement Trust 126 Holgate Road York YO2 4DL
Printed by	G. H. Smith & Son The Printers Easingwold York YO6 3AB

FOREWORD

As with the first volume of this work I am extremely grateful to the Trustees of the York Settlement Trust for their help in producing this one. I am also deeply indebted to Brian Kesteven who designed the cover of Volume one and did the line drawings for it. He also designed the cover for this work and did the line drawing of Arnold Rowntree, taken from a family photograph. Alan Gebbie has helped me enormously over many years and he is responsible for the photographs, taken, as is noted elsewhere, from original newspaper sources which had usually deteriorated very badly over the last 75 years or so. I am deeply grateful, too, to Pip Stevens, who typed and prepared my manuscripts for publication and Nicky Cunniff, who arranged and typed the index for me. I hope all of them enjoy the book.

A.J. PEACOCK

ILLUSTRATIONS
(between pages 414-415)

1. Arnold Rowntree, a line drawing by Brian Kesteven from a family photograph.

2. An early patriotic advertisement.

3. Left, one of Lord Kitchener's appeals for volunteers. Right, an advertisement for one of the first war films to be shown in York.

4. One of George Coverdale's wartime advertisements.

5. Top row, Mrs Edwin Gray and Miss Edith Milner. Bottom row, Dr W.A. Evelyn and C.E. Elmhirst. Photographs taken from The York Historic Pageant Souvenir, 1909.

6. One of the York Zeppelin alarms.

7. Rowntree's advertisements illustrating how women took men's jobs as the war went on.

8. Two advertisements for popular war films.

9. Newspaper photographs published just after one of York's Zep raids.

10. 'HAXBY ROAD MILITARY HOSPITAL (Rowntree's Dining Block).'

11. Left, a Leak and Thorpe blackout advertisement. Right, Reg Smith had had several deferments, but the draft finally caught up with him.

12. The York NCF kept detailed records of its members' court appearances

------

Note. Most of the photographs have been copied from York newspapers of the 1914-18 period. Many of these were printed on very inferior paper and consequently have deteriorated very badly.

CONTENTS

VOLUME 2
YORK 1900 TO 1918

			Page
Chapter	10	The Outbreak	289
Chapter	11	Compulsion Coming ?	327
Chapter	12	The Blackout, Price Rises - and Drink	353
Chapter	13	1916, The Tribunals and Conscription	375
Chapter	14	Zeps and Films	421
Chapter	15	Allotments, Prices and Rationing	445
Chapter	16	Food Control and the End of the Party Truce	467
Chapter	17	The National Federation, the Comrades, and Thomas Raftery	493
Chapter	18	The Tribunals 1916-18	511
Index			540

CHAPTER 10

THE OUTBREAK

On Tuesday 5 August 1914 the York newspapers announced 'WAR DECLARED ON GERMANY' and four years of appalling sufferering were ushered in. It had been August Bank holiday week-end and, although it would be quite wrong to say that there had been a state of alarm in the last weeks of peace, there had been incidents enough to put those who thought about these things on the *qui vive*. These had not been enough to spoil the holiday - one of the very few that many got - but on 25 July the *Yorkshire Evening Press* had told its readers 'War Confronts Europe' and troop movements might have been taken to indicate that, this time, there really was something serious afoot. The West Riding Territorial Infantry Brigade was in camp on Scarborough race course - there was nothing alarming about this, it was a normal thing - but the 1st East Yorkshire Regiment, which had left the city for a two month stint at Llanidloes, had been recalled and was back in barracks at Fulford on 1 August. (1) Almost immediately many of its members left for Cottingham singing lustily, it was said, a song called 'The Army of to-day is all right.' The same paper which reported that fact (2) told its readers that the Scots Greys were still at the cavalry barracks in York and that the 3rd and 4th West Yorkshires (also recalled from Wales) were at Fulford. All government subsidised horses in the area had been called in and many sent off to unknown destinations, the army reserves had been called up and many were stationed in the city. Two hundred naval reserves were seen at York railway station en route for Chatham and pilots had left Montrose to await orders on the Knavesmire. Several of these (members of No 2 Squadron, RFC) were well-known in the city - the Knavesmire had been for sometime a regular stop-off point for aviators flying to and from Scotland.

The citizens of York may not have really believed that war would come, but, just in case, those who could afford it had engaged in an exercise of denuding the shops of everything edible they could lay their hands on. The *Press* of 1 August reported an unprecedented run on the grocers establishments and quoted W. Banks, of Banks and Company, provision dealers of Nessgate. He said that he had sold dozens of sides of bacon and around 400 hams at a time he would normally have expected to sell 30 or 40. Prices would undoubtedly rise, Banks said, and already flour was up from 1s.8d. to 1s.10d. a stone. The run on the shop, with people 'laying up' went on into the first days of the war, naturally, (3) but by the second week of the conflict the government had stepped in and fixed maximum prices for some food items including sugar, imported butter and colonial cheese. (4) This was a portent, it was also probably the beginning of a black market.

Another indication of unease amongst a population which nevertheless thought war would not come is the fact that early in the Bank Holiday it was reported that Scarborough had had 15,000 fewer visitors than usual. (5) The resort's business community would not have been helped by the fact that the North Eastern Railway cancelled all excursions and on the last day of peace the York papers reported an intensification of war preparations (just in case). There was tremendous activity involving the loading of military personnel and equipment at the old railway station at the foot of Lendal, it was recorded, and from this the public were forcibly kept away. The 5th West Yorkshires (Territorials) had been called from their camp at Scarborough and the St Peter's School Officers Training Corps camp at Rugeley had been broken up. York's schools were to be taken over as barracks, it was reported, and prominence was given to a government notice ordering all banks to remain closed on 4, 5 and 6 August. Strensall camp, it was noted, was deserted - all the members of the King's Own Yorkshire Light Infantry and the Notts and Derby regiment having left for Pontefract, Sheffield and Derby. The papers reporting all this would have finally shown that war really was near perhaps. Banner headlines on 4 August recorded the 'INVASION OF BELGIUM'.

York, in the first few weeks of the war, was to become crowded with servicemen, but it had been a garrison town for many years. Military establishments were supposed to have been created in York in the early years of the 18th century but in the 1790s land at Fulford had been purchased and the cavalry barracks which became such a prominent feature of the city were built and occupied in 1795. (6) Improvements were made to the site and it was enlarged during the 19th century. In 1854 a new military hospital was built, a church was built in 1867, 'and a prison in 1884; the prison accommodation was supplemented in 1900 when York castle was used for military prisoners.' In 1876 35 acres of land on the southern side of the cavalry barracks were purchased and infantry barracks built there, enabling the depot of the 2nd West York Light Infantry to be moved there from Lowther Street at the end of 1880. Two years before this the headquarters of the north-eastern military district moved from Manchester to York as a result of General Order No 97. In 1905 York became Headquarters of Northern Command, and when the war broke out the GOC was someone who was to become one of the most successful field commanders of the Great War. This was Lt General Sir Herbert Plumer. (7) Outside the city another large military camp was established at Strensall - with the 3rd West Yorkshire regiment stationed there by the mid '80s.

The columns of York's press on the day it reported the outbreak of the Great War, particularly the letter and advertisement columns, reveal much about what the city was like. There was a letter from Edith Milner, of Heworth Moor House, attacking the suffragettes (of all kinds). Edith was a 'bigoted political partisan', (8) the sister of a Tory MP and ex supremo of one of York's sections of the Primrose League (the Milner Habitation). Edith will feature prominently in the following pages of this work. Her letter about the women agitators of her time went as follows. (9)

> Will no one protest in the name of our common womanhood against the conduct of our Suffragettes ? That they have become a deadly peril to the national life has long been apparent, but when deputations of women, calling themselves non-militant, importune our King and Ministers with senseless petitions when the militants continue to endanger life and property, and when, as on Sunday last, they interrupt the solemn services in our churches, the women of England who deserve that noble title should rise in their millions and protest. I would venture to suggest that the Press should from henceforth ignore the Suffragettes in toto, neither publishing their letters nor describing their outrages.

Had Edith read the columns of (for instance) the *Press* of 4 August she would have seen that there were other things than politics to concern the women of York. Isaac Walton and Company, for example, had a clothing sale on. Walton's must have paid thousands of pounds to the local papers as they regularly took considerable space in them (and during the war used a drawing featuring what must the ugliest dog ever). Their sale of August 1914 offered men's straw hats to their customers at prices from 1s.3d. to 3s.6d. (compared with 1s.6d. to 4s.6d.); men's rain coats were on offer at 28s.11d; youth's trouser suits were down from 18s.11d. to 10s.6d.; and white cellular shirts had had 9d. knocked off them and were retailing at 2s.2d.

The fact that the motor age had arrived was demonstrated regularly in the press by letters of complaint about cars, accounts of accidents involving them, and court cases ending with fines for speeding. In mid August Robert O. Irwin Dees of Husthwaite was prosecuted for that other infuriating offence, obstructing the highway, when he was accused of leaving a car for 37 minutes in Coney Street opposite another one. Dees, a county magistrate of Northumberland and Berwickshire and a borough justice for Wallsend should have known better. He was proceeded against under the Highways Act of 1835 and was tried by two justices - a bad practice - who could not agree, and he got off. His trial was enlivened by the answer a policemen gave to a question from Norman Crombie, the prominent York lawyer. 'What was the distance between the cars ?', Crombie asked. To which the constable replied 'Thirteen and a-half feet by my feet, but I am 13 inches to the foot.' The *Press* of 5 August had a whole column of small ads devoted to motor cars and cycles. A Hobart two stroke, two and a quarter horse power motor cycle was offered at 25 guineas, and there was an ad for the kind of device which came to be very popular in this country in the late 1940s and early '50s.

HAVE YOU
seen the Little Auxiliary MOTORSET, The J.E.S., which fixes to any Ordinary Cycle, INSIDE THE FRAME ? The very latest. Easy to manage. Very light. Economical running. Come and try it. Sets from £12.12s.0d.
Sole District Agents.
BENSON'S For BIKES and Auxiliary
MOTOR SETS
51 & 53 LOWTHER-ST., YORK

The columns of the York papers also demonstrated the fact that society in 1914 was still one in which people usually treated themselves in times of illness, buying patent medicines or, sometimes, resorting to the quacks who abounded. Thomas Ison, Oculist, and Aurist of Ison's Eye and Ear Dispensary, Leeds, anounced that he would be visiting York and Scarborough, and at York would effect 'CURES WITHOUT OPERATION' on or for the 'DEAF AND BLIND'. Where were his clinics to be held ? At the Black Swan Public House! A more regular advertiser was the producer or retailer of Blanchard's Pills for Ladies. On 5 August he, or she, or they, announced that Blanchard's speedily afforded relief, and that 'They supercede[d] Pennyroyal, Pil Cochia, Bitter Apple &c.' They had competitors, however. 'SANTAL MID'Y', readers were told, was 'Superior to copaiba, Cubebs and Injections, and a Mrs Stakman Morris, of Stoke Newington Road, London, had what was said to be a useful product. So had a Mrs Ellis of Surrey Lane, Battersea. She was advertising 'Pills' which, she said, superseded 'ordinary apiol, pennyroyal, and steel &c.' What were all these things for ? Undoubtedly the producers would have said, in classic fashion, that they were 'cure-alls' like those sold by the medicine men of the Wild West, and that they were 'efficacious in everyway', like Lilian Pinkum's famous remedy. It is a fact, however, that many of the ingredients mentioned above were, or were reckoned to be, reliable abortificants.

Isaac Walton and Company were regular advertisers in the York papers, and so too was the firm of George Coverdale, of Parliament Street. They were chemists. They had a complete range of services from dentistry (and the making of dental plates - you got the tooth extracted free if you had the falsie afterwards) to sure-fire cures for piles. On the day war was announced they advertised a product which would have been useful in York's slum areas. This was KILLO, which no-one living in some of the places described by Seebohm Rowntree in his book *Poverty* should have been without. Coverdales were rapidly into 'war' advertising, recommending products as useful aids to the young men who were soon flocking to the colours. Many men were being turned down for the Army because of bad teeth they said - which was true. Have them out at special prices at Coverdales and get in they suggested. Foot ointments of various kinds were advertised in this way (Tiz was the most popular) and E.J. Wood announced one for sale on 5 August - and in doing so explained a trick of the trade of the charlatan.

IN OLDEN TIMES

quack doctors trod on the feet of men in a crowd to find if they had corns. We chemists don't do that. Cure yours with Magical Corn Silk, 7d., from my pharmacy.

E.J. Wood, Chemist, 69 Bootham, York.

Coverdales, naturally, sold Corn Salve and what looked like a splendid Antiseptic Foot powder. It was recommended at the end of August for various groups, (10)

TERRITORIALS, Have you tender feet ?
SCOUTS, Have you tender feet ?
PEDESTRIANS, of all occupations, have you tender feet ?

A little earlier than this George Coverdale had noted that run on the food shops and the possible need for substitutes. 'USE SACCHARIN AND SAVE YOUR SUGAR BILL' he recommended. (11) The first trader to really incorporate politics into his advertising, however, seems to have been a butcher. The following appeared in the *Press* of 14 August.

NOTICE
Swales' Meat stores
Notice!
During the war we have contracted with a *British* firm to supply our Customers with *British* meat brought from our Colonies in *British* Ships at Prices very little above our Ordinary Charges.

York was liberally endowed with places of entertainment and the Theatre Royal was playing 'The Story of the Rosary', when war started, which does not look the most enthralling fare, but had 'Charley's Aunt' booked for the following week. The Empire was more down market, a music hall, playing twice nightly, and in that first week of war Fred Keeton and Alfredo topped the bill, with, lower down the bill, 'VERA AND SID' and 'LE ORIGINAL PERCIVALY', who must have been really something.

The Empire always included films in its programme, but York had no less than four permanent cinemas. The Electric, in Fossgate, was one of the newest of these and another was The Hippodrome, where 'All the Pictures [were] accompanied by the Hippodrome Orchestra.' The Victoria Hall was run by an enterprising businessman called Bert Rutter, also active in the York City Football Club, and, in the first week of the war, charging popular prices of 2d., 3d. and 6d., he was showing 'The Master Crook turns Detective' ('A detective story which holds the interest throughout') and 'The Stolen Code' ('An exciting story of the Diplomatic Service'). The City Picture Palace, Fishergate, which had been a roller skating rink during the short lived craze for that pastime, was showing 'The White Lie' in three parts, a film by William le Queux. This was accompanied by 'The Frenzy of Fire Water', 'The Lovesick Maids of Cuddleton' and 'The Story of an Equine Spy'. William le Queux was an author who had written much about the possibility of impending war incidentally. (12) At the time that his work was showing in York two other cinemas were applying for certificates or being built, one in Coney Street, the other in Skeldergate.

When war was declared York went into a turmoil, and nothing caused greater annoyance and upset than the commandering of horses for the forces. The government subsidised animals were called up just before the outbreak of hostilities, as has been mentioned, but by the end of the first week of the war officers were reported to be scouring the countryside for animals. (13) A day after this was reported farm rulleys were stopped in Blossom Street, the horses taken, the money for them paid over, and the drivers left high and dry. (14) These actions, which caused great chaos in the countryside, led an enterprising York businessman to insert an advertisement in the *Herald* headed 'COMMANDERING OF HORSES'. Use the motor vans of 9.5 horse power he stocked instead, he said. They could be obtained for £185 from Myers and Burnett of the Davygate Garage.

The farmers' problems, made serious by the taking of their horses, were made worse by the number of farm hands who left to join up. Lord Kitchener's famous poster 'Your King and Country Needs You', asking for volunteers between 19 and 30 years of age, appeared in the columns of the York papers on 8 August. Two days before this the executive of the Yorkshire Farm Workers' Union called off a strike they had planned before harvest, (15) the Wagoner's Special Reserve was mobilized and passed through York ('a grand set-up body of men') (16), and there was a rush to join Viscount Helmsley's Foreign Service Contingent of the Yorkshire Hussars. (17 Many country lads flocked into York to join up at one of the two recruiting stations, where they still had an opportunity to join a regiment of their choice. Their numbers made the overall figures enlisting look good, but under close scrutiny they were not a matter of pride for the civic dignitaries of Old Ebor. Recruits were coming forward 'by the hundred' it was reported on the last day of August, and by then the chaos of the last few weeks had been overcome. The officers and clerks, a report said, 'Have reduced the work of attestation and acceptation to a science, taking an incredible length of time, and they cannot keep up with the influx of volunteers for service.' (18) That may have been so, but five days earlier a similar report had looked closely at the figures. Then there had been an average enlistment of 34 men a day for 'Lord Kitchener's special army', it was said. 'These are excellent figures,' the report went on, 'but the city of York can take little credit for them, as more than 93 per cent of the enlistments emanate from outside the boundaries. York itself is reputed to be one of the most difficult in England for obtaining recruits.' (19)

Responsible opinion in York (not always among those of military age it should be pointed out) took unkindly to young men (and not so young men) being unwilling to offer themselves for slaughter. What could be done ? One suggestion was that York should try to raise a Pal's battalion of the kind being raised elsewhere, (20) and some inducements were offered. At the end of August a big meeting was held at the Guildhall at which a recruiting committee was created. Newbald Kay, a Methodist solicitor who had been prominent as a rates resister in the aftermath of the passing of Balfour's Education Act, spoke of the apathy that he said prevailed in York. Alderman Birch declared that until recently he had been effectively 'a peace-at-any-price man', but now supported the war effort, and J.G. Butcher dangled a carrot before the young men of his city. Butcher was one of York's two Members of Parliament (the Tory) and he said that he had been authorised to say that 'one interested in York ... will pay during the continuance of the war 10s. per week to the wives of the first fifty men who join Lord Kitchener's Army from Monday.' (21) The general opinion then was that the war would be a short one, and the generous donor may have thought so. If so he would have had a rude shock, and his promise would have cost him something like £5,000. The first person to qualify for a chunk of this was A.G. Barclay of 13, Wilson's Yard, Layerthorpe, (22) possibly the pre-war militant painter.

There was very genuine concern among prospective volunteers in York about their jobs and their families - and this undoubtedly had an affect on recruiting, as contemporaries realised. Agricultural labourers, it was pointed out, hired then under a yearly contract, were being held back by the fact that they risked losing almost a year's wages by joining up, (23) and many townspeople were being held back by fear about their jobs. Would they get them back when the war ended ? And what would happen to their families ? (24) Their fears might well have been fired by the comments at a meeting held in York by Major General Baldock. There were many men 'off the strength', Baldock said, and 'the Government did not recognise them at all' and 'they often suffered.' Territorial army wives, he pointed out, got separation allowances, but there would be suffering if the TA went overseas - at present, he concluded, though, they were to remain at home. It is a fact, however, that a 'large percentage of TA members volunteered for service abroad, and the first Territorial units of the British Army were with the BEF in France before the end of 1914. (25)

Anxious to do their bit (and probably not thinking too far ahead) many local employers of labour acted to relieve would-be recruits of worries about their families and their jobs. The firm of Henry Leetham, flour millers, notified the local branch of the Soldiers and Sailors Association, in mid-August, that their men who joined up would get full wages (by which they meant the soldiers pay would be enhanced to his peacetime wage) 'during the war.' (26) Rowntree and Company were pressed to say what they would do (and were doing) and they made a statement on 16 August. Rowntrees, the statement said, would see that all families affected by the enlistment of an employee would be 'looked after' at least until the end of the year; that jobs would be kept open for all their reservists and TA men; and that all pension premiums would be paid. (27) In early September it was announced that the directors of the NER had applied to the Secretary of State for War asking for permission to recruit an NER battalion. Already, they said, some 3,500 of their employees had joined up and men were leaving still to do so at the rate of 150 to 200 a day. (All these had been offered good terms.) (28) Now they wanted about 1,100 for the new unit and they promised recruits that: full salaries would be paid (or army pay made up) to the 'end of the current pay period'; that there would be adequate provision for families (the company would supplement the separation allowance a family was entitled to to four fifths of his salary when he left); that jobs - or job equivalents - would be kept open; that pension costs would be paid by the NER; and that families could still occupy company houses. (29) A little later it was announced that recruiting of officers for the NER battalion (to be in the Northumberland Fusiliers) would open at York and Newcastle, and that the men would be trained at Hull. (30) By 24 September it was reported that 5,000 NER men had joined up - 1,100 in the now completed NER battalion, of which Colonel D'Arcy B. Preston of Askham Bryan, 'late of the Garrison Artillery', was temporary colonel. (31)

The generous gesture of Leethams, Rowntrees and the NER would have meant great expenditure (recouped by higher prices maybe) but individuals made similar moves. The anonymous 'donor' described by J.G. Butcher has been mentioned. Another patriot from Askham Richard - W.F. Wailes - Fairburn - offered bounties to his men for volunteering either for overseas or home service. (32) The following appeared in the papers

NOTICE

It is the duty of every unmarried man of right age, and medically fit, to fight for his country; if he won't do this, he is no man and his neighbours should shun him and the women look down upon him.

To any man in my employ who enlists for active service abroad for the period of the war I will give a bounty of £5, and keep his place open for him on his return.

To any man in my employ who enlists for home defence, I will give a bounty of £2, and keep his place open for him.

W.F. WAILES - FAIRBAIRN
Askham Richard, August 29th, 1914.

Wailes-Fairburn had another suggestion for getting what were to become known as 'slackers' into khaki. It was hinted at in the notice above and it was a suggestion which was seized on and refined by stupid girls and idiots of the other sex in years to come. 'There are heaps of young fellows hanging about doing nothing but amuse themselves,' Wailes-Fairburn wrote, 'who are to all outward appearances fit to fight; I wish the women and girls would make a point of ostracising all such, and for very shame that they would have to do their duty.' (33) That splendid piece of prose contained one suggestion of how to swell the numbers in the forces; a letter from the Sedgefield Union contained another. This was sent to the York Board of Guardians and asked for support for legislation which 'in some way' would utilise the services of all able bodied vagrants between the ages of 18 and 30. Surprisingly this got some support, but to their credit the guardians threw the idea out. A Mr Tredale pointed out that 'voluntaryism' was in existence 'and if compulsory service was to apply it should apply all round, and not only to those people whose footsteps had been dogged by misfortune.' Quite right too, and Councillor Horsman - an outspoken Labour member - agreed. Compulsion, he said, 'should apply to the men at the top of the social 'scale' if it was to apply to the young vagrants. (34)

The bench, naturally, had things to say about recruiting. At the East Ainsty petty sessions, held at the York Castle, the landlord of the New Inn, Askham Richard, where Wailes-Fairburn came from, asked for an hour's extension (from 10pm to 11pm) for a cricket supper, whereupon the chairman 'said it did not seem a desirable time for cricket suppers when all young men ought to be serving their country'. To this the hapless landlord replied that most present at the annual bender would be aged between 40 and 50, but his worship in the chair was not to be put off. The landlord should become both mine host and recruiting sergeant. (35)

The chairman said the application would be granted but the magistrates would expect the applicant to say to any young men who came that they ought to be learning to defend their country and not hanging about. He should say a few kind words to the young men on their duty, and use a little influence with them.

A reason why recruiting fell off to add to worries about family and pay (and getting killed) was that the standards for recruits was rapidly put up. After Kitchener got his 'first hundred thousand' men, volunteers had to be at least five feet six inches tall and have a chest measurement of 36 inches. This requirement was followed in York by a drop of enlistments from 100 a day (from all areas) to just five on Saturday last the *Herald* recorded on 21 September. Four days later the same paper reported that only one man had enlisted the day before and the York Recruiting Committee (whose secretary was the prominent Tory politician C.E Elmhirst) suggested that the government should lower requirements. In October they were changed. Now men of five feet five inches will be taken the *Herald* told its readers, (36) 'with proportionate chest measurement.'

It seems reasonable to suggest that certain other things may also have had an effect on some of the young men of York. The possible consequences of enlistment quickly became all too apparent for example. Bootham School had been rapidly equipped as a hospital by the St John Voluntary Aid Association under the supervision of Dr W. A. Evelyn, a local celebrity and an important figure in the fight against TB. (37) The Royal Military Hospital, Fulford Road, had also been got ready for men from the front, (38) and the first war picture was shown in York by the end of the third week of August. This was 'The Looters of Liege' put on by Bert Rutter at the Victoria Hall, and with it were locally made films of the departure of the Scots Greys from the city and some of the Seaforths and Warwickshires going through or from York. (39) On 26 August (it seems) the first 'wounded' photograph (of Lt the Earl of Leven and Melville) appeared in the *Press*, then news began to come through that the Scots Greys, so recently peacetime soldiers based in York, had been severly cut up during the retreat from Mons. (40) Then also familiar local names began to appear as casualties. Stoker Petty Officer George F. Banks who had been born in Lord Mayor's Walk and had gone to Queen Street school was killed. (41) Sgt Orderly Room Clerk Alexander Hutchison of the 1st Cameron Highlanders, who had been educated at Fishergate was killed on the Aisne on 25 September. (42) Corporal W. Newton was another of York's first casualties. He was in the 6th Dragoon Guards (Carabineers) and was killed on 24 September. He had served eight years in the army and was stationed in York when he finished his time and stayed there. He went on to the reserve and after 12 years signed on, on 14 June 1914, for another four. He had been called up the day after war was declared. (43). Private Walter Rickard, an ex-Rowntree employee had joined the Scots Guards in 1913. He was killed on the first day of the Battle of the Aisne. (44) Major Swetenham, well known in York as one of the Scots Greys, was killed and his death reported early in September. (45)

The faint hearted may have been put off enlisting by the war news and the casualty lists, but in the aftermath of the lowering of standards recruiting did pick up. All 'records at the York ... depot' were broken, the *Press* reported on 31 August, 'and all past figures greatly exceeded.' Some of those who had joined gave rise to some good stories. Cuthbert Storey, of Harrogate, for example was prosecuted for driving a motor car along Boroughbridge Road without lights. He appeared in court and told their worships that he was going to York to enlist (at night time), and that since the offence he and his two mates 'had ... enlisted in Lord Helmsley's troop.' (46) In mid August G. Emerson, 32, a labourer from Gainsborough was charged in York with being drunk and thumping Private Henry Wilcock. Emerson had been trying to get into the West Yorks depôt at Fulford using force (he had served in the 3rd battalion in the past). The Lord Mayor adjourned his case to see if the military would have him, and he reappeared in the dock a week later. (47) He now answered to the name of Garsell, said he was with the colours and the case was withdrawn. Only two days after war was declared Private J. Winterburn, 24, of the 5th Royal Irish Regiment appeared before the Lord Mayor and A.P. Mawson, a labour pioneer, in York. Winterburn was charged with deserting at York in 1910, and had given himself up. (48) Had he read the papers carefully he would have seen that there was no need to do this. (49) James Booth, a painter, also appeared before the Lord Mayor, Councillor Henry Rhodes Brown and Cuthbert Morrell. He had pinched a clock and a coat at Selby and was arrested in York. The Chief Constable, who did the prosecutions in those days, said Booth was a time expired reservist 'but was trying to join the Royal Reserve.' The defendant said he had been smashed out of his mind at the time of his crime, and was bound over for six months - 'The Lord Mayor [however] said the nation wanted soldiers, and the magistrates thought the accused would make a good soldier' even though he had done 'this thing.' (50) What the owner (or owners) of the coat and clock thought is not recorded.

By the time Booth was appearing in court stories of German atrocities at places like Vise, (51) and later Dinant, were being reported in the press, and arrested aliens were being brought to the city. Sometimes the actions of the police were nothing short of farcical. A Mr Schumacher, a man in his sixties, and an 'experimental engineer', was arrested getting on to a tram in Acomb. He had served in the Franco-German war and his period as a reservist was only completed a year earlier. He had an English wife and one of his sons was serving in the Royal Garrison Artillery. (52) Nevertheless, he was put into York Castle, along with

Julius Koch, the manager, and several employees of the Selby Olympia Mills, Herbert Lindenburg of the Ardol factory, and eight men arrested at Market Weighton who had been drilling for coal as employees of the International Boring Company. (53) By the second week of September the Castle was full of Germans and the Exhibition Buildings had had to be used for the overflow. To meet the demand a concentration camp' [sic] was built in Leeman Road on land once occupied by the York Engineering Company. (54) This was got ready in rapid time and was open for business in October, (55) when amongst its inmates were enemy prisoners of war as well as aliens. It became a great tourist attraction and thousands went to look at it and its occupants on Sundays - taking with them fruit and gifts which they threw over the wire. (After having read terrible atrocity stories in their daily papers.) (56) This got so bad that the authorities had to take steps to keep the crowds away and, as the *Herald* of 26 October reported, a 'boarding' was 'placed round the camp' in 'order to arrest public curiosity'. In October a tragedy occurred in the camp which aroused much interest. August Beckert, an engineer from Selby, was interned on 26 September. 'He was a registered alien, and was detained because he was likely to become dangerous' the *Herald* told its readers. Beckert died and was buried in York. Several internees were allowed to attend the funeral and a photograph of them in procession appeared in the papers. (57) They, incidentally, were now taking on a more modern look, and using photographs quite liberally. The *Herald* produced a weekly edition in which most of the illustrations of the previous week were reproduced.

German prisoners had appeared in York quite early in the war, to a by no means hostile reception if the accounts of the crowds at Leeman Road are correct, and not long afterwards wounded Belgians and Belgian refugees made their appearance. (58) Very rapidly the local community began to care for them, and this was but one way in which the citizens rallied round. There began a mass of collections and community efforts which, seemingly, did not slacken off during the war. A call for blankets and crockery for the troops who were flooding into York was rapidly over subscribed. (At the end of September it was reported that there were 3,500 members of the West Yorkshire Regiment in the city, 2,400 men - overwhelmingly New Army men - in the cavalry barracks while the 5th Cavalry Reserve was on the Knavesmire, where the race course grandstand was equipped with 1,500 beds. By the end of October 'between 6,000 and 7,000' were at Strensall to add to these.) (59) Soon there would be collections for cigarettes for the troops, appeals for binoculars and saddles (from Lord Roberts no less) and circles of people knitting for the troops. Edith Milner was connected with the latter. She got so that she became York's number one jingo artist, writing to the papers sometimes twice a day, always hectoring, always patriotic, usually predictably so. She undoubtedly meant well, and she undoubtedly did good, but her good works were conducted with such a patronising, superior, know-all attitude that she must have terrified the working class women and kids who came within her orbit. The latter did so when they attended one of her two Girl's Clubs. When hostilities started Edith rapidly put these on a war footing. She wrote to the highest in the land and affiliated them to the York branch of Queen Mary's Needlework Guild - Her Majesty, she said, 'graciously signified her approval of increasing the branch.' When she met the girls about to knit for the troops, Miss Milner said she agreed with Mrs Edward Lytellton's 'wise suggestion' about how the dead should be mourned, (60) then read to them 'the King-Emperor's stirring address to his peoples beyond the seas.' She also read out the Lord Mayor's address 'praying the mothers and girls of York to do their part and not lower the standard of our common womanhood by interfering with the soldiers, and especially the recruits' and emulating the 'unseemly conduct of too many girls and women on the streets.' In the same paper in which Edith's stirring address to the Guild appeared there was a letter from her on the second subject she spoke to the needleworkers about. She cried, she said, when she saw the girls of York chasing the fellows in khaki. (61) It is difficult to envisage Edith Milner crying.

Rhodes Brown's manifesto asking the young girls of York 'to refrain from levity and from making difficulties for the recruits' was issued in early September 1914, (62) and the theme was taken up by others as well as Edith. In October the Archbishop preached in the York Garrison Chapel and made an impassioned plea to the soldiers assembled there to keep their hands off the ladies of York and not to go on the booze. (63) It seems fairly certain that his pleas (and those of Rhodes Brown and Edith) went unheeded. The Archbishop also pleaded with the populace at large not to treat soldiers to alcoholic drinks. Restrictions on its availability had already been imposed.

Lt General Plumer, like the government, had become alarmed at what the effects of readily available alcoholic drink might have on the thousands of men under his command, and he wrote to York's Licensing magistrates asking them to curtail pub opening hours in their city. They agreed, and were very quick off the mark as they used an Act which had become law only a week earlier. Henceforth, they announced, all pubs, clubs, eating houses and confectioners' shops (that sold drink presumably) would remain closed from 9 pm to 6 am (64). The York initiative was followed in neighbouring areas. Towards the end of September, for example, the Ouse and Derwent Licensing Justices made an order under the same legislation, (65) and closed their pubs at the unearthly hour of nine o'clock. (66)

The populace of York, it seems, took the outbreak of war in their stride, gave a good welcome to the German prisoners and the Belgian wounded, and knuckled down to perform good works under the supervision of the likes of Edith Milner. But closing the pubs at a time when many were just getting into their stride was something else. The protests started, and letters began to appear in the press. 'Our liberty is being curtailed,' wrote one irate toper, with awful predictability, 'and devoted husbands must henceforth seek the domestic fireside three hours before the stroke of midnight.' (67) Another correspondent said their worships had used 'the proverbial "bull at the gate" principle' in dealing with the possibility that soldiers might get too much drink. (68) (No-one seems to have considered the fact that most of them would not get enough money to make drinking to excess more than an occasional feature of their lives.) The 'trade', of course, went up in arms. In October C. Palliser, of the Malt Shovel, Walmgate, that area of York where pubs were as numerous as shops, wrote to the clerk of the York court (now H.V. Scott) on behalf of members of the York and District Retail Licence Holders' Protection Association. He revealed that Scott's reply showed that the justices had discussed the terminal closing hour for a second time on 23 September and had decided to keep it at 9 pm. (Pontefract, and another garrison town, allowed pubs to remain open until 10 pm on week days and 10.30 pm on Saturdays.) (69) On the day before Palliser's letter was published it was revealed that the military authorities had approached the Licensing Bench with a further suggestion for 'reform'. They wanted drink sales to soldiers prohibited, except between 7 and 9 pm. (70) An Army Order, however, dealt with this problem, restricting the hours when soldiers could visit pubs. (71) These were originally fixed as between 2 and 4 pm, and 6 and 8 pm. In November the second 'session' was extended by one hour. Robert William Colley, incidentally, of the York City Brass Band Club and Institute, Merchantgate, was one of the first to break (or to be found breaking) the justices' instructions of 23 September. He was prosecuted for allowing boozing in his establishment after 9 pm. He was fined 5s. and costs, and he thoroughly deserved what he got. (72)

When Colley was being proceeded against there was an invasion scare on, with the east coast regarded as the obvious landing place, and a month later Scarborough was bombarded from the sea. Many of the soldiers who joined up from York, or in York, put their reminiscences down on tape in the 1970s and many of them recalled their first duties 'protecting the coast and digging trenches on the beaches'. (73) In those circumstances it was inevitable that a 1914 version of Dad's Army should come into being, and one did so in York, early in December (after, perhaps, any threats of invasion had passed). H.E. Leetham presided over a meeting of what came to be known as the York Volunteer Training Corps. They had been called, Leetham said, 'an army of ineligibles' by the press. 'They were formed for defence against invasion', he went on, 'and against invasion only.' He thought they would become the fifth line of defence, eventually, Leetham said, with rifles and uniforms, and in York they had 23 military instructors. They were to be affiliated to a central association in London and only wanted recruits from men ineligible for the regular army, the new army and the TA - hence their nickname. (74) Their call was well supported, as had been an earlier one for special constables. (75)

Lloyd George very early on in the war coined a phrase which the public adopted which ran 'business as usual', but during those early weeks nothing could have been further from that as a description of York. The banks had been closed, and when they opened began issuing paper money, and the press had to reassure the citizens that they could use it just like coin. 'ACCEPT IT, USE IT, AND DON'T WORRY', they were urged. (76) This did not last long, and within a few weeks Lloyd George introduced a bill 'to enable the Treasury to call in the new £1 and 10s. notes', largely, it seems, because they could be easily forged. (77) The horses that had been such a feature in the streets had been severely depleted in number, the city was now crowded with soldiers, prisoners and refugees - and the pubs closed at 9 pm. The Boy Scouts were doing war work, and there were other changes. It had been decided that cricket fixtures should be stopped, the York races were abandoned for a time, and amateur football games were cancelled. Professional football, however, still went on, a matter for grave concern and the cause of a prolonged campaign led by one F.N. Charrington.

York City were a professional side in the Midland League, and they began the season, war or no war, with great hopes. Archie Taylor was then manager and over the August Bank holiday weekend it was reported that he had signed left half back Henry Brough. There had been some grumbling about the increased price of season tickets, it was reported, but, it was pointed out, 'it should be borne in mind that if the directors are to secure a team that will have any chance of winning the ... League championship they must get first-class men, and first-class men can only be secured if the club are prepared to pay top wages.' (79) The team made an excellent start to the season (80), though without the services of Henry Brough, who volunteered for military service in the first week of the war. (81)

Giving up sport was a sacrifice for many - but there were other sacrifices of a much more impressive kind in the first weeks of the war. It has already been mentioned that the agricultural labourers had a strike planned for the period before harvest, and that this was called off. They eventually dropped their claim for higher wages, despite the fact that the rush to the colours by country lads must have put them in a relatively strong bargaining position. (82) Other groups of workers also dropped wage claims. On 15 September it was reported that the demand put forward to the York Council by the Municipal Employe's [sic] Association for a halfpenny an hour had been withdrawn - 'it was felt by the Association that owing to the war it was not a proper time to bring it forward', it was stated. (83)

The pre-war years in Britain had been years in which labour relations were frequently at fever pitch and sometimes violent. The gesture by the Municipal Employe's Association is both remarkable and part of a wave of political and industrial trucing 'for the duration' which went on everywhere, but which, in York, was less than complete, as will be seen. On 13 August it was reported that the Liberals, at a meeting presided over by J.B. Morrell and K.E.T. Wilkinson, had decided to suspend propaganda for the duration, (84) and the day before it had been announced that all activities of the Milner Habitation of the Primrose League would stop, and that its offices in St Helen's Chambers would be put at the disposal of the Red Cross. (85) Edith Milner had presided over the Milner Habitation for many years, and, as has been noted, she was vehemently anti suffragist. One of the organisations she hated - the York branch of the National Union of Women's Suffrage Societies - announced it would give up agitating for the vote at least for the time being. The suffragette movement was split over whether to take this action or not, and the United Suffragists, for example continued their campaigning, (86), but they had no representation in York. The Labour party prevaricated. Over that momentous Bank Holiday weekend of 1914 labour movements throughout Europe had held meetings of protest against the war, but when war was declared, rallied to the support of their respective governments. They did so in Britain, and York's leading labourite of 1914 did so too. Councillor Will Dobbie, who had replaced J.H. Hartley as the city's most outspoken socialist, addressed a meeting on the Knavesmire. He was on the executive of the National Union of Railwaymen and had told his hearers that he would try to bring about a national strike if war was declared. He was not allowed to forget this and at a Walmgate Tory meeting to adopt a municipal candidate in October, for example, both S. Scruton, presiding, and T. Harrison, one of the candidates, lambasted Dobbie for his remarks. (87) Walmgate was Dobbie's ward, where he was up for election in November. By then he had done a U-turn and offered to join up. Some said he had been turned down, but eventually Dobbie did enlist and become an enthusiastic supporter of the war. In fact he became a jingoist given to making some appalling speeches.

The Labour party was split over support for the war nationally, with the bulk of it going along with its leaders, and the York party adopted a similar attitude. The Independent Labour Party (the ILP), however, was resolutely against and remained so throughout the war. There was a small, yet quite influential ILP branch in York and in it were many of the protesters of 1914-18. Much more will be heard of them.

The party truce did not extend to municipal politics yet. In the last years of peace York had had, for a short time, a spell of government by the Liberals - or the Progressives, as they called themselves. They had brought in new men to politics and much-needed reforms which were expensive, and this and their own stupidity had led to their downfall. In 1913 the Liberals gained only one success in the November elections and lost their majority. The Tories, in control again, immediately vetoed one of their predecessors' favourite schemes (a municipal cemetery) and during the year increased their majority. They did it by doing what Alderman W.H. Birch 'called "packing" the aldermanic bench.' (88) J.H. Hartley, an outspoken Labour alderman, over whom a bitter controversy raged in 1913, took up employment with the City council as a school attendance officer, and had to resign his seat. It was taken by the Tories, as it would have been in the days of George Hudson. (89)

In 1914 there were the usual 12 seats up for grabs - nine held by Liberals, three by Tories, and one of the Liberals seeking re-election was John Bowes Morrell, the chairman of the York Liberal Association,

A constitutional rule had grown up over the years in York which said that the Mayoralty should be offered to the most senior alderman who had not held the office, and who would accept it. This meant, in 1913, that the office 'should' have gone to the troublesome J.H. Hartley, but in his stead Rhodes Brown, a councillor, had been selected and the tradition well and truly broken. Brown would not stand again in 1914 (he was asked), and a sub committee of the Council declared that it was not prepared to go outside the Council chamber for a candidate. Eventually J.B. Morrell accepted. (90) This effectively increased the Tory majority by one as Lord Mayors, unless they were like George Hudson and one or two of his lackeys - and to some extent like Rhodes Brown - kept aloof from politics during their term of office.

Should the party truce be extended to municipal affairs ? A heated and nasty controversy broke out over the matter. Labour (91) would not agree and the two main parties argued for an arrangement which would suit their purposes. The Liberals were losing popularity and they said they would agree to a truce for one year. In 1914, they said, they would agree to the parties holding their seats as they were at the outbreak of hostilities. There was no way the Tories would agree to this. They saw it as a sly way of retaining seats (which it probably was). The tide was running their way they thought (and they were right), and they saw the Liberals' suggestion as a means of hanging on to seats they would probably lose. They proposed, instead, a three year truce which had a definite logic about it (three years was a municipal term of office), but if the Liberals agreed to this, of course, they were definitely out of power for that time (during which the Tories could take up any aldermanic places that became available). The negotiations came to nothing and elections were held. Was this not against the spirit of the times ? Was it not against the national feelings expressed in the party truce at a national level ? That had already been broken, some York Tories contended, by the government forcing measures through parliament. Would York be unique in holding what could be bitter elections at a time of great crisis ? One of the candidates (O.F. Rowntree) thought York might well be the only place in the country where such contests would be held. (92)

Electioneering began late in September 1914, and one of the most interesting contests would be, as always, in Walmgate - 'something of a Labour-Liberal stronghold' in the *Herald's* words (which were correct). There Will Dobbie, who had been running hot and cold over the war, as has been said, was retiring, along with Councillor T. Morris, a Liberal representative who also stood for re-election. The Tories decided to try to unseat both - and it is interesting to note that Morris claimed he would be at a considerable disadvantage because no less than 257 Irish and Roman Catholic voters in the ward were away in the forces. (93)

The Tories chose two candidates for Walmgate - Lancelot J. Foster, the son of an alderman, and T. Harrison, a fruiterer. These two attacked the Liberals' manifesto as 'a sham, a hypocrisy and a humbug' (they had said they would donate the money earmarked for the election to charity if a truce was agreed) and laid into Dobbie for his anti-war speeches. To call the public announcement from the Liberals a 'Manifesto' (and they called it that themselves) is something of a misnomer, as it simply reiterated their terms for a truce. (94) It looked as if a contest like those of old might develop, but, truth to tell, the election turned out to be a dull affair. The Tories failed to unseat the sitting councillors and Morris, despite his comments about many of his supporters being away, easily headed the poll. Dobbie was also returned, but well behind Morris, perhaps the result of his war speeches. Out of an electorate of 3,050, 1,946 voted and the returns showed: Morris 1,226; Dobbie 805; Foster 699; and Harrison 544. (95)

In Micklegate J.B. Morrell and J.F. Glew (Labour) were re-elected without a contest and in Monk the retiring councillors (96) were unopposed. In Guildhall the two retiring Tories were allowed a walk-over. (97) In Bootham, however, there was a fight.

In Bootham Councillors Dennis Vivian Scott and W.H. Sessions, both Liberals, sought re-election, though the latter had originally intended to retire from civic life. He had been one of the young 'Progressives' who had swept into power before the war and the Bootham Tories put up two candidates. They were A.E. Hewitt and Capt W.A. Pearson. The latter had been serving in the Boer War while on the council and his seat had become due for re-election while he was abroad. Then, to the Tories' disgust, the Liberals had opposed him - and they did so again in 1914. Pearson was away training Territorials and took no part in the campaigns. His supporters were sure he would be elected, but they were wrong. He came last.

The Bootham election was enlivened by an acrimonious dispute on the platforms and in the press between Hewitt and Scott. In addition to contending that Liberal government would be expensive government, (98) Hewitt attacked Scott's record while on the council, maintaining that his attendances were not what they should have been. This did not produce the desired results, however, and Scott and Sessions were quite easily returned. The latter was a member of the Society of Friends and a pacifist, and it is interesting to note that he beat Pearson who had been presented as the sturdy, country first patriot that he undoubtedly was. (99) Elsewhere a Quaker candidate lost his seat.

G.H. Mennell had been on the council for two years, and he and another Quaker (O.F. Rowntree) sought re-election in Castlegate. Mennell's father had done relief work on the continent in the aftermath of the 1870 Franco-Prussian war, and early in the war Mennell went to the French and Belgian battlefields. He described his experiences at meetings in York (100), and perhaps this high profile drew attention to his pacifist beliefs - which, of course, were also held by his colleague, a member of the most prominent Quaker family in the north of England. Anyway he was ousted and Rowntree was pushed into second place by T.F. Clark, a Tory. (Clark 868; Rowntree 865: Mennell 798; Edwin Piercy, Tory, 787.) During the Castlegate election Rowntree (Mennell was on the continent for quite a part of the campaign) had to defend past Liberal policies. He said they had cleared the slum area of Hungate, were considering 'thinning' the equally bad area of Walmgate, and that a housing scheme for Heworth would start shortly. This was a scheme initiated during their period of office, and it was a fact that housing needs were pressing in York. As was revealed at a later enquiry, while the population was increasing, and while slums were being pulled down, no provision for rehousing those dispossessed was in existence. Piercy would have none of this. The Liberals, he said, had a cemetery scheme and a bridge scheme, both were expensive and he was against both. Clark, making his first appearance in York municipal politics, put forward some unbelievably reactionary views. Showers were being provided in some York schools, he said; they were a waste of money! He was also against (or would look carefully at) proposals to extend the city's tram network. (102)

The Tories made a gain of one in November 1914, and were securely in power, particularly as J.B. Morrell, the city's 526th Lord Mayor, was a Liberal. Henceforth there would be no 'progressive' policies and the Liberals accepted the fact that war time was not a time for social reform. What had municipal politics been like in the few months that the war had been on ?

Almost as soon as war broke out York's civic leaders, headed by Rhodes Brown, set up a Recruiting Committee. This has been mentioned before, and it campaigned throughout the autumn of 1914 (stopping its activities during the municipal elections). J.G. Butcher was prominent on its platforms, while the city's senior MP, Arnold Rowntree, was conspicuous by his absence. Set up at about the same time was also an extremely energetic Relief Committee, an organisation in which there was much more of a cross section of the influential and powerful in York. Sebastian Meyer, for example, played a very active part in its work - and Meyer would not have been seen to be a party to recruiting. His political and religious views were those of the Rowntrees, Sessions and Mennell.

The Relief Committee was created within three days of the war starting, and it held its first meeting on 10 August. It was broadly based with many prominent York people serving on it. Among them were Canon Argles, a pre-war temperance activist and F.T. Beney of the I.L.P. Sir Joseph Sykes Rymer, an influential Tory was a member as were K.E.T. Wilkinson and Sebastian Meyer of the Liberal party. Will Dobbie was a member insisting on workers representation - 'especially seeing that the workers would be the people who would be hardest hit, and the first hit' by the war. (103). A.P. Mawson, the Labour JP, was a colleague Dobbie would have approved of and a number of ladies were members of the committee from the outset. Edith Milner joined them a little later. By the end of the first week of hostilities they had raised some £4,000 - £1,500 of which had been passed over to the National Relief Fund. (104)

What did the organisers of the Relief Fund think would be their prime concern? Clearly the relief of the families of servicemen whose employers had not been as generous as the NER, or Leethams, but they were also sure that the poor would suffer from unemployment and the price rises which came with every war. Were they right?

The periodic reports, published at some length in the York papers showed that unemployment (they did not mention under employment which, it has been contended, was the real curse in York) did not in fact go up, though in the early days of the war there were great fears that it would. In mid-September G.W. Halliday reported to a meeting of the York Traders' Association that 'practically every trader in the city ... was feeling the ill-effects of war by a decrease in his weekly takings of 30, 40 and 50 per cent., and in some instances even more ... Very shortly', Halliday went on, 'unless the public rise to the occasion, assistants and workmen would have to be dispensed with, because it was impossible to go on indefinitely paying wages unless there was a corresponding influx of orders to find the wherewithal to keep the wheels of commerce running smoothly.' The patriotic knitting groups ('public working parties') of the kind Edith Milner promoted were putting women out of work, Halliday concluded. (105) In October things seemed to be getting as bad as Halliday had predicted. In the first week of that month there was a meeting of the York branch of the National Amalgamated Union of Shop Assistants, Warehousemen and Clerks at which H.G. Bassett, the district organiser, spoke of firms cutting wages and reducing wages by a third, others cutting wages and not hours, and elsewhere of 50 per cent wage cuts. In York, he reported, wages were being cut in proportion to hours, though some employers, Bassett said, were generously keeping up both hours and wages. (106) There were fears, too, that Rowntrees would have to go on short time. (107)

Those troubles, worrying though they were, proved to be of a temporary nature, and the fears of the city council (which had prepared public works schemes for the unemployed) (108) were shown to be ill-founded. After a month or so of total confusion trade in York began to pick up, and the extent of the recovery was detailed in a series of reports in the *Yorkshire Herald* at the end of 1914. It is interesting to note that the period when things were bad was also the period when workers were voluntarily giving up wage demands.

The *Herald's* surveys of business included one on the drugs trade in York, when Bleasdale's Ltd reported that the price of opium (an essential element in many of the do-it-yourself remedies of those days) had gone up by five per cent by the end of 1914, and another from Gibbs and Company. The latter sold motor vehicles, and reported that trade had improved because of the commandering of horses. (109) Hills Brothers, in the leather trade, reported that their trade had had a shock when the war started. Army orders, then, had been small and prospects had looked bleak until, in September, the French government placed orders for boots worth one million pounds. Between October and November enormous orders had been made by the home government and at the end of the year the trade was experiencing boom conditions. (110) This was a common story. A little before this (half way through November) the Citizen's Committee had shown that 1,424 men had been taken from industrial employment for the forces (938 married and 486 single) and that the unemployed in York amounted to 196 compared with 370 for a year earlier. Once again these figures are not an indication of suffering because they do not include people on short time, but they certainly do indicate that things were not developing as many had feared. For the week ending 30 October the number of women out of work was 66, compared with 37 a year earlier, and 41 boys were unemployed as were ten girls. (111)

Somewhat earlier than the end-of-the-year surveys which have just been mentioned, the *Herald* (on 6 November) had confirmed that after the first two months of war York's trade had picked up. No Rowntree workers had been laid off, it was recorded, but the drapery trade had fallen off somewhat (and later on there were some bankruptcies). (112) The glass trade, however, was prospering as a result of German imports being cut off, and T. Cooke and Sons, of Buckingham Street, scientific instrument makers, had received massive orders and its employees were working overtime. At the NER's carriage and wagon works there had been a massive installation of woodworking machinery and already between 700 and 800 military vehicles had been made in addition to railway stock.

The city council, then, did not have problems of unemployment on a large scale to contend with. What did concern it between the outbreak of war and the end of 1914 ? Just after hostilities started the York Corporation Bill which had been started on its way when the Liberals were in control of the city received the royal assent (113) but it was clear, indeed it was agreed, that there would be little innovation until after the war ended (which most people thought would not be long). However, as a result of moves or applications started before the war, an enquiry was held into an application for authority to prepare a town planning scheme for 'an area situated partly in the City area and partly within the rural districts of Flaxton and Escrick, and including the districts of Heslington, Osbaldwick, Heworth, Hull-road, Clifton, New Earswick, and Burton Stone-lane.' This was a scheme very close to Liberal hearts, and the enquiry was held during the municipal election campaign. (114) It was by no means enthusiastically received in all the outlying areas, and at it the inspectors heard from the Town Clerk that, whereas the city had powers to construct trolley bus routes to the Burton Stone/Clifton area of the city and to Heworth, it was the intention to try running electric omnibuses there first. These were duly started after some considerable delays and letters in the press from Edith Milner (and others). (115) In December 1914 there was another Local Government Board enquiry in York - into an application from the Corporation for permission to borrow £6,214 to enable it to purchase 48 acres of land for council housing at Heworth. (116) At the hearings it was revealed that private enterprise was failing to keep pace with the demand for new housing, and a very nasty fact was revealed about the slum clearances that had already gone on. It has already been mentioned in these pages. The Corporation had demolished slums in places like Hungate, it was said, but, except in Alma Grove, no alternative accommodation had been made for those made homeless. Dr Smith, the city's Medical Officer of Health, said that he thought 220 houses were needed immediately; that up to 300 more ought to be demolished; and that between 50 and 100 new dwellings would be needed each year just to cope with population growth. The City Treasurer was asked what that growth was like. The area of York, he said, was 3,230 acres, and the population had grown from 77,914 in 1901 to 82,282 at the time of the last census. When he spoke York's estimated population was 83,802. (117)

Council housing was something that the Tory government of York was not enthusiastic about, but which had to be accepted as an undesirable necessity. It was not likely to become a great issue in 1914, and it did not, seemingly, feature greatly in the elections of that year. What issues did concern the council in that early part of the war ? Few, before November, it must be said, and the *Herald* drew attention to the fact that the full council meeting of October 1914 took only two hours 50 minutes - compared with 14 hours in the identical meeting of 1913. A main reason for this, the paper said, was the disappearance from that august body of two windbags - J.M. Hogge, now an MP, and engaged in a libel suit with Horatio Bottomley, no less, and J.H. Hartley.

After the November elections one of the first questions the council dealt with - to its great credit - was dependant's allowances. Perhaps prompted to take action by the death of one of the city's tram conductors - killed in action in France - (118) Councillor Horsman persuaded the council (by a majority of 39:0) to make up the wages of employees killed during the war. At the meeting at which he did so (in November 1914) it was revealed that at that time 101 Corporation workers had joined up, 21 of whom were 'at the front'. Later there was a move to curtail what were undoubtedly generous arrangements made for the Corporation workers. In April 1915 the Electricity and Tramways Committee revealed that these arrangements were costing £4,000 a year and were, they reckoned, the most generous in the country. (119) They recommended that the system of grants to recruits and 'full pay without reductions for those who go to the front' should remain for those already enjoying it, but that future recruits should simply have their wages made up, after deductions of amounts equal to pay and separation allowances. The separation allowances themselves were a source of considerable agitation and controversy.

The Labour party, consisting of people like Will Dobbie, had been thrown into disarray by the outbreak of war, but rapidly rallied round to supporting the government (with some notable exceptions it must be said). Quite incredible agreements to waive wage demands were made, as has been said, but with a determination that the war should be fought 'fairly' - and quite rightly so. Very early in the conflict those attitudes centred on what was considered to be a totally unacceptable level of allowances paid to the dependants of men who had been killed. Nationally Labour leaders like James Sexton and Ben Tillett campaigned for more money for widows and families (with Tillett saying as early as November 1914 that there would be a national strike if conscription was brought in) (120) and in York F.D. Wood and J.H. Hartley took part in an eve of council meeting in November at which demands were made that every wounded soldier should receive £1 a week until fully recovered and that widows should get the same amount plus children's allowances. (121) The very next day Horsman persuaded the York City Council first of all to support a resolution demanding better treatment for bereaved wives, then to continue to pay the wages of those killed who had been in their employ. (122)

The question of separation allowances, pensions to the disabled, and to war widows were all interconnected and, although the government had had little time to address itself to the matter, it got little credit for this and people as dissimilar as J.M. Hogge and Sir Frederick Milner began to pressurise it - to their everlasting credit. Hogge took the matter up in the pages of the *Globe*, for example, quoting among others, the example of a woman receiving 12s.6d. for her husband, who had been earning 37s. a week when he joined up. (123) Milner was Edith's brother, and an ex MP. He had been persuaded to give a lecture in York on the war. He did so, then returned and at a public meeting over which his formidable sister presided, he announced that he was considering a campaign to get 'adequate' pensions for the disabled. Like Hogge he gave examples of great suffering and told of a man who was now 'maimed and helpless' who, he said, would never be able to 'look after himself' on the 15s. a week he had been awarded, and of another who would never be able to work again, who had been receiving wages of 6s.8d. a day before enlisting, and who now had to exist on 14s. a week. (124) A little later Milner wrote a powerful letter to the *Herald* in which he drew attention to a circular of 23 November authorising pensions of 23s. maximum to wounded seamen of the lower grades (and proportionately higher amounts to more senior grades). This had not yet been implemented, Milner said, and some 2,000 had been discharged (some of whom had had pre-war wages of 45s.). Their treatment was 'a disgrace', and the maximum they were receiving - if totally disabled - was 17s.6d. Like the good contraversalist he was Milner contrasted this meagre amount with the 25s. the government was paying some people to keep remounts for the cavalry and the sums of up to 25s. paid to others for billeting. (125)

The issue of the local paper which reported Milner's bitter and justified comments about Britain's treatment of her war widows and the disabled, carried a note saying that Mrs Charlotte Despard had been in the city lecturing the local Independent Labour Party on 'The War and After.' Mrs Despard was a prominent worker in pre-war years for female suffrage and the sister of Sir John French, the Commander-in-Chief of the British Army. Mrs Despard would undoubtedly have had some very strong views on what some were saying about what was happening to the separation allowances which were being paid out already. What were they saying ? Mrs Despard had been the leader of a deputation to the government about what they were saying (and doing). (126)

It was contended regularly, and persistently, that women were spending their separation allowances in the pubs, and that the incidence of female drunkenness everywhere was going up alarmingly. In November 1914 a deputation met a government minister about the question of women drinking and Mrs Millicent Fawcett, another famous suffrage fighter, wrote a letter saying that the allegations were grossly exaggerated (which they most certainly were). (127) That allegations are exaggerated, however, does not stop them getting wide acceptance, and much ink was spilled complaining about separation allowances going straight to the publicans. It happened in York and the army took the issue very seriously (it was their actions which prompted the Despard deputation). In January 1915 a suffrage paper reported that an Army Council circular had gone the rounds on the question of soldiers' wives, in which the possibility of them being confined to their homes and not served drinks was discussed. This infuriated Mrs Despard, as has been said, and in February she signed a petition to Lord Kitchener drawn up by the Women's Local Government Society which said that although she and other signatories, like the equally famous Mrs Jane Cobden Unwin, had been told it would not be put into force, the circular was still in existence and was a cause for concern. (128) This did not happen in York, but in Blackburn, because of the belief that separation allowances were going on booze, the licensing justices held a solemn debate on 'the advisability of making a restrictive order, referring to women only, with regard to the serving of intoxicating drinks.' They asked the Home Secretary if they could do this and he told them what they should have known already - that 'the Intoxicating Liquor (Temporary Restrictions) Act did *'not allow a restrictive order applied to females only.'* (129)

Women, then, could go into pubs. They could not 'treat' soldiers, but it looked very much as if they, and everyone else, would have to pay more for their tipples. In early 1915 the Chancellor, Lloyd George, launched an attack on the drink industry. He did so, he said, because of the effects of drinking on industry, (130) and he did so, certainly, to raise revenue. A great deal of evidence was produced about the effects of drink on the work force, and that of Rear Admiral F.L.T. Tudor, for example, got a great deal of press coverage. (131) Tudor reported that time lost by 135 men working on submarines in the north east in the first week of March lost between them time equalling a full week's work by 28 of them - or, put another way, every man on average lost three quarters of a day. At a ship yard in the same area, Tudor stated, for the period 26 January to 9 March, time lost equalled 35 per cent among rivetters, 26 per cent among platers and 22 per cent among caulkers. In the north east and elsewhere, the pubs opened at 6 am (they did in York) and early morning drinking was a real problem, with many, presumably, preferring the hostelries to work, and others turning up in a state that would not have earned them the title of Stakhanovite in another place at another time.

Lloyd George who had put a penny on a pint in November (and 3d. a pound on tea) proposed to tax beer and spirits, and the trade and the drinkers were outraged. The brewers lobbied parliament, and all over the country meetings of protest were held. In York members of the local Licenced Victualler's Association added their collective voice to the outcry. T.J. Betchetti told his members what the new taxes were to be in a hastily convened meeting held less than a week after Lloyd George first announced his dreadful news. There was to be, Betchetti said: 'a double spirit duty; a sur-tax upon ... beer which was above a certain strength, which would be graduated from 12s. to 36s. per barrel; a quadrupled duty upon ordinary still wine, an increase on sparkling wine of 15s. per gallon; or six times the amount of the present duty'. (132) The proposals would meet with determined opposition, Betchetti went on, and of course prices would go up and a list of what they should be was prepared. The York and District Retail Licence Holders' Protection Association met at the Mason's Arms to adopt the new scale and J.H. Atha of the Locomotive Inn wrote to the papers to say that his organisation thought it could mean 'absolute ruin.' (133)

By the time Atha's group met, Lloyd George had been forced to retreat - he had lost the 'opening round' in his fight for 'high taxation of alcoholic beverages, dilution of spirits and encouragement of lighter beers' he wrote. Much of the trouble in the north east was caused by the consumption 'of raw cheap spirits of a fiery quality', the Chancellor said, so it was now proposed to substitute for his tax proposals a complete prohibition of the sale of this fire water, which would stay in bond for three years. The beer duties were withdrawn, and so were those on wine. The York LVA issued a circular saying that the old price list should be reverted to.

The short-lived threat to the price of beer had been accompanied in York by a hysterical controversy kicked off by a hysterical cleric. This was the Rev Henry Brett who talked of themes touched on by other members of his profession, including the Archibishop, but who for some reason or another stirred up a lot more trouble for himself than they did. Henry Brett preached a sermon in which he attacked soldiers stationed in York for getting drunk (despite 'no treating' and early closing hours) and he attacked girls for getting themselves in the family way. The columns of the press became filled with rebukes to the reverend gentleman (including one from Edith Milner). In a sermon at Groves chapel early in May Brett tried to reply to his critics by saying that his contentions were true, which they probably were, and Edith Milner, it will be recalled, had already written to the press saying so. The girls were chasing the fellows, Edith had told one of her Girl's Clubs, and had said the sight of it made her cry. Miss Milner, incidentally, had a suspicion of one group of girls in the city who she maybe thought imbued suffrage ideas from their membership of a certain organisation or, worse, ran after the soldiers. 'I hope none of the club girls in whom I am interested belong to the Girl Guides', she told readers of the *Herald* in a bizarre letter, 'That scheme will never gain my approval. The Boy Scouts have my hearty support and all my available bicycles.' (134) A little earlier Edith had come out solidly on the side of those who said dependant's allowances went to the likes of Betchetti and J.H. Atha. Opening a bazaar in the Ebor Rooms, Coney Street, Edith carried on something alarming about treating soldiers and 'a terrible evil in our midst which', she said, 'must be faced.' She meant, she went on, 'the terrible drunkenness which prevails amongst women in York, especially a number of those who are provided for by the State during their husband's absence at the front.'

So, a great many married women spent all their money on drink, according to some, which was certainly untrue, and the girls ran after the soldiers and got themselves in trouble (and perhaps increased the sales of Blanchard's Pills). That was certainly true. What could be done about the latter? Well people like the Archbishop could ask them to desist. People like Brett could condemn them, and people like Edith Milner could write to the press, but all this seemed pretty ineffective if the speakers and writers themselves are to be believed. What else could be done? Well in York, as in many places, 'patrols' could be started - patrols which might conjure up an image of those in D.W. Griffith's great film 'Intolerance' to the cynical. In November, perhaps having been put on the *qui vive* by the likes of Brett and Edith Milner, the York and District branch of the National Union of Women Workers (which was not a trade union and with which Edith Milner was not associated) met to consider the possibility of 'promoting the "League of Honour for Women and Girls of the British Empire" in York.' One of the NUWW members was Mrs Edwin Gray, wife of a prominent Liberal, and she, in addition to holding many other offices, was a Vice President of the League of Honour, and she persuaded her colleagues to set up a branch in York. (135) Little was said about what the League's aims and objectives were, though they would not seem to be too difficult to infer. Anyway the patrols were started as they were elsewhere, and in June 1915 the York NUWW heard a report on them by Mrs Tupper-Carey. (136) These patrols are generally reckoned, nationally, to have been important precursors to women's police units. They had the enthusiastic support at the time of the Home Office, Lord Kitchener and the Chief Metropolitan Police Commissioner.

The girls who hung around the soldiers (and drank and so on) were not the only group on the receiving end of hostility from the likes of Edith Milner. The aliens also had a bad time. The rounding up of the likes of Julius Koch in the early days of the war has been mentioned. They were put into the Leeman Road Concentration Camp (which closed because of overcrowding) then were treated royally by the crowds who went to look at them and throw gifts to them. But, outside the camp, they were still likely to be harrassed. There were many prosecutions for 'failing to register as an alien' or for travelling more than five miles from his address if he was registered (contrary to section 22 of the Alien Restriction Act) (137), and there is plenty of evidence that the lives of some perfectly loyal and respectable people were made miserable by idiots using patriotism as a disguise for downright loutish, prejudiced behaviour. In September the Lord Mayor received a letter from Guy Bedan Alexander Lt RN retired who suggested the setting up of a civil Secret Service Corps of York - the members of which had 'no other duties than to obtain and follow up evidence against anyone of German nationality, and to supply the police with such information as they obtain.' (138) His advice was not acted upon, but plenty of people fingered others in a way he might well have approved of. As early as 9 August, for example, Tom Hawksby, an ice cream vendor, appeared in court on a charge alleging notorious conduct. For some reason or another he had made one of his children lie on the pavement in Walmgate and had shouted across the street to 'Mrs Frankle, also an ice cream vendor, "You - German dogs, you put the police on me."' (139) If she had he probably deserved it. In October Joseph Foster Mandefield, a hosier of 12a Monkgate, wrote to the papers to protest against rumours that he had been arrested as a German who had tried to poison the water in the York reservoir. He was British born but of French extraction. (140) A month earlier W. Kitching, of Holgate Road, also wrote an extraordinary letter to the papers telling readers that he did not own either an airship or an aeroplane with which he might assist the enemy. (141)

All aliens tended to be regarded as enemy agents, and attitudes to them hardened in the aftermath of what were regarded as particularly deplorable incidents in the war. In December 1914 Scarborough was shelled from the sea, an incident made much of by the press, (142) and many of the victims of the shelling were sheltered in York. Edith Milner blamed the aliens, said the German fleet were guided by them, and demanded action. (Her second point would seem to be quite unjustified.) (143) She wrote angrily as follows

> I see that very stringent measures are being taken in other places with regard to aliens. Why is York exempt? No one can doubt that treachery has been at work, or this raid on our coasts could never have been carried out. The danger is in our midst. Will York sleep on?
>
> God helps those who help themselves. I am not in a panic, I am only repeating what I have said ever since the war began.

In May 1915 a German submarine sunk the *Lusitania* off the coast of Ireland and one of the survivors was a local York resident - Mrs Lassetter, the wife of the Brigadier commanding the 3rd West Riding Infantry Brigade stationed at Strensall. (144) The Germans, foolishly, gloated over the incident and in its aftermath there were serious anti-German, anti-alien riots throughout Britain. There were incidents in Liverpool, where scores of German pork butchers' shops were wrecked (and emptied of course) and where Lord Derby said the sinking had shocked the nation more than had the use of gas on the Western Front. (145) At about the same time there were serious incidents of a similar nature in London where, on one occasion, a baker's shop was wrecked even though he had two sons serving at the front. (146) Nearer to York there were incidents at Bradford, Sheffield and Mexborough, and very serious trouble at Goldthorpe.

The Goldthorpe riots took place on 11 and 12 May and were perpetrated mainly by miners from Goldthorpe and Bolton on Dearne - two of whom were brothers called George Edward and Robert Owen Milner, but that they were not related to the redoubtable Edith might perhaps be inferred from the latter's christian names. People were injured in the incidents, and the main object of attack on the first night was the shop of Frederick Shonut, a man who had lived in England all his life, and whose wife was English. The riot took a fairly typical form with Milner and the others drunk, using their victim's name as an excuse to cause trouble, then engaging in downright criminal activity (demanding money and looting). The very first account to appear in print about the rioting of 11 May referred to the man who was the main object of the rioters hatred being Councillor Shonhut (the usual spelling) a pork butcher of High Street, Mexborough - a naturalised man who had been 'established in business in the town for fifteen years, and until the outbreak of the war ... one of the leading townspeople.' He had been on the Mexborough District Council.

The Goldthorpe rioters were arrested under the provisions of the Malicious Damage Act of 1861, and several of them appeared in and were sentenced in the Doncaster Magistrates' court. Forty six were charged and convicted of stealing or receiving and were given fines ranging from £2 to £3. Others were committed and bailed to appear at the Assizes. (147)

Twenty three men charged with riots at Goldthorpe appeared at the Leeds Assizes in July 1915. There a dreadful story was unfolded. The incidents were spaced out over two nights. On the first the pork butcher with the German sounding name was attacked, his house invaded, his shop cleared out and fired - and damage to the amount of £1,300 was done. Then 17 men were indicted for rioting on 12 May. On that day they attacked John Robert Bakewell's London Tea and Drapery Stores. Bakewell, Mr Justice Rowlatt said, 'had not a drop of

German blood in his veins'. He was struck on the head with a brick and knocked down, three attempts were made to fire his premises, there were baton charges, there was looting and shooting and one John or Jack Fades, a miner of 27, was killed. (148)

At the trial it was revealed that Fades was shot by people defending Bakewell's property and that damage to Bakewell's stock and property amounted to £3,000. During the course of the trial 13 men withdrew their pleas of not guilty 'and admitted having committed a misdeamenour.' The judge accepted these pleas, saying 'he thought misdeamenour was quite enough to cover the case, because he thought what the men did was more looting than demolition', and the hearings went on against the remaining four. These were found not guilty - not surprisingly in two of cases as they produced evidence that they were in the mines when the riots occurred. Sentences ranging from two months hard labour to 15 months hard labour on the others were then imposed. For the attack on Shonut's shop George Edward Milner, Henry Hepworth and David Griffiths received two months hard labour and Joseph Smith got six months hard labour. The ages of these last four ranged from 19 to 30. At a preliminary hearing it was revealed that John Bakewell was an ex chairman of the Goldthorpe District Council and 'an ex-officio member of the Doncaster West Riding Bench'. He had gone to Mexborough from Derbyshire about 15 years before he was attacked and had seemingly aroused the anger of the mob by expressing his disapproval of the attack on Mr Shonut. Bakewell had not made matters any better by declaring that 'he would shoot the first man to appear on his premises.' He or his friends did just that.

There was an ironic sequel to the Goldthorpe riot story of 1915. Above use has been made of a quotation made at the time saying that poor old Shonut was a naturalised person - he was not. On Monday 26 July 1915 the *Yorkshire Herald* reported his appearance in the Doncaster Police Court two days earlier. Shonut had made 'a claim on the public authorities' for the damage done to his premises and for this it was 'necessary to produce his naturalisation papers.' He had none, and George said that 'having served in the Doncaster Yeomanry he did not know it was necessary.' He was charged with 'being an alien subject' he 'failed to register himself.' Shonut's solicitor gave some interesting details about his client. He was born in Obehof in 1861 and 'in consequence of his dislike to the military system in Germany' went to England 'where his brothers and sisters were registered' in March 1878, 'when 16 years and ten months old.' There was then, Mr Ellison said, a law in Germany saying that anyone between the ages of 16 and 17 could 'denaturalise themselves provided they left Germany within six months and [they] could not then be called upon for military service'.

Mr Ellison said he did not know whether Shonut 'took out a denaturalisation certificate' and neither did his client. It would have been extremely difficult to check in 1915, of course, but having gone to Mexborough in 1888 Shonut joined the Queen's Own Yorkshire Dragoons three years later, and in 1897 was made a sergeant. In 1891, at the time of the Jameson Raid, he had consulted a London solicitor about naturalisation and been told 'that having taken the oath of allegiance to His Majesty's Forces it was not necessary to go through the form of naturalisation.' This was bad advice and George was fined a fiver. After what he had been through this seems a little harsh, as does the chairman's summing up. He said the magistrates were there to administer the law 'as it stood'. 'The fact that the defendant enlisted in the Yeomanry did not prove patriotism. Taking the oath of allegiance did not naturalise him. The law provided that at the outbreak of the war ... Every German must register ... [however] He had consulted his solicitor, and ... there had been a mistake, therefore the Bench were prepared to consider it a trifling offence.' Nevertheless 'The least' they could do was impose 'a fine of £5.'

The Goldthorpe riots (which the judge said were 'mere looting' and an 'outbreak of ruffianism and dishonesty') had their counterpart in York - but on a much smaller scale thankfully. The main recipient in Old Ebor of the attention of the likes of George Edward Milner caused a statement to be put in the papers in May 1915 saying that the writer had been living in England well over 34 years and that he had been naturalised in 1898. (149) He was G. Steigmann, a pork butcher of 28 Goodramgate, and his was not the first letter from people who were suffering from slanderous allegations and were fearing worse. As early as 3 September F.H. Wickenden, a jeweller and watchmaker wrote as follows. (150)

> Sir, - It having come to my knowledge that rumours are current that I am a German and under supervision, I should esteem it a favour if you could find me space in your columns to give a most emphatic denial of these absolutely unfounded statements, which have caused me much annoyance. I am English and of English descent and have never been in Germany and have no connection with that country in any way.

Perhaps the best know 'alien' to be harrassed in York was not Mr Steigmann or that poor fellow who was suspected of owning an airship, but the city's Labour parliamentary candidate. He was a barrister called Schloesser, who was selected by the party before the war began. Not long after hostitities started he changed his name to Slesser and rumours went round that he was 'pro German' (like some of the Rowntrees). This was helped, in his case, no doubt, by the ambigious attitude towards the war adopted by some of his party. In an attempt to put matters right he wrote to the press saying: that he was not German; that he had never been to Germany; that he had no relatives there; and that furthermore he supported the war. (151) 'I have satisfied myself' he wrote, 'that the breach of Belgian neutrality by Germany has fully justified England in entering upon the war.' This was not strong enough for one 'FUNNY BONE' who wrote an 'amusing' letter to the *Herald* attacking Mr Tribich [sic] Lincoln, (152) Arnold Rowntree and 'Mr H.H. Slesser (revised Yorkshire version)' all in one go. His daft effort was headed

> "If Lucy is Lowsey, as some folks miscall it,
> Then Lowsey is Lucy whatever befal it."
> The immortal Will - not the Kaiser.

It went on, heavy handedly, and offensively, to deal with Slesser's attitudes. Had he *really* changed ?

> One is reminded of the tale of the old nigger, who was a suspected poultry thief, and who was arraigned before the church authorities. "Brudder Sam, did you steal Brudder Johnson's chickens ?" "No. minister, I did not." "Did you steal his geese or his turkeys ?" "No, minister." But after an acquittal the delinquent remarked "Bless de good Lord, he didn't mention ducks."

There were other letters about Slesser, and they appeared at a time when the papers were full of the story of the wreck of the hospital ship *Rohilla* off Whitby. It was a bad time to be an 'alien', and just a few days before the *Rohilla* tragedy Vernon Wragge had told the world what he thought should be done with them. Wragge, a reactionary if ever there was one, was an important figure in York politics and in 1914 was the Recorder of Pontefract. He regularly used the Quarter Sessions there to give vent to his ideas and he did so again in October. His chosen topic was 'aliens' and the prisoners with German sounding names (if there were any) would not have felt reassured when they heard old Vernon carry on. '... he thought no-one would feel really secure until more drastic remedies were adopted with regard to enemy aliens', he said, (153)

> Those who had not been naturalised at all should be deported until the end of the war. Those who had been naturalised during the past 10 years, since when Germany had been competing with England for naval power, should be interned under supervision, but allowed to conduct their businesses, and those naturalised over 10 years ago should be allowed to live on their own premises under a substantial bond for their good behaviour and under police supervision.

Arnold Rowntree was as unpopular as the likes of Slesser, as FUNNY BONE'S letter indicates, and he would certainly have been on a Vernon Wragge hit list had there been such a thing. Rowntree, to people like Wragge, was 'pro-German' and as the war went on so attacks on the city's senior MP and the company with which he was associated grew more nasty. Arnold had spent little time in the Commons since the war started, but when he went there his actions were always criticised. In February 1915, for example, he came under heavy fire for a speech he made in the Commons when he said that the mind of the working man was in a 'serious condition' and that wages should be raised to achieve national solidarity. (154) This was sure to go down badly in some circles. Later there were quite unjustified hints that Rowntree and Company were acting unfairly, suggestions that he should resign and more letters to the press about his few attendances in Westminster. (155) Arnold Rowntree was extremely unpopular in the summer of 1915 - he was to become even more unpopular in the following year for acting in a way which observers now might well say was honourable, justified and, without any doubt, extremely brave.

1. *Yorkshire Evening Press* 13 July, 1 August (special edit) 1914. Hereafter *Press*
2. *Ibid* 3 August 1914
3. *Ibid* 7 August 1914
4. *Ibid* 11 August 1914
5. *Ibid* 3 August 1914
6. *Victoria County History. A History of Yorkshire. The City of York* (1961) pp 541-2. Hereafter *VCH*. G. Heelis, 'The Army and a City',thesis deposited in the York City Reference Library. C. Caine, *Martial Annals of the City of York* (1893)
7. See eg C. Harington, *Plumer of Messines* (1935) There is a memorial plaque to Viscount Plumer in the little church at Bilton in Ainsty, between York and Wetherby. Plumer left York to take up duties in the war zone at the end of the year. See eg *Herald* 2 January 1915, supplement
8. She was referred to thus by a *Press* correspondent called Rawleigh Humphries. Quoted in A.J. Peacock, 'A Nightmare (In Three Acts)' in *Gun Fire* No 10. The article is on Lawrence Rowntree. Humphries' exact words (from the *Herald*) were that Edith was a 'bigoted political partisan who can see no good come out of Nazareth'.
9. *Press* 5 August 1914
10. *Yorkshire Herald* 31 August 1914. (Hereafter *Herald*)
11. *Ibid* 12 August 1914
12. le Queux wrote a sensational novel called *The Invasion of 1910* (1906) as a part of Lord Roberts' campaign to get conscription. It was serialized by Lord Harmsworth in the *Daily Mail*. On le Queux see I.F. Clarke, *Voices Prophesying War* (1966)
13. *Press* 6 August 1914
14. *Ibid* 7 August 1914
15. For 22s. a week for 60 hours work. *Ibid* 6 August 1914
16. *Ibid*. There are many articles about the Wagoner's Reserve, and there was a recent (1990) TV programme about them. See eg "Contact", 'Yorkshire Waggoners with the A.S.C.', *Journal of the Royal Army Service Corps* and 'Old Soldiers the story of a waggoner', *Around the Wolds* No 12 (1990). See also *A History of the Wolds Waggoners Special Reserve* published by the Museum of Army Transport, Beverley (1988)
17. See eg *Press* 27 and 31 August, 1 September 1914, particularly the letters from F.W. Green. On the last date Green announced that recruiting was finished - that Helmsley had got his numbers up to strength. Conditions of enlistment were an agreement to serve abroad, familiarity with horses and an ability to ride, and enlistment for the duration at 'regular' army rates.

18. *Ibid* 31 August 1914
19. *Ibid* 26 August 1914
20. See the letters in *Herald* 10 September 1914 (signed 'AUX ARMES') and 11 September 1914 (signed 'A Recruit'). The nearest York got to having a Pals battalion were the two Heavy Batteries of the RGA, raised in 1915. See later
21. *Ibid* 31 August 1914
22. *Ibid* 2 September 1914
23. *Ibid* 1 Septembr 1914
24. *Ibid* 26 August 1914. At this date the NER announced that it would keep jobs open, allow servicemen's families to continue to live in company homes and would make a family allowance. The Baldock mentioned in this paragraph was T.S. Baldock of Monk Fryston Lodge, South Milford, a Boer war veteran who commanded the 49th Brigade, West Riding Territorial Division. Baldock, then 61, was wounded in action in July 1915. See eg *Ibid* 15 July 1915
25. These were led by the London Scottish. TA units were invited to volunteer for overseas service on 10 August (three days after Baldock's speech). Recruiting for the TA was stopped until Kitchener got his 'first 100,000 men' then restarted (for both home and overseas service). For a local report of the London Scottish going into action see *Ibid* 3 and 7 November 1914. There is a poem on the event in *Ibid* 8 November 1914
26. *Press* 17 August 1914
27. *Ibid*
28. See fn 22 supra
29. *Press* 9 September 1914
30. *Ibid* 14 September 1914. On the raising of the battalion see J. Shakespear, *A Record of the 17th and 32nd Battalions Northumberland Fusiliers 1914-1919* (1925 Chap 1)
31. *Herald* 24 September 1914
32. It was possible to volunteer for home service only up to mid 1915
33. *Press* 31 August 1914
34. *Ibid* 3 September 1914
35. *Herald* 31 August 1914
36. *Ibid* 13 October 1914. The NER battalion was raised after the regulations were altered
37. *Press* 8 and 13 August 1914
38. *Ibid* 13 August 1914
39. *Ibid* 24 and 25 August 1914. 'The Looters of Liege' was the story of a war correspondent trapped in the Belgian city of Liège. That was a place surrounded by forts which held up the German advance for a time until subdued by giant siege howitzers brought up specially
40. The Greys were the 2nd Dragoons and they were a party of Allenby's Cavalry Division, and the 5th (Independent) Cavalry Brigade. The papers rapidly became filled with personal accounts of the war. For a letter on the Scots Greys being 'cut up' see, eg, *Herald* 3 October 1914
41. *Ibid* 21 and 22 September 1914
42. *Press* 12 October 1914. Sgt Hutchinson's death is recorded in one of two interesting log books held at Fishergate School. The headmaster recorded the deaths of many if not all ex-scholars of the school and the logs make fascinating reading
43. *Herald* 4 October 1914. *Press* 3 October 1914
44. *Herald* 12 October 1914
45. *Ibid* 3 September 1914
46. *Press* 29 August 1914
47. *Ibid* 13 and 20 August 1914
48. *Ibid* 7 August 1914
49. Deserters were pardoned (if they joined up again) by Army Orders 297 and 327 of 1914. On the pardon see eg B. Webster, 'The Deserters of 1914 (1)' and A.J. Peacock, 'The Deserters of 1914 (2)', *Gun Fire* No 8 (no date)
50. *Press* 6 August 1914
51. See eg *Ibid* 7 August 1914. Some of the very worst German atrocities were committed at Dinant where a huge number of civilians were shot, including a very young baby. On the massacres see eg *The Legend of the "Francs-Tireurs" of Dinant* (Gembloux 1929)

52. *Press* 8 August 1914. Presumably the son was serving in the York detachment of the RGA. If this is the case he may well have ben one of those who volunteered ('practically the whole of the men ... nearly 200' did) for foreign service at Lumley Barrcks, a fact reported the day before Schumacher's arrest was.
53. *Ibid*. There is a picture of Koch in *Herald* 26 October 1914
54. *Herald* 5 and 12 September 1914
55. *Ibid* 5 October 1916
56. *Ibid* 12 and 14 October 1914
57. *Ibid* 17 October 1914
58. *Press* 7 October 1914
59. *Herald* 25 September and 27 October 1914
60. This was raised in the *Times* by several ladies, who wrote about the best 'method' of mourning the dead. See A.J. Peacock, 'How to Mourn', *Gun Fire* No 16 (no date)
61. *Herald* 12 September 1914
62. *Ibid* 8 September 1914
63. *Ibid* 19 October 1914. The Archbishop addressed himself to this 'problem' again in his monthly letter to the diocese in October. See *Ibid* 1 November 1914
64. *Press* 8 September 1914
65. 4 and 5 Geo V, Chap 77. The Intoxicating Liquor (Temporary Restriction) Act, 1914, passed 31 August. By this justices, on recommendation from the Chief of Police, could restrict pub openings to 9 pm. An order for even earlier closing had to have the approval of the Secretary of State. Maximum fines for breaches were £50. The Act was to remain in force for one month after the war ended - how this was to be calculated is not clear.
66. *Herald* 21 September 1914
67. *Ibid* 11 September 1914
68. *Ibid*
69. *Ibid* 15 October 1914
70. *Ibid* 14 October 1914
71. *Press* 18 November 1914
72. *Ibid* 26 November 2914
73. They were made by A.J. Peacock and are now deposited in the archives of Churchill College, Cambridge
74. *Ibid* 2 December 1914. They were to affiliate to the Central Association of Volunteer Training Corps. See the letter signed by the joint secretaries (H.W. Pulleyn and H.L. Greer) in *Herald* 4 November 1914. See also the appeal for volunteers on the front page of *Ibid* 5 November 1914
75. *Press* 12 August 1914. Many of the specials then joined up and a further appeal for men up to 50 to volunteer was made in November. *Herald* 6 November 1914
76. *Press* 7 August 1914
77. *Ibid* 26 August 1914
78. See eg *Ibid* 13 August 1914. Baden-Powell visited York en route to the east coast where Scouts were acting as 'coastguards'. In York he inspected the local Scouts and the inspection was filmed and the film screened at the Victoria Hall. *Ibid* 8 December 1914
79. *Ibid* 24 July 1914
80. They began by beating Rotherham County, champions for the last three seasons
81. *Ibid* 12 August 1914
82. Their rates seem to have increased anyway, for obvious reasons, if the reports of the York Martinmas hirings are reliable. Labourers there, of course, were hired by the year; the union's demand was for weekly paid workers. Nevertheless pay was 'considerably higher' than that contracted for in 1913. *Ibid* 28 November, 15 December 1914
83. *Herald* 15 September 1914. *Press* 15 September 1914. The railwaymen dropped a national wage claim a little later. *Herald* 30 October 1914
84. *Press* 13 August 1914
85. *Ibid* 12 August 1914
86. See the files of their paper *Votes for Women*
87. *Herald* 8 October 1914

88. He said this at a meeting to select a candidate for Walmgate. *Ibid* 14 October 1914
89. The Tories took the aldermanic seat by elevating Councillor J.B. Inglis. This caused a by election. Henry Hopkins of the York Traders Association and the Master Builders Association, a Tory, was returned unopposed. See eg *Press* 7 and 21 July 1914
90. *Ibid* 15 and 17 September 1914. *Herald* 18 September 1914
91. At first Labour said it would not 'force' elections. *Ibid* 9 September 1914. Later it agreed to the Tory suggestions. *Herald* 3 October 1914
92. *Herald* 14 October 1914. He was wrong. Elections were held in Scarborough, Ripon, Middlesborough and Hull for example. *Ibid* 26 October 1914
93. *Ibid* 14 October 1914
94. Published in *Press* 8 October 1914.
95. Results published eg in *Ibid* 3 November 1914
96. W. Robie Robinson (Tory) and R. Petty (Liberal)
97. A. Fox and E. Allen
98. A vote for Sessions was 'a vote for Progressive extravagance' Hewitt said. *Herald* 17 October
99. The results were: Scott 1,204; Sessions 1,204; Pearson 1,083; Hewit 1,023. This must have been one of the very few occasions when successful candidates got exactly the same number of votes. On Sessions' prevarications (he clearly thought his pacifism would lose him his seat) see eg *Herald* 3, 13 October 1914
100. See eg *Press* 26 October 1914
101. 'Spray baths' were being installed at Knavesmire Council School. There was a considerable amount of school building going on at that time. See eg *Herald* 24 September 1914
102. It was proposed to extend the tram system along Hull Road, see later. The tramlines were extended, for the military, in Leeman Road and Fulford quite early in the war. See *Ibid* 8 December 1914
103. *Press* 8 and 13 August 1914
104. *Ibid* 2 September 1914. The fears of unemployment (see later) were common to other cities. See eg J. Belsey, *The Forgotten Front, Bristol at War 1914-1918* (Bristol 1986) Chap 2 *passim*
105. *Herald* 19 September 1914
106. *Ibid* 6 October 1914
107. *Press* 8 August 1914
108. *Herald* 24 September 1914
109. *Ibid* 23 December 1914
110. *Ibid* 2 January 1915
111. *Ibid* 12 November 1914
112. See eg the bankruptcy of Benjamin Cohen trading as Clegg and Clegg in *Ibid* 11 and 25 March 1915. Cohen's case is mentioned in 'Jews in York in More Recent Times' in *Clifford's Tower Commemoration* (York 1990). This is an extract from an 'unpublished dissertation' by M. Hilton titled *Economic Jewish Activity in York since 1753*
113. *Press* 11 August 1914
114. *Herald* 7 October 1914
115. 'When are the motor buses coming to Heworth?', Edith wrote, 'We are not getting younger and work seems to be increasing. The rain it raineth every day.' *Ibid* 9 February 1915
116. *Ibid* 22 December 1914. A Local Government circular advised corporations to cut major developments by half, but York maintained that the Heworth development tramway extensions and other schemes (the building of tram workers cottages and electricity supply to Strensall, Poppleton and Naburn) should go on. See *Ibid* 11 and 24 April 1915
117. For detailed figures from the city's annual accounts see eg *Ibid* 7 November 1914
118. *Ibid* 10 November 1914
119. *Ibid* 29 April 1915
120. *Ibid* 9 November 1914
121. *Ibid*
122. *Ibid* 10 November 1914. The York Citizen's Committee also lobbied the government to pay £1 a week. *Ibid* 12 November 1914
123. Quoted *Ibid* 11 April 1915

124. *Ibid* 30 April 1915
125. *Ibid* 12 May 1915
126. Votes for *Women* 29 January 1915. The York papers regularly carried accounts of frauds regarding separation allowances tried in the local magistrates court
127. *Herald* 10 November 1914
128. Votes for *Women* 26 February 1915
129. *Ibid*
130. See eg the War Memoirs of David Lloyd George (1934) Vol 1, Chap 9, section 5
131. See eg *Herald* 3 May 1915
132. *Ibid* 4 May 1915. *Lloyd George Memoirs* op cit Vol 1 p 202
133. *Herald* 7 May 1915. On public opinion in Britain on the drink question at that time see eg T.N. Carver, *War Thrift* (New York 1919) - No 10 in the series Preliminary Economic Studies of the War edited by D. Kinley
134. *Herald* 10 December 1914. Edith's 'women are spending their allowances in the pubs speech' reported in *Ibid* 5 November 1914. In January 1916 (the allegations went on) the Lord Mayor of York, addressing the local branch of the NSPCC, gave the lie to the charges of Edith and her like. There were then, he said, 1,200 soldiers wives in York receiving separation allowances, and out of them 'there have been only 25 offenders through drink, and of these 17 had been under the notice of the Society' previous to the war. 'Once again', he went on, this gave 'the lie direct to the loose and foolish changes that are made from time to time, as to the conduct of the womenfolk of those who are fighting our battles'. *Ibid* 28 January 1915
135. *Ibid* 3 November 1914
136. *Ibid* 30 June 1915. The very first organised patrol began work on 27 October 1914. M.S. Allen, *The Pioneer Policewoman* (1925) p 22
137. Eg *Press* 14 August 1914, the case of Karl Lorentz, who had gone from York to Harrogate 'to enquire about a situation'
138. *Herald* 8 September 1914
139. *Press* 10 August 1914
140. *Ibid* 5 October 1914
141. *Herald* 30 September 1914
142. The bombardment of Scarborough (and Hartlepool and Whitby) took place on 16 December. see eg *War Illustrated* 26 December 1914
143. *Herald* 21 December 1914
144. *Ibid* 12 May 1915
145. *Press* 11 May 1915. The Germans first used gas on the Western Front in the Ypres Salient
146. *Ibid* 12 May 1915
147. For the events leading up to the Assize trial., and those dealt with at lower courts see eg *Ibid* 13, 14, 15, 21 and 27 May, 6 June 1915. *Herald* similar dates
148. On the Assize trial see *Herald* 16-23 July 1915. For an appeal by Joseph Goulding against this sentence of six months (which was dismissed) see *Ibid* 21 August 1915. The Bakewells appeared in the magistrates court at Lancaster
149. *Press* 22 May 1915
150. *Ibid* 3 September 1914
151. *Herald* 31 October, 2 and 3 November 1914
152. Trebitsch Lincoln was the ex MP for Darlington, once an associate of Seebohm Rowntree
153. *Herald* 31 October 1914. For another of Wragge's Quarter Sessions 'charges' - when he had no prisoners - see *Ibid* 10 July 1915. Also *Ibid* 28 October 1915
154. *Ibid* 20 February 1915
155. *Ibid* 2 August 1915, letter signed, predictably, 'Cocoa'.

CHAPTER 11

COMPULSION COMING ?

Arnold Rowntree was unpopular (amongst some sections of York's populace) because he was a pacifist, and because he was reckoned to be (indeed was) sympathetic to organisations which were (unfairly) reckoned to be pro-German. One of these was the Union of Democratic Control, a branch of which appeared in York. The city was a happy hunting ground for emissaries of the UDC the *Herald* said in an editorial of 19 July 1915. It was commenting on a meeting presided over by Sebastian Meyer at which R.D. Denman MP spoke on 'How can we help in securing Peace ?

The UDC had been set up just a month after the war started and its major aims were to halt the war by negotiation and make sure that the diplomatic methods used before the war were brought to an end. E.D. Morel was the secretary and he led the attacks on 'secret diplomacy' - attacks which must have seemed overwhelmingly justified when the Bolsheviks eventually released details of the deals which had been done with Italy to bring her into the war. Ramsay MacDonald of the ILP was the major politician of the UDC - a future prime minister, but at that time dreadfully unpopular for his anti war attitudes. (1)

Meetings of the UDC were frequently broken up, often by soldiers on leave. In July 1915, for example, A.W. Ponsonby was unable to get a hearing after B.N. Langdon Davies had been interrupted with cries of '"How much German money do they get out of this sort of thing ?"' (2) Ponsonby's attitudes brought great trouble for him in his constituency. (3)

The York branch of the Union of Democratic Control was, inevitably, regarded as a Rowntree creation and, equally inevitably, as 'pro-German'. It was small, and in July 1915 it took part in a meeting to create a York branch of the Council for the Study of International Relations. Prominent at that meeting was K.E.T. Wilkinson, the Quaker solicitor and a prominent Liberal, and Arthur Greenwood, then a Leeds University tutor, later to become a famous Labour politician. By the time the new organisation was set up in York the war had been going on for nearly a year and many of the organisations present at its inauguration were among those expressing if not explicit anti war views, certainly views about its origins and sometimes its conduct which would be enough to get them labelled unpatriotic, 'pro-German' or whatever tag occurred to those who thought like Vernon Wragge or Rhodes Brown. The Adult Schools and the New Earswick Village Guild were two organisations which were definitely equated with Quakers and pacifism. The Railway Institute and the Railway Women's Guild also took part in the creation of the new Council, as did the Fabian Society, the YMCA, the Church of England Men's Society, the York Liberal Club, the Lendal Literary Society, and the Cooperative Women's Guild. The York Trades Council also took part but, surprisingly, the local ILP was not represented.

It could be said that the creation of the Council for the Study of International Relations represented simply a desire of people in York (a small minority it must be admitted) to be better informed about international affairs, but that is not the way it was seen. It was seen as an anti-war or a 'peace at any price' organisation, and there was clearly an element of that in it. It was also seen as Rowntree inspired and that impression would not have been lessened by the fact that W.A. Kay and Wilfrid Crosland were its first secretaries, and that the meeting was hosted by the Educational Settlement which has been mentioned before in these pages, and of which Crosland was one of the administrators.

The Settlement got a lot of press coverage in those early years of the Great War. It formed a Club Belge (4) for the refugees in the city, provided language courses and others on aspects of theology, but what attracted most attention were its offerings on international affairs. Like the UDC, perhaps influenced by the UDC, it put on courses which looked at the events that led up to war and the secret diplomacy involved in them, and it got clobbered for doing so. The courses were presented as pro-German (of course) and were said to have purveyed 'Rowntree' ideas - which they certainly did. One in particular aroused some York patriots to great heights of indignation and brought Mrs Arnold Rowntree some very adverse publicity.

The Settlement ran a course on 'The Problems of the War', taken by F.J. Gilman, an adult school enthusiast, commencing in April 1915, (5) just after the bombardment of Scarborough and just before the sinking of the *Lusitania*, but this seems to have escaped hostile comment (surprisingly). In October Professor Macgregor of Leeds University, began a series of lectures on 'War and Nationality' at the St Mary's centre. (6) In January 1915 the York Adult School Union ran a week-end school there presided over by K.E.T. Wilkinson and Philip Burtt, two Quakers, on the war at which the lecturer was W. Bradshaw of Mansfield College, (7) then a few days later the Settlement's spring term began. Its main course was to be on European history from 1713 and Mrs Arnold Rowntree presided at the first meeting. She gave a 'UDC' type introduction to the speaker, maintaining that the war was the result of 'wrong thinking'. (8) Immediately the vitriol began to be thrown. Rachel McClelland of Heworth Green wrote to the *Herald* saying, profoundly, and stupidly, that 'Mrs Arnold Rowntree evidently speaks from the German standpoint', whereas what Mrs Rowntree said was that a better understanding of foreign affairs might prevent the excesses of pre war balance of power diplomacy. Rachel, however, was sweetness and light compared with Una Pope-Hennessy's contribution to the letter columns. She attacked Mrs Rowntree and Quakers like that lot at the Settlement. Mrs Rowntree's speech, Una said, was 'detached, vapourising [and] academic' and because of their pacifism people like her 'cannot suffer as others suffer the loss of beloved husbands and sons and brothers; they cannot sacrifice as others sacrifice their professions, their incomes, their lives on the altar of our country as many an unknown civilian had done during the last few months'. Edith Milner, naturally, weighed in with some profundities. Such a shocking misstatement of the causes of the war could only have been made by a pro-German, Edith said, going on to say that Arnold Rowntree should resign and revealing that she 'was ignorant of the existence of the "Settlement"' and was still 'quite in the dark as to its object or objects'. Edith was ignorant about many things, but not to have known of the existence of an institution run by someone as well-known as Richard Westrope in a city the size of York is incredible.

Una Pope-Hennesey's onslaught on Mrs Rowntree was typical of the hysterical attacks some people were making on aliens and innocents like Mr Steigmann. It was grossly unfair and H.C. Hunt wrote to the press pointing out that not all Quakers were pacifists and that some had in fact enlisted. Another writer told Una that about 100 Friends were working in ambulance units near Soissons in what was (then) the French sector of the Western Front, and that the MP for Leeds was among them. (9) He also said that two or three of Mrs Rowntree's brothers were there and Una herself might well have read a report in the *Herald* on 7 November 1914 which said that no less than 14 old Bootham schoolboys, Quakers, were already working with the wounded at Dunkirk. He could well have mentioned the fact that Lawrence Rowntree, another member of the family, was one of them; someone who had already seen more action than many men saw during the whole war. He was to see even more.

Lawrence Rowntree joined the Friends Ambulance Unit and very early in the war was helping the Belgians in the Ypres area, where he came under shellfire on more than one occasion. He wrote a description of his experiences which was published in the 1980s. (10) After some time in the war areas the need for voluntary work declined (as the army got its act together) and Lawrence returned home. When war broke out he had been a medical student at Cambridge and, back in York, he helped at the hospital at Haxby Road, the old Rowntree dining block which, like the Friends' Meeting House and, more recently Nunthorpe Hall, had been turned into a hospital. (11) (Rowntree workers voted to give up their dining block and it was let as a hospital rent free.) The workers at Haxby Road, like the members of the Army Pay Corps stationed in York were continually criticised as 'slackers' - the then in-word. They wore a uniform and were mocked for this. Anyway it seems very ikely that Lawrence was on the receiving end of abuse from people like Una Pope-Hennesey and the silly girls who handed out white feathers (one wrote to the press calling the hospital helpers 'the fakirs of the cant and cocoa brigade'). Whether because of all this or for some other reason Lawrence Rowntree decided to join up, and he did so as a private soldier, and he held that exalted rank when he took part in one of the most significant battles of the First World War. On 15 September 1916 tanks were used on the Somme for the very first time, and the one which got most publicity and attracted most attention was one in C Company called *Creme de Menthe* which attacked a sugar factory at Pozieres. It returned from action with its driving wheels smashed and when it stopped its doors opened and a young driver stepped out, only to be hit by a stray bullet or a piece of shrapnel. It was Lawrence Rowntree and there is something sublimely ironic about a scion of one of the most famous Quaker families being a part of the crew of the most famous of the first tanks.

Lawrence Rowntree was sent back to England for hospital treatment and while on leave was persuaded by Frederick Milner no less, Edith's brother, to apply for a commission. He did so and went back to France as an artillery officer. He was killed during the Battle of Passchendaele.

Una Pope-Hennesey and the other bigots could have found out about people like Lawrence Rowntree, but hating is easier if one does not know what one is talking about. Nevertheless Una had to answer the point made by one of Mrs Rowntree's defenders - that Quakers were serving in the Friends Ambulance Unit (for example) in hot places like Soissons. What did she say ? In the same paper in which Edith Milner's 'I am ignorant of the Settlement/sack Arnold Rowntree' letter appeared Una fatuously wrote that she admitted that 'Ambulance work is good work, but', she went on rhetorically, 'can it be compared to the divine folly of honour or to that truer and adorable faith which leads a man to toss his life like a flower at the feet of his country and its cause ?'

The creation of a study group on international affairs, the Settlement courses and the weekend schools indicate a growing concern about the war, its aims (the belligerents' war aims were not formulated until the conflict was half spent), its causes and what should happen at the end of it. The organisations directing their attention this way mentioned so far were undoubtedly Liberal or Labour in complexion, but they were not alone. They were not, as has been said, stop the war organisations, but they reflected a growing unease about what had gone on. Such courses as those the Settlement provided grew in numbers. In September 1915 that splendid institution started another on 'Democracy', which Edith Milner it is certain did not enrol in, (12) and a month later Dr M.E. Sadler, the Vice

Chancellor of Leeds University took part in a series of lectures that were started in Lendal Chapel. His topic was 'The conflict of ideals, absolutism and compromise'. (13) At about the same time the York University Extension Society (an organisation which was not accused of being pro-German) promoted a series of lectures by a Mr Ian Hannah on 'The Map of the World, its Making and Re-making'. (14)

All this activity produced great and unjustified hostility, and that hostility might partly be explained by the German atrocities of the time, partly by sheer stupid jingoism, partly by the fact that many people (like Arnold Rowntree) were also making protests against conscription (of which more later) and partly because it may have been seen as a possible cause for the fall off in recruiting. It is a fact that after the initial enthusiasm of the first months of the war, recruiting fell off drastically. Frantic attempts were made to get men to enlist in the last three quarters of 1915. The York Recruiting Committee worked overtime.

After the first great rush to the colours a hectoring tone crept into recruiting posters ('THE MAN TO BE PITIED' one published in the *Herald* on 28 April was headed) indicating that men were needed in greater numbers than expected, and the fall off in enlistments at the end of 1914 that has been commented on. Various ploys were resorted to to get men. For example special 'Bantam' battalions were created wherein men too small for normal entry in the army were taken. Recruiting of these little persons started in York in December 1914, with the requirements being five feet to five three in height with a chest measurement of 33 to 34. (16) York claimed that the nation's very first Bantam was a local lad (though he joined in Birkenhead). He was R.S. Parker (17) and the city was equally proud of the first two York men to join the Hull Bantams (J. Howard and T. Middleton). (18) Elsewhere Lord Derby, soon to become very prominent as a recruiter, organised a Docker's battalion, and in the York area the Earl of Feversham was authorised to raise a battalion in the Northern Command which came to be known as the Yoeman Rifles. (19) In York itself attempts were made to raise a second Heavy Battery. (The first - 'In every sense a Pal's Battalion of York lads' - was completed by the middle of April 1915.) Whereas Feversham got his numbers, however, recruiting for the York Battery went abysmally. In a three week recruiting drive held in October 1915, only 37 men joined, despite the fact there was reckoned to be 10,000 eligible in York. (20) A campaign by the West Yorkshire Regiment earlier had been less than completely successful too. (21) Even a visit by Harry Lauder's pipe band failed to get men flocking to the colours (it may have had the opposite effect).

The recruiting posters, by the early months of 1915, had begun to try and shame men into joining up, and the girls with the white feathers and the recruiting officers themselves began to finger whole communities and groups within those communities. Major General H.M. Lawson, involved in the West Yorkshire's campaign wrote to the Electricity and Tramways Committee of the York Council, for example, asking it to take on women as conductors to release those males of military age for the front. (22) Recruiters went round the hiring fairs of parts of North Yorkshire and tried to shame those who lived there by pointing out that in some villages hardly any men had gone, and a Colonel Saltmarshe declared at a Rural District Council meeting that Leeds was absolutely full of 'slackers'. (23) Lt Colonel Raleigh Chichester-Constable, a little earlier, singled out Scarborough for condemnation, saying that recruiting at that seaside resort was a disgrace. (24) He was right in one way at least. Sometime in the summer Brig Gen N.T. Nickalls was on horseback when he saw Enos Thompson Horsman, an official at the town's Labour Bureau, walking along the street in civvies. The Blimp on the horse asked Enos why he was not in the army, just as a recruiting band was going by. Enos said he had made four attempts to join up already, his employers (the government) refused him permission to enlist, but that he now had that permission. Despite this he was assaulted by the irate representative of all that was commendable about the British Army. He struck Enos across the face with a stick. Nickalls was prosecuted and quite rightly so. The following dialogue went on in court. (Royle was Thompson's solicitor.) (25)

> Perhaps the recruiting methods you employ will not encourage anyone to join. You will not use these methods again.
>
> No reply was given.
>
> A moment later the General said: "I should like to see compulsion adopted."
>
> Mr Royle: So should I.

Nickalls was fined two guineas and costs for his assault, and three ladies tried on something similar in York (well if not similar they tried to 'recruit' someone). The ladies involved were a Mrs Ward, a Mrs Wharram and a Mrs Barber, and they were eventually charged with assaulting a 48 year old employee of the North Eastern Railway. He was William Hodgson and he was followed by the three charmers into the Red Lion, Micklegate, where Mrs Barber called him 'A —— —— shirker'. He went home but returned to the Lion where Mrs Ward thumped him and his housekeeper. These two then went home followed by the three patriots, where another hassle started. Hodgson tried to escape through the window but was siezed by the nose and beaten up again. The ladies were bound over for a year with costs, and a report of their trial was headed 'TOO VIGOROUS RECRUITING BY WOMEN'. (26)

It is unlikely that Mesdames Ward, Wharram and Barber secured many recruits for HM Forces, though one or two might have thought that facing the dreaded Hun was preferable to facing them - particularly after they had had one or two in the Red Lion. (One wonders what work of national importance they did.) In an attempt to get more recruits the authorities relaxed their standards, but still only dented the problem of shortage of men. Height requirements were lowered for the Bantam battalions as has been said, and they also lowered other standards. A James Rafferty had been refused enlistment because of his illiteracy and his case became well known. The Director of Recruiting, in a letter to William Murray Burgess, the Procurator Fiscal of Haddington, said that henceforth illiterates would be taken into the infantry and some other units. (27) This was to be enshrined in an Army Order, and another order said that soldiers should wear their uniform at all times. One reason for this was to stop imposters using them, another was because the wearing of uniforms just might aid recruiting. (28) In 1915, also, the *Yorkshire Herald* began to publish a list of the names of those who signed up - maybe in an attempt to shame others into doing so too.

The most prevalent way of getting recruits - which still did not get enough - was to threaten those who were holding back with the ultimate sanction, compulsion. The National Service League, of which there was a branch in York, had stopped its agitation for compulsory military service when war broke out, but in August 1915, recognising that voluntaryism was failing, it decided to restart its campaigns of pre-war years. Announcing its decision to restart its fight for universal national service it declared that meetings would be held throughout the country and drew up specimen resolutions to be put to them. (29) This move, the NSL had Lord Milner as its president, must have made it very clear that unless things picked up, compulsion would be on its way. There were many who said the same thing, frequently from the pulpit. In April 1915 the *Press* contained a series of headings in bold type about the country's premier recruiter which read 'COMPULSION COMING? LORD DERBY'S BROAD HINT. WHAT EARL KITCHENER TOLD HIM' (30) and a week earlier the Earl of Harewood dropped dark hints about what might be in store at a meeting of the West Riding Territorial Association when he said that a two week campaign they had conducted had led to only 7,036 recruits, 'a very inadequate result for so thickly populated a county with a population equal to the whole of Wales'. (31) The Archbishop of York added his voice to that of the recruiters. 'No man who might go ought to wait to be called twice', he said, 'for obedience to the second call will be robbed of the sense of freedom and honour', (32) while a letter writer who signed himself RGA went at the subject a little more recklessly and attacked the 'flaccid, backboneless slackers' who, he said, either would not or did not 'realise their duty and responsibility'. (33) The Rev R. Harrington Johnson preaching in St Mary's, Castlegate also gave the reluctant-to-join-up some stick. In a sermon on 'service - now and afterwards' he demanded conscription forthwith. 'It seemed pitiable', he said, 'that one's country should be forced to stoop so low' as to resort to recruiting posters. (34) (A famous one was produced by York artists.) (35) The vicar of Hipswell, near Richmond, wrote in his parish magazine that 'shirkers must sooner or later be made to toe the line. Compulsory service', he went on, was 'the only way' to make them do so. (36) Sir Eric Swayne who reckoned three million men were needed, made what could have been taken as a rather unfortunate appeal at a recruiting meeting when he asked 'the men of York to come forward without further hesitation if they were desirous to be in at the death', and his colleague on the platform, J.S. Shannon, asked (37)

> would men of York refuse to hand down the sacred flag of liberty less sullied than they had received it from those who handed it down to them ? Was it not better to enlist as a volunteer and do one's duty in that capacity than be forced ? Unless young men flocked voluntarily to the cause of the flag of liberty there was the taint of conscription waiting in the immediate background for them.

Sir Frederick Milner had made similar comments and his formidable sister Edith agreed with him. 'We have a right to ask who are the slackers, and where they are', she wrote, 'Only national service or conscription, call it what you like, will find them'. (38) Just a week before Edith's letter was published 40 MPs had written to the Prime Minister asking him to receive a deputation which would present facts and arguments to prove 'that only by the early adoption of a measure of compulsory service can the war be brought to a successful termination.' Asquith refused to meet them. (39)

Given the poor recruiting figures, and given the strength of the demands for compulsion, it must have seemed inevitable that it would come, or at least that some attempts would be made to impose it. Opposition to it was declared, and among the most vociferous opponents was the labour movement. It, like the other objectors, regarded compulsory military service as 'un-British', an intrusion into its hard-fought-for liberties, 'Prussian', but also, almost as important, as a precursor to industrial conscription. From the very top to the lowest party levels all sections of the movement protested.

Large sections of the labour movement supported the recruiting campaign enthusiastically (James Sexton, a famous leader, was acting as 'consultative officer in the raising of Lord Derby's Docker's battalion for example) (40) but the very hint of compulsion antagonised them. John Hodge MP circularised socialist MPs to see if they would support the relaunched campaign of the National

Service League. Their replies were against it, he reported, '"The general tone of the replies I have received so far is absolutely against," he said. 'We are fighting against militarism, why then should we go for compulsion, that is the argument.' (41) A couple of days later the offices of the national ILP, where the *Labour Leader* was printed, was raided, and some ILP members (including Fenner Brockway) were charged with offences under the Defence of the Realm Act. (42) The reason for this was the intention of the party to print a statement titled 'Trade Unionists and Conscription, by Clive Bell'. A few days later the parliamentary committee of the TUC protested 'against the sinister efforts of a section of the reactionary press in ... attempting to foist on their country conscription, which always proves a burden to the workers, and will divide the nation at the time when absolute unaminity is essential.' (43) In early September the president of the TUC protested 'against a sinister and diabolical attempt to rush this country into compulsory service', and Robert Smillie, another labour leader, said 'Capitalists and landowners were in this cry for conscription, and it would be the duty of organised labour to resist it to the last.' (44) J.E. Williams, the secretary of the National Union of Railwaymen, interviewed by the French newspaper *Le Matin*, told it of labour's attitude to compulsion and what he feared might be a result of it. 'We remember how the French railway strike was crushed by bringing in to play the military organisation', he said. (45) Williams' logic is rather difficult to follow (there was already in existence a huge British army which could be used however the government decided), but his remarks embodied long-held beliefs about the evils of conscript armies. His opposition to conscription was echoed in York. T.H. Gill, chairman of the York Trades Council, attended a meeting of the Yorkshire Federation of Trades Councils at which Councillor Ben Turner of Batley spoke of 'military debauchery' and attacked 'the armament profit monger, the financial-sharper, and the secret diplomat' - all UDC targets - then say 'the curse of conscription should be fought against ... [as] Huge standing armies are a menace to continued peace.' (46) In December 1915 the York ILP 'pledge[d] itself to resist the imposition of any form of conscription' in a resolution communicated to the press by F.T. Beney, its secretary, (47) and earlier the York Trades Council had put its opinions on record. It viewed 'with considerable apprehension', it said, 'the strenuous efforts that are being made in reactionary circles to induce the ... Government to put into operation a measure of compulsory service.' This, the Council said, was unnecessary and unjustified because of satisfactory voluntary enlistments and it was 'contrary to the sentiments and principles of the British people; subversive of the free and democratic character of their institutions, and involves a serious menace to the liberty and freedom of the Labour movement.' (48) The Trades Council was undoubtedly correct when it said compulsory service was un-British, but its contention that voluntary recruiting was satisfactory flew in the face of very obvious facts. York No 1 branch of the National Union of Railwaymen protested against conscription 'in any form' and sent their resolution to J.G. Butcher. (49) He was unsympathetic.

Some of the churches, like labour, viewed the possible introduction of compulsion with alarm, though, it must be said, not many. On 17 September the York Free churches passed a resolution condemning compulsion (and asking for the pubs to be closed on Sundays) (50) but later seem to have had a change of heart (about compulsion not about closing pubs). Either that or they did not stand up for their beliefs. It was the Quakers among the religious who stood out against national service, and it was they (and the ILP) who took most of the flak for doing so.

Many members of the Society of Friends (like Lawrence Rowntree) went to the front very early in the war, often as members of the Friends' Ambulance Unit. They were pacifists and the most notable of their number actually left the fighting zone to go back home to become a resister - a conchie - when the time came. (51) People like Una Pope-Hennesy ignored the bravery of young men like these, (52) but many of those left at home made no secret of what their attitude would be if and when they were told they *had* to join up. As early as January 1915 Councillor S.H. Davies of York took part in a debate in Leeds on 'the desirability or necessity or otherwise of compulsory military service' with a Capt S.M. Mercer of the National Service League. (53) Davies was one of a number of Liberals who had wrested power from the Conservatives in York before the war, a chemist working for Rowntree and Company and someone who was to become very prominent in York politics in a very short time. Davies resigned from the council in October 1915 (his fine of £5 for doing so was remitted) (54) and, there being a party truce on, and so no November elections, his Castlegate place was filled by nomination. Arthur Wilkinson took his place, (55) and at the same time York got a new Lord Mayor. John Bowes Morrell had been approached to serve for a second term but had refused and he was replaced by Alderman W.A. Forster Todd, whose sheriff was C.W. Shipley (the 'first one selected from the ranks of the wage-earning classes'). (56) Morrell was not a Quaker, but was associated in most people's eyes with the Rowntrees, but, unlike Arnold Rowntree, he had taken part in recruiting meetings. (57) What his views on compulsion were were not made public (he really was a non political Lord Mayor during his term of office) but he perhaps did not relish the troubles that he must have seen were in store for him and his colleagues if and when compulsion came. (Morrell's sheriff was Oscar Rowntree who would seem to have been singularly ill-equipped to hold high municipal office in 1916.) They had made no secret of their opposition to it in headline grabbing speeches throughout 1915, their comments becoming more frequent (like labour's) after the National Service League entered the political arena again. During the municipal election campaign of November 1914, S.H. Davies had been pressed about his pacifism, if not his attitude to compulsion as he might well have been, because *as early as October* 1914 there was talk of it. Only 20 recruits came forward yesterday, the *Herald* reported on the 29th. If enough volunteers do not come forward by 30 November, it said, 'some form of compulsory service will be put into operation'. There would be no difficulties 'if the military authorities decided to bring into operation the Militia Ballot Act, which has not been availed of since the days of Trafalgar'. Compulsion was further away than the *Herald* thought, however.

Throughout 1915, through courses at places like the Settlement and lectures at the Adult Schools, the members of the Society of Friends put forward their views on the war, then on compulsion, and just occasionally on temperance. What they believed was well aired in a voluminous correspondence in the columns of the *Yorkshire Herald*. This had been triggered off by Arthur Dearlove, a socialist, a member of the ILP, and a pre-war rates resister along with Newbald Kay, now the king pin in the York Recruiting Committee. Much more was to be heard about Arthur, but he reappeared on the York political scene with a letter complaining (rightly) about the fact that the *Herald* had advocated shooting a few Clydeside strikers, (58) then later criticised the York Free churches for their apparent change of heart on conscription. Thereafter abuse became the order of the day with the Friends and the ILP (and particularly Arthur) getting it in the neck in the way supporters of unpopular causes sometimes do.

When Arthur Dearlove was vying with Arnold Rowntree to become the most unpopular York citizen among Old Ebor's bigots, a last great, national voluntary recruiting scheme was under way. It, too, was a failure, but it was extremely important in preparing the way for compulsion. It was the 'Derby Scheme'.

S.H. Davies made his views on compulsion known early in 1915, but voices against it were not raised in their thousands at the time - and the reason was definitely the assurances that were given by the Prime Minister that there was no intention of resorting to national service. Most of the opponents of compulsion were Liberals, Asquith was a Liberal, the government was Liberal, so they had nothing to fear they reasoned. His word was his bond. But, from the middle of May 1915 Asquith's cabinet was no longer completely Liberal - in that month (on the 17th) the Prime Minister agreed to the formation of a coalition, and into the cabinet came supporters of compulsion (like Bonar Law). (59) From 17 May compulsion looked more likely. The cabinet 'now contained a nucleus of politicians whose desire to prosecute the war was not inhibited by a devotion to the principle of *laissez-faire*. On the issue 'of compulsory military service' this nucleus was most likely to press for a decision.' (60)

Asquith engaged in a balancing act, putting off the abolition of voluntaryism with considerable skill, but was continually embarrassed by the falling off in the monthly recruiting figures (the first significant decline being in July). Lloyd George was for compulsion but Asquith persuaded Kitchener to agree to one last attempt to get men to come forward for the forces voluntarily. It was launched in October and was the Derby Scheme. The Prime Minister cleverly chose the Lord Derby, a Tory, a conscriptionist and a Vice President of the National Service League to head it.

Discussions about recruiting were carried on 'in ignorance of the exact numbers of men available for military service' in the first half of 1915. Many estimates were made, and an attempt was made to get reliable figures by a canvass of several million families, but this was a failure. In the aftermath of this it was decided to obtain a register of the nation's manpower resources, and an Act (5 and 6, Geo V, cap 60) was passed in July enabling one to be compiled. Some saw it as a step towards compulsion. Was it? Lord Derby, speaking at Liverpool, dropped one of many hints that he thought it might be. While the National Service League was saying the country should be placed under orders, Derby was a little more optimistic about men (still) coming forward voluntarily (he said). 'Some people, he said, would tell them that it meant compulsory service. He was not going to argue with those who said that; [but] he was going to be more optimistic than many. He was going to raise a pioneer battalion himself'. (61)

Details for the national register were taken on 15 August of all persons aged between 15 and 65, and there were (of course) objectors. Harold Pugmire, a schoolmaster, was committed to prison at Heywood in October for refusing to pay a £5 fine imposed on him for refusing to fill in his registration forms, (62) and at Croydon Amelia Elizabeth Hewitt a spinster and a draper was prosecuted. She was similarly fined £3 and costs (with 21 days in default). (63) Annie Wren Hutty was seemingly the first person prosecuted for refusing to fill in the registration forms, and she did so on suffragist principles. Annie refused to reveal any particulars about herself on the grounds that she was a woman, had no vote, and was therefore not a citizen. (64) She was fined on several counts, refused to pay and was distrained upon. There were no objectors to the registration in York, though there were to be later on. This is perhaps a little surprising. One might have expected Arthur Dearlove to have made a stand on this issue, for example. Perhaps he was saving himself for later.

In York 130 persons gave their services as enumerators and they were briefed at the Guildhall on 9 August. The enumerator 'must not get cross' with people it was stated and forms were distributed throughout the city during the week prior to signing on day. During the week the newspapers carried information about filling the forms in - urging people to give precise answers to ensure an efficient register. (65)

The national register showed that 2,179,231 single men of military age had not joined the forces, and the government produced the Derby Scheme. It was launched in October. This time there was no beating about the bush - if it failed, it was announced, then conscription *would* be brought in. Asquith said so in an ambiguous letter to Kitchener, Derby said so, and so did Lloyd George. If the numbers produced by this last effort at voluntary recruiting demonstrated 'to every unprejudiced person that voluntaryism has exhausted its utility,' the Welsh wizard said, and 'that nothing but legal pressure can give us the armies necessary to defend the honour of Britain ... I have not yet heard of a man who would resist compulsion under these circumstances.' (66)

Kitchener's cousin, a Miss Kitchener, also said the same thing to some ladies at Blackburn, but she laced her remarks with some rather acid comments or suggestions. The war would last another year, Miss K said and (67)

> They must also help, as women, in Lord Derby's recruiting scheme, for unless there was a satisfactory response ... it was almost certain that on December 1st conscription would come into force, and their relatives or boys would then have to walk the streets with the letter "C" marked on their khaki. Would they not rather their lads died for their country than that they should remain skulking at home ?

What was to happen under the Derby scheme ? There was to be a personal canvass of all available men between the ages of 18 and 40, and they were to be asked to agree to serve if and when they were needed. Those who agreed were placed into one of 46 groups, according to their age and their marital state - it being clearly understood that the 23 groups of young single men would be called upon first. At Edinburgh, late in the campaign, Derby reiterated his 'absolute pledge' to married men that this would be so. The method of calling up men only when they were required was referred to as the group system. The national register was to provide the information for the canvass.

J.B. Morrell, the Lord Mayor, called for canvassers to undertake the work involved in the Derby Scheme and an embarrassing situation developed. Men were being harassed to get them to volunteer, yet Morrell's call for canvassers was also badly supported. A letter in the *Press* said that only about 100 had offered their services, showing 'a very poor spirit of patriotism', and the writer went on to say that people would have flocked to help if the work was paid. He was probably right. And what response had there been from the councillors ? It had been abysmal, he said.

Despite the poor response in York the Derby canvass went on, and nationally, Derby said, in six weeks, his staff acknowledged and replied to 48,606 letters, issued a million and a quarter leaflets, 452,000 posters and 15 million circulars. (69) York was in the 14th Recruiting area and the campaign ended at eleven o'clock on Sunday 12 December. What happened ? On the day the scheme ended it was reckoned that a half of those men eligible in York attested, but that most had done so in the very last days of the scheme. There had been a last minute rush to attest, so much so that the recruiting office had been opened for a couple of hours on the day after the official closing date. (70) Why had men delayed (both in coming forward anyway and waiting until the last minute of the Derby scheme)? They were asked, and some said they had had trouble in getting an agreement that they could have their jobs back after the war, some said they were small tradesmen unable to make arrangements about their businesses, and others said they worried about the inadequate separation allowances then being paid. (71) To these reasons might surely have been added another fact. Many of those employers who, when the war started, had said they would make up their men's wages while they were serving their country had, understandably, had second thoughts. The last minute rush can also be explained, to some extent, by the fact that men realised they would almost certainly be called up if they did not volunteer, and they felt (like Miss Kitchener) that it was better to be a volunteer than a conscript, particularly if they were to be badged for everyone to see as she suggested. The extent of that last minute rush to sign up was incredible. The busiest day of the last week of recruiting was, not surprisingly, the very last day (11 December) when no less than 336,075 attested. On that day and the three days preceeding it a total of 1,070,478 signed up.

The report on the Derby scheme appeared in January 1916. Nationally it showed that (72)

The total number of men of miltary age available for service was	5,011,441
The total number attested and enlisted or rejected was	2,829,263
The total remaining was	2,182,178
Single men available was	2,179,231
Single men accounted for was	1,150,000
Single men unaccounted for was	1,029,231

For the York recruiting area the figures relating to the Derby scheme were published when the government relaxed the embargo it had hitherto imposed on recruiting figures. They mirrored those for the nation as a whole. There had been a 'poor response of single men', for example. (73) The national register had shown 'there were some 26,500 men of military age remaining in the area, divided roughly into 12,250 single and 14,250 married men'. Of this total of 26,500 'approximately 4,900 single and 7,900 men had enrolled under the group system, a total of 12,800 or less than half of the eligibles.' In addition to these figures it must be noted that about 2,150 single and '1,300 married men' either enlisted direct (74) or were rejected on medical grounds, so that 'the approximate number who came forward was 16,500, or slightly more than 62 per cent., as compared with 56$\frac{1}{2}$ per cent. for the whole country. The single men represented 38 per cent. of the attestations under the scheme, and the married men 62 per cent., figures which are, of course, disproportionate.' A comparison with Leeds showed the percentages were '37 per cent. and 63 per cent. respectively, which is a trifle worse.' The 14th Recruiting area consisted of 'York, Harrogate, Selby, Ripon, Wetherby, and many smaller places. York and district contributed 5,483 recruits under the scheme, Harrogate 1,468, Selby 1,058, and Ripon 996. In the whole area 5,200 single and 5,000 married men failed to attest.'

The Derby scheme had clearly failed to get the young single men to come forward and the results must have been a bitter disappointment (if not an unexpected one) to the likes of Asquith. Many of the married men clearly chose to attest under Derby in the hope that maybe the war would be over before their turn came, and the scheme also had attractions for some who were less than one hundred per cent enthusiastic for war service, in that if they had special skills or were reckoned to be essential to an employer they could be 'starred' and so not be called on. (Men in reserved occupations could also attest under Derby and live in the knowledge - with an armlet that proved the fact - that they had signified their willingness to go, but were unlikely to do so.)

The national figures quantified the numbers of attestees who were both single and 'starred'. (Figures for the York area do not seem to have been published.) The 'POSITION AT A GLANCE' the *Press* reported on 4 January 1916 was

Total of "starred" single men	690,138
"Starred" single men attested	312,067
"Starred" single men not attested	378,071
"Unstarred" single men not attested	651,160

The 'unstarred' single men, of course, would have been expected to go to the colours more or less straight away, and it is not surprising, therefore, that they did not present themselves.

Lord Derby claimed that 'starring' had been a hindrance to his scheme with many men, particularly agricultural workers, claiming they were 'carmen and horsemen, etc, though in many cases it is known they are not really so engaged.' These would all have to be looked at, Derby reported, and so too the list of men in reserved occupations. To do this work a series of local tribunals were set up. They were to be the precursors for others later.

A letter from the president of the Local Government Board was laid before the Finance Committee of the York Corporation early in November 1915, and it addressed itself to the fact that some Derby attesters may have been attempting a con. With a view of 'disturbing as little as possible the essential industries of the country men had been "starred"', it said, 'that is barred from enlistment, but', it went on, 'it would probably be found on investigation that some of these men could be spared'. In some cases 'questions' about classifying people might arise, and these questions should be referred to a local tribunal, at which a recruiting officer could be present with a right of appeal to a district committee. The York tribunal chosen consisted of: the Lord Mayor, J.B. Morrell; Alderman J.S. Rymer; Councillor K.E.T. Wilkinson; H.V. Scott; W.F.H. Thomson; and Councillor Shipley. (75) Forster Todd and Shipley, of course, were to be Lord Mayor and Sheriff for 1915-16. John Gulland, in a letter to the *Press* published on 8 November, criticised the composition of the new tribunal. A third of the members were lawyers, Gulland said, and there were 8,000 men of military age in York. The tribunal would soon be adjudicating on cases and would have to balance the needs of York against the needs of the army - so there ought to have been businessmen on it.

Who could present cases to the tribunal? Lord Derby, during the course of his recruiting campaign, and maybe in an attempt to dissuade some of his potential soldiers from trying it on, told a gathering of canvassers in Glasgow that he would instruct 'the Advisory Committee[s] to go through the starred lists with the War Office representative' and that cases would then go before the tribunals. 'Every case would be investigated on its merits' he went on, 'and he hoped to put every man in the right place, whether in the army, the navy, or the civil employment of this country.' (76) But not only that. An attestee himself could apply to be put into a different group and an employer could appeal against an employee being called up on the grounds that he was essential to his business.

By the end of November detailed instructions on the advisory committees and the local tribunals had been received. An advisory committee was to be set up in every parliamentary area and on it (five strong) were to be representatives of the local recruiting committee and industry. They could vet applications for postponement of call up and look at the categories men were in and make decisions, which, if agreed, would not go before local tribunals. What were considered 'unreasonable requests' would go for deliberation at the tribunal and the Advisory Committee's military representative would put their case there. (77) The York Tribunal got its detailed instructions at the same time, as has been said, and these were outlined in the *Herald* of 26 November. Coal miners, munition workers, railway and agricultural workers were usually to be regarded as exempt, though claims that they were improperly described could be brought. Apart from these special groups, both men and employers could apply for a man to be put in a later group 'on the grounds that he is individually indispensable to the employer', but 'In no case can the Local Tribunal place a man back more than ten groups, and notice of claim for postponement of service must be delivered not later than ten days after the issue of the proclamation calling up the particular group in which the man has been placed'.

The Derby scheme brought with it a formidable bureacracy intended to catch out the slackers, yet attesting under it still looked a reasonable bet for those who were not too anxious to experience what conditions on the Western Front were like. Married men might have reckoned they had gained some time (they had been assured that they had) and some men with sympathetic employers stood a good chance of staying out. The more one looks at the results of the Derby Scheme, the more one realises that among the men who had joined it were a huge number who were very reluctant to do so. An indication of this is the massive increase in the number of weddings that took place before the scheme started - among men who would then go into a later, 'married' group. Lord Derby recognised this and decreed that men who had married after his campaign began should simply be entered into his lists as if they were single.

It should not be forgotten that running in tandem with the Derby scheme were 'ordinary' recruiting campaigns, and these experienced the same things as did Derby. Enlistments were very slow in York, as has been said, but just as there was a last minute rush to attest under Derby, so there was a rush to join up in the normal way. That compulsion was on the way, everyone now realised, and some men thought it better to be a volunteer than a conscript, and attested under Derby. Others realised that it was perhaps better to join a unit of one's choice (though you could not be certain you would stay with it) and go in as a 'Kitchener' man. Many did this in York. Response to calls to join the second York Heavy Battery had been dreadful, then everything changed. In a three week recruiting drive, it will be recalled, they secured only 37 men. This was in late October. Before the end of the first week of November the battery was oversubscribed! (78) Feversham's Yoeman Rifles similarly got more men than were needed.

The second York Heavy Battery had had the support of two prominent York Labourists, J.H. Hartley, and Will Dobbie. Both these illustrate well how the Labour party now supported the war effort. Dobbie had started off as an opponent, then changed and eventually joined up. As Bombardier Dobbie he vied with the girls with their white feathers, (79) indeed he encouraged them. A letter writer to the *Press* said that one of the things Dobbie told a recruiting meeting was that he 'encouraged the lasses of York to walk on the other side of the road when passing a civilian who was not in khaki.' (80) This was grossly unfair, as Dobbie should, indeed must, have realised. A modern leader of the York Corporation on attaining office said that Dobbie was one of his idols, someone he looked up to as a model York politician. (81) One hopes that he was not referring to this aspect or period of Will's career when, though perhaps still a voluntaryist, he actually encouraged stupid girls to shun men who could well have been wounded and attacked many of his pre-war political colleagues who were soon going to make a determined and brave stand for what they thought was right.

Running alongside the last great recruiting campaign of 1915 were attempts to persuade men to join up of a kind which had lasting importance. There had been that request by the military authorities to the Tramways Committee asking it to take on women and so release male employees for national service. This was agreed to, women tram conductors made their appearance in York, and the pressure thereafter was on employers and employed to allow women to take over jobs which had hitherto been male preserves. A Munitions Bureau was set up at which people could enrol for war service, and pressure was exerted to have the clerical work there done by either women or wounded servicemen. (82) As early as March 1915 there were suggestions that women should be employed by the North Eastern Railway as ticket collectors and booking clerks, (83) and by August women were employed there as porters. (84) In June a Mrs Simpson of Terrington was employed as a temporary postman (85) and it was not long before ladies were doing many jobs of this kind in York. There seems to have been little opposition to this new phenomenon locally, though the Trades Council did make some protest. In Hull, however, men working on the tramways referred to proposals to employ women as 'an attempt to introduce an obnoxious system of casual labour' and a dispute ensued. The men lost, however, when the authorities dug their heels in, and perhaps workers elsewhere took note. (86) It might be worth noting that when women replaced men on the York tram system they were paid the same wages as their colleagues. (87) This was in November, and when the ladies appeared on the trams they received 28s. for a 56 hour week. Within a few months women had appeared in many hitherto male preserves as workers.

When the lady tram conductors started work the reports of them doing so mentioned that 45 per cent of the male tram workers in York had enlisted before the Derby scheme started, that six left on the preceeding Saturday, and that no man eligible for national service had been hired during the past 12 months. This draws attention to the fact that employers had frequently pressurised men to leave, and that jobs had been identified as either non-essential or jobs that women could do, so directing attention even more fiercely on fellows who were reluctant to go. The NER identified men who could go, for example, and in May J.G. Butcher urged York traders to employ women instead of male shop assistants (for example). (88) Two days after this a conference of York traders was held at which it was definitely decided to reorganise their businesses so that men could be released. (89) Whether this meant that, in the last resort, men of military age would be sacked is not clear. In October the Finance Committee of the York Corporation announced that it would not stand in the way of any clerks who wanted to join up. (90) The way to using women's labour had been well prepared in York and it started when an attempt was made to organise what was called 'the reserve force of women's labour in the city' in April 1915. On the 10th of that month the *Herald* reported that a Miss Thornton of the Board of Trade had been to York where she had met representatives of the local ASLEF, the Gasworkers' and General Labourers' Union and the Trades Council. The meeting clearly cleared the way for women taking on many hitherto men-only tasks, and Miss Thornton told her hearers that women railway porters had already appeared elsewhere and that she saw no reason why they should not be employed on trams. She said that in some places the Factory Acts which regulated conditions in workplaces had been suspended and spoke of what conditions women should work under. These should be, she said, those negotiated by Lloyd George and recently explained at great lengths by Sylvia Pankhurst. W. Shilleto of the Trades Council demanded equal pay and the labour members seemingly went along with the new proposals without demur, clearly delighted that the forces they represented were being consulted. The meeting was a splendid example of the public relations techniques that could have been used more extensively in the Great War and at which Lloyd George, at this time, was a master. Miss Thornton's appearance in the city cleared the way for the traders' meeting mentioned earlier and a painless introduction to the city scene of the lady tram conductors, and so on.

The recruiting drive of 1915 opened the door to women's employment, and work opportunities for them were to increase as the war dragged on. York never became a great centre of the arms industry as many places did, but in August moves were started to get a munitions factory set up there which would undoubtedly employ many women and girls. Early in the month a meeting of lathe owners, engineers and others was held at the Mansion House. Its task was to consider organising the whole county for war production and at the end of it a York Munitions Committee was set up to look at the possibility of siting there a factory for making shell cases. Their work was successful and in September it was announced that Armstrong, Whitworth and Company had rented two sheds from the NER adjacent to Queen's Street, and that shell producing plant was to be installed straight away. It was anticipated that a work force of 1,000 would be needed. (91)

The better work opportunities enjoyed by young women and the increased wages they received gave them greater independence and allegedly led to a dropping of moral standards which people like Edith Milner thought had already dropped far enough. The York branch of the misleadingly titled National Union of Women Workers had set up their patrols to first frighten girls out of - well- misbehaving, then reason with them. In the summer of 1915 they also set up a place where there was provided alternatives to whatever went on at and near the fair ground. In September a Girls Patriotic Club was formed, with Mrs Edwin Gray and Canon Tupper-Carey prominent among its founders. The Lord Mayor and Corporation gave the club a site at a nominal rent in Piccadilly and it duly opened for business. Its objectives were declared to be to 'provide a place for social intercourse under the best possible conditions for the girls and their men friends, [and] supply healthy influences to counteract the excitement of the present time.' How effective it was in this is unknown. (92)

The York Girl's Patriotic Club had that patronising air about it that so many organisations 'for' the working class had, and there can be no doubt at all that the club did not compare with the Stage Door Canteens of the Second World War in any way. But the good ladies who ran it were contributing to the war effort and their work should not be knocked (really). They were not of a class which could or would fill shell cases, and their war work had to be found other than in the factories. The patrols must have seemed useful and undoubtedly interesting and helping at the Patriotic Club worthwhile. They could also have joined the Women's Volunteer Reserve, which really did seem more valuable than the Patriotic Club (which opened as the Lady Wilma Lawson Hut in January 1916).

Edith Milner once said she would support the creation in York of a Women's Relief Corps, and no fascetious comment will be made about that. (93) This does not seem to have come into being, but by mid July 1915 there was in existence a York branch of the Women's Volunteer Reserve. (94) This had offices at 34, Coney Street and was intended to provide trained women to release men for the front. It was open to ladies aged 18 to 50 and 120 had enrolled in York by mid 1915. It had a cadet corps of 14 to 18 year olds and elsewhere was manning canteens in munition works. By the end of the year the Reserve's numbers in York had increased to 200 and they held what was in reality a recruiting meeting of their own at the Mansion House. Lady Wilma Lawson presided and the meeting heard a Mrs Charlesworh say something about the origins of the movement. It had begun, she said, as a rifle corps raised by the Hon Evelyn Haverfield, 'a very warlike lady, who did a great deal of scouting in the South African war.' The movement then changed, because 'however enlightened a Government might be ... it would [n]ever allow women to go to the trenches.' So they became what they were, a movement which ran canteens, wore khaki and drilled. Lady Londonderry was largely responsible for its present form, and the organisation ran courses in nursing, telegraphy and other subjects and aimed to provide drivers for hospital work and so on. (95) A great deal of time was spent talking about what they could do in the event of air raids or an invasion, the risk of which had surely gone by late 1915. The York Council's Education Committee also provided classes in the city for women to train to take over men's jobs.

There were tremendous outlets for women anxious to do voluntary war work, though the outlets would not seem to have been ones in which working class women might have been able to play a great part (certainly if they were working a 54 hour basic week). The Voluntary Aid Detatchment did marvellous work and so did the St Johns Ambulance Association. In July 1915 Mrs Lycett Green gave a report on its work, mentioning the Clifford Street hospital and that at Nunthorpe Hall, given by her father in law for use as a 50 bed hospital. A Capt Anderson reported that they had been given cars valued at a phenomenal £4,270 for use in transporting wounded men from one hospital to another. These included a Mawdsley, a Simms, a Belsize and a Studebaker. (96)

The enthusiasm for joining up had quite clearly gone by the end of 1915, but the amount of voluntary work being done had not declined at all. Perhaps it is easier to retain enthusiasm for helping the wounded (for example) than it is to maintain enthusiasm to get wounded, but York, like most places, had dozens of schemes for helping the war effort. In addition to those already mentioned there was a scheme for setting up a well-remembered and certainly much appreciated Soldiers and Sailors Canteen which opened on Monday 15 November 1915 on number three platform on York railway station. The NER gave three carriages placed at the buffer end of the platform for this purpose, and the initiative in creating this venture came from the National British Women's Temperance Association, and the Rev G.F. Richardson, a prohibitionist. (97) In addition to this there was a York Naval Vegetable Depot, from which supplies which had been donated were sent off to the senior service, (98) and the sandbag making groups started by Edith Milner and others still collected funds and made sandbags. (99) Edith's knitting circles still knitted and there were dozens of collections for cigarettes, eggs and other comforts for the troops, for prisoners of war and civilian internees. Later great campaigns for collecting horse chestnuts and sphagnum moss were organised. (100)

Edith kept up her letter writing to the press, urging readers to see the war as a means of Britain regenerating herself, to get Arnold Rowntree to resign, to watch out for spies, to support conscription and so on. Just occasionally she ventured into deeper water. She fulminated against dancing after whist drives (a 'very serious form of diversion') for example, (101) and her 'We have a right to ask who are the slackers' letter has been quoted. She had things to say about people ignoring the lighting regulations. Why are the soldier's billets in Haxby Road always a blaze of light, she asked? They made an 'excellent target for an enemy air raid'. My lamp is out, she went on, but 'I do not complain, but grope my way down my dark steps, dazzled by the distant blaze' from the soldier's digs, which was 'all the more evident from the near darkness. There are many puzzles which seem difficult to unravel, and I strongly feel there are many spies at large.' (102) There were many puzzles difficult to unravel indeed, and one of them must have been why the editors published so many of Edith's whining, simple, sometimes odiously prejudiced letters. Her appeals for charities like the Soldiers and Sailors Aid Society, and for money for troops comforts and sandbags were worthwhile and laudable, but her sallies into wider issues of the day were dreadful. She was one of those, incidentally, who believed the story of the Angels of Mons. A journalist called Arthur Machen wrote a story about a heavenly host appearing over the battlefield which he went to great length to explain was pure fiction. It was, but many people refused to believe him, maintaining that he had been divinely used to tell a great religious story. The whole thing became simply dotty, (103) with people like Edith swallowing the religious version of the story hook line and sinker and basing their arguments on the belief that if you could find a biblical quotation which suited your purpose, then that was it. (104) Edith had no difficulty in doing that, she could probably have found a quotation to support any of her ideas. On Sundays she helped at the Melbourne Terrace Soldiers' Club which met in the Assembly Rooms, and, she told readers of the *Herald* on 2 December 1915, she provided picture puzzles for the servicemen who went there. A night out in Old Ebor which took in both a session at the Melbourne Club and another at the Girls Patriotic Club must have been one to remember.

1. On the UDC see eg M. Swartz, *The Union of Democratic Control in British Politics During the First World War* (Oxford 1971) and H.M. Swanwick, *Builders of Peace: Being Ten Year's History of the Union of Democratic Control* (1924). Arnold Rowntree actually severed contact with the UDC very early in its history - his reason being that he thought it wrong to criticise the pre-war Liberal government in war-time.
2. *Press* 22 July 1915. Langdon Davies visited the York UDC in March 1915. *Herald* 22 March 1915
3. *Press* 27 August 1915.
4. *Ibid* 18 November 1914. *Herald* 19 November 1914.
5. *Press* 10 April 1915. It also ran one on 'The story behind the war', *Herald* 2 January 1915.
6. *Herald* 9 October 1914
7. *Ibid* 12 January 1915.
8. Mrs Rowntree's speech and the subsequent letters to be found in *Ibid* 14 to 19 January 1915.
9. Soissons was where the British crossed the Aisne during the retreat from Mons. They had fought there again in September but shortly afterwards the BEF was moved to Flanders. A letter writer to the *Times* also pointed out that 'all the direct descendants' of John Bright the famous 19th century Quaker politician had 'answered their country's call'. Quoted *Herald* 14 January 1916.
10. A.J. Peacock, 'A Nightmare (In Three Acts)' *op.cit.*

11. There were 50 beds at Nunthorpe Hall. See the report of Mrs Lycett Green describing how her father in law gave the hall for use as a hospital in *Herald* 16 July 1915. She was speaking on Red Cross work in York and mentioned that the Clifford Street hospital opened on 25 March. It had 118 patients when she spoke.
12. *Ibid* 24 September 1915
13. *Ibid* 11 October 1915
14. *Ibid* 13 December 1915. Report of the last lecture of the series.
15. On the bantams see S. Allison, *The Bantams; the Untold Story of World War1* (1981)
16. *Herald* 1 December 1914
17. *Ibid* 2 December 1914
18. *Ibid* 4 February 1914. Another York bantam who enlisted in the 15th Sherwood Foresters was H. Cambage. *Ibid* 13 October 1915, article with photograph. Yet another was J.W. "Stuff" Brown who had been a York rugby half back. He was in the same unit as Cambage and in January 1916 he received a special medal from the Mayor of Nottingham for being 'one of the best shots in the Battalion'. *Ibid* 27 January 1916.
19. *Press* 28 July 1915. For the war experiences of a 'Yoeman' from Hull, see, eg A.J. Peacock, 'A Kitchener Man's Bit', *Gun Fire* No 3 (no date). This is the story of Gerald Dennis of Hull and the title (a misleading one) is taken from his MS autobiography. There are fascinating tape recordings of Mr Dennis in the archives of Churchill College, Cambridge.
20. *Herald* 3,10 and 21 October 1915
21. *Ibid* eg 26 July 1915. Major General Lawson said in the Museum Gardens, York, that they had raised 300 and wanted 90 more men. He had great hopes that the ancient city of York would produce them. He was disappointed. *Press* 25 July 1915. He criticised York as others had Scarborough. *Ibid* 6 August 1915.
22. *Herald* 26 July 1915
23. *Ibid* 2 August 1915
24. *Ibid* 13 July 1915. For Scarborough's reply see *Ibid* 10 July 1915
25. *Press* 2 June 1915
26. *Herald* 15 June 1915
27. *Ibid* 13 October 1915
28. *Ibid* 11 October 1915
29. *Ibid* 20 August 1915
30. *Press* 28 April 1915
31. *Ibid* 26 April 1915
32. *Ibid* 1 November 1915
33. *Herald* 30 July 1915
34. *Ibid* 30 August 1915
35. This was from the Admiralty Recruiting Committee and was of a sailor with two guns behind him using the words "Remember!" "England Expects". It was designed by H.L. Oakley and a Mr Horsley of the advertising department of the NER. The earlier "Think" poster had also been designed by Oakley who enlisted in the Public Schools Brigade and was commissioned into the 11th Yorkshire Regiment.
36. *Herald* 6 September 1915
37. *Ibid* 4 October 1915
38. *Ibid* 14 September 1915
39. *Ibid* 15 September 1915
40. *Press* 31 March 1915
41. *Ibid* 16 August 1915. Hodge was very prominent as a recruiter and he appeared as such in York. *Ibid* 5 May 1915
42. *Ibid* 19 and 24 August 1915.
43. *Press* 1 September 1915
44. *Ibid* 7 September 1915
45. *Ibid* 20 September 1915
46. *Herald* 2 August 1915

47. *Press* 14 December 1915
48. *Ibid* 2 July 1915
49. *Ibid* 6 December 1915
50. *Herald* 20 September 1915
51. This was Corder Catchpole.
52. A well-known York personality of the post Second World War years, a Rowntree employee, was in the FAU. He was Harry Locke and tape recorded interviews with him are in the archives at Churchill College.
53. *Herald* 21 January 1915
54. *Ibid* 5 October 1915
55. *Ibid* 5 November 1915
56. *Ibid* 6 November 1915. *Press* 9 November 1915
57. See eg *Herald* 11 October 1915, report of a meeting to get recruits for the second York Heavy Battery.
58. *Ibid* 1 March 1915. The *Herald* had done this on the 27th
59. Bonar Law was at the Colonial Office; the Cabinet from 17 May contained eleven Liberals, nine Tories, one Socialist (Arthur Henderson) and Lord Kitchener.
60. J. Rae, *Conscience and Politics* (1970) p.5.
61. *Press* 16 August 1915
62. *Ibid* 12 October 1915
63. *Herald* 10 September 1915
64. *Ibid* 4 September 1915. See also the case of Frederick George Higgs of Chester in *Ibid* 6 September 1915. The report about Higgs said there were only two other cases of 'contumacious persons refusing to fill up the forms' in the UK. The *Herald's* report about Amelia Elizabeth Hewitt made the same claim.
65. Eg *Press* 11 August 1915
66. *Herald* 20 September 1915
67. *Press* 25 October 1915
68. *Ibid* 3 and 15 November 1915
69. *Ibid* 24 November 1915
70. *Ibid* 11 December 1915
71. *Ibid* 13 December 1915
72. *Ibid* 4 January 1916
73. *Herald* 8 January 1916. *Press* 8 January 1916
74. See later.
75. *Herald* 4 November 1915
76. *Ibid* 19 November 1915
77. *Ibid* 26 November 1915
78. *Ibid* 4 November 1915. The medals rolls of the Public Records Office show that Dobbie enlisted on 17 May 1915; rose to the rank of Corporal; and had the regimental number of 312492.
79. There are some letters about these delightful people - detailing how they handed out their silly symbols to wounded ex-servicemen for example - *Press* 1, 9 and 11 1915.
80. *Ibid* 23 October 1915
81. This was Councillor Rodney Hills
82. *Press* 10 and 12 July 1915, letter signed SPES.
83. *Herald* 22 October 1915
84. *Ibid* 7 August 1915. There is a photograph of the lady porters.
85. *Ibid* 23 June 1915. Picture of Mrs Simpson.
86. *Press* 9 July 1915. *Herald* 17 July 1915. The workers might well have taken note of what went on in London where there was a strike. All the strikers of military age were ordered to hand in their badges and uniforms, and men over military age invited to apply for their jobs. *Ibid* 22 May 1915.
87. *Herald* 22 May 1915
88. *Ibid* 8 May 1915
89. *Ibid* supplement 22 May 1915

90. They actually said they would not ask the Derby Tribunal to hold men back. *Ibid* 4 November 1915
91. *Ibid* 7 August, 28 September 1915
92. *Ibid* 29 September 1915. There are pictures of the Girls Patriotic Club in *Herald* 23 March 1916 (and a letter from Lady Wilma asking for money to pay off its debts). When Lady Wilma left York Lady Maxwell took over as president. In the first year of its existence the club got 900 members. For a report of its year's working and the annual general meeting see eg *Herald* 17 March 1917.
93. *Press* 5 November 1914.
94. *Ibid* 17 July 1915
95. *Ibid* 12 October 1915. On the Education Committee's decision to provide classes for training munition workers see eg *Ibid* 13 November 1915.
96. *Ibid* 16 July 1915
97. *Ibid* 15 and 19 October, 13 November 1915
98. See eg *Ibid* 17 January 1916
99. The energetic Lady Wilma Lawson organised working parties in the Assembly Rooms. See *Ibid* 5 August 1915. So did Mrs Mends the wife of a General. *Press* 15 August 1915.
100. Sphagnum moss was collected and dried, then cleaned and eventually used for dressing wounds. The first mention of it being collected by parties in the York press seems to have been in *Herald* 27 August 1915, an account from the village of Bainbridge. By mid 1916 the collecting of moss, available in 'bountiful measure' near York, was well organised. It was collected on the moors and sent to the Assembly Rooms and 26 St Saviourgate, where it was picked over by voluntary teams of workers. See the letter from A. Anderson in *Ibid* 14 August 1916.
101. *Herald* 7 December 1915
102. *Ibid* 9 February 1915
103. The work in which Arthur Machen gave the story of the Angels of Mons to the world is *The Bowmen of England* and the literature it spawned is voluminous. Quite a lot of the literature is mentioned in eg A.J. Peacock, 'The Angels of Mons. The Truth', *Gun Fire* No 16 (no date) and P.T. Scott, 'The Angels of Mons. More Truth', *Ibid* No 17 (no date)
104. Edith's letter (to which there were replies) in *Herald* 8 October 1915.

CHAPTER 12

THE BLACKOUT, PRICE RISES AND DRINK

Great use was made by the York press of letters from the front wherein soldiers berated the 'slackers' left at home who, they said, were not only earning good wages (which they certainly were compared with a Tommy's pay) but were agitating and striking for more, and so endangering the war effort. Nationally interest was centred mainly on the miners, but there had been wage demands backed up by threats of industrial action in York. The situation in which groups willingly dropped wage demands in the national interest did not last long. To suggest that it should have would be a little less than fair.

One of the first groups to put off calling a strike when war broke out was the agricultural labourers, who had planned action for harvest time 1914. (1) By February 1915, however, they had put in demands that were backed by threats of industrial action. They wanted 22s. a week and 5s. a day for threshing and 4s. a day for casual work. (2) They were only one group among many, and the reports of the demands going in (and often being agreed to) are fascinating and reliable guides as to how long people worked and for how much. The same paper which mentioned the farm workers' demands recorded that railwaymen had been given a rise, which later reports said they were dissatisfied with. (3) The formula agreed to for NER workers said that men then receiving less than £1 a week should get an additional amount of 3s., and that men receiving £1.10s. should get an extra two shillings. The York bakers (three quarters of whom were unionised) demanded a rise to 30s. for a week of 54 hours in February, (4) and early in March the city's tram workers asked for increases on their existing pay of 28s. for conductors and 32s. for drivers. (5) At the same time employees at the York Cooperative Society demanded an extra half crown a week (6) and men working at the Ordnance Stores threatened to strike for an extra 1d. an hour. (7) A letter in the *Herald* described their plight. They were on 5d. an hour it said and had been working between 72 and 80 hours per week. Now, however, overtime opportunities were decreasing and many men working there, with a wife and two children, were receiving 21s.8d. a week. The York city police put in a request for a pay rise which was turned down by the Watch Committee in March (8) and corporation workers demanded an extra 3s. at about the same time. The Streets and Buildings committee of the Council knocked a shilling off the claim and sent it forward to be debated by the full council in March. During the debate, in which Rhodes Brown opposed any concessions, it was revealed that the lowest paid council worker was paid 6d. an hour for a 56 hour week - giving a wage of £1.10s.4d. (9)

The York Corporation, whether controlled by Liberals or Tories, had always claimed to be a good employer, and a comparison of what its labourers got and what the city's bakers got would seem to substantiate the claim.

The letters criticising workers making wage demands (and usually getting them) were grossly unfair as a rule because they simply did not taken into account the price rises which had hit the country since the war broke out. Had workers not made claims many would simply have not been able to exist. As it was it must have appeared as if some of them were losing out anyway. A Mr G.H. Bowman of York put his finger on the matter when he told a meeting of the Railway Clerks Association at Selby that whereas the £100 a year men had recently 'got a bonus of 5 per cent., ... prices had gone up about 25 per cent.' (10) People like those Bowman was speaking to were relatively well off, however, as some of the figures quoted above will show. The agricultural labourers who were demanding 22s. got £1, despite the fact that labour in the villages was short, and some railwaymen, who would not have got the perks that the rural worker (sometimes) got, earned below a pound at the start of 1915. S. Holmes, chairman of the Northern District of the Operative Bakers organisation pointed out, correctly, that a married man with a family (whose wife was not working) would be having a very difficult time indeed if he received something like the average wage. It was 'impossible', Holmes said, 'for a man in receipt of less than 30s. a week to be a respectable person and do his duty to his wife and children.' (11) Of course if a man in receipt of thirty shillings, had a wife and children working, things might have been comfortable compared with pre-war days, but the kind of person Holmes had in mind, presumably, was a workman with small children and a wife unable to work. For them times were indeed bad.

What of the extent of inflation in these early months of the war ? Prices began to go up almost as soon as hostilities commenced - at first for reasons of profiteering, perhaps, but later for more laudable reasons. Early in January 1915 the cost of a quartern loaf of bread was 7d. compared with 6d when the war started. The reasons given for this were that the Australian harvest had failed, that freight charges had gone up, that there was a ring operating in the USA, and that British merchants had been gambling with corn. (12) At the end of the first week of 1915 the Board of Agriculture issued some comprehensive figures comparing price increases which (with the exception of fish) showed no extraordinary advances, but made it evident that what price rises there had been, were larger on the inferior qualities of meat, for example. Some of the figures were (13)

	Week ending 6 January 1915	Week ending 6 January 1914
Second Quality beef per cwt	68.10	60.8
Dozen eggs second quality	2.0	1.7
Irish bacon per cwt	87.0	80.0

In late January figures like those above were given by G. Dickenson, the secretary of the York Grocers' Association. He gave prices for Danish butter and flour, and said the reasons for the rises were those given before - higher freight charges, 'an artificial "rig"', and farmers holding grain back. (14) Dickenson contended that Danish butter now cost 1s.7d. compared with 1s.4d. twelve months earlier, and that flour had gone up from 25s.6d. to 42s! At the annual general meeting of the York Gas Company it was announced that from March its charges would go up by 2d. for every 1,000 cubic feet consumed. (15) In July a correspondent to one of the York papers claimed that, for reasons he did not give, prices were higher in York than elsewhere, and gave examples. Cod, he said, which cost 6d. in Leeds, cost 8d. in York, while sugar, bacon and other items were a penny a pound more than elsewhere. There had been a glut of pineapples (!) in London, he had concluded, which were selling at 10d. In York they were retailing at 3s.6d. (16) Towards the end of the year there were further increases caused, this time, by the Chancellor.

In September 1915 Reginald McKenna produced what was in fact the third war budget, and it came as a very unpleasant shock. It seems incredible, but no new taxation whatsoever had been imposed in May (in the second war budget). McKenna however added 40 per cent to income tax by putting it up to 3s.6d. in the pound and reducing the limits downwards so that a man with no children earning £2 15s a week paid £2.8s.4d. a year. Duties of 33 1/3 per cent were put on 'luxury' imports (like cars) and an excess profits duty of 50 per cent was put on pre-war company profits to meet any outcry against war profiteers. (It soon became known as the EPD and was raised to 80 per cent in 1917.) In addition to all this sugar was taxed, and the duties already levied on tobacco, tea, coffee, chicory, and dried fruits (except currants) were raised by 50 per cent, and the duty on patent medicines was doubled. Postal charges also went up, and the halfpenny post was abolished. McKenna's budget was a departure from the principles of free trade and the cause of many complaints among Liberals who maintained that the party was being broken by it. (By taxing the overseas luxuries McKenna stimulated production at home and thus reintroduced protection.) Petrol duty was also raised by 3d. a gallon.

To the man in the street the increases in 'essentials' were serious indeed. Tea went up by 4d. a pound; sugar by a halfpenny; and tobacco by 1d an ounce. Cigarettes went up by 3d. or 3^1/$_2$d. a packet. Any advantages that had been gained by York workers earlier in the year were almost certainly swallowed up. In addition to this rents had been rising in the city.

In December 1915 a deputation of York 'Labourists' went to lobby the City Council about rents, demanding also that the city should be included in the Rents Bill which was then before parliament. A great deal of attention had been directed on rent rises by agitators in Scotland and J.H. Hartley, Mrs Fawcett of the York Womens' Federation, W.H. Farrar, the president of the local ILP, and Mr Hutchinson, the secretary of the Trades Council and joint secretary of the War Emergency Rent Committee produced similar stories about York. (18) In October Councillor Horsman had protested at a council meeting about rent rises (19) and this provoked the inevitable letters to the *Press*. One of the first spoke of the 'bloodsucking business' of letting in which 'miserable' food of 'microscopic dimensions' was 'served out by ... grabbing niggardly landladies for 16s., 17s.6d, and £1 a week' (20) He seemed to have the experience of clerical workers brought into York to work in army or government offices in mind, and he was challenged (21) but there is no doubt whatsoever that rents both for housing and lodgers *had* gone up. Horsman, when making his presentation to the Council, had used statistics and arguments which had been presented to the country at a York conference of the War Emergency Workers' national committee at which he, Hartley and the famous Henry Myers Hyndman had been present. They showed that shortage of rented accommodation had produced a problem of crisis proportions in York, and that the shortage had forced rents up. There were, when the conference met, (22) 700 houses then available for rent, and of those only 50 were available at less than £30 a year. In the last two years in York there had been 1,300 marriages and only 110 new houses built. Horsman's solution, of course, would have been to build council houses, but given the political complexion of the York Corporation and war time restrictions that was not a possibility. (Walter Long, president of the Local Government Board had recently ordered local authorities to exercise strict economy, and it was only with difficulty that York was able to complete its tram extensions.)

Horsman's protests about rent rises and the associated lobbying by the city's left wing organisations (or some of them) came as near to upsetting the political truce, which had now been extended to municipal affairs, as anything did in 1915. A year earlier York has stood out in holding municipal elections, but since then the Labour party had swung over to supporting the war and it agreed to honour an agreement not to engage in politicking on a local level. In November there were no elections and municipal affairs became extremely dull. Only questions relating to education in the city raised the standard of debate or interest in the Council's proceedings in 1915. (That and wage demands.)

Rent rises, the cost of essentials like gas and food price increases meant that, as before the war, and despite labour shortages, (23) life must still have been extremely hard for many in York. For those who could afford it, however, there was still plenty of professional entertainment. The Theatre Royal and the Empire still flourished, with the latter still mixing films with its music hall turns, and bringing the very famous, on occasion, to perform there. In May 1915, for example, Syd Walker appeared there in Fred Karno's first revue 'Parlez Vous Francais?' (24) The Empire was frequently given over to celebrity lectures which were part of the war effort. In the week in which Syd Walker appeared there Fred T. Jane gave a talk on the naval war, for example, and on another occasion Crawford Price, a *Times* correspondent, lectured on 'SERBIA'- THE TALE OF A GALLANT NATION.' (25) The local cinemas also regularly took part in the recruiting campaigns and fund raising efforts.

The cinema was the most popular form of entertainment with the populace in 1915 and when the war started York was already well served with picture palaces - one of which was purpose built. In April, without ceremony, another was added to them. This was New Picture House in Coney Street, (26) erected at a cost of £10,000 by the York Picture House Company. It had 1,000 tip up seats, an orchestra under the direction of one W. Bartley, and by all accounts it was a splendid place indeed. It proudly announced that 'Jane Shore' would be shown in May, (27) but its opening programme consisted of 'When East meets West,' a film based on a story by the Marchioness Townshend, 'The Manicure Girl', a comedy which like most films probably promised more than it delivered, and 'A Partner of Providence', a detective film. The bill was completed with a film consisting, the papers said, of Lightning sketches of the Kaiser'. (28)

Edith Milner did not weigh in with any criticisms of the cinema, though others did, and a tiny advance was made in the early months of the war by the York film industry (if that is what it was). Several 'topicals' made in York in the early days of the conflict have been mentioned, and the creation of a film making department in Debenhams, which first filmed a York race meeting, was also noted. In May 1915 the firm made a version of Henry V for Eric Williams, a London actor, shooting some of the scenes in the Museum Gardens and using troops of the 5th

Cavalry Reserve as extras. Debenham's earlier made 'The Lifeboatman' for and with Williams at Scarborough. (29)

The great spectator sports of the North of England were football and rugby, and when the war started the York City professional team carried on with its programme to the accompaniment of much criticism - not the least of which was that the players should be in the forces. The season then went badly, at least from a financial point of view. The club had offered very generous terms to its players and had had a heavy bill for wages during the summer. From the beginning of the season to January a weekly wages bill of £27.10s. had to be found when gate takings were down to £50. (30) Season tickets, which had realised £207 in 1913-14, had produced only £50 in the season so far and wage reductions had been imposed with the players receiving two thirds of the takings at the turnstiles for home gates (a move which brought the wage bill down to £7.10s a week). Sod's law had also prevailed, with the bad weather keeping spectators away and the club had a loss of £318 with the season half way over. They had four home and eight away games to play (for which they would get little income) (31) and they had made an appeal for cash. This had brought in the magnificent sum of £1.1s.0d from Oscar F. Rowntree. It was reckoned they needed £185 to complete the season.

York City completed the 1914-15 season, but then bowed to the inevitable. They made a loss of £373, which does not look too bad when it is recalled that they were £318 down with 12 games to go (in March), and in the summer announced that there would be no professional football in York in 1915-16. (32) A programme of local matches, with scratch sides, often from the Army, was announced, and very attractive it looked too. The first game was between teams representing the Army Ordnance Corps and the Durham Royal Engineers and the second was between York City and the AOC. The weather then was 'delightful', the ground was 'excellent', but the crowd was 'small'. In the third week of the season 'There was [again] only a small attendance to see the 5th Cavalry Reserve beat the City by three goals to one.'

The decision to abandon professional rugby in York, also, was given some 'recruiting' overtones. Should the Clarence Street Club continue to provide entertainment for the slackers at home, a meeting of the Northern Union Rugby Club was asked in the summer? Fifty one members of the club had joined up, Alderman Forster Todd reported, and it was resolved that henceforth there would be no professional games played in York. In the following season, it was announced, the club would play only friendly home matches . (33) It does not seem to have occurred to anyone that this might still possibly provide entertainment for the 'slackers at home'. Not only that, but without doubt the club would eventually tout for customers, gratefully taking their money whether they were slackers, 'conchies', Quakers or whatever. People and organisations were as adept at compartmentalising their attitudes during the Great War as they were at any other time.

So York changed enormously with the disappearance for the duration of professional sports, and it changed in another way too. Lighting regulations made the city a gloomy place, as Edith Milner said, and they were the subject of a good deal of criticism and a large number of prosecutions. No doubt those who were alarmed at the goings on at the fairground and the dropping of certain standards laid a great deal of blame at the door of Old Ebor's 'darkened streets'. Perhaps the potential of the darkened York streets, however, for those on the lookout to take advantage of them was negated to some extent by the NUWW patrols. (In 1911 they had eleven on the go and they said quite categorically that things had been made worse by the black-out, and that the 'danger point' of York was the fairground.)

The nation was worried about attacks from the air, of course, and it was because of this that blackout restrictions were imposed. The first seem to have been made in January 1915, when the Chief Constable issued notices about lighting and what would happen in the event of an air raid. (34) Mr Burrow ordered shopkeepers to stop using lights outside their premises, and said that all windows were to be screened. The electricity supply, from York's municipally owned generators, would be cut in the event of an alarm, and citizens were urged to get a secondary source of lighting. The gas supply would be turned off at source in the case of an emergency and the street lamps doused at the earliest opportunity. In April there were what seem to be the first prosecutions for lighting offences in York. (35)

The early lighting regulations were clearly the result of local initiative, but in April York became subject to the provisions of an order issued by the Home Secretary under the Defence of the Realm (Consolidation) Regulations of 1914. These ordered that from one hour after sunset until one hour before sunrise: illuminated signs must be extinguished; market flares extinguished; public lights doused or shielded; car lights kept low; blackouts implemented; and rear lights used on cars. In addition to this factory roofs had to be blacked over. (36) By the middle of April the order was in force and on the 14th the *Herald* gave a long description of what the city was now like at night (well it said what the city was like without lights). 'The novelty of the darkness under which the city will exist at nights is perhaps appealing to the people of York more than the experience itself', the *Herald* said. By nine o'clock all the shop lights which had aided pedestrians, like the arclights on shop fronts, 'were gone' and 'as these evenings there is no moon, from that time onwards the streets were in utter darkness. This was particularly so in the case in narrow streets, such as Coney-street, which was naturally far from being so full of people as it usually is. That is one of the most noticeable effects of the new regulations - the comparative emptiness of the streets at an early hour of the evening. The difficulties of traffic' however, 'were greatly reduced by the use at corners and crossings of low-power lights.'

At the end of the month the first York prosecutions under the DORA regulations were held, and the first malefactor to be dealt with was William Ellis, a butcher of King's Square who was unable to appear in court because of that affliction of the over indulgent - the gout. Clearly people like Ellis had not taken the new restrictions as seriously as they should have, and the police were out to make an example of one or two of them. The Chief Constable said so. The case against Ellis was brought, Mr Burrow said, 'for the purpose of making it known that something would have to be done, and done seriously, to compel people to comply with the order' which was dated 8 April and became effective four days later. The Chief Constable revealed that under the order it was necessary for the offenders to be reported, first of all, to the military authorities for permission to prosecute. The offender could also be dealt with by a court martial, Mr Burrow went on, but on this occasion Colonel Lord Basing had given permission for proceedings to take place before the beaks. Ellis, rather ungraciously, blamed his wife for his crime, saying that she had turned the lights on by mistake. (37)

Also in court, along with butcher Ellis on that memorable day in 1915, were Jonathan Dunningham, a tailor of Church Street, and 15 cyclists. Dunningham had broken the blackout regulations in the way Ellis had, at his house or shop, and he was told he could have got a £100 fine or six months in the nick. (He got away with ten shillings as did Ellis.) Fourteen of the cyclists were done for having no rear lights, and got away with costs of 5s. each with no conviction registered. Poor old Dunningham must have had a fright when the consequences of his unpatriotic behaviour were pointed out to him, but justice would seem to have been done - and Chief Constable Burrow's warning must have got across. The last of the cyclists also revealed that the new order would have been welcomed in some circles. 'Alfred Anfield stated that he was hurrying home to see his child who was ill, and [he] had tried to get a rear light but could not as the shops had sold out'. The rest of the cyclists must have cursed their luck when they heard that Alf's case was dismissed.

The dousing of the street illuminations allegedly led to a spate of accidents (as well as much else if the fears of Edith Milner and the NUWW were justified). The Yorkshire Insurance Company saw an opportunity for increased business, and under a heading that read 'DARKENED STREETS AND ACCIDENTS' readers of the *Herald* were urged to get 'a "YORKSHIRE" Policy.' (38)

The ordinary people who showed lights when they should not have shown lights ran a serious risk of being accused of being spies or collaborators, but some well-known York citizens were also found guilty; people who were beyond reproach (as patriots anyway). Canon Bell - he who revived the Mystery Plays- got done and so did premises belonging to H. Rhodes Brown, the ex Lord Mayor. (39) There were many others, and there were people, too, who objected to the gloom that had descended upon the city, saying that it was the cause of some danger. One letter writer to the *Herald*, for example, wrote asking if a cage lamp 'such as was formerly on Scarborough Bridge, [could] be placed near Lendal Bridge, just at the corner where the steps descend by the waterworks ?' Placed there, he said, it would not be visible from the air, and people found it, he went on, 'a very dangerous corner in these days of "lights down".' (40) He may have meant by that last remark that people were in danger of falling down the the steps. He probably did, but he may have meant that and something else. Anyway he signed himself 'GROPER'.

As old Groper revealed, and as mentioned before, the country, and York, were afraid of Zeppelin attacks, and they had every right to be. Zeppelin raids had become fairly common throughout 1915. (41) They were frequently reported in the press and were the cause of constant scares during the raiding season. It became imperative that the local authorities should devise a scheme of air raid warnings, though 1915 ended without an attack on York. They thought they had solved the problem by the end of the year, but events were to prove them wrong.

Chief Constable Burrow had outlined what would happen in the event of an air raid early in 1915, (42) but his instructions then had more to do with blacking out what lights remained once a raid had started. What could be done to warn the citizens of enemy aircraft approaching so that they could take shelter ? The blackout seemed to be operating fairly well in the last summer months of 1915, helped on by numerous prosecutions particularly, so it was said, in the Acomb area, (43) but experiments with a warning had been going on for months without being completely satisfactory. In April '"Like a thief in the night"' a Zeppelin - known in German official records as Z9 - 'stole over the North-east coast ... just after dark, and accomplished a circular tour of bomb dropping for about 50 minutes ... '(44) It was, 'it appears, ... first observed by a Shields pilot off the Tyne, steering northward' and was next seen above terra firma at Blyth at 8.05 As soon as the visitor was identified as a Zeppelin the news was rapidly telegraphed over the whole of the North Country, and lights were extinguished. At Selby mills which were engaged on night work were closed and the mast lights on shipping were doused'. In Leeds the alert was received at 10.30 and 'A pre- arranged code signal, summoning all special constables to duty, was thrown on the cinematograph screens at various places of amusement and proved very effective' and at Goole the National Reserve and the Customs officials 'assisted the police in extinguishing the public lights in the docks, the river, and in the town.' Halifax was in total darkness by 10.30, and in York 'the men of the York Volunteer Training Corps (45) and the special constables' clicked superbly into gear for what was expected might be the city's first air raid. They were summoned by a siren and reported to the police station, then patrolled the city to assist the police in seeing that all windows were properly obscured and that no lights were burning which would be likely to attract the attention of enemy aircraft. The VTC went to posts previously allotted to them and the York Voluntary Aid Detachment, 'numbering 70 men, under Captain Anderson, were on duty ... with every requisite for rendering first aid to the injured should necessity arise.' The detachment, which spent a week in camp recently, had been 'training for three years' the *Herald* told its readers, 'and it is thoroughly efficient.'

It will have been noticed that air raid warnings in York, Halifax and other places were audible signals, but it was the practice of the Zeps, sometimes, to switch off their engines and hover in the skies, maybe above the clouds, and use the noise from a town to home in on their targets. Air raid warnings of the kind used in 1915 could almost have been designated as Zeppelin aids, and an alternative (or alternatives) had to be found. They were eventually. Arrangements were made whereby citizens would be warned of a raid by interrupting the supplies of gas and electricity. The electricity would be cut off and the gas pressure raised and lowered a number of times. This way the Zep commander would be denied the help of an audible alarm of the kind hitherto used. But what if the alarm came when people were in bed and not using their lights, and what about those people who did not have gas or electricity ? By the time these silent warnings were implemented, however, (46) York had been raided.

By the end of the first month of 1916 new lighting regulations were in force in York, becoming operative on Monday 10 January. They decreed that 'the intensity of inside lighting of shops and shop fronts must be reduced or the lights obscured so that no more than a dull, subdued light is visible outside, and no part of the pavement, roadway, or any building is distinctly illuminated. In particular', the order went on, 'all sources of light must be shaded with some opaque material so that all direct light is cut off from the windows and doors.' (47) In hotels, dwelling houses 'and premises of all descriptions' lights had to be reduced or shaded so that no more than a subdued light could be seen 'from any direction outside'. For all vehicles the lighting up time was altered to half an hour after sunset and the order that they carried lights was 'extended to all vehicles using the road-way, including hand vehicles', which would have to carry single lamps 'with a red disc throwing light to the rear, but all other vehicles' had to have 'a seperate lamp showing a red light carried at the rear.' Motorists would learn with interest, the *Herald* said, 'that the use of headlights of all kinds is prohibited'.

Just before the new order came into force, the York Council debated on the state of the city under the regulations existing then. Henry Rhodes Brown was a bit rattled (because he had been prosecuted presumably) and he maintained that the new order was one which was '"tantamount to tradesmen having compulsorily to close their stores"' at a certain hour, and questioned whether the regulations were 'absolutely necessary'. To this Alderman Norman Green replied that it was not a matter for debate, as the dictates came from the Home Office. Horsman contended that the Chief Constable had gone over the top in interpreting the first order (a contention which Rhodes Brown might have agreed with). In York they always went to extremes, Horsman said, 'and it was a bye word in the city that the Council usually did the wrong thing. ... In Leeds where munitions were being manufactured electric lights were lit, with no shades at all. In York they had allowed the Gas Company to take away certain illuminating factors from the gas and substitute flat flame burners for incandescent mantles, consequently the lighting had been greatly modified, and to reduce it further would be against the interests of public safety.' Alderman Inglis agreed with Horsman, saying that 'he was afraid they in York were liable to "panicky legislation"', and that 'the state of darkness ... was a matter of grave danger to the public' but Green replied to these critics with statistics saying they were wrong. Chief Burrow's annual return to the Home Office, Green said, 'showed that during 1914 there had been 100 street accidents reported to him, before any any lighting orders were in vogue, whereas there had been only 81 in 1915.' (48) The figures were disputed, as indeed they should have been.

On the day the new order came into force the well known York firm of Leak and Thorp, of Coney steet, was prosecuted for a lighting offence committed on 20 December, and the principal of the De Bear Shool was done for one committed on Christmas Day. Fines of 5s. were imposed. By the end of January prosecutions were going to the courts galore. On the last day of the month for example, Sing Lee, a Chinese laundryman, who could not read English and did not understand the law, got done for 2s.6d., Edwin Peat of Anderson and Sons, Coney Street and Susan Rose of Leeds House, Holgate Road, were similarly fined. Sergeant Burnett of B Squadron, 5th Reserve Cavalry, Fulford Barracks was prosecuted and had his case dismissed while Kate Scrivener got clobbered for the half a crown which had clearly become the bench's norm. Kate's case was bad in that she worked at, and committed the offence at, the house of Major Weigall, MP, Deputy Assistant Quartermaster-General Northern Command. PC Parker said that he saw a very bright light coming from the attic of Knavesmire Lodge (Kate's pad) and that the light 'could have been seen for miles over Knavesmire'. Kate did not turn up in court when her case was heard but a lady who did that day was Theresa Robertson, of 66, St Olave's Road. She should have been a lot more careful as she was a German, who not only kept her lights on, but banged the door in the face of PC Brinton who was only doing his duty (after all), and then kept it on for another half an hour. She was fined a very reasonable 2s.6d. Ralph Stamp and Sarah Dalby, neighbours in Brunswick Terrace, were also done. Alderman James Melrose, the chairman of the bench that day, announced these two would be fined a shilling each, and Ralph asked for time to pay as he had only got 4d. on him. Sarah was broke and chairman Jim very generously 'paid both fines for the defendants.'

It is an interesting (and not all that important) point to note that the blackout legislation of the 1914 war brought into court people who would never normally had found themselves before the beaks. The likes of Susan Rose would never have been forced to attend at a magistrates court (except as a motorist maybe) in the usual way of things. The blackout had a lot to answer for, but before a year was out the courts would be dealing regularly with members of sections of the community which were normally completely law abiding. They would be objecting to national service.

The drink trade might have been thought of as a cause for concern when the lighting regulations were imposed, but it had already felt the heavy hand of legislation and was already drastically restricted. By the end of 1914 the pubs were closed at 9 o'clock at night, and servicemen were restricted to a limited period when they could (legally) partake of a few glasses. (49) Lloyd George had put prices up, and had had to back down when he tried it again, but there other assaults on the trade. In August 1915 the treating of soldiers in pubs in Liverpool and Merseyside was prohibited (50) and in York similar regulations (along with prohibitions on slates and long pulls) were brought in in November. (51) In October the trade had held a well publicised meeting in Leeds to discuss opening times, (52) when a delegation from the Central Control Board (Liquor Traffic) met under Lord D'Abernon to consider 'evidence for and against a further reduction' of permitted hours and to discuss even more restrictions. They were given conflicting evidence by Chief Constables and military personnel about the current situation and told that whereas the incidence of drunkeness in York and Leeds had gone down, Halifax had seen a 20 per cent increase. In November it was announced that the Liquor Control Board would be implementing a new scheme for York (that mentioned above) but that hours would be slightly extended - to allow six hours drinking on week days (12 to 2.30 pm and 6 to 9.30 pm) and five hours on Sundays (1 to 3 pm and 6 to 9.00 pm). (It had been rumoured that they would be cut to five and a half per day.) (53) It will be noticed that Sunday lunchtime closing time was that that was restored in the late 1980s.

Announcing the new rules the *Yorkshire Herald* told its readers that whereas some pubs remained closed during prohibited hours, others kept open selling coffee, mineral waters, Bovril and other non-alcoholic beverages. It welcomed the extra half hour opening at night and told its readers, perhaps rather irresponsibly, that the no treating order - which now applied to everyone, not just soldiers, could be circumvented. (54) Referring to happenings on what it called 'THE APPOINTED DAY' it said the later openings in the morning 'caused dissatisfaction to many' who could not get a dram before midday (now), but that basically the new regulations had had 'a mixed reception ... some treating the matter with a certain amount of levity and others looking on [them] with great seriousness and concern.' In many places, the *Herald* went on,

> the "no treating order" was made fun of, and numerous jokes were passed. One thing to be observed was the entire absence of such phrases as "Going to have one ?" "What's yours ?" etc. You may be treated to a drink of lemonade or any non-intoxicant. Two men entered a hotel in the centre of the city, and one asked the other what he would have. "I'll have a soda water," was the reply; "All right, then I'll have a Scotch." These drinks were taken. The one who had been treated then desired to "take his turn," and asked his friend the question. "Mine's a lemonade," replied the other, and the generous one in his turn had a Scotch. Thus treating did take place, but in a very roundabout way, although we believe it was quite legal.

What did licencees think of the new arrangements ? One said he was 'very pleased that they [had] made soldiers and civilians alike' and said his customers had 'fallen in with' them 'splendidly', but there were the inevitable prophets of doom and despair.

> Another licensee was very bitter ... and said that if the present Government had fought the Germans in the same way as they had fought the publicans, the Germans would have been beaten by now. He was sure that unless something was done there would be trouble. The new restrictions would ruin the trade.

The Liquor Traffic Board meeting at Leeds received deputations from the licensed victuallers and from temperance workers, and the trade must have expected more blows in the future (if only because the glorious product it sold was easily taxable). Because of these threats the York trade's two protection agencies had amalgamated as perhaps they should have done years earlier. In July the LVA and the York Retail Licence Holders' Protection Society joined together to present a united front whenever necessary. They rapidly made their views on the new rules known. The supplement to the *Herald* of 27 November reported a meeting of the York LVA under J.T. Betchetti and described a resolution moved by W. Boddy which was couched in language which would not have seemed out of place in one by Arthur Dearlove protesting about conscription. The Victuallers wanted an enquiry into the actions of the Control Board 'in issuing Orders unnecessarily for the compulsory suppression of the liberty of His Majesty's loyal subjects who have conscientious objections to any form of compulsion to deprive them of the reasonable use of alcoholic beverages.' The resolution also spoke of the Board 'ignoring the constitutional rights of the people', and of the 'national scheme of restriction involving serious inconvenience to the working classes at a time when the great majority of those who are best able to afford protection are away from home fighting for King and Country'.

It was inevitable that the no treating regulations would be challenged in the courts. They were, and in the very issue of the *Herald* which told of the changes on 'THE APPOINTED DAY' in York there was a report of a case brought to determine the legality of the Control Board's order 'prohibiting treating in licensed premises' in a part of Scotland. It was heard before the Justiciary Court of Appeal, Edinburgh, and a bench of three judges presided over by the Lord Justice General. It involved a landlord called McKechnie who supplied a lady with 'a nip of port wine which was ordered and paid for by another woman'. There were other challenges elsewhere. In late January 1916, for example, an appeal was heard in the King's Bench which was reported in the *Yorkshire Evening Press* on 1 February. The appeal was lodged by the Cardiff police against a stipendiary magistrate who had refused to convict a licensee in whose pub a sailor was bought four glasses of nectar. None of these appeals were successful and no treating remained the rule of the day.

Frederick Randall a 40 year old York labourer of no fixed abode did not approve of the new drinking times (or he seemed not to). Fred was up in court on Thursday 25 November, a couple of days after the new regime to control such as he was started. He was up for being smashed at 8.40 pm on the 24th. He admitted 'having had a drink or two' but denied that he was kettled. 'Time now did not permit him to get a lot of beer', he said. He was not done for perjury but was fined 10s. (55) (Less than a week later George Barrett, the licensee of the Blue Bell was charged with permitting drunkeness in his pub, and fined 5s.) (56) The first prosecutions proper under the Central Control Board (Liquor Traffic) Order were heard on 13 December, (57) and the first person to be done was Mrs Winifred Cargill, of Hope Street. Her offence was that she took beer from the Brown Cow at 9.25 pm on 4 December, after the time for sales had passed. (58) Winifred said she did not know she was breaking the law, said the beer was for her husband who was on leave 'from the front', and had her case dismissed. Agnes Rowlands was similarly prosecuted. She had been seen taking beer from the Crown Brewery Inn, Walmgate at 8.30 pm. This was on a Sunday when such transactions had to stop at 8. Agnes had been in the Admiral Hawke, then went to the Crown, and on leaving there PC Lumley asked her what she had under her shawl. Her case too was dismissed (she said she had bought the booze at seven o'clock and simply went back to pick it up). The bench went to some lengths, however, to put the city's drinkers on the *qui vive* and told the likes of Agnes and Winifred just what was permissable. They 'wished it clearly understood that the law stipulated that intoxicating liquor could neither be sold nor delivered after hours,' they declared. Same as now.

It was not long before 'treating' prosecutions were reported in the York area. In January Thomas R. Smithson, landlord of the Reindeer Hotel, Donaster was done. (59) PCs Woodward and Enfield went to the Reindeer and Woodward bought two glasses of beer from Florence Woodhouse, the barmaid. When Flo was told 'she had supplied beer to a person who had not paid for it' she replied, candidly, 'I was busy and forgot'. Enfield and Woodward left the pub, and their beer, and went on to the Palace Buffet. Mr Andrews for the defence argued that as the beer (4d worth) had not been consumed no offence had been committed. His argument was not accepted and Smithson was fined £5. None of the licensing reports to the local Brewster Sessions of 1917 seem to have singled out prosecutions for treating (though many, including that at York, dwelled on the increase of drinking amongst women).

The new licensing regulations were challenged in the courts (and unoffically in the public bar of many many a pub it must be assumed). They were also challenged on the hustings, and the challenge involved Britain's greatest patriot, Horatio Bottomley.

In late 1915 Herbert Samuel was made Chancellor of the Duchy of Lancaster, and had to fight a by election in Cleveland as was the rule in those days. Joe Terrett of the Labour Protest Committee, with the support of the National Union of Railwaymen, was approached to fight Samuel, and incidentally break the party truce. For some reason or other Terrett did not stand, but Reginald Knight did, put up by Bottomley, who campaigned in the constituency for him. Knight allegedly represented the Business Government League and he, and they, were against the recently imposed drink restrictions. The Central Liquor Board was, in Knight's words, a sop to the 'teetotall crank, [and] the cocoa men' for the help they had given the Liberal government over national insurance. (60) This was nonsense and Samuel was returned with an increased majority. (61)

The legislation creating the Central Control Board was the Defence of the Realm (Amendment) No 3 Bill, and it was introduced by Lloyd George to control 'the trade' after his proposals to nationalise the industry had failed. It was decreed that in defined areas (defined in July by a series of Orders in Council) the Board could make regulations of the kind applied in York, after due investigation, and 'no treating' saw the light of day in October 1915. (Well in a legal sense it did; every drinker will have come across 'no treaters' at sometime in his career.) The publicity surrounding it justifiably dwelled on the fact that it was intended primarily to help solve the problems in munition centres, but York was not one of those. This was frequently pointed out, and it was pointed out by them when members of the Corporation met three members of the Central Board in January. 'York, apart from the railway and cocoa works, was a purely agricultural centre', they said, 'and at no time were there great fluctuations in wages. There were no munition works worth speaking of in the city, and there was therefore no reason for harsh restrictions'. (62) These contentions nicely turned one reason for the regulations into the sole reason and they deservedly got nowhere. (The penalties for breaking the regulations, incidentally, were very heavy - six months hard labour and/or a £100 fine.)

The regulations of 1915 were intended to cut down drinking, and they were supplemented by appeals to the nation at large to give up altogether. The King took the pledge for the duration. (The King's Pledge it became known as - not surprisingly.) He gave 'up all alcoholic liquor' himself, and issued 'orders against its consumption in the Royal Household, so that no difference' should be made 'so far as His Majesty is concerned between the treatment of rich and poor in this question.' Some followed His Majesty - but not many. Lord Kitchener did; Lloyd George did not; and Asquith certainly did not. What happened in York? Well it is fairly certain that Fred Randall did not sign, though the Archbishop urged people to follow George V's example. So did Canon Argles, the temperance stop-a-pub-in-South Bank agitator. (Argles, incidentally, was responsible for spreading a rumour that Rowntree and Company were cornering the market in milk in York and so forcing up the price.) (63)

So, at the end of 1915, York's drinkers (like those everywhere) could only drink for a few hours a day and had to go home (well they should have gone home) at 9.30. Their drinks were less potent and more expensive, and they were forbidden to treat members of the forces and their friends. What was the city like when these dreadful restrictions appeared? Chief Constable Burrow revealed all in his report to the members of the licensing bench (64) in late January. (65) There were now, Burrow reported, 298 licenced premises in his area, representing one to every 276 persons according to the last census. (None had been closed since the war started.) In the year 286 people had been convicted of drunkeness. Since the new regulations had been in force, Burrow went on, the streets had been clear earlier at night and there had been less riotous behaviour. In spite of that York was second again in the drunkeness league table which has been mentioned before. There had been a rise in boozing at home, the Chief Constable concluded, and spirits were 'purchased and taken to the homes', he said, 'to be consumed, payment for same being made by those partaking thereof'. Good jargonese; the piece about 'payment for same' was in there presumably to make the point that there was no longer any tick.

The convictions for drunkeness figure (286) was an increase on that given for the year ending in January 1915 (274) and it could have been interpreted rather more seriously than it was if the state of the police force had been taken into account. York in 1915 had a much larger population than a year earlier, if the troops are taken into account, with a very different constabulary from that of pre-war days, which may not have been as good at arresting the likes of Fred Randall as its predecessor had been. (Equally it could be argued that the force was not as good at preventing or defusing incidents.) During the Derby scheme period, in a well-publicised episode, no less than 22 of York's coppers joined up together in a stage managed exercise, (66) and the Chief Constable reported on the state of his command to the Recorder at the Quarter Sessions of January 1916. He had an authorised strength of 109, Burrow said, and since the outbreak of hostilities: two men who were army reservists had gone; 34 regular policemen had volunteered and gone; two men who had joined the police for the duration had joined the forces; three men had been sent to the army as drill instructors; and no less than 39 PCs had attested under the Derby scheme and so could be lost very shortly. It would have been impossible to police York without the use of specials, the Chief concluded. (67)

The year 1915 ended with analyses and sets of statistics being produced other than those relating to the police, 'the trade' and recruiting, which all add to the picture of what York was like after 17 months of war. (68) The *Herald* carried its usual survey of business in the city, for example, and it showed, not surprisingly, that firms like Gibbs and Company and Wales and Son, motor traders, were doing only moderately and selling only American cars (which had been taxed as luxuries of course). (69) John Gray and Sons, musical instrument salesmen and repairers, reported a good year, but Waddington and Sons Ltd, the piano makers, were working at only half capacity. Messrs H. Bushell and Sons, agricultural engineers and implement makers, however, reported that they had had a year of 'general satisfaction, the amount of business for the past twelve months having been well maintained'. The cost of raw materials was high, and many of their suppliers had been closed 'having been taken over by the Government for the manufacture of munitions.' They had lost 40 men to the forces and this had further curtailed their 'capacity to turn out goods of their own manufacture'. Work had had to be turned away because of this and the firms' inability to deliver goods. However the loss of business was more than compensated for by an unusually heavy demand from farmers for labour saving devices which would 'replace the men who have left the land and joined the colours.' (70) At one stage during the year Bushell's whole labour force had been engaged on this work, and oil engines, chaff cutters, double-furrow ploughs, cream separators and many other devices had been sold and installed. The great feature of the year, however, was the advent of the light oil tractor engine, which with two men could do the work of 'eight horses and four men'. So great had been the demand 'for this new labour-saving device, that double the number would have been readily purchased by farmers had it been possible to procure them.'

Messrs Kay and Backhouse agricultural engineers, ironmongers and hardware merchants, had a similar report to that of Bushell. They complained of great delays in the delivery of machinery. ('The large firms have lost 30 per cent to 50 per cent of their staffs; a good proportion of the remainder, and in some cases all, are working in munitions ...'.) Rowntree and Company reported an increase in demand during the year, 'especially ... marked in connection with the sale of plain chocolate, such as "Elect", "Queen", "Milk", and "British"'. Demand had gone up in the autumn and full employment had been maintained throughout the year, and overtime was worked in some departments'. 1,282 Rowntree men had 'joined the colours.'

The building trade, it was reported, was slacker than it had been for three years, with few large works in the city being built (the new Picture House, Coney Street, was an exception). Mennell Brothers, wood turners of the Ebor Works, reported that it had government orders making tent poles, and handles for trench tools, but they had acute labour shortages. (The work force of the City Council had been short for many months.)

In war time some businesses grow and some (like Waddington's) suffer. Early in January 1916 there appeared the Official Receiver's report for the York Bankruptcy District wherein were details of some of those who had gone to the wall. (71) During the year 33 petitions had been received, all 'more or less, of an ordinary character', and the bulk of them had been in the first quarter of the year, and among those who failed were mechanics, grocers, joiners, tailors and butchers. The total estimated liabilities were £16,624.

A month before the appearance of the bankruptcy figures the York civic accounts for 1914-15 were made public in a volume of over 350 pages. (72) These only went up to 31 March, but showed that the borough rate, made in April 1914, raised £60,613. Expenditure on education was given in great detail and the tramways accounts showed that income from 'the electric cars, rents, etc.; was ... £30,027 9s. 9d., an average per car mile of 9.45d. and the expenditure, £20,640 15s. 2d., an average cost of 6.51d. per car mile.' Income from the motor omnibuses for 15 February to 31 March was £99 8s., an average of 7.55d. per car mile, and the expenditure was £103 14s. 3d., an average cost of 7.88d. per car mile. Allowances to men on military service came to £910 9s. 6d.

In March 1916 the Chief Constable's annual report on York was made public, dealing with the year ending 31 December 1915. (73) It gave figures relating to the police, many of which had already been given to the Brewster Sessions, but added that the cost of the force for the year ending 31 March had been £12,777 6s. 4d. costing the city (after grants) £6,769 5s. 1d. or a sum equal to £62 per constable which equalled 19.74d. per inhabitant and 3.82d. in the pound rateable value. Thirty five calls had been made on the fire brigade, 24 to fires within the city, eleven to fires in the country. The approximate value of property at risk in the city was £40,100 and the actual damage amounted to £4,276 16s. 'In 1914 property at risk within the city was £7,500 and the actual amount of damage £1,348'. There had been three false alarms and the cost of the fire brigade establishment (for the year to 31 March) was £1,321 14s. 5d. A sum of £379 15s. 1d. had been received for attending country fires and other sources, so that the 'net cost of the brigade to the city was £941 19s. 4d. In 1914 the cost was £926 19s. 4d.'

The Chief Constable's report gave crime statistics for 1915. Three hundred and fifty five crimes were reported, 'and for these 232 persons were proceeded against, 150 by apprehension and 82 by summons, which is 95 above the average of crimes for the past five years, whilst the number of persons proceeded against is 75 above the average.' Of the 355 crimes, three were offences against the person, 26 against property with violence, 316 without violence, and ten in other categories. Of the 232 proceeded against 23 were committed for trial, 32 tried summarily and acquitted, 102 dealt with under the Probation of Offenders Act of 1907, 70 were summarily convicted and five discharged. Robberies of all descriptions during the year (included in which were the crime figures above) amounted to 342 and the people proceeded against for them came to 220. There was an increase of 57 in the number of crimes, and the value of property stolen was £302. Property in excess of £122 was restored to owners.

In addition to the above figures, Burrow continued, 1,108 persons had been proceeded against for non indictable offences - an increase of 99 over the average for the preceeding five years. Of these: 877 were males and 231 females; 502 were proceeded against by arrest and 606 by summons; 599 were convicted; 91

were discharged; 273 were dealt with under the Probation Act; and 145 were 'otherwise disposed of'. As 'compared with the number of persons proceeded against for non-indictable offences for the previous year', the Chief Constable concluded, 'there is an increase of 201'.

Mr Burrow concluded his report with a number of other statistics and facts, including the following, the first of which could be taken to demonstrate the final victory of the petrol engine over older means of transport.

> During the year 81 persons were injured on the streets by vehicles, 48 by mechanically propelled vehicles, 16 by pedal cycles, and 17 by horse drawn vehicles.

> At the end of the year the register of traders contained the names of 183 children not exempt, and 26 exempt from school attendance, making a total of 209.

> The sum of £595 12s. was received from licenses under the Motor Car Act, 1903, and paid over to the city treasurer, an increase of £133 14s. on the previous year.

The annual report of the York Education committee for the year ending 31 December appeared somewhat later than did that of the Chief Constable, and it contains information of value. (74) The effects of the war had been deeply felt on education, it said, and 45 male teachers had enlisted or attested - the equivalent of 38.4 of the total male teachers in elementary schools or 62.5 of those of military age. The Council were making up their pay including allowances, and were keeping their posts open. The cost of making up pay was £1,446 a year. The education rate, which had been 2d. in 1890, was $22^{1}/_{2}$d. in 1915 and had increased mainly in the last decade. The total costs of salaries for elementary teachers was £41,779 (compared with £31,486 ten years earlier). There had been a decrease in the number of necessitous children for whom school meals had had to be provided from 75,364 (a weekly average of 319) in 1914, to 59,951 (an average of 253 a week). The cost of the meals had gone up, nevertheless, to £876 6s. from £767 18s. 4d. a year earlier. (75)

1. See earlier
2. *Herald* 16 February and 8 March 1915
3. *Ibid* 22 February, 11 June 1915
4. *Ibid* 22 February 1915
5. *Ibid* 2 March 1915
6. *Ibid* 27 February 1915
7. *Ibid* 24 and 26 February 1915
8. *Ibid* 12 March 1915. The police wanted a pay scale rising from 30s. to 41s. spread over 12 years. *Ibid* 5 April 1915
9. *Ibid* 11 and 16 March 1915

10. *Ibid* 16 March 1915
11. *Ibid* 8 March 1915
12. *Ibid* 6 January 1915
13. *Ibid* 11 January 1915
14. *Ibid* 19 January 1915
15. *Ibid* 26 February 1915
16. *Ibid* 12 July 1915
17. F.W. Hirst, *The Consequences of the War to Great Britain* (1934) Part 2, Chap 1. *Herald* 22 and 23 September 1915
18. *Herald* 3 December 1915
19. *I bid* 5 October 1915
20. *Ibid* 18 October 1915
21. Later letter writers pointed out that the workers got an allowance of 17s. 6d. to cover living expenses.
22. *Herald* 15 November 1915. Hyndman was leader of the Social Democratic Federation.
23. There were constant reports in the *Press* that labour was hard to get for the land, and the Corporation reported that it was understaffed.
24. *Herald* 4 May 1915. Syd Walker became extremely famous in the late 1930s when he appeared regularly in the BBC Radio show Band Waggon, where he gave the nation one of those catch phrases which annoyed everyone when they were repeated *ad nauseum*.
25. *Ibid* 13 April, 4 May 1915. On the cinemas taking part in recruiting see eg *Ibid* 27 September 1915.
26. *Ibid* 12 and 13 April 1915. When the war broke out two new cinemas under planned. The second, in Skeldergate, was never built.
27. Jane Shore was a historical film described in *The British Film Catalogue* as 'HISTORY 1480. Goldsmith's wife becomes King's mistress to save husband's life.' There was a version made in 1908 and another in 1911. This one was almost certainly the 1915 version with Blanche Forsythe playing Jane Winstead and Roy Travers playing Edward IV. Yet another version of Jane Shore was released in 1922. It had Sybil Thorndike and Lewis Gilbert in the cast.
28. *Herald* 13 April 1915
29. *Ibid* 6 May 1915. The film was actually called 'The Lifeboat' and was made by Eric Williams Speaking Pictures. Its description explains: 'DRAMA' (Shown while Price Williams recites from stage).
30. *Ibid* 5 March 1915, report of a special meeting of York City FC.
31. They got £15 from the away game with Bradford, £14 from that with Goole, £16 from that with Grimsby.
32. *Herald* 20 July, 3 September 1915
33. *Ibid* 25 August 1915
34. *Press* 26 January 1915
35. *Ibid* 29 April 1915
36. *Herald* 11 April 1915
37. *Ibid* 30 April 1915
38. *Ibid* 5 May 1915
39. Rhodes Brown's case in *Ibid* 13 January 1916. Bell's first conviction reported in *Ibid* 29 February 1916
40. *Herald* 3 December 1915
41. On the Zeppelin raids and the air war at that time see eg A. Norman, *The Great Air War* (1968). Also A. Whitehouse, *The Zeppelin Fighters* (1966) and H.G. Castle, *Fire over England* (1982)
42. *Herald* 16 April 1915
43. See letter in *Press* 14 September 1915
44. *Herald* 16 April 1916. The Zep dropped bombs at Bedlington (6), Cramlington (4), Dinnington, Benton and Wallsend.
45. The York Volunteer Training Corps was then some 600 strong.
46. *Press* 25 February 1916
47. *Herald* 8 January 1916
48. *Ibid* 4 January and 8 January 1916 (supplement). Also edition of 11 January 1916.

49. This had been made general throughout the Northern Command by the military authorities using the powers given them in January 1915. It applied to places where troops were 'actually stationed for training'. This was considered and noted at the York Brewster Sessions in late January. *Ibid* 1 February 1915
50. *Press* 6 August 1915
51. *Ibid* 13 November 1915
52. *Herald* 4 and 6 October 1915. On the creation of the Liquor Board (the creation of which led to the state control experiment at Carlisle) see eg Lloyd George, *Memoirs. op cit* Vol 1 Chap 9 section 5.
53. *Herald* 4 October 1915. It was anticipated that closing time would remain at nine o'clock.
54. *Ibid* 23 November 1915. The full order is published in *Press* 13 November 1915. It deals extensively with such things as off sales (12 to 2.30 and 6.30 to 8.30 weekdays), and the acceptance of orders for off sales of spirits. Regarding treating the order was tightly drawn in a way magistrates today (1992) would like to see some regulations drawn. For the purpose of the treating regulation 'consumption on the premises [included] consumption of intoxicating liquor in or on any highway, open ground or railway station adjoining or near to the licenced premises or club in which the liquor was sold or supplied.'
55. *Herald* 26 November 1915
56. *Ibid* 2 December 1915
57. *Ibid* 14 December 1915
58. See fn. 54
59. *Herald* 24 January 1916. The York Brewster Sessions of 1917 reported in *Ibid* 10 February 1917.
60. *Ibid* 2, 8, 9 and 10 December 1915.
61. Samuel 7,312, Knight 1,453. In 1910 the result had been Samuel 6,870, J.W. Lewis 5,343
62. *Press* 1 February 1916
63. *Herald* 8 October 191564. As will have been noticed - as has been pointed out - the Lord Mayor was traditionally the chairman of the Licensing Bench. This was a ridiculous arrangement with, frequently, a non-magistrate presiding over important matters with no training or experience whatsoever. In February 1915 D.S. Mackay, an ex president of the Law Society, became chairman. *Ibid* 1 February 1915.
65. *Press* 1 February 1916. It will be noted from what follows that convictions for drunkenness in York were up compared with 1914. This is not what Burrow tried to get the Liquor Board to believe when he lobbied them as described earlier.
66. *Herald* 27 October 1915. The incident of the police joining up was filmed (the men marched from the Law courts to the recruiting office).
67. *Ibid* 7 January 1916
68. Or rather there were tables and articles relating to the end of the year which came out at various times.
69. *Herald* 30 and 31 December 1915, 3, 8 and 31 January 1916
70. The extent of the labour shortages in the farming areas might be gleaned from eg the reports of the annual hirings in the local newspapers, where 'boys' were demanding men's wages, it was said, and female labour was being used more and more. See also the reports of the annual meeting of the Yorkshire Union of Agricultural Clubs and Chambers of Agriculture held in York in February 1916. *Herald* 4 February 1916.
71. *Ibid* 1 January 1916
72. *Ibid* 1 December 1915
73. *Ibid* 17 March 1916
74. *Ibid* 12 une 1916
75. The school meals figures are for years ending 31 March. In 1913 the figure had been in excess of £824. The Board of Education made a grant towards the cost of school meals. In 1915 it amounted to £433.8s.9d.

CHAPTER 13

1916, THE TRIBUNALS AND CONSCRIPTION.

Not long after the new year began there were changes made of monumental importance in the system of of obtaining recruits for Britain's armed services. Compulsion 'came in'.

The recruiting campaign that ran alongside 'Derby' was impressive in its results, but the attempt to get men to attest was in reality nothing more than a qualified success. Just over a week after the results of his campaign were published in York it was announced that Lord Derby and his Central Recruiting Committee had decided to run just one more 'energetic' recruiting campaign 'To Save Volunteerism' in the words of the *Press*. (1) By this time men who had attested were being called up - and if any of them had joined the Derby scheme merely to put off the dreaded day of enlistment they had, in fact, bought very little time. Early in the third week of January notices were issued in the York area instructing recruits in groups 6, 7, 8 and 9 to report for service, (2) and three days later they did so at Fulford Barracks. Just over a week later notices were posted in York calling up Derby groups 10 to 13. (3) Between these two call-ups the Lord Mayor made yet another appeal to single men to enlist under the Derby scheme 'which has now been re-opened'. (4) Men in classes 2 to 12 were given a month's warning that they would be called up (these were men aged from 19 to 30) (5) and repeated notes appeared in the papers telling men that the very last day for voluntary enlistment was 1 March. "'If you intend to enlist voluntarily, do not delay', the *Press* told its readers of military age on 22 February, 'You may be left out in the big rush at the end." This is the official intimation to those who wish to embrace the opportunity of avoiding compulsion.' Better be a Derbyman than a conscript was the essence of messages like that. (6) Why? Had the situation altered? It had. A Military Service Act had been passed which became operative on 10 February. Compulsion had arrived. Through its provisions, one of the York newspapers told its readers, all unmarried, fit, men would be called up by 17 March, and thereafter the authorities would start to deal with older men. (7).

Before the end of the Derby scheme, and before Derby gave the results of his campaign to the cabinet, Asquith had given his approval to the drafting of a bill for compulsory military service. He had given a pledge to married men that their single contemporaries would go first and the bill was to honour that pledge.

The Military Service Bill, drafted by a cabinet committee which was only appointed on 15 December, was presented to the Commons on 5 January. It provided that 'all men who had been unmarried on 2 November 1915 (the date of Asquith's pledge) and between the ages of eighteen and forty-one on 15 August 1915, the precise age-group canvassed under the Derby Scheme, should be deemed to have enlisted for the period of the war.' (8)

For political reasons Asquith had to tread a very delicate path, and present the Military Service Bill as a redemption of his pledge to take single men into the forces first, as a continuation of the Derby Scheme (which it was not) and as a conscription measure that would satisfy the Tories. He presented the bill to the House in a masterly fashion, blurred certain issues quite deliberately, and reopened the Derby scheme as mentioned above, saying that he hoped that sufficient men would come forward at that late hour to make the new bill a dead letter! He got his majority, persuaded Labour not to oppose him, (9) and the bill became law. Later, in May, the Military Service Act 1916 (10) extended liability for military service to all men aged between 18 and 41.

A most important feature of the compulsion legislation was its conscience clauses, clauses which recognised the right of some groups to opt out of military service in a variety of ways. During the (first) bill's progress through Parliament discussion had been lengthy on what rights (if any) conscientious objectors should have in law, and much was made of precedents under the Militia and Vaccination Acts, and the examples of colonial legislation. Eventually a subsection was agreed upon which dealt with certificates of exemption to military service for those who had a conscientious objection to taking part in the war. It was ambiguous, and led to considerable confusion later on. 'Any certificate of exemption may be absolute, conditional, or temporary' it said

> as the authority by whom it was granted think best suited to the case, and also in the case of an application on conscientious grounds, may take the form of an exemption from combatant service only, or may be conditional on the applicant being engaged in some work which in the opinion of the tribunal dealing with the case is of national inportance.

The ambiguity of the conscience clause came as a result of Walter Long inserting the word also in the text, and administrators frequently stood on what they thought was the letter of the law which, they said, distinguished between conscientious objectors and others, whereas it is clear that Long intended that the section dealing with conscientious objectors was in addition 'to the general power to grant absolute exemption to all classes of applicant'. (11) It would seem fair to say, however, that in York the administrators were well aware of the Act's real intention, as they had to be, given the nature of the place. Many Quakers were given absolute exemption 'on the nod' as will be seen later.

Who were to be empowered to exempt men from national service ? Long and his colleagues (Long was president of the Local Government Board when he was given the task of steering the compulsion bills through Parliament) decided they should be the tribunals set up for the Derby Scheme, which were given statutory authority.

It was absolutely inevitable that the conscription legislation would be the cause of great debate and acrimony in York, not only because of the influential Quaker community, but because its senior MP had been an ardent opponent of the legislation. Arnold Rowntree had been prominent in the opposition to the Military Service bills and was one of 36 MPs who voted against the first of the bills on its second reading and the 35 who voted against it in its final stages. (12) His actions increased the number of hostile letters about him in the *Press*. He was one of 'these 36 paltry friends of Germany' in the words of one of them, while another wanted them all either interned or deported. ' ... it is time some pressure was put upon them either to intern them', wrote another irate reader to the *Press*, 'or to let them have a press pass to the land they love.' (13) Earlier, in January, and while the first of the Military Service Bills was in Parliament, the 'York Liberal Thousand' held two meetings to consider Arnold's attitude towards the legislation. Sebastian Meyer was chairman and Rowntree was present, but it is not clear what happened (beyond the fact that the party did not disown him). Certainly Rowntree's popularity was at an all time low, at least among great sections of York society. Someone recalled one of his speeches against one of Lord Roberts' proposals for compulsory military training for 18 year olds in 1913. Jack Seely (14) had changed his views since then, it was pointed out; Arnold Rowntree had not. He 'sticks to the old phrases and obsolete views' it was contended. Another writer said, of course, that Arnold should resign. (15) At about this time, too, there were questions in the Commons about the export of cocoa in which Rowntree and Company got some very hostile - and unfair - criticism, which those in York hostile to the firm and family siezed on with great glee. (16)

Hand in hand with the passing of the Military Service Bill, the cocoa question and the last despairing efforts of Lord Derby to get men to enlist voluntarily went an increase in the activities of those who shouted 'slacker' - the current buzz word - at the deserving and undeserving alike. The more articulate wrote to the *Press* and named names in a very unpleasant episode. Both the *Press* and the *Herald* of 5 February, for example, carried a column headed (in one of them) 'Two White Feathers', in which it allowed correspondents to finger one John J. Wilson. He had been the recipient of two white feathers and 'COMFORTABLE SLACKER' asked why two were not enough. Wilson, he said, had a job which would be guaranteed him after the war, and his salary would be made up while he served. 'G.E.C.' entered the fray against Wilson and 'Scottie' said the feathers were well sent. This kind of thing was to become even more common in the months that lay ahead.

The passing of the conscription measures at last brought about some cohesion among the organisations which were sometimes anti-war, certainly anti conscription. The Labour party had taken the decisions at Bristol mentioned earlier to support the war, but not to oppose conscription if and when it came in. That was of immense help to the government, but other organisations set about organising themselves as never before, either to opppose the war or conscription (or the way it was administered) or both. Sections of the Labour movement did so. The Women's Labour League, in January, declared itself against conscription, for example, (17) and the Independent Labour Party, always an opponent of the war, naturally did so too. The UDC contained many people who made anti-war statements and were prominent pacifists, and the No Conscription Fellowship became prominent in the life of the nation. The Society of Friends and (a few) other religious organisations were anti war and therefore anti conscription, and many of these bodies were represented in York and added their contributions to what became extremely volatile political times, in which attitudes were polarised as never before. (Though not equally.)

In mid January 1916 the UDC held a meeting at the Ebor Rooms in York at which the cross membership of such organisations mentioned above was demonstrated. (18) S.H. Davies, the ex-councillor, pacifist, Rowntree employee was present and he said that the UDC did indeed contain all kinds of people, as well as 'confirmed pacifists like himself'. Davies on that ocassion demanded a statement of war aims, while Andrew Maclaren inveighed against the activities of the private armament makers. 'War was brought about to suit the interests of the armaments makers', he said, 'who, when out to do business, did not fight about such things as the Kaiser and Belgium.' The local secretary of the UDC seems to have been F.E. Pollard of Clifton Dale, a Quaker, and shortly after the Ebor Rooms meeting he was bitterly attacked in the *Press* by the male counterpart of Edith Milner. This was Charles A. Thompson who carried on something alarming about the 'Quaker Little-England, love-the German Section of the community' to which, he said, Pollard belonged. (19) It does little credit to the historical record of the *Herald* and the *Press* to have to record that they published - indeed encouraged - such hate drivel as emanated from the pens of people like Thompson and Milner.

There were other York organisations which were loud in their protests against compulsion, and the issue raised political activity to heights in York which had not been seen since the days of the People's Budget. In mid January, while the first bill was before Parliament, people like Arthur Dearlove attended a protest meeting over which S.H. Davies, once more, presided. He read a letter from Seebohm Rowntree in which his views were put succintly, and in which he said compulsion was not necessary. 'It was sad to think that we began with free military service, a free Parliament, and a free press', Rowntree wrote, 'three of the greatest safeguards we enjoy, and [that we] end in compulsory service, a Parliament gagged, and a muzzled press'. (20) O.G. Willey posed a rhetorical question and got an answer which showed that the meeting contained several shades of opinion. If there had been a real necessity for compulsion, Willey asked, why did the government not bring in 'a real whole-hearted Compulsion Bill.' They did that in the not very distant future, but a heckler told Willey one was not brought in then because the government was 'quibbling to the Quakers," [and] to the Cocoa press".' F.F. Beney, another speaker told everybody what they knew already. He represented the ILP, Beney said (as did Dearlove), and the ILP had fought conscription proposals for 21 years, 'and if the Bill [ever] occupied a place on the Statute Book, they would still fight, whether above board or underground.' The ILP had been in existence in York for many years, playing a minor though not unimportant part in the city's political life. It was now to move centre stage and occupy the role which its members thought should have been occupied by the Labour party. The ILP was bravely to oppose the war and conscription until the Armistice and some of its members were to suffer for their beliefs. Arthur Dearlove who had courted imprisonment for years was one of its main spokesmen. In early 1916 he was well into the press controversy over conscription, annoying the likes of Charles A. Thompson, with letters saying conscription was 'un British' (which it was) and accusing politicians of being bent on 'militarising and Prussianising Britain (21) (which given certain definitions of those terms might also have been true, though it was in the cause of winning the war).

Fred Bradley of Stockton Lane was, like Dearlove, associated with the ILP and other radical organisations in York, and in January he sent letters to Asquith and Lloyd George telling them that another York meeting had been held at which pledges had been made that great resistance would be offered by certain individuals to the call-up as and when it affected them. At a large Quaker meeting of Friends of enlistment age, the No Conscription Fellowship and the Fellowship of Reconciliation, Fred wrote, a resolution was passed saying that those assembled together declared 'that under no circumstances can we submit to any form of compulsory military service; and therefore, though recognising the grave consequences which may follow our decision, solemnly declare our determination to oppose to our uttermost the priciple of compulsion as embodied in the Bill now before Parliament.' (22) On the very day that that resolution was passed the Friends' Guild of Teachers held its annual conference at the Mount School in York, and there Arnold Rowntree certainly did not add to his popularity among the likes of C.A. Thompson and Edith Milner when he proposed a resolution which included a statement saying that we 'wish to express profound sympathy with those who, under a deep sense of conscientious conviction, feel compelled to stand aside from the country's call to arms as a part of their loyalty to the eternal state, the eternal city of God.' (23)

The passing of the Military Service Bill(s) concentrated minds on those who could refuse service, and those who had hitherto been denounced as 'slackers' now became 'conchies' and the scene was well set for when they made their protests. The *Herald* in an editorial in February 1916 said they had started a 'crusade' financed by ample funds from Quakers from York, Scarborough and London, (24) and one is tempted to ask 'why not' when the way they were denounced is taken into account. William Joynson Hicks, later Viscount Brentford, called the Military Service Act wherein the right of conscientious objection was enshrined, a 'Slacker's Charter' and R.H. Vernon Wragge used the judicial bench to give vent to his views (again) in January 1916. He compared criminals with 'those who had conscientious convictions which prevented 'them from joining up.' 'For his part', Vernon told the Pontefract Quarter Sessions, 'he unreservedly preferred the former to the latter.' (25) Using the bench to purvey hate messages against a section of the community which had not yet begun to object seems deplorable, but in character for the unpleasant Wragge. Using the pulpit to stir up hatred against people brave enough to stand up for their beliefs looks even worse. A little later the Rev D.P. Winnifrith, senior chaplain to the forces in York distinguished himself when preaching in St Paul's church. The conscientious objectors, Winnifrith told his congregation, 'smirched the name of Englishman.' (26) So did he.

A York branch of the No Conscription Fellowship was certainly in existence by the spring of 1916 (28) and by April a York and District Anti-conscription Council was in being. (29) J.H. Hartley was connected with the latter and both organisations represented objectors. The former helped them prepare their cases for the tribunals which deliberated on them, and members of that Educational Settlement mentioned in these pages before, did so too. They got in early and on 12 February 1916 the following advertisement appeared in the *Press*. Once more S.H. Davies was involved, and so too was the sub warden R. Wilfrid Crosland.

TO CONSCIENTIOUS OBJECTORS.

MILITARY SERVICE (No. 2) ACT.

Local Members of the SOCIETY OF FRIENDS will be glad to hear from any genuine conscientious objector to compulsory military service who requires advice on the presentation of his case before the Tribunal. Enquiries may be addressed to:

R.W. CROSLAND, 31, St Mary's, York
S.H. DAVIES, Ryecroft, New Earswick, York.
F.L.P. STURGE, 10, Grosvenor Terrace, York.
R. DAVIES, 30 Leadhall Lane, Harrogate.
J.W.EDMUNDSON, Rothbury, Sowerby, Thirsk.

How was the York tribunal to work? It had been set up during the Derby scheme and the Military Service Act required bodies of not less than five and not more than 25 persons, with 'adequate representation of labour', and 'suitable women', if the authorities thought it 'desirable' to appoint them. Men should, naturally, be over military age. Members were appointed by the local authority at council meetings and in many areas the directive by Walter Long to elect labour representatives was ignored. But not in York. The Trades Council demanded a two fifths representation (and the York Butcher's Association wanted two members). (30)

The York City Council considered the creation of the local tribunal on 7 February 1916, and a heated debate took place over whether or not traders should be represented, and whether or not labour had a right to two members. Councillor Bury found his name was taken out of the original list in favour of Rhodes Brown (who said he had earlier declined an invitation to stand), and the results of the election were as follows, plus two members to be nominated by the Trades Council. (31)

The Lord Mayor, Alderman Forster Todd, a Tory.

The Sheriff, C.W. Shipley, Labour, a J.P.

Alderman Sir Joseph Sykes Rymer, a Tory and a J.P.

Mr W.F.H. Thomson, JP.

Mr H.V. Scott, clerk to the magistrates.

Councillor K.E.T. Wilkinson, Liberal, Solicitor, Quaker.

Councillor H. Rhodes Brown, Tory, ex Lord Mayor, tradesman.

Councillor W.H. Sessions, Liberal, Quaker, printer.

The Labour nominees seem to have been a Mr C. Boyce and W.H. Farrar, the chairman of the York ILP. Out of a total membership of ten, there were, then, in York, three representatives of labour and two Liberal pacifists. There is no way this was a typical tribunal. There can have been few ILP tribunal members anywhere.

There was considerable confusion about what the tribunals could do in their early days, and some thought their powers were less than they really were (to begin with that in York thought the mximum power it had was to put a Derby man back ten groups). What they could do was to award 'conditional' exemptions from military service - conditional upon taking up some specified work or keeping in the job the applicant had. They could also put off a man's call up, and they could give men total or 'absolute' exemption from military service. Many of the most famous of the conscientious objectors became known as 'absolutists', unwilling to accept anything less. The tribunals could also order that a man be taken into the forces and given only non-combatant duties. They could, of course, also totally reject a man's application. The applications could be made either by the man concerned or someone on his behalf - perhaps a parent, more often an employer. All these options were used in the first meetings of the York tribunal and what went on there will be described at some length. The pleas, the rebukes, and the details of personal circumstances given to the tribunal tell the reader much about what York was like in 1916. They tell of hardship, personal losses, and the difficulties of employers. They also tell, again, very often, the story of just how many men had already gone to the colours.

The York local tribunal met for the first time on 17 January 1916 to consider applications from men in four of the groups of the Derby scheme. (32) It had 103 claims before it for either exemption or postponement of call-up, and half of these were dealt with without the claimants making an appearance. The tribunal dealt with no less than 55 cases of people who presumably turned up, and 70 per cent of the applications were refused. There were no exemptions granted (perhaps because at this stage members thought they could not give them) and most of the applications the tribunal considered were from employers who maintained that the men under threat of call up were indispensable, or men themselves who were only sons, who contended they had to stay behind to look after parents or small businesses or both.

The York tribunal next met towards the end of February when it sat as reconstituted by the new regulations made on the passing of the first conscription legislation. (33) It now had to deal with both Derby men and men called up under the Military Service Act, but on that first day it dealt only with Derby men. It was a crowded day's work it had, and it is clear that there must have been many a man who regretted attesting, even though he would have been picked up anyway. The Lord Mayor presided over the deliberations, which were open to the public, and as usual a military representative was in attendance. The press was persuaded not to name the applicants, the first of whom was a land agent who managed estates of 43,700 acres in 37 parishes in the North and East Ridings. It was said on his behalf that all his staff had joined the forces and that the estates he managed produced pit props and timber for government services. He was allowed a six month's postponement of call up.

The land agent's case was followed by that of a school teacher. He claimed he was the sole support of an invalid widowed mother and his case was heard in camera and no decision was announced. He was followed by a whitesmith and engineer who appealed for exemption for one of his men. Before the war, he revealed, he had engaged eleven persons, and five of them had enlisted. He now had only two men and three boys under the age of 16 left, and would have to close his business if this man went. He supplied work to military contractors, he went on, but his application was refused.

The *Press* and the *Herald* never missed an opportunity of taking a swipe at the Rowntrees and Rowntree and Company and rather than name the latter it sneeringly told its readers that the fourth person to appear before the York tribunal was a 'wood yard labourer' at a 'cocoa works' who had, neverthless, some skilled trade behind him. Perhaps the *Press* was trying to convey the idea that this fellow had moved to work at the Haxby Road factory to get a sympathetic employer who would support him. If this is true, then it was grossly unfair because the man applied for exemption on personal grounds. He was the sole support of his mother, he said, though he had a sister. In cross examination he revealed that his mother had five lodgers who paid her 15s. or 16s. a week, and from that point on he did not stand a chance. His application was refused, and quite rightly so.

A baker with army contracts asked the tribunal to exempt the manager of one of his shops - a man fit for home service only - telling tribunal members that he had already lost nine men to the forces who had gone voluntarily. He was asked why he did not employ a woman to do the manager's job, and succeeded in getting his man's call up put off for three months. He then made a similar application on behalf of his sole remaining van driver (he had four rullies or vans and only one driver he said). This person made deliveries to army camps. Why was he not replaced by a woman, he was asked? Because a woman could not lift ten stone bags of flour, he explained. Try to employ a discharged soldier, the military representative suggested, and the tribunal gave him a month to make some such arrangement.

The York tribunal demonstrated that it now knew what it was about when it gave absolute exemption to a chemist's son who managed his father's business, then dealt with another labourer from 'a cocoa works'. This man applied only for a deferment of his call up and explained that since he had attested and become a Derby man he had married and now had to help support his wife's aged parents. Too bad; his application was refused. Somewhat luckier was a tobacconist who got a three month deferment during which he could teach his wife the art of selling his foul merchandise and a partner in a saddlery business which had suffered from loss of employees was similarly treated. A dental surgeon then applied on behalf of a dentist who was employed entirely as a school dentist, and the application was supported by Dr E.M. Smith, the local Medical Officer of Health. They were unsuccessful, and the man they supported presumably went off to pull the teeth of men dressed in khaki. A motor engineer also got short shrift. He was one of two partners, and he heard his application refused. A railway employee said he had attested in group 22 of Derby's scheme, and declared that he was the sole support of his mother, apart from the 3s. 6d. a week she got from a soldier son. He told the tribunal that his employers made up salaries to those who enlisted, but thought he would get nothing. He got nothing from the tribunal either, and they refused his claim forthwith.

A second chemist appeared before the tribunal at its first real sitting asking for exemption on behalf of his assistant who acted as both a dispenser and a porter, which seems a bit much. 'The assistant was absolutely necessary to the continuation of the business', it was claimed, 'as he was the only man left.' Thomson asked 'Are there no qualified girls in the trade ?', and he and his colleagues gave the man short shrift. A temporary sorting clerk and telegraphist asked if he could be put back as far as possible as he was the sole support of his 69 year old mother, and he too got the thumbs down. Only slightly more lucky was a boot maker and repairer who asked for exemption on the grounds that he too was the sole [sic] support of his mother and a sister who was unable to work. His employer spoke up for him, but to little effect, and the man simply got a deferment of two months. A temporary Post Office sorter then told the Lord Mayor and his colleagues that he received 30s. a week wages and that he was the sole supporter of his mother who paid a rent of £13 a year. He was deferred for one month.

Next to appear before the tribunal was a flour miller who asked for exemption for 'three specially trained clerks.' He revealed that 66 per cent of his office staff and 51 per cent of his milling staff had joined up and if 'any more were allowed to join it would be a question of whether they could carry on, as the firm was hovering between the balance of stopping and continuing.' He went on to hint that some workers, now that there were labour shortages were, for the first time, getting a bit bolshie. 'Many of the left [sic]', he said, '"could not be spoken to," and one had recently left because the foreman had "looked disrespectfully at him."' That was certainly a change from pre-war years when the railwaymen, for example, were picked off at will if they showed any signs of militancy or independence. The miller got nowhere, however, or almost nowhere. One man's case resulted in a refusal; the other two were deferred for just one montth.

A grocer and provision merchant persuaded the tribunal to put his only son on 'the exempted trades list', which amounted to conditional exemption. He employed three assistants and did carry a large credit trade, he said. A jobbing printer asked that 'the only compositor and machine minder he had left' be exempted. He was not employing any girls he replied to a question which was fast becoming routine, and before the war he employed three men and two apprentices. His employee was put back for but two months and a packer who wanted total exemption on the grounds that he had to look after an invalid father and a sister had his application turned down flat.

Rowntree and Company (34) then applied for deferment for a chocolate moulder and a storekeeper in a packing and stores department and total exemption for a mechanical draughtsman and a specially trained audit clerk. They revealed that the firm had lost 13 men so far who had been called up under the Derby scheme, and they heard they were to lose three more. The moulder's application was refused; the draughtsman was exempted; and the other two got a month's deferment. A solicitor's clerk who had attested on 11 December (a last minute man) applied for total exemption on the grounds that he was indispensable. He said he had been declared medically unfit on 5 January, but was unable to produe a certificate saying so. He should have known better than to go before the tribunal unprepared and his case was adjourned for him to produce the magic piece of paper. A painter and joiner made a better go of things than did the solicitor's clerk. He told the court that his business 'would be ruined if he were forced to give it up. He had also a widowed mother dependent on him. The labour he employed was mostly casual, and there was no one who could take his place.' A railway clerk with a widowed mother and an epileptic brother dependent on him asked to be put back. He was. For one month! A wages clerk made a similar plea (as far 'back as possible'). He had a dependent mother and an invalid father, and his case was refused.

A dealer in hunters and chargers applied for exemption for his groom but got only a month's deferment for him. The groom was 'absolutely indispensible to the continuance of the business', he contended, he 'had made every endeavour to secure a substitute, but had not been successful.' Disappointed, the applicant accepted a suggestion 'that he might give a trial to a discharged soldier.' The managing director of a firm of ironmongers who had attested asked for 'total exemption, on the ground that the whole of his capital was invested in the business, which if he were called up, would have to be closed down.' Of his six employees, he said, only two knew anything of the internal working of the business. That may have been so, but the managing director only got a two month deferment. That was all the last applicant wanted. He was supporting a widowed mother, he revealed, and wanted deferment. He was a lorry driver who was 'willing to join either the Motor Transport Service or the Royal Flying Corps', but not just yet. He got a one month dispensation.

It is clear that all the applicants dealt with by the York tribunal on 21 February were single Derby men (with the exemption of the one who had got married after he had attested). Between that meeting and the next, the group system for single men ended. More Derby men were called up, (35) and rumours abounded that married Derby men were to be taken. (36) The papers were full of letters of the kind Charles A. Thompson wrote about 'conchies' and it must have been known that the first of these would appear before the Lord Mayor and the tribunal when it met on 1 March. They did, but the adjudicators had to deal with a mix of Derby men and men called up through the Military Service Act. Proceedings began, however, with an application presented by Kenelm Kerr, representing the general manager of the North Eastern Railway Company and he did so, he said, on the direct instructions of the Minister of Munitions. At the start of the war, Kerr said, the NER employed 54,000 men, of whom 32,000 were of military age in 1914. By 1 March 1916 over 30,000, representing 56 per cent of its total staff and over 95 per cent of the male staff of military age, had presented themselves for military service. 17,000 had attested under the group system and 11,000 had already been released 'for service in either the Navy or the Army.' Kerr had added 30 more men to those listed in his letter and all 387 were given conditional exemption.

The railwaymen all seem to have been Derby men and among the first men dealt with under the Military Service Act were two brothers employed by an engineering firm doing war work, a ledger clerk at an ironmongers and a manager for a fish and poultry dealer. The first two were represented by that Councillor C.A. Bury who was a first choice as a tribunal member until ousted in favour of Rhodes Brown, and both his men got conditional exemptions. The ledger clerk got a two months deferment, and the fish shop manager's case was put by his employer, a lady. Her application on his behalf was refused. (37) A baker had rather more luck. He applied for conditional exemption on behalf of one of his men and revealed that he had lost five of his workers and two thirds of his business since the war started. He would have to close if this last man was called up, he said, and that man was given conditional exemption.

A steel worker at a 'cocoa works' told the tribunal that four of his brothers had already joined up, and that he was an only son remaining at home. It is not clear what he applied for, but he got six month deferment. A young man who ran his mother's business as a licensed victualler got a one month postponement of call-up, and a butcher's application on behalf of his slaughterman was turned down. A firm of colour printers applied for exemption on behalf of an employee - unsuccessfully, and a cycle agent who said he had sunk £200 in his business which would fail if he went into the army, had his call-up put back only until 6 April!

There were other applications similar to those above before the York tribunal in March. Three Derby employees at a 'local institution' were put back three months and five attendants at other unnamed institutions were given conditional exemption. A hospital attendant got three months deferment, a single man supporting a widowed mother had his application (undefined in the reports) refused, a tinsmith wanting total exemption was refused and a china, glass and hardware merchant, wanting total exemption for a son he said was essential to the business, had his application turned down. A boot repairer and a builder applied for total exemption for their sons and were unsuccessful and a businessman wanting total exemption for a branch manager/slaughterman failed. He revealed that the 'society' he represented had 368 employees (78 of whom were females) and that 98 men had already been lost to the forces. A grocer's assistant who presented himself before the tribunal seems to have been a very reasonable young man. He simply asked for a deferment long enough for his boss, who had lost ten men to HM forces, to replace him. Very reasonably he got a month's deferment.

An aged farmer who appeared before the Lord Mayor and his collagues had an uphill task as he must have realised. He wanted total exemption for two sons and said their business involved general smith's work and shoeing 40 horses a week. The military representative, predictably, told him that farriers were much needed in the army and the bench very reasonably, it seems, granted one son conditional exemption and decreed that henceforth the other would shoe horses while wearing khaki, and quite right too. An application from the York sanitary authority, perhaps surprisingly, got nowhere. Dr E.M. Smith wanted the call-up of an assistant in the 'disinfectant department' put back for an 'indefinite period'. He had worked at his present job for 18 months, Smith said, and the work he did was essential. Measles had now become a notifiable disease and was a problem, Dr Smith went on, and in the recent past seven memebers of this vital department had left - six joining up, and the other leaving for higher wages elsewhere. The man was told his deferment would last only until 6 April next.

A window-blind maker and fitter asked 'for total exemption because he was the sole support of his widowed mother', and perhaps his case should be quoted if only to show that such cases sometimes were received sympathetically

> he was 17 years of age he had supported her and it had been a hard job. He himself was in bad health, and had been continually paying doctor's bills. If he went into the army there was nothing for his mother but the workhouse.
>
> Exemption was granted on the condition that applicant continued to care for this mother.
>
> Applicant: Thank you. My mother looked after me when I was young, and it is my duty to look after her in old age.

So far, in the cases that have been quoted, the tribunal had dealt with Derby and MSA men seeking deferment or exemption on the grounds of personal hardship or their indispensability to either a home or business or both. They had yet to deal with a man applying for total exemption on the grounds of conscience, as he had every right to do. The first person to be dealt with who fell into this category appeared late in the day on 1 March 1916. He was Basil Neave, who worked as a commercial traveller for Rowntree and Company. His case was to get wide coverage because of a daft remark by one of the tribunal members.

Neave was a lifelong member of the Society of Friends, he told the tribunal, though not a 'speaking' member. As a Quaker his beliefs were those of a pacifist. But are there not Quakers who have joined the forces as combatants, Rhodes Brown asked? There were, Neave agreed, and he could well have cited Lawrence Rowntree as one of them, a young man who, it has been suggested, was forced into the forces by the activities of York's white feather merchants. (In fact over 36 per cent of young Friends enlisted.) Then came the question which, it has been said, cropped up again and again - a 'trick' question which Wilfrid Crosland and S.H. Davies had probably seen coming a mile off.

> Mr Scott: Should you attempt by any force to protect the chastity of your Sister ? - I should hope not. I think that the whole system of militarism, is against one of the great natural laws under which we all have to live.

The military representative weighed in with a tricky one of his own, asking Neave if he would serve on a minesweeper, a vessel bent on saving lives. He would take no part in an armed conflict, Neave replied, then the following remark was thrown at him.

>Alderman Sir Joseph Sykes Rymer: I think God has made a great mistake in sending you forth before the Millenuim [sic].

Neave was given a conditional discharge which he apparently accepted and the next 'case' involved another Quaker. He was Charles T. Hodgson, a teacher for 15 years who was a senior housemaster at Bootham school. He revealed that he spent three quarters of his spare time training men in the Friends' Ambulance Unit, but declared he would not undertake military service as it was contrary to the teachings of Christ. He was given total exemption as was a second Bootham schoolmaster, James Leadbetter, who had been born and bred a Quaker. Scott tried on one of the standard questions with him. 'Mr Scott: Would your conscience allow you to stand by and see three innocent people killed by a rascal without your making any attempt to stop him with a revolver or by some other means ?' The man's reply was that he would not use force. 'While I should do my best to otherwise stop him killing before my eyes, I should not kill him', he said. To this Scott replied that in his opinion the man 'would be guilty of murder, or at least [be an] accessory after the fact.'

The last conchie case heard that day was reported in the *Herald* of 3 March under the heading 'A VEGETARIAN'S PLEA' and was that of Robert Cecil Bilton, wholesale and retail stationer 'who said he had belonged to the Society of Friends since the outbreak of war and the Vegetarian Society since 1904.' The *Herald* clearly intended that the applicants fairly recent conversion should cast doubts on his motives for joining the Society of Friends, which would have been very unfair because few would have envisaged compulsion in 1914, and Bilton annotated the report on a cutting which is in a collection of such things kept by York objectors. 'I *distinctly* said I was not a *full* member but an attender', he wrote. Bilton was represented by a solicitor (J. Hague) who stressed that, as a member of a vegetarian society, his client held that 'there should be no shedding of blood.' Bilton refused to join either the AOC or the RAMC, and his case was adjourned.

From this first meeting of the York tribunal which had to deal with conscientious objectors (the really difficult part of its work) it is clear that some members were as ill disposed towards them as were some of the letter writers to the press. If I had my way I 'would send the lot of them ... to fix barbed wire and sand bags to protect our dear Tommies at the front', wrote Walter Blakey, of Harrogate, for example. (38) Colonel R.F. Meysey-Thompson held similar views. He suggested they should be dressed in red and 'distributed along the front in the firing line ... their task to be the digging of graves for the heroes who have fallen. ... Verdun would be an excellent place at which to commence.' (39) As more and more 'conchies' appeared before the tribunal so, taking their cue perhaps from offensive remarks from the likes of Sykes Rymer and Scott, more and more letters of the kind quoted above appeared in the press.

What were the attitudes of the Liberals and Quakers on the tribunals? They seem to have been determined to help applicants by putting leading questions - not all of which got the answers they might have expected. Wilkinson, skilled as a lawyer, gave one of the schoolteachers an opportunity to say that he recognised that there was 'a special duty laid upon people with conscientious objections - that they should do all that lies in their power to help forward work of a most useful nature in the national interest' for example, and Sessions allowed the same man to say he considered he would 'be doing better work by trying to evade, by peaceful means', an invading army, as was 'done at Brussels ... rather than by meeting them by force with intent to kill'. He had asked the first schoolmaster to be dealt with if he 'would take part in a peace meeting?', to which the answer was, perhaps surprisingly, 'I do not think I should.' The Labour members do not seem to have distinguished themselves in any way. Shipley made few interventions in the proceedings as reported and Farrar's questions reveal little. Somewhat later conchies of a different kind would make their appearance including close political allies of Farrar. They would tax his loyalties.

Reports from the proceedings of tribunals elsewhere kept feelings against objectors high (and sometimes produced both amusing and complex cases). Selby's tribunal met for the first time at the local court house in March and before it appeared a permanent way inspector employed by the NER. He objected to service on non-religious grounds and revealed that the company had not applied for his retention. He got the standard treatment and the standard questions thrown at him. (40)

> The Clerk: Would you allow a German to criminally assault your mother or sister?
> Applicant: I should protest against it.
> The Clerk: How would you protest. Would you pray to them?
> Applicant: No, I should not pray to them. I belong to no religious body. I have my objections on moral grounds, not religious ones. I might give way and do something, but my objection is to taking life.
> The Chairman: Would you let a burglar in your house with a revolver shoot you?
> Applicant: I should try and stop him.

The NER man was given non-combatant service and said he would join the RAMC, and in the same paper which reported his case the following appeared

THE ONE-EYED COACHMAN
GIVES PROOF IN COURT OF HIS DISABILITY

At the Hertford tribunal Thomas Grove, a coachman, applied for exemption because he had only one eye. When asked for evidence of this he dropped his right-eye into his hand. The court allowed the claim.

The one-eyed coachman seems to have had a genuine disability, but was perhaps better equipped for war than a man whose appearance before the Salford tribunal was reported in the *Herald* on 5 April 1916. He wanted exemption on the grounds that he 'had a conscientious objection' to military service and 'stepped forward with the aid of a crutch.' A member of the tribunal said that the applicant had only one leg, and the chairman 'said he had noticed that' too. The following exchanges then took place.

> Applicant: I have a conscientious objection.
> The Chairman: I think you have more than a conscientious objection. You have an objection on material grounds.
> Applicant: Well, I wish to go on with the conscientious objection.
> The Chairman: It is no use wasting the time of the court. There must be an exemption.
> The Military Representative: On what grounds ?
> Applicant: Conscientious grounds.
> The Chairman: On the ground that he has only one leg.
> Sir William Stephens: We have a conscientious objection to calling up a man who has only one leg.

At the Flaxton tribunal a few days after Tom Grove dropped his glass eye into his hand, a clerk employed by Rowntree and Company asked for conditional exemption under the Military Service Act, on religious grounds. He was, he said, 'a member of the religious body known as the Philadelphians.' He was refused, but not before he had told his tormentors that 'he would not take up the sword under any consideration', and not before he had got the, by now predictable treatment. Taking up arms, he said, was 'against the law of God to kill' whereupon he was quizzed as follows. (41)

> The Chairman: If anyone was coming to slay your mother would you sit and watch them ? - I should trust in faith as Daniel did in the liorn's [sic] den.
> Do you object to Red Cross work ? - Yes, because it is aiding and abetting warfare.

What would you do if the Germans came ? - I should still trust in the Lord.
The applicant said he joined the Society three years ago, and no decision of the tribunal would alter his conviction, he would carry the matter as far as he could.

The applicant's father spelled out what the latter remark meant. 'His son would ... suffer imprisonment rather than serve', he said.

If the York *Press* meant that the Rowntree's clerk was a Christadelphian (and it did, because that is how both the *Gazette* and the *Herald* described him) then it was reporting one of the first appearances before a York area tribunal of a member of the religious group which provided more objectors than any other sect. It is a commonly held belief that the Quakers occupied this position, but in fact only 45.4 per cent of young Friends of military age objected during the war and, as members of the York tribunal were well aware, a far greater proportion of them served (33.6 per cent) than is often realised. However, the population of York seem to have lumped them all together as conchies. The Christadelphians, however, were a group which refused to take up arms and were not prepared to accept anything less than absolute exemption. Many of the Quakers, of course, and indeed many other groups adopted a similar attitude. Frequently a tribunal would offer them non-combatant service, or conditional exemption (as was offered to Basil Neave). This was not enough and they lodged appeals. They became know as 'absolutists'.

The first York meeting of the North Riding Appeal Tribunal was held on 19 March 1916, (42) and a member of it was the opinionated Recorder of Pontefract and the scourge of the pre-war York conscientious objectors, R.H. Vernon Wragge (43).

The appeal tribunals heard challenges to the decisions of the local organisations, and the appeals could be laid either by the dissatisfied man himself, or by someone on his behalf, or by the military representative who thought the lower 'court' had been misguided or too lenient. On the first day they met in York, Wragge and his colleagues had 26 appeals before them, four of which were withdrawn. Of those that remained 15 were disallowed and among the decisions the military representative challenged were those which gave total exemption to a York chemist's son, and that Rowntree draughtsman.

So far the North Riding Appeal tribunal had not had to deal with a conscientious objector, but that experience was not to be long delayed, and one of the people it had to deal with was R. Wilfrid Crosland, the 40 year old secretary and sub-warden of the Educational Settlement, a man who would undoubtedly have been shocked by the way his centre was killed off in the 1980s. His case had been heard by the York body early in March, when Crosland told the members of the tribunal that he had been born a Quaker and that he gave up his work some ten years before to work in adult education. The following exchanges took place, with Sir Joseph inviting a fairly obvious reply. (44)

> Sir Joseph Sykes Rymer: What do you think would become of your country and mine if everybody held the same views as you ?
> Claimant: I think it would be heaven upon earth.
> Sir Joseph: I think it would be hell upon earth! (loud laughter and a voice from the gallery: "It is now!")

Crosland was given exemption on the condition that he continued to work at the Settlement on what was a marathon day for the York tribunal. Its workload then will be described, because it is indicative of the problems that the members had to confront, and among those appearing were some whose stories, again, illustrate facts about the life of York at that time.

Crosland's case was followed by that of Fred Bradley a Fabian and the secretary of he York No Conscription Fellowship, a confidential clerk at Rowntrees who said he had been putting forward his pacifist ideas since the South African war. He wanted absolute exemption and was excused combatant duties only. There then appeared an 'alien' who had an Austrian mother and a German father. He was a watchmaker called Kaiser who said 'He believed the killing of human beings to be totally wrong, even in self defence.' His father said the boy was indispensable to the business and revealed that he had been naturalised for 18 years and that his business had been established for half a century. He also revealed that he (they) had been on the receiving end of racial, hostility and he got what looks like a little more. 'We only rely on repairs now', the father told the tribunal. 'Jewellery is "off".' The Lord Mayor then asked the name of the shop, to which there was the reply that 'We had my name up, but after the Lusitania outrage the police told me my shop was not safe and that I must hide my name. I tried to insure my shop, but the Yorkshire Insurance Company would not do business with me. I covered up my name on my other shop, but the mob smashed my clock.' Sykes Rymer then laid it on.

> Sir Joseph Sykes Rymer: What made you come to this country originally ? - I expected it was a free country. (Laughter.) Nobody asked you to come, but if you do come the country expects you to fulfil your duties.
> Applicant: They let me come, and they imposed no condition or restriction upon me.

Kaiser's application for exemption was refused 'on both grounds' and he was followed by a man who had 'been cradled in the tenets of the Lyceum Spiritualist movement', a sawmill worker who demanded absolute exemption from all forms of warfare because it was 'opposed to the beliefs of brotherhood of nationalities'. He also said he believed it cowardly to engage in 'non-combatant service if such person declined to engage in combatant service' and his case was adjourned indefinitely while he engaged 'in some work suitable to his own conscience and also in conformity with the best ideals of the national interest.' The next applicant was a Rowntree's clerk, a Wesleyan who had lived in York for only eight weeks, a Sunday school teacher who said 'He had been cradled in pacifism.' He criticised his church's attitude to the war and was given exemption from combatant service. He immediately gave notice of appeal saying that 'during the five years that he had been a Sunday School teacher he had endeavoured to imbue the principles of pacifism in the minds of the scholars he taught. "Christ died for His principles," he concluded, "and I am prepared to die for mine." (Loud applause, and sharp cries of "Order!")'

A York Council teacher, a Quaker, was given exemption while he continued in his post, and a second year student at St Johns teachers training college (probably D.M. Davies) told the tribunal he had been an ILP member for five years and had organised an anti war meeting. The grounds he objected on were not overtly political. He declared 'his conscience would not allow him to take human life, believing that human life was sacred.' A picture framer declared that he believed 'all war was wrong', though he was not a member of 'any religious organisation holding these views.' K.E.T. Wilkinson asked him what had led him to his conclusions, and the applicant rather surprisingly (and not too helpfully from his point of view one would have thought) said 'The bringing in of compulsion.'

O.G. Willey, who had addressed one of the conscription meetings, applied for total exemption. He was a member of the NCF and the Peace Society and taught economics and the philosophy of religion at the Swarthmore Educational Centre in Leeds, a sister organisation to the Settlement in York, set up at the same time as the St Marys Centre. He was given conditional exemption, and was followed by a Wesleyan local preacher (a tailor). 'He would serve his country where God had placed him', he said, 'and he would not be dictated to by the tribunal. He was willing to go to prison or to be shot rather than disobey the voice of God'. He was given exemption from combatant service and gave immediate notice of appeal.

A Rowntree clerk applied for exemption on conscientious grounds 'and set up the theory that no armed nation would attack an unarmed nation. He would have let the Germans come over to this country', he said, 'and believed it would have been in the best interests of humanity. He did not believe in competition, either in trade or between nations. He did not belong to any religious organisation holding views against the war, nor was he a Socialist. He attended the Church of England because it was the least orthodox of any'. His case was adjourned and followed by those of three brothers. The first was a clerk on the NER, aged 20, a member of the Brotherhood Church movement who said he had objected to wars since he had first heard of them in history lessons. His first brother was a certified teacher at the Park Grove Council School, who was given exemption from combatant service, as was his second brother, a Weslyan who worked as a clerk in the York education service. He said 'all warfare was against the teaching of Christ.'

Two British sons of unnaturalised Russians had their cases heard privately and were given deferment until 20 May, and two people did not turn up. The first sent a letter containing biblical quotations, which got him exemption 'from non-combatant service' [sic] and the second was a 'sweet confectioner' employed by Rowntrees. His communication contained but seven words - 'Conscientious Objector. I don't believe in fighting.' His application was refused.

A second watchmaker and jeweller appeared before the tribunal sitting at the end of March. He had a brother who had been a mariner for 14 years, but wanted exemption on conscientious grounds. He would not accept non combatant service, he said, 'because it would help the war and was part of the military machine.' His claim was refused, and the last person to appear on the day he did was a bookseller's assistant. He objected to any kind of military training, but said he 'was willing to adapt himself to other work of public utility.' He did not appear in person, and his claim was turned down.

The tribunal meetings which have been described at some length contained examples of some who objected on religious grounds and about whom members had great difficulty. The Quakers were usually recognised as genuine pacifists and were frequently given absolute exemption as a matter of course - but not yet, it will have been noticed. The tribunals had more difficulty with lesser known sects or organisations like the Brotherhood movement, (45) and even more trouble with members of groups (like the Wesleyans mentioned above) who did not go along with general thinking of their church.

So far a case of an out and out York political objector has not been described, though the St Johns College ILP man looked at the outset as if he might fill that bill. Just a little earlier than he appeared before the tribunal, though, Arthur Hatfield had done so, unsuccessfully. (46) Arthur was in the ILP and the NCF. He was 32 years old and a carriage cleaner working for the North Eastern Railway

Company. He described himself as a socialist and an advocate of internationalism who considered 'that the workers' had everything to lose and nothing to gain by war. The suppression of free speech and the limitation of the press since the war broke out confirmed these views.' The Sheriff asked Hatfield if he would be 'opposed to joining the R.A.M.C.' and Arthur replied 'Yes, because I have a conscientious objection to patching a man up to send him back to the hell in Flanders.'

Arthur Hatfield appealed and appeared before R.H.V. Wragge and others in April 1916. (47) He demanded that his exemption be made absolute and said, again, that 'he believed militarism to be the greatest curse to mankind, and he therefore refused to have anything to do with it.' Wragge taunted him with cleaning carriages which were used to carry troops, and said the 'work you are doing to-day is just exactly the same as if you were carrying a wounded soldier on a stretcher.' To which Arthur replied 'Oh, no it is not. Our Company and the Conciliation Board control our labour.'

Arthur Hatfield's application was refused and he appeared before the York tribunal again in May applying for his original certificate giving him non combatant service to be reviewed. His justification was that Wragge had said that the work he was doing was a 'national service.' His objection, Arthur said, 'was a political, rather than a conscientious, one', but Wragge had said he was a 'useful member of the community at present'. I am 'prepared to give you my word that so long as the Railway Company employ me I will continue' to work there, he went on, in a rather strange statement, 'but if you turn me down I shall have to go to prison, and shall then be useful to nobody.' Arthur, a product of the Central Labour College, got nowhere, the military representative contending, quite rightly, that there had been 'no additional facts' put forward. 'There is no change of the previous decision concerning your case' the Lord Mayor told York's best known carriage cleaner, whose case has all the appearances of one prepared by the local NCF.

Many of the 'religious' objectors appeared before the North Riding appeal tribunal. Wilfrid Crosland did so and he got absolution. (48) They did not seem to realise he was a Friend, Crosland said, but when they did they became almost apologetic and gave him what he wanted. The military authorities objected to the 40 years old Crosland's award saying that, as a fully qualified ambulance man, 'he would be better employed in non-combatant service', and they did so against that made to O.G. Willey. He resolutely refused to do any work ordered him by the Pelham Committee, (49) and the military's appeal was dismissed. Two of the three brothers who were before the York tribunal in May appealed themselves and had those appeals dismissed, as did young Kaiser. The secretary of the York NCF had his appeal against non combatant service dismissed, and the Park Grove teacher had his award of conditional exemption successfully challenged (50) by the military on the grounds that he would be of more use to the country 'in a non-combatant corps.' (51)

> The respondent said it took six years to train him, at considerable expense to the State and himself, and he had 13 years' experience with the result that he was now rendering the highest and most efficient service that he could render to the State. He objected to in any way advancing the war.
>
> The Chairman: You are advancing war by education. If education had not been so far advanced we should not have had such far-advanced discoveries with the implements of war. Zeppelins, aeroplanes, big guns and howitzers are all the result of education. Although you little know it, you may be instrumental in bringing out some great discovery in connection with war.
>
> Respondent: That would be quite by chance. I might be instrumental the other way as well.

The North Riding tribunal heard appeals from employers (like Colonel Meysey-Thompson who wanted to keep either his cowman or horseman), from the military representatives, and from the men themselves, either on the grounds of hardship, indispensability or conscience. Those with religious objections who were either out of step with their co-religionists, were members of minority groups or who based their objections on their own interpretation of the scriptures (like the York education clerk or the Wesleyan Sunday School teacher) frequently got nowhere, and the few political objectors were on a hiding to nothing. What happened after the appeals? Well to all intents and purposes that was the end of the line, and, if exemption was refused, or if non combatant service was awarded or given instead of something else, men became subject to the call-up and were eventually ordered to present themselves for military service. Many did that, but some, whose objections were usually based on a mixture of religion and politics, ignored their enlistment papers and waited instead to be arrested as they had always indicated they would if they did not get what they wanted. The first batch in York were arrested and appeared in the magistrates court in May.

On 22 May 1916 James Ritchie Henderson a 21 year old who had appealed against an award of non combatant service, and Harold Deighton, of Fenwick Street, appeared before the magistrates. Henderson lived in Vyner Street, and so was a near neighbour of Arthur Dearlove. He was a Rowntree worker who should have reported for military service on 3 May and both he and Harold Deighton were handed over to the military authorities, but not before Henderson had heard some extremely sympathetic remarks from one of the two JPs on duty that morning. This was Robert Kay, from whose remarks Alderman Purnell publicly disassociated himself. These two declined to fine the pair, and Kay said that (52)

> I should like to state that I am very much in sympathy with this young man, and I may say that I honour the man. It requires as much courage to say and do what he has done as to do other things, but there is no alternative but to hand him over to the military authorities.

Henderson's remarks which promoted Kay's statement included the following:

> He was not there that day to "save his skin," but to oppose the present military system which threatened to make slaves of the future generations. It was the liberty of the individual to act according to the dictates of conscience as to what was right and what was wrong in a matter of life and death. He had a deep admiration for his friends, the heroic soldiers who were giving up their lives in the cause they believed in, but the Court would never make him depart from the principles which he believed to be right, and for which he was willing to stand up to the end.

Harold Deighton was a young man of 24 when he was arrested and a resumé of his attitudes and court appearances appears in a collection of York NCF archives held by a man in York whose father was a (later) conscientious objector imprisoned during the Great War. (The son was similarly imprisoned in the Second World War.) In these documents, some of which were illustrated in the journal *York Historian*, (53) there is as comprehensive a record of the local objectors as one is likely to find anywhere. It is from them that Wilfrid Crosland's remark that the tribunal gave Quakers almost automatic exemption was taken. Arthur Hatfield's record is there, and so too are those of many others whose names will appear in this narrative. Harold Deighton's and James Ritchie Henderson's court appearances are also recorded in those fascinating documents and in the 1980s tape recordings were made with two York NCF members which are now deposited in an archive along with other recordings mentioned in these pages. (There is also a recording made with the son of that Robert Kay, JP, who said he admired young Henderson.) Harold Deighton was one of those interviewed at his home in the north-east. One of his colleagues described what an earlier age would have called the 'hole in the corner' meetings the Federation had behind drawn curtains, and Harold described his time in prison, because that is where he went.

After their court appearances Deighton and Henderson were charged with insubordination (they were now deemed to be soldiers) and tried by court martial at the Infantry Barracks at Fulford. Harold's crime then was that he refused to get his kit ready for a planned move to Richmond, and Henderson had first of all refused to take his boots off, then refused to put army ones on. They both got 28 days detention, (54) and went on to a career of disobedience, repeated court martials and prison sentences. Harold Deighton was as sure of the rightness of his actions in the 1980s as he had been in 1916. He was amused then at the way he and his colleagues were then (now) being looked at by historians.

Harold Deighton never complained about the way he was treated while 'in the army', but another York conchie had every reason to do so. Just under two weeks after Deighton and Henderson appeared in the York magistrates court, five of their friends had a similar experience and were handed over to the military authorities. Like Harold they had all been before the North Riding tribunal wanting absolute exemption instead of what they had been given at York, their appeals had been dismissed, they had ignored their call up papers and were charged under the Reserve Forces Act of 1882 with being absentees from the Army. (55) They were William Preston of Emerald Street, Charles E. Barnes of Surtees Street, Arthur Scott Dyson of Heworth Green, William Judson, of Field View, who declared that 'war was contrary to the Sermon on the Mount, and to the whole teaching and example of our Lord', and Andrews Britan (whose name was frequently rendered incorrectly). Britan was that teacher at Park Grove School who said 'He resolutely refused to become a deserter from the peace cause.' That Robert Kay who had said such complimentary things from the bench about Henderson (a Quaker) was Andrews Britan's boss. He was the headmaster of Park Grove School.

The appearance of the five York objectors in court provoked a tremendous outcry of a most unpleasant kind. Almost certainly the hostility shown to them was enhanced by such things as the current Zeppelin raids and the death of Lord Kitchener, whose memorial service was held in York Minster on the day the appearance in court of Scott Dyson and the others was reported. Anyway a torrent of abuse was heaped upon them, with a character who signed himself (or herself) 'PHRENO' excelling himself (or herself). 'Never in the whole course of my life have I seen such a disgusting spectacle as I witnessed a few days ago in the York Police Court', he wrote, 'when five animated pieces of clay, formed after the fashion of human beings, essayed to give reasons why they should not be handed over to the military powers.' (56) One 'took the Sermon on the Mount as his guide', wrote Phreno, but forgot that 'The Deliverer of that sermon enjoined His chosen disciples to take no thought or prepare no defence for their conduct when they were brought before magistrates and judges.' This is the way a large proportion of newspaper controversies went on in those days, with one disputant quoting an extract from the scriptures to support his argument and another, like Phreno, countering with another. It was all unedifying but Phreno was good at coining silly jingoistic rhetorical flourishes with which to end his absurd letters. 'Young men, put away childish manners', he said.

> don't make yourself a public laughing stock to be admired by a few girls in short frocks. Quit you like men. Up and at the devil's own agents; Huns, who slay innocent babies and commit unspeakable horrors on helpless women, and here in York have dropped their bombs from the clouds as liberally as you would expect blessings, after the way England has treated them.

Phreno did not tell his readers how he was able to afford the time to attend court to hear the 'five animated pieces of clay' argue their case and he would have written his diatribe before he read S.H. Davies' letter about what happened to one of them. Davies, as has been said, was active in the NCF and frequently appeared before the York tribunal to help men present their cases. On 16 June the *Herald* published a letter from him in which he described what had happened to Andrews Britan. It was a dreadful story he had to tell. Britan (who was not a Quaker as Davies said he was), was arrested on 12 June,

> handed over to the military authorities, forcibly dressed in khaki, handcuffed, and taken to Richmond. On arrival he refused to obey an order, and was assaulted by a corporal - bruised and cut on the face. On Tuesday morning, on refusing to parade, he was knocked down by another corporal (or sergeant), and forcibly carried to the Parade ground. Britan quietly endeavoured to explain his position to a captain, and removed his tunic. The captain ordered him to be stripped naked, except for his shirt, and placed against a wall in the public square of Richmond Castle. Here he endured the gibes of the passers by, women being excluded by the military. A young civilian who raised his cap and spoke respectfully to Andrews Britan was arrested. Britain was then locked up in a cell, with floor space of about 8ft. by 5ft., with no seat or bed and a concrete floor. Notwithstanding the definite pledge of the Prime Minister, he and others of like faith at Richmond are told that they will be drafted to France to-morrow (Friday), where the prospect is held out of severe penalties.

It was inevitable that Edith Milner would reply to Davies and comment on Andrews Britan. She did, saying she simply could not 'believe that such treatment would be imposed in England under any conditions, whether deserved or not.' (57) This was as dotty as quoting one piece of scripture to deny the contentions of another, and a J. Campbell of Hetherton Street demanded proof of his charges from Davies, which was a lot more logical than denying something went on, as Edith did. (58) Before he did so Arthur Dearlove gave the *Herald*'s readers a list of the ill treatment of other objectors elsewhere (his letter appeared under the heading 'CONSCIENTIOUS OBJECTORS' WHINE BUREAU'). (59) Davies wrote on 23 June saying that he now had 'independent testimony' to support his earlier contentions, and, not only that, but 'Britan was exposed to similar treatment the next day, and was then confined for 48 hours on bread and water diet.' Like Dearlove he concluded, truthfully, by saying that 'Unhappily' the Britan case was 'not unique' as although 'the majority of conscientious objectors have been decently handled in detention barracks and military prisons, there are scores of cases of brutal ill-usage.' (60)

Britan was mercilessly attacked in the press. 'A REAL BRITON' said that he was 'like a circus clown', and that far from beating him up 'the sergeant in charge' of him 'acted like Job's own brother'. (61) 'A SOLDIER'S WIFE' said Britan deserved what he got, and that Dearlove and Davies were not 'men'. (62) 'W.H.F.' said it would be 'a sorry day for England were the majority composed of such creatures as Messrs Davies and Britain', (63) and 'THRINO' thought Britan 'got off very lightly' for taking off his uniform. (64) Philip Ramsay, who had the courage to sign his letter, however, and it is good to record this, wrote of Edith Milner's 'ignorance', (65) and John Masefield asked if she really thought Davies did 'not know what he is talking about?' (66) Was it likely, he asked, that a man of Davies' 'scholastic ability' would 'sit down and weave a yarn like a short-story writer of fiction simply for sale and to be gulped down the ever open mouth of a credulous public.' It was about time someone wrote like this. 'Some people have lived so long in a bed of roses', Masefield went on, 'that they will not believe that there are such things as thistles, and if somebody tells them that outside their own garden thistles grow they will not believe it. They simply look up to the sky and say, "No, I will not believe it; in this fair land thistles do not grow; they only grow in wicked ruritania, or somewhere else; here everything is perfect and good, and everyone is kind and just, particularly in the - whatever you like.' J. Rendel Ridges attacked Edith in a similar fashion, and so did Fred Bradley, of Stockton Lane. Both these were objectors and NCF men, and Fred said it would be 'no surprise to anyone acquainted with Miss Milner that she finds herself unable to believe the plain statement of facts given by ... Davies', because 'people of her type of mind always find it difficult to believe anything that does not square with their accepted notion of things.' (67) He had before him, Bradley wrote, a letter from an eye-witness who saw the assault on Andrews Britan. In the same paper in which Fred Bradley's letter appeared there was another from Mark

Tapley who poked fun at Phreno, saying he would 'make a comic cut in the box, if compelled to speak impromptu', and yet another from S.C. Watkinson of Marygate. He pointed out now stupid it was to take pieces of scripture and quote them to serve one's immediate purpose, and suggested that Phreno should sign his name. Edith Milner, who would not have seen the letters from Fred Bradley and the others, also contributed to that day's correspondence column. What did she say? She still challenged Davies to prove his contentions, said that the current pro-Britan agitation was 'evidently got up by the peace-at-any-price party', and demanded that the correspondence on it be closed. Well she would do that seeing she was at last getting her come-uppance, but she wanted the last word. 'There is only one opinion of Britan', she wrote, 'he is a coward.' (68) That was a stupid remark from a very silly woman, and perhaps the true state of affairs was much better put in a much better letter to the *Herald* of 9 May 1916 by Fred Bradley. 'No man who is a coward', Bradley wrote, 'would choose the position of the conscientious objector unless he was also a fool; there are so many easier ways of shirking that by openly resisting the law.'

Edith's last letter built up to her attack on Britan. Prior to that she had made her contribution to another hate campaign that was going on in the city, also no doubt largely the result of the air raids and the lumping together of objectors, Quakers and pro-Germans. York was 'honey-combed with aliens and pro-Germans', she said, and it seemed a pity that they should be allowed liberty 'to air their views'.

By the time Edith wrote, the York 1916 anti-alien campaign had reached hysterical proportions, if the correspondence columns of the *Press* and the *Herald* are an indication (which they are). Why do not aliens trade under their own names, one writer asked, and why can Germans still set up business? The answer to the first question should have been perfectly obvious; it was to protect themselves from people capable of the hatred he was showing in his letter to the *Press*. In the same paper that printed all this (69), a Scotsman said there were 'more aliens ... with businesses ... in [York] than any other place I have been in yet.' He urged the public to boycott them. 'Do as our great and magnificent Navy did last week (70) - wipe them out ... if we can't intern them ... shun them.' This was dreadful stuff, and there was a lot of it. (71) On 19 June 'SOLDIER' had a letter published which asked York people

> What is a stranger [like him] to think of your own peculiar brand [of], "Conscientious objectors?" and the alleged swarm of German tradesmen who infest your city? Has York any interest in the war? Judging by your correspondence column is to be relied on [sic], it surely cannot be very deep. Otherwise the people here would do

what others have done - boycott the enemy, neither trade with them, deal with them, drink with them, or even speak to them; in short intern them in their own homes.

The really sad thing about the anti alien feeling expressed at various times during the Great War is that very often the 'aliens' had not only been in the country for many years, but frequently had sons serving and dying in the armed services. Perhaps it was inevitable, however, that fairly easily identifiable people should become the objects of hatred by the stupid and prejudiced, but just occasionally that hatred was inflamed by people in positions of authority who should have known better. It happened in York when Henry Rhodes Brown gave the bigots his support.

Solomon, Israel and Lewis Morris were three sons of Austrian parents who had changed their name from Saul and had tried to join up but were told they could not. But then British sons of alien parentage became liable for military service from 1 March 1916 as a result of new rules. The three Morris boys appeared before the York tribunal early in April. (72) They asked for deferment so that Israel and Lewis could join the RFC as tailors and for exemption for Solomon 'to carry on their tailoring business in York.' Another brother, it was revealed, was already serving, but the applications were refused, though Solomon was given leave to appeal to the North Riding tribunal. By the time the higher body sat, his brothers had joined up, and Solomon was merely given deferment until 1 October. Rhodes Brown was furious and not only attacked the appeal body, but declared that 'one Solomon Saul, otherwise Solomon Morris, an alien,' is extending his business in York 'to the detriment of our own citizens,' including himself, presumably. Councillor J.F. Glew attacked Rhodes Brown for his intolerance and stupidity, (73) but the ex Lord Mayor pressed on and contributed to the correspondence columns of the press dealing with 'the problem'. (74) A Bavarian with 15 years' service 'with one of our city's most respected firms' had, along with his daughter, 'born of a Prussian mother', commenced 'business last year in our city', complained Rhodes Brown, the great exponent of the free market. It was all wrong, and 'Why are aliens not compelled to put up and trade in their own names, so that we may know with whom we are trading; and why should they be able to change their names, taking new ones ?' Charles A. Thompson, it seems almost superfluous to add, supported the ex Lord Mayor. In a letter to the *Herald* of 7 June, an issue almost entirely devoted to the memory of Lord Kitchener, Thompson wrote of the 'iniquitous shame' and the 'gross evil' of unnaturalised aliens trading in York, capturing, often, 'the loyal Englishman's business in his enforced absence.' The authorities, he said, 'should prohibit alien enemies trading at all', and 'The names of property owners who let their premises to them should be published, with what verdict the public care to pass upon them.'

Mixed up with the arguments about aliens and conchies, and indeed a part of it, were attacks on members of the Society of Friends who were working at the hospital in Haxby Road which had once been the Rowntree dining hall. These young men wore a uniform and it sometimes led to them being saluted, because the uniform looked like that of an officer. (Rhodes Brown in the silly letter just quoted complained of this.) In actual fact the FSA unit at Haxby Road was made up mainly of men who were unfit for military service or who were over age, but this did not matter. They were lumped together with the conchies and the Quakers and attacked as bitterly as were the aliens. The soldier who had said aliens flocked to York from Tyneside 'a year or more ago' to get 'a safe and congenial refuge within the city walls' - something which York might have prided itself on - called the FSA men a 'parcel of humbugs.' (75) An idiot who signed himself 'ONE OF BOTHA'S NON-COMS' excelled himself in a letter published under the heading 'THE "SWANK" QUAKER UNFORM'. He spoke of 'the sexless creatures who comprise the Rowntree orderlies', who were pretending to do women's work. They would be better dressed in 'short petticoats and skirts, frilled underclothing, white socks, low shoes, and corsets, the latter to be worn outside of khaki serge jackets'. he concluded. (78)

Hostility towards workers at the Haxby Road Auxiliary Military Hospital would not have been lessened by the way they were given exemption. Tribunals were in the habit of accepting groups of applicants together (more or less), as when the NER submitted its claim on behalf of nearly 400 workers. The York tribunal also heard, or agreed to, exemptions for the FSA members at Haxby Road en bloc. On that occasion, reported in the *Press* of 14 March, the military representative accepted the applications, and it must have looked as if strings were being pulled on behalf of what one fool called the 'fakirs of the cant and cocoa brigade' when it was revealed that the military did not object on specific instructions from Sir George Newman of the Army Council.

Eventually the 'alien' question was discussed at a meeting of the York City Council held on 31 July (a meeting at which Rhodes Brown was elected as an alderman to replace the late Thomas Carter). This was the day when the country got to hear of the murder of Captain Fryatt by the Germans, and Alderman Purnell moved the adoption of the report of the Finance Committee wherein there was a minute supporting 'a resolution from the Wolverhampton Corporation calling upon the Government to intern all enemy alien subjects resident in the country for the duration of the war.' Alderman W.H. Birch and Councillor T.H. Rowntree demanded the deletion of this stupid suggestion, but it got support from predictable sources. Alderman Inglis went on about an 'unseen hand' which 'had been working in our midst, and' said he 'was glad people were beginning to be alive to this danger.' The country was 'honeycombed with spies', Inglis went on,

'During the last ten days aliens had been sent from York for a holiday in the Isle of Man, and if the Government did their duty they would send a large number more to that salubrious resort.' Vernon Wragge did not quite go along with Inglis. He recognised that some 'aliens' had children fighting for the British, but nevertheless wanted them all put 'under varying obligations so as to prevent them doing harm to this country.'

It was a fact that a large proportion of the applicants at the York tribunal were Rowntree employees - which is not surprising as the firm was a large employer in the city - and the company was always the subject of hostility during the war years. Perhaps it was inevitable that at the time of the air raids, when the first objectors were appearing before the tribunals, and during the manufactured alien row, the anti Rowntree feeling should reach something of a peak. It did. It perhaps started with a union meeting, or, if not, that meeting spurred it on.

In June 1916 the York branch of the National Union of Gas and General Workers called a meeting of unorganised women. There Shilleto said that the Minister of Munitions had laid it down that women over 18 employed on time work 'customarily done by men shall be rated at £1 a week', but one York firm was paying half that amount, and an instance was given of a worker who received only 14s.2d. for a 71 hour week, or less than 2d. an hour! Furthermore, the official said, 'he believed that Messrs. Rowntree were the only firm in the country who were not paying war bonuses to women.' (77) A correspondent to the local papers signing his letter 'A Sufferer' said that Rowntrees were only paying the 3s. war bonus to married employees. Shilleto later corrected his story about the lady earning 14s. 2d. and said she worked only 60 hours a week, and it appeared that the company did in fact pay £1 a week to women doing men's work. However, there were other complaints about the firm and the *Press* of 28 April carried numerous letters about it. How can Rowntrees find work for new hands 'but cannot keep their old hands in work' asked one, who went on to complain that 'when we speak up for our rights all we get is "You had better leave".' (79) Rowntree girls did not get a war bonus, wrote another, and in a great many cases wages there were 'less than they were before the war'. This looks rather unlikely, but another complainant in the same paper said they got less than did local munitions workers. These workers earned more, she wrote, 'and have more privileges than anyone else, and could get 2s. discount knocked off what they bought in the last seven days at Leak and Thorp's' (a large local store).

Clearly all was not well at Rowntree and Company and mixed in with the attacks on it were what looked like genuine workers' complaints. The comparisons the girls made with munition workers were comparisons with what girls working at the munitions factory set up by Sir George Armstrong, Whitworth and

Company got for example. The proposal to create this was mentioned earlier, and it was set up and running by the spring of 1916. The girls there did indeed receive good wages - and they worked very hard for them. While training as machinists (the factory turned out shell cases) they received £1 for a 53 hour week. When fully trained they received the same wages as men, and this meant that girls on lathes could get £2 a week, and girls on milling machines or slotting machines could get 30s. or 36s. respectively. 'There was no cheap labour' at the factory, it was declared, and the lowest wages mentioned were 28s. to 30s. Details of the conditions they worked under were: a 12 hour day (from 7 to 7); shift work; one and a half hours for meals; with ten and a half hours standing at a bench.

The details of wages and conditions at Armstrong, Whitworth, were taken from an account of what seems to have been the first sitting of the York Munitions tribunal or court, (80), another regulatory body which signified that government control was making itself more and more evident in everyday life. At that first hearing a Mrs Florence Humphries, a soldier's wife, was charged with leaving her work as a machinist, and much was made (very reasonably) of the cost to the firm of training such as she, and many threats were made - for public consumption - of the fact that without a leaving certificate from the tribunal people like Mrs Humphries would be unable to obtain work elsewhere. In July Edith Smith, a young married lady of 21, made a complaint to the York Munitions court (which only had jurisdiction over government controlled works). She was represented there by Shilleto of the National Gas and General Workers' Union, and she complained that the firm of Adams Hydraulics would not give her a leaving certificate, and she demanded compensation. Mrs Smith told the court that she went to the firm as a learner on 9 May 1916 and asked for a rise on 9 June, a request which was refused by the senior members of the Adams family. 'Complainant [then] asked how it was that girls employed at the Queen-street works [Armstrong, Whitworth's] got £1 per week while they only got 10s. per week. He said they only got 10s. because they were learning [which was not true], but added that he would pay 15s. as their work was satisfactory. On the following Friday night complainant was given her notice and told that she was inefficient at her work. 'Mrs Smith had not worked her notice, but had gone to Cooke's, another firm, but they could not take her on because she had not got a leaving certificate. She then went back to Adams senior who told her 'that as she was going to another munition place he was not forced to free her.' (81)

Old habits die hard, the days of labour power were well in the future, and people like Adams could still victimise people like Smith (though he would not have seen it that way). But things were changing, as a result of the war, and Edith Smith was not only able to take her case to court, but win it and have her employers heavy handedness exposed in the press. Shilleto told the court that Edith had gone to see him and revealed that conditions at Adams Hydraulics were 'very unsatisfactory'. It was her information he had used in his speech on 1 June, and it was Adams Hydraulics he was referring to when he revealed that a certain 'firm in York on munitions and a Government controlled shop ... were not complying with the instructions from the Ministry of Munitions, as they were violating the schedule relating to wages.' Shilleto's statements and Edith Smith's case must have done a power of good (though it may have marked Edith as a trouble maker). The lady got 30s. damages and her leaving certificate. On the same day Adams Hydraulics were fined 5s. for dismissing Gladys Annie Collins within six weeks of her undertaking to work in a controlled establishment.

Clearly conditions were improving for the workers in York, a result of government legislation and, one imagines, labour shortages. People like Edith Smith and Gladys Annie Collins would not have had access to the courts a few years ago, but their court appearances were not those which attracted most attention. As the weeks went by more and conscientious objectors ignored their calling up papers, and found themselves in the courts, and the subject of the usual hostility. In June Arthur Hatfield, the carriage cleaner was up. He lived in Cromer Street and was arrested there at 7.30 on the morning of 29 June and whisked off to the law courts. He had been left at liberty for what looks like a fair length of time, having been ordered to report at the Infantry Barracks on 10 April. He told the magistrates that he had been sacked from the NER. He 'pleaded not guilty to being a soldier', Arthur said, 'According to the Pelham Committee, railway work was considered to be of national importance. He had been employed by the North Eastern Railway Co. for 11 years, and because he had not attested he was discharged. If he was taken into the Army he should not obey orders, and they would simply have to keep him. ... He was not a soldier, and had not taken any oath, and therefore could not be a soldier.' Arthur was handed over to the military authorities. (82)

With Arthur Hatfield in court on 29 June was Fred Bradley, the Rowntree clerk and the secretary of the NCF. Fred had been arrested at work after failing to present himself for service. He was 40 years of ago and, like Arthur, a political objector. He described himself as a socialist and an internationalist and told the court about the NCF. He joined it in its earliest days, he said, and when they formed it they confidently expected that the penalty for refusing to serve would be death. When conscription came in the NCF decided to oppose it in every way. He had been given conditional exemption but went to appeal, where he was ordered to take up non-combatant duties. But 'Non-combatant service was more objectionable than combatant service. He was', Fred went on, 'perhaps, a fanatic, but he was not a coward, and he would not obey a single army order if handed over.' He would 'not even march from the Police Station to the Barracks. He would be perfectly passive, but they would either have to carry him or something. From that moment he must become a burden upon them. There was no alternative for him.' Like Henderson Fred was complimented by one of the magistrates - A.P. Mawson, the veteran Labour politician, but he was handed over and was as good as his word. He, Arthur Hatfield and James Walsh were taken away in a VAD ambulance. Large crowds witnessed their going, but there were no demonstrations as there were on one occasion at Malton, where two men were treated appallingly (though one would have tried the patience of most justices).

George Robinson, a shepherd, appeared before a Malton bench presided over by Sir William Worsley, charged with having failed to report for military service on 23 May. Asked why, Robinson, a socialist and an 'internationalist', said all war was wrong and that 'he had not reported himself because he considered that this would have been a voluntary surrender of himself to military service, which his conscience told him was wrong.' He had failed to convince two tribunals that he should be given absolute exemption and the announcement was made in court that the 'Defendant was a criminal of the worst type, and his crime was one against his country.' He was fined £5 and handed over to the military along with Frank Dean, a butcher's assistant, who was told from the bench that 'they were ashamed of the prisoner ... he was a disgrace to his country.' Large, hostile crowds watched as Robinson and Dean were marched to the railway station. Had there been trouble it would have been possible to argue that the bench had had something to do with starting it. (At the time Robinson and Dean were in court the Malton Rural District Council was debating a proposal that it should refuse to employ people with conscientious objections to military service. To its everlasting credit the council decided it would employ objectors.)

It is not too difficult to find examples of benches and tribunals being unbelievably offensive to conscientious objectors, and in July the Malton magistrates did so again. Tom Gascoigne, a Malton tailor, appeared before them as an absentee, when Alderman Robert Metcalfe told him he was 'A BLOT UPON THE SPLENDID RECORD OF THE DISTRICT', but that rebuke seems mild when compared to that delivered to a weaver from Saltaire, a NCF member who appeared before the Wetherby tribunal, a member of which said 'it was a good thing he had no children as they did not want any more of his breed.'

A few days after Hatfield and Bradley were forcibly enlisted, Frederick Charles Watkinson, a shoemaker's apprentice, appeared in court and was handed over. He had been given absolute exemption at York but his award had been appealed by the army representative and he had been ordered to do non combatant service instead. (83) A few more days went by and then the York education clerk appeared before Robert Kay and Cuthbert Morrell. He was Herbert Coupland, a 27 year old who lived at 53, Skeldergate. He had appealed to the North Riding tribunal, where he received a severe wigging from R.H. Vernon Wragge, had his case dismissed, and received his call up papers for 6 June. His case led to a spirited attack on the tribunals by Robert Kay who pointed out that the Military Service legislation exempted genuine conscientious objectors from national service and said he knew Coupland to be 'an honest, hard-working man and a conscientious objector - not a shirker, but a real man.' (84) Kay said he did not think the military had any right to Coupland and declared that he objected to handing someone over who might be treated in the way certain others had been. Morrell said he thought Coupland should be handed over; the Chief Constable said he did not think the bench had the power to dismiss the case, but dismissed it was. Tlhe *Herald* of 19 July carried a furious editorial demanding that Kay and 'certain [other] magistrates who deliberately refuse to carry out the law' regarding objectors be dismissed. (It never criticised the tribunal members who refused to carry out their obligations.)

Coupland was not at liberty for long. He was rearrested on the night of his court appearance and taken before a fresh bench the next day, consisting this time (sensibly) of three members who were Donald S. Mackay, Alderman Norman Green and Councillor J. Hardgrave. Coupland asked for an adjournment to obtain legal advice, saying that he was of the opinion that he could not be indicted twice for the same offence. This was refused and Mackay, the chairman, set about Coupland. 'You are a soldier', he told him

> and the fact that you objected to being a soldier cannot influence us to-day. The case seems perfectly clear. You may have your own opinion as to what you term conscientious objections, and other people have theirs. To most people it appears the most selfish possible position to take up; you are willing to take all the benefits you can get out of the country under its laws, but you are not willing to do anything for your country. We have no sympathy for you; you will be fined 40s., and handed over to a military escort.

Coupland was duly handed over and on 20 July went before a medical board which found him 'unfit for service'! A brother of his, however, objected and was drafted. This was Frank who was handed over to the military, then appealed to the North Riding tribunal, asking for his case to go before the Pelham Committee (which had not been formed when he first appealed). Frank, who was 23, was then in khaki, and he told the tribunal that he was awaiting a court martial 'for having refused to parade when ordered to do so.' (85) His appeal was dismissed.

Others followed the Couplands. In August George Broadley, a 25 year old tailor, was handed over to the military and fined by the York magistrates. (86) He had been before the York and North Riding tribunals, but it must be worth adding that there were people being reluctantly taken into the forces who had not done this, and who have to be added to the numbers of objectors (in some way, though categorising them would be extremely difficult). These were people who simply ignored their call up. A publican in one of the country areas near York did so and took off (taking the till money as well to help him on his way). There were many others, John Robinson Harding of Sycamore Place, New Earswick for example. He was a 36 year old man who simply ignored his calling up papers in March, and found himself before the York magistrates charged with being an absentee on 9 May. Henry Shepherd, a labourer of Skeldergate, was similarly up in court five days later, but classing him as an objector would be rather difficult. Henry had simply ignored his papers when they came through the post. He said 'he did not think he was liable for service as he was over age. He said that he did not know, however, exactly how old he was. He might be 41 or he might be 48.' He was 'handed over to the military, but no fine was imposed.' There was, however, at least one case where it is quite clear that a man refused to join the army on conscientious grounds who did not go through the tribunals, and it came from near York. William Frederick Balderson appeared before the magistrates at Helmsley for not reporting himself for service. This was on 14 July 1916 and evidence was given that Balderson should have reported four days earlier. He had sent a letter to the authorities saying 'he had conscientious objections to military service, and therefore could not submit himself' and a warrant was issued for his arrest. He was told he would be fined £10 and handed over, and the following dialogue took place

>Defendant. All right, sir, but don't expect that you will get it.

>The Chairman. You ought to be ashamed of yourself.

>Defendant. I am not.

On the day that Frederick Charles Watkinson appeared in the York courts charged with being a deserter, 14 men appeared before a court martial at Ripon, amongst whom was 'Private' Andrews Britain [sic]. (87) Two days later Arthur Hatfield, James Watson and Fred Bradley appeared before a similar court at Ripon. Privates Bradley and Hatfield appeared in their shirt sleeves and the former declared himself a socialist who 'believed in the ethical teaching of Jesus Christ', while the latter told his judges of his membership of the ILP. (88)

The issue of conscription, and the unpleasantness that accompanied it had a polarising effect on attitudes and led to something of a revival in politics in York, and everywhere else for that matter. The Tories and the Liberals still adhered to the party truce, and the Labour party, after a period of indecision, decided to carry on doing so too, with many of its members in York, like Mawson, active either on the tribunals or on the benches which sent the likes of Arthur Hatfield off to become very reluctant soldiers. But what was going on disturbed many Labour supporters, and they began to protest, and so both highlighted attitudes and divided people. In June 1916 W.H. Hallaways, secretary of the York No 1 branch of the NUR, wrote to the papers to say that he and his members had discussed what had been happening to the likes of Andrews Britan and protested strongly 'against the brutal and cowardly treatment meted out' to them 'in the various military camps and barracks.' (89) Whilst some protested against the behaviour of the military towards such as Britan others criticised the tribunals for simply ignoring the law - and they were right to do so. On 21 July the *Press* carried two letters to this effect, the first by someone signing himself 'Justice', and he said, quite correctly, that 'The law allows a class of men calling themselves "conscientious objectors" to be free from military duty. This being the case', he went on, 'the law should be obeyed' yet 'the Appeal Tribunal deliberately (and the chairman avowedly) ignores the law', it 'deliberately refuses to carry out the law.' The second correspondent was the indefatigable Arthur Dearlove, who applauded Robert Kay for his remarks from the bench and referred to the 'scandals' of the tribunals. On this occasion Arthur got an editorial rebuke which said that his one 'ambition in life seems to be to justify any and every man who tries to avoid serving his country in her hour of need.'

The *Press*'s editor was unfair to Arthur Dearlove, but were the charges that he and others were making true ? It seems certain that they were. The York tribunal must have known about the beliefs and the character of people like Wilfrid Crosland for example, and yet they refused him absolute exemption. Robert Kay testified to the integrity of young Henderson, and Mawson did so for Coupland. This was in a magistrates court, of course, but people like Crosland would have been as well known to tribunal members as they were to Kay and Mawson. The North Riding tribunal also resolutely refused absolute exemption to many who clearly merited it, like the young man who was actually training with the Friends' Ambulance Unit, who was represented by K.E.T. Wilkinson, and whose case was reported in the *Herald* of 31 May. His parents were attenders at Quaker meetings, and he attended a Friends' Sunday School, and, of course, there was every chance that he would go to the front line somewhere. All this was presented and got the young man absolutely nowhere, and he left the court presumably to be arrested eventually with Beresford Pierce's words that 'it would look better if the applicant was fighting for his country' ringing in his ears. William Judson a Sunday School teacher and lay reader at the Groves Methodist chapel in York was another young man seemingly badly treated. He was refused absolute exemption, drafted and eventually tried for refusing to obey orders before a District Court Martial at Richmond. There a Mrs M. Thompson appeared on his behalf and said the members of Groves Chapel had prepared a memorial on Judson's behalf, and that 'She thought the Tribunal's decision in this particular case was wrong' and that 'many in the city of York thought so too.' People like R.H. Vernon Wragge, who were members of the tribunal, certainly knew what the law was, and must have realised that it intended exemption for the likes of Judson and Wilkinson's client, but he, at the county level, and Rhodes Brown and Sykes Rymer, for example, at the city level had no sympathy whatsoever with pacifist views and simply ignored them, and their own duty. Arthur Hatfield said that the York tribunal split equally on his case, and that he was sentenced by the casting vote of the chairman, and Henry Tennant, once Under Secretary of State for War (and then Secretary of State for Scotland) admitted that this kind of thing had gone on. Speaking at Dun, in July, Tennant said that on the whole the tribunals had worked well so far but that 'there was good reason to believe [some] genuine conscientious objectors, had been sent to the Army.' That was one of Tennant's massive understatements, and many men from York had found themselves before court martials and in the army nick at places like Ripon and Richmond. In Richmond Castle there can still be seen the prison cells into which conchies were incarcerated and the prisoners did what most prisoners do, they defaced the walls, and their - high class - contributions to the art of graffiti can still be seen. Fred Bradley recorded the fact that he was there on 2 and 3 July, and James Walsh that he was there from 3 to 6 July, at least. William, James, John and Stephen Fowler, four brothers aged between 18 and 24 from the Bentham branch of the NCF were there, and so was Arthur Hatfield. Arthur's contribution to defacing HM property was rather predictable. 'Workers of the world unite', he wrote, 'You have nothing to lose but your chains, you have a world to win.' (90)

In addition to the unwillingness of tribunals to do what was clearly their duty on many occasions, there were repeated administrative blunders which made the lot of objectors (conchies or not) difficult. It was by no means uncommon for the North Riding tribunal to sit and find men brought before them in khaki, and to hear that an applicant had already been drafted before their appeals procedures had been completed. Men frequently were simply not being allowed to pursue their applications through, and in June 1916 this led to criticisms by Councillor Glew. The *Herald* of Thursday the 8th reported that a Carlton farmer's son who was to appear had 'gone into the Army' on 1 June. Glew angrily said 'It was not the first [case] by any means which he had heard of where men had been called up by the Military authorities, even when appeals had been lodged and were pending' and Beresford Pierse agreed with him. The tribunal clerk said 'a serious error had been made, and someone would no doubt get into trouble.' It is hoped that he was right.

Arthur Hatfield, as he never stopped telling his tormentors, was a very active member of the Independent Labour Party, a body which never strayed from its anti-war, anti-military service stance. Before 1914 it had existed in York, acting as a ginger group to the local Labour party, never getting a large membership, but nevertheless atracting some of the most able working class leaders in the city (who could well have been members of both organisations - and the Trades Council too - of course). When the official Labour party agreed to the party truce, and, more particularly when it decided not to oppose the operation of the Military Service Acts, the ILP moved centre stage in York and became extremely active, with members answering the likes of Edith Milner in the *Press* and holding regular meetings, frequently in Exhibition Square, at which no doubt that lady of the 'ever active pen', as one admirer described her, was mentioned. York, in the first half of 1916, saw as much political activity as it had done in many pre-war years, with many famous, and many not so famous names gracing ILP platforms. The party had rooms in Micklegate and there on a Sunday in April, for example, a Mr Hancock spoke on 'War and Peace'. (91) In February the contents of the Military Service Act were publicised at a meeting at which, without doubt, the conscience clauses of it were dealt with, (92) and a little earlier a Miss E. Pickard had spoken about 'The days that are to be.' (93) Mrs Fawcett, the famous suffragette, lectured for the ILP on 'Women in Industry', J. Wardropper, a local man of whom much was to be heard in the future, spoke on 'The Future of Trades Unionism', and W.A. Kay addressed an open air gathering in Exhibition Square on 'Education After the War'. (94)

The ILP, lumped by most people under a generic heading that called it 'pro-German' or 'peace at any price' was, in fact, carrying on a vigorous campaign on a wide range of political issues, attempting to make people aware of the pressing issues it considered important and were, perhaps, likely to be as ignored in post war times as they had been in pre war years. And it highlighted local issues or problems too. A.V. Iredale, for example, gave a lecture asking 'Is the York Board of Guardians a Failure ?'; J.H. Hartley, the school attendance officer, must have lived dangerously when he spoke on 'Questions that need the immediate attention of the York City Council'; and Councillor W. Horsman spoke on 'A Municipal Milk Supply for York' when that was a topical issue. (95) Arthur Hatfield had, so far, been the most prominent ILP member to be prosecuted for his beliefs, but a few days after he had played host to Fred Jowett, the ILP secretary appeared before the York tribunal demanding absolute exemption on political grounds. This was F.T. Beney, a 36 year old leather worker, who was also active in the trades union movement. (99) He was a Rowntree employee and the tribunal was told that he was one of several men for whom the company had made representations and got tentative agreements about. His case was put back, and he clearly got exemption, because he remained active in York.

It seems strange that Beney should have gone for exemption in the way he did. He might have been expected, perhaps, to have persisted in his demand for exemption on political grounds and provided the city of York with something of a show trial. Had he done so it would have been serious stuff no doubt, and entertaining, though maybe not quite so entertaining as that of an ice cream vendor, represented by Norman Crombie, whose case was reported in the *Herald* of 26 July 1916. C.W. Shipley, presiding, heard that this captain of industry had married an Italian lady some eleven years earlier, 'who could not speak English.' Her sisters had joined the family, 'but neither of them could speak the English language which, applicant had been informed, was very difficult to learn.' If he was called up the man said, his business would be ruined. Shipley asked him if he could speak Italian, and he said no, though he had lived amongst Italians in Hull. He 'had found the language impossible', he said, and 'His wife and her sister[s] had had a similar difficulty with English... they did not even understand the coinage.' Eleven years 'of married life and neither man or woman understands the language of the other!' gasped a tribunal member, 'this takes the biscuit.' It did. The man got temporary deferment 'for one month, this to be final' and the kids of York were deprived of what may well have been a splendid product.

It was inevitable that there would be cries for the ILP to be banned (in effect) and there were. In August Arthur C. Taylor wrote to the newspapers complaining that the likes of Arthur Hatfield were putting out their 'pernicious views' with impunity, and complaining that they were distributing pamphlets, magazines and books, at less than cost. When 'will the City council stop those meetings held in the Exhibition Square every Sunday', he asked, 'and thus follow the example of Leeds and other patriotic towns ?' Arrogantly he spoke of those the ILP might influence as 'weak-minded people who need to be protected against themselves' and engaged in that ploy of using a slightly esoteric word when something more straightforward would have done just as well - a ploy resorted to with irritating predictability by present day writers to BBC programmes like 'PM'. Taylor wrote of 'purblind pacifists' and was taken to task by James Wardropper. (100) Perhaps Taylor had attended a York meeting called to 'celebrate' the second anniversary of the start of the war at which J.G. Butcher and the Labour MP for Merthyr, C.B. Stanton, had been present, and perhaps he got some ideas about invective from there. Stanton had there moved a resolution which, he said, 'nobody could take any exception to' except, perhaps, 'his old comrades of the I.L.P., the peace-at-any-price, and some of the "Please kick, I do not mind" people.' Conchies, Stanton went on, were 'social lepers' and 'weak-minded individuals' who ought to be transported. (101) Social lepers some of the objectors might have become, but the contention that they were weak-minded is simply patronising stupidity. The similarity between Taylor's letter and Stanton's speech will be immediately apparent.

*Arnold Rowntree, a line drawing by Brian Kesteven
from a family photograph*

All the Rome newspapers express the opinion that the reported sale of the Goeben is a violation of neutrality.

CREWS NOT DISEMBARKED.

Despatches received in Paris to-day from Constantinople state that according to information received from the Dardanelles the crews of the Goeben and Breslau, contrary to the statement of the Ottoman Government, have not yet been disembarked.

the Canadian Expeditionary, and the surplus above the required strength, will undoubtedly form the nucleus of a second contingent.

The "London Gazette" records the appointment of Lord Arthur Francis Henry Hill as a second lieutenant in the 2nd Dragoons (Royal Scots Greys). He is the younger son by the first marriage of the sixth Marquis of Downshire, and was born in 1895.

SWALES' MEAT STORES.

NOTICE!

During the War we have contracted with a **British** Firm to supply our Customers with British Meat brought from our Colonies in British Ships at Prices very little above our Ordinary Charges.

SEE OUR WINDOW DISPLAY TO-NIGHT (Friday) and TO-MORROW (Saturday).

FRESH SUPPLIES EACH DAY.

PLENTY OF GOOD MEAT at Prices to suit the anxious times in which we live.

"OUR EMPIRE AND OUR TRADE."

19, GOODRAMGATE, YORK.   Telephone No. 589.

An early patriotic advertisement

Left, one of Lord Kitchener's appeals for volunteers.
Right, an advertisement for one of the first war films to be shown in York.

COVERDALES'
Antiseptic Foot Powder.

TERRITORIALS,
Have you tender Feet?

SCOUTS,
Have you tender Feet?

PEDESTRIANS,
Of all occupations, have you tender Feet?

If so, dust freely with "Antiseptic Foot Powder" and you can march to the end of the world.

Thousands of Territorials to-day, through much marching, find the feet begin to get troublesome. The feet seem to expand, and the restriction and compression results in a tired, aching feeling, often too distressing for words.

By the use of this "ANTISEPTIC FOOT POWDER" a condition of freshness, sweetness, and cleanliness is the sure result.

Sold in tins, 10½d. (postage 1½d. extra).
Special prices for 1 gross and 5 gross quantities.

Geo. Coverdale & Sons,
Chemists,
PARLIAMENT STREET, YORK.

One of George Coverdale's war time advertisements

Top row: Mrs Edwin Gray and Miss Edith Milner
Bottom row: Dr W. A. Evelyn and C. E. Elmhirst
Photographs taken from the York Historic Pageant Souvenir, 1909

ZEPPELIN ALARM—YORK MAN'S NOVEL APPARATUS.

To the EDITOR of the YORKSHIRE HERALD.

Sir,—I enclose a sketch of a Zeppelin alarm I have fixed in my house, and so far it has worked satisfactorily. It is very easily made of a length of ⅜in. gas pipe bent as shown, and filled with water, in which floats a glass plunger, to which is fastened a piece of fine copper wire. When the gas is on the pressure raises the water in the tube, which in turn raises the plunger, which in turn raises a copper wire arm. When the gas pressure is removed the plunger sinks and depresses the arm, thus making the electric connection. The plunger is simply a fountain pen filler without the bulb, and is sealed with candle wax. It is very buoyant in the water. I have my alarm fixed in the hall, with a gas tube from the hall gas. I have tapped the electric bell wires from the front door, hence it is that bell which rings.—Yours truly,

J. E. R.

York, Aug. 21, 1916.

One of the York Zeppelin Alarms

Rowntree's advertisements illustrating how women took over mens' jobs as the war went on

Two advertisements for popular war films

Newspaper photographs published just after one of York's Zep raids

HAXBY ROAD MILITARY HOSPITAL. (Rowntree's Dining Block).

Left, a Leak and Thorp blackout advertisement.
Right. Reg Smith had had several deferments, but the draft finally caught up with him.

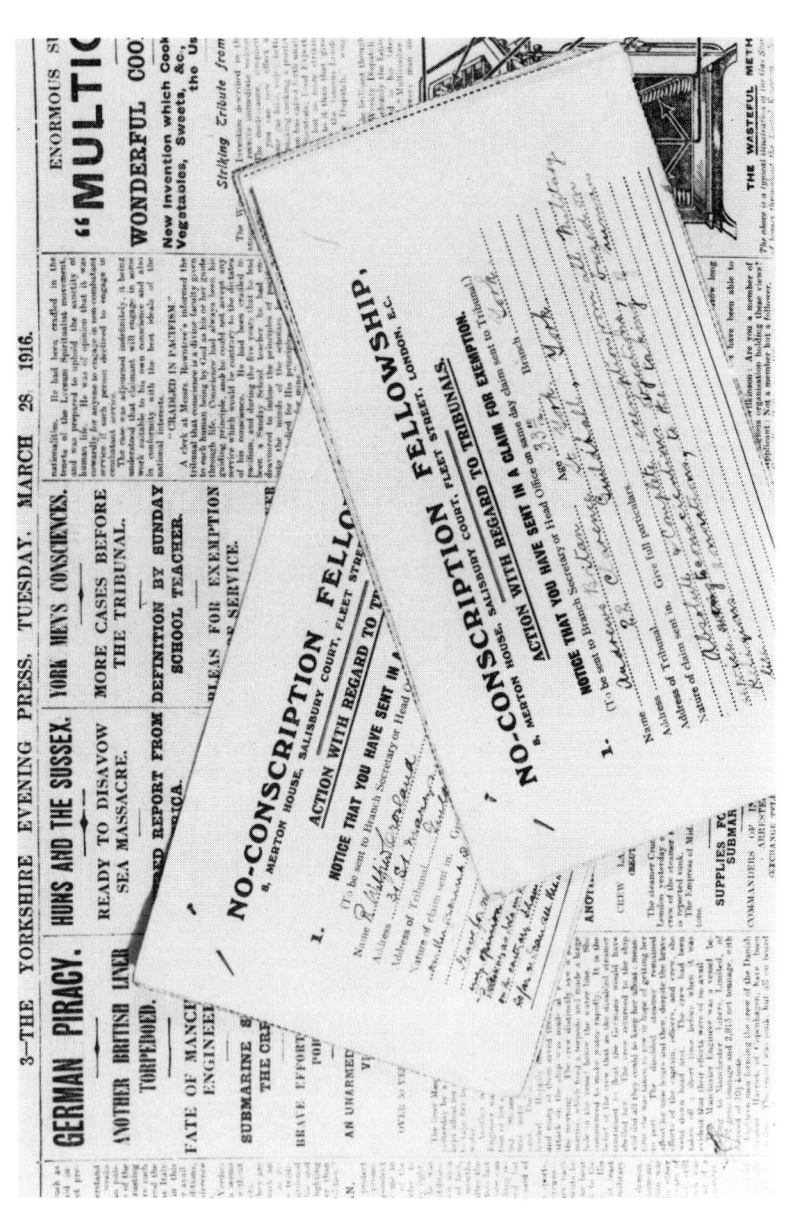

The York NCF kept detailed records of its members' court appearances

Hatred of the conchies probably reached a peak in the summer of 1916, though there are indications that some people unconnected with the Quakers or the ILP (like the members of the Groves Chapel) thought the tribunals were going too far and not facing up to their responsibilities under the law. However, the pacifists were not helped by the actions at about that time of Seebohm Rowntree who applied for exemption for no less than five of his employees. The first was simply a coachman of 40 years of age, and Seebohm said he needed a competent coachman because his wife was ill. The second two men worked in his nursery gardens. York had once been the centre of the chicory growing industry of Britain, but this had been killed off by free trade legislation in the 19th century. (102) When the Great War began there were attempts to revive it in the York area, and Rowntree had been a part of them. He was not having a great deal of success, the tribunal was told, though he had the support of the Board of Agriculture, and was still experimenting (though concentrating more on vegetables). He needed his men, and he needed, too, the Homestead gardener. Rowntree lived at The Homestead, in Clifton, and his application to keep this fellow must have looked as if it ran very much counter to what Avner Offer has called 'war socialism', (103) where everybody supposedly suffered alike. Rowntree's last request was on behalf of his private secretary (F.D. Stuart), and he handed in a letter from Lloyd George, no less, in support of his demand. At that time Rowntree was working with the Welfare Department of the Ministry of Munitions, reporting on social conditions in the munitions establishments. (104)

Some of Seebohm Rowntree's applications that day before the York tribunal must have given some the (not totally unreasonable) impression that he was simply a rich man trying to maintain his standard of living and luxury (like many others) regardless of the manpower needs of the time. His family firm also continued to apply for exemptions for many of their workers and, and as has been said before, there were always people anxious and willing to knock it. The company had lost many men to the forces; it had tried to make up for their loss by installing labour saving machinery; but still had problems, and so it applied for men to stay there on the grounds that they were essential workers. This led to many complaints which ignored the firm's justification of their acts and a conspiracy theory was constructed which went something like this. The firm enticed men to go to work for it (the skilled man who went as a labourer will be recalled) and in return it agreed to try to get them exempted, presumably for a mixture of economic and political motives. This was patently absurd, if only for the fact that such an agreement would have been sussed out and blazoned out in headlines in the *Press* and the *Herald*, but it was widely believed, as letters in the papers show. In August 1916 one spoke of the 'scandal' of the way Rowntree and Company had applied for exemptions for their workers. 'We read', the writer went on, 'that committees are making a careful scrutiny of the lists of "exempts".

It is to be hoped', he concluded, 'that the list of Messrs. Rowntrees "indispensables" will get more than a cursory examination, and that a crying scandal may be cleared up.' (105)

That people did join Rowntrees and other works where they might become 'indispensable' or 'essential' is beyond doubt. To infer that the firm conspired with them is simply preposterous - yet there were incidents which persuaded the uncharitable to draw such conclusions. The letter writer quoted above referred to a scrutiny of the men of military age. On 24 July every man over 18 became eligible for national service, but many simply ignored their obligations. The police had a right to insist on the production of documents and in September there was held in York what the Chief Constable called 'a raid on eligibles' who were 'evading military service' which, it was said, was conducted with the utmost politeness and decorum. Detectives were was placed outside all places of amusement and civilians of military age were asked to produce certificates of exemption when they left. (106) Eventually one of these appeared in court before B.S. Rowntree and J.J. Hunt, a temperance advocate and a brewer, two people who might have been expected to disagree on some things, when clearly there should have been three justices present. They were confronted with Robert Bodgener, a man of 38 who had been taken on by Rowntree and Company without a certificate of exemption. It was revealed that Bodgener had lied to his employers, saying he was 44 'so that the firm was in no way to blame for having given him employment.' Without doubt some would not have believed a word of that. (107)

1. *Press* 19 and 22 January 1916
2. *Ibid* 18 January 1916
3. *Ibid* 29 January 1916
4. *Ibid* 22 January 1916
5. *Ibid* 9 and 14 February 1916
6. See also *Ibid* 3 February 1916
7. *Ibid* 4 February 1916
8. Rae *op.cit*. p.24. Enlistment under the Derby scheme ended on 1 March 1916 for single men. Married men could still enlist (or attest) under it afterwards. *Press* 24 February 1916. By the end of May 1916, when groups 42 to 46 (married men over 36 and under 41) were called up it was reckoned that all Derby men with the exception of those who had gained exemptions would have been called up. *Ibid* 11 May 1916. Recruiting under the Derby scheme closed in York at midnight on 7 June. There was no last minute rush to enlist on this occasion.
9. The Labour party in conference at Bristol in January declared its opposition to compulsion and its support for the war effort, but decided it would not agitate for its repeal if the Military Service Bill became law - which it was clear it would. Labour members stayed in the cabinet and government
10. 6 and 7 Geo 5 Chap 15
11. Rae *op cit* pp 47-48
12. *Press* 5 January, 5 and 17 May 1916
13. *Ibid* 10 and 11 May 1916
14. Jack Seely, a Liberal cabinet minister at the time of the Curragh Mutiny. He resigned and at this time was a serving soldier

15. *Press* 13 and 31 January 1916
16. See eg *Ibid* 14 and 18 January 1916
17. *Ibid* 25 January 1916
18. *Ibid* 14 January 1916. In February at another York UDC meeting addressed by Charles Roden Buxton the claim was made that the UDC was not a 'stop the war' organisation and had no policy on conscription. This was true, but many of its members had. J. Gulland, S.H. Davies and W. Farrar were all anti conscription.
19. *Ibid* 24 January 1916
20. *Herald* 12 January 1916
21. *Ibid* 7 January 1916.
22. *Ibid* 10 January 1916
23. *Ibid* 7 January 1916
24. *Ibid* 25 February 1916
25. *Ibid* 27 January 1916
26. *Ibid* 13 March 1916
27. An interview with a member is contained in the collection of tape recordings mentioned earlier which are held at Churchill College
28. When the secretary appeared before a tribunal. *Press* 28 March 1916
29. *Ibid* 8 April 1916. The latter of these was set up to get the first MSA repealed and to stop the extension of compulsory military service. For a report of its first meeting see eg *Herald* 13 April 1916
30. Because of 'the hardships of master butchers, owing to so many of their employees being taken.'
31. A great early criticism of the York tribunal was that it contained too many legal representatives. By this the critics must have meant too many magistrates
32. *Herald* 18 January 1916. This was the meeting at which the tribunal thought its powers were limited to putting men back a maximum of ten groups
33. *Press* 22 February 1916
34. It is assumed it was Rowntree and Company
35. See eg *Press* 25 February 1916. Report of notices being posted calling upon men of group 1 and class 1
36. A considerable campaign on behalf of *married* men was run in the first half of 1916
37. Proceedings at the second meeting of the York tribunal reported in *Press* 2 March 1916, *Herald* 3 March 1916
38. *Press* 18 March 1916
39. *Ibid* 22 March 1916
40. *Ibid* 3 March 1916
41. *Ibid* 7 March 1916
42. *Ibid* 20 March 1916. *Herald* 2 March 1916
43. Councillor J.F. Glew of York was another member. Sir Henry Beresford Pierce and T. Sunley of Kirbymoorside were the others in the early days. They sat with a military representative and a representative 'of the agricultural interest.' They met at York and various other places in the area
44. *Press* 28 March 1916. *Herald* 29 March 1916. *Gazette* 1 April 1916. An annotated *Press* cutting in a collection of cuttings from the NCF gives the names of the objectors
45. Alfred G.S.Higgins was a member of the Brotherhood Church. He and his brother were conscientious objectors and a tape recording made with him is in the collection which has been mentioned several times in these pages. On the movement see A.G. Higgins, *A History of the Brotherhood Church* (Stapleton 1982)
46. *Ibid* 23 March 1916. *Herald* 22 and 24 March 1916
47. *Press* 23 April 1916. *Herald* 4 and 5 April 1916
48. *Herald* 1 June 1916
49. The Pelham Committee was in reality the Committee on Work of National Importance to which cases could be referred 'for advice as to what service of national importance an applicant for exemption on the ground of conscientious objection should undertake ...' It could only make recommendations and therefore had no real authority. Pelham was T.H.W. Pelham, an assistant secretary at the Board of Trade.

50. He was given non combatant service insted of the conditional exemption which would have enabled him to continue teaching
51. A non-combatant corps was formed early in 1916. See eg *Press* 11 March 1916
52. *Herald* 23 May 1916
53. A.J. Peacock, 'Conscience and Politics in York. 1914-1918', a Sheldon Essay published in an edition of the *York Historian*
54. *Herald* 30 May and 2 June 1916
55. *Ibid* 13 June 1916, *Press* 12 June 1916
56. *Herald* 17 June 1916
57. *Ibid* 17 June 1916
58. *Ibid* 19 June 1916
59. *Ibid*
60. His letter was not published until the 27th. *Press* 27 June 1916. Five days earlier Edith Milner had written to say Davies could not answer her 'challenge'
61. *Ibid* 22 June 1916
62. *Ibid* 23 June 1916
63. *Ibid* 24 June 1916. 'Personally, I think the trenches are the proper place for them', W.H.F. concluded
64. *Ibid* 26 June 1916
65. *Ibid*
66. *Ibid* 27 June 1916
67. *Ibid* 29 June 1916
68. Of course there were attacks on conscientious objectors in general published day after day. See, eg, the clutch of particularly offensive ones in *Ibid* 29 March 1916, and 23 April 1916. In the latter there is a soldier's letter saying 'If you see or know any of these conscientious objectors, go and shoot 'em, also some of the members of the Tribunals.'
69. *Ibid* 9 June 1916
70. A reference to the Battle of Jutland
71. See also, eg, *Press* 8 and 13 June 1916
72. *Herald* 5 April 1916
73. *Ibid* 30 May and 1 June 1916
74. *Press* 9 June 1916
75. *Ibid* 23 June 1916. A letter saying the FSA men were medically unfit or over aged in *Ibid* 24 June 1916
76. *Ibid* 24 June 1916. The 'mass' appeals by FSA members mentioned in the next paragraph reported in *Ibid* 14 March 1916
77. *Ibid* 2 June 1916
78. *Ibid* 8, 9 and 15 June 1916, letters
79. *Ibid* 28 June 1916, letter signed 'THOSE WHO HAVE SUFFERED'
80. *Herald* 23 March and 26 April 1916. The second sitting was taken up largely with the case of Martha Wilkinson of Fairburn, who had left her work 'at the York Munition works without notice'.
81. *Press* 5 July 1916. There is a letter from girls working at Adams Hydraulics challenging some of the statements made in the Smith case in *Herald* 8 July 1916
82. *Press* 30 June 1916. The Gascoigne case, and the Shipley bricklayer mentioned later are reported in *Herald* 10 and 14 July 1916. The decision of the Malton RDC to employ objectors referred to later reported in *Herald* 1 May 1916
83. *Press* 10 July 1916
84. *Ibid* 15, 18, 19, and 20 July 1916
85. *Ibid* 31 July 1916
86. *Ibid* 2 August 1916
87. *Ibid* 10 July 1916
88. *Ibid* 13 July 1916. Arthur Hatfield and his mates seem to have been members of the 9th York and Lancaster Regiment
89. *Ibid* 24 June 1916. The Judson case mentioned below reported in eg *Herald* 8 July 1916
90. There was an attempt to get the cell at Ripon preserved a few years ago
91. *Press* 8 April 1916

92. *Ibid* 26 February 1916
93. *Ibid* 12 February 1916
94. *Ibid* 15 January, 5 February and 3 June 1916
95. *Ibid* 1 and 21 January, 29 April 1916. For the council debate on a municipal milk supply see eg *Herald* 4 July 1916
96. *Press* 22 January 1916
97. John McLean was a Glasgow socialist who was eventually sentenced to three years imprisonment
98. *Press* 15 July 1916
99. *Herald* 19 July 1916
100. *Press* 17, 18 and 21 August 1916
101. *Ibid* 12 August 1916
102. Attempts were made to restart the industry at the outbreak of the war. On the first two years of operation see eg the article in *Herald* 28 August 1916
103. In his superb book *The Great War. An Agrarian Interpretation*
104. *Press* 25 July 1916. Results of Rowntree's application were that the coachman's call up was postponed to the end of September; the nursery gardeners were given conditional exemption; the gardener got deferment to 20 October; and the secretary was given conditional exemption
105. *Ibid* 14 August 1916
106. *Ibid* 7 September 1916. *Herald* 7 September 1916
107. Bodgenor, from Leeds, was eventually discharged. It seems he had attested and that his papers had been sent to his Leeds address. Why he lied about his age was not explained.

CHAPTER 14

ZEPS AND FILMS

The *Yorkshire Herald* of Tuesday 4 May 1916 was number 30,310 and the paper, its banner announced, was in its 191st year. Its front page was as always devoted to advertisements which included one from the Theatre Royal announcing a visit by the Carl Rosa Opera Company, and another from the Electric Theatre, which told readers that showing then were 'Getting Even with Hubby' (A Comedy in three parts) and 'Gussie's Day of Rest' (A two-part exclusive Keystone Comedy). The Picture House was showing 'The Marriage of Kitty' and the Yorkshire School for the Blind announced that there was a 'CONCERT TO-DAY AT 3.0'. There was half a column of advertisements from moneylenders and the usual puffs for various peoples' 'Female Pills', one of which offered free an interesting book called *The Manual of Wisdom*. Next to one of them, perhaps put there by a typesetter with a sense of humour, was an advert for baby carriages and Thomas Horsley and Sons Ltd of Blossom Street offered for sale the 'HUPMOBILE CAR, "The Car of Established repute"', and Bradbury's Cycle and Sewing Machine Department of Davygate promised immediate delivery of 'Bradbury, Rover, Calcott & B.S.A. Cycles.' George Coverdale and Sons, the pharmacists, announced that 'YORK is again visited with an epidemic of MEASLES' but that all would be well if the populace took 'Croskell's Yellow Mixture' which was 'THE medicine' and cost 1s.2d. a bottle. The *Herald* and the other York papers must have made a fortune from George Coverdale and Sons.

Inside the *Herald* of 4 May there was a report of the annual meeting of the York Tuberculosis Flower Crusade where the well-known Dr Evelyn presented accounts and Mrs Edwin Gray told listeners how they had helped the Council's TB officer and made a passionate appeal for the building of houses for rent at 'not more than 5s. a week'. Her husband also had a letter in the correspondence column headed 'LESSONS OF ZEPPELIN RAIDS'. In it he attacked (or seemed to attack) conscientious objectors. After referring to raids on 'Scarborough, Hull, etc.' Gray wondered what 'the views and attitude of the conscientious objectors here and elsewhere' were 'towards the vicious vagaries of our clever cultivated, and God-invoking friends' were. Below his letter 'CITIZEN' said he was worried about the 'facilities for egress in case of fire or panic' from the Theatre Royal. On Tuesday last, he said, all the lights were turned off and the audience was near to panic, and trouble was only averted 'by the admirable presence of mind of the orchestra, who, emulating the historic scene on the sinking of the Titanic, struck up a favourite tune and thus prevented the audience from losing their heads'.

The news columns of the *Herald* carried details of some house sales in York, mentioning that six freehold properties in Scott Street and Fairfax Street went for prices ranging from £152 to £235. Miss Amelia Rainer's bankruptcy was also reported. She had a lodging house at 53, Bootham and said her failure was 'due to lack of boarders', which seems strange at that time. The Carl Rosa Company had given a matinee performance for the Lady Mayoress's fund for providing comforts for York soldiers and Florence Peacock of St Cuthbert's Band of Hope was crowned May Queen of the York and District Band of Hope Union before an audience of 'upwards of 400' in Councillor Willie Dixon's orchard at Heworth. The parliamentary report contained an account of the introduction of one of the Military Service Bills and the international news announced that the Prince of Wales had visited Khartoum. War news was about a 'SHARP FIGHT IN ARGONNE' and 'FRENCH PROGRESS AT VERDUN', while other reports were about the courts martial sentences of some of those involved in the Dublin Easter uprising. 'In the House of Commons yesterday', it was reported, 'Mr. Asquith said that Pearce, J. Clarke, and T. McDonagh, leaders of the Irish rebellion, had been found guilty by court-martial and shot that morning.'

Many sports ceased 'for the duration', but it was inconceivable that in the Britain of the early 20th century the 'sport of Kings' should go the way of football, and the back page of the *Herald* of 4 May 1916 was equally divided between reports of the share markets and the card for that day's racing at Newmarket - and a report on the Two Thousand Guineas run the day before. Inside the paper there was the second of two articles on the 1915 annual report of the Yorkshire Insurance Company. Just above that was a report on an inquest into the death of Edward Woodcock, a 51 year old shotfirer from 'a north-east coast town' who 'had caught a severe cold while hiding in a cellar during a Zeppelin alarm.' On the same page there was an account of the meeting of the Convocation of York at St William's College. Topics discussed there included a question to the Archbishop about military service and 'those who were at present in training for the ministry.' This was raised by the Bishop of Manchester and the Archibishop told him that the War Office had advised tribunals that men under 'immediate preparation for Holy Orders' should be exempted. What did 'immediate preparation' mean? The Archbishop said he was speaking for all the Bishops 'of that Northern Province and of Canterbury' when he said 'they had no desire to facilitate the exemption of any man of military age and physical fitness who would be ordained after Trinity next. ... the exemption of anyone able to serve his country, but entering Holy Orders after Trinity next, would not be facilitated in any way. ... the Bishops ... had determined to do their very utmost to assist the country to bring its whole resources to bear in this supreme struggle.' The Archbishop said he had been glad the question had been raised - it gave him an opportunity 'of letting the country' know 'how eager the Bishops were in every possible way to give to the service of the country at this supreme moment all the possible strength of the manhood whom the church hoped, at a later stage, to dedicate and consecrate to the priesthood'. That was a pretty definite statement of support for the war effort by the Church of England. The Upper House then went on to consider the booze question.

The Bishop of Chester proposed a resolution saying that the present controls 'on the liquor traffic' should remain after war or even be 'extended in ... scope'. Supporting him a Bishop referred, of course, to the fact that the King had taken the pledge of 'personal total abstinence' and said that Russia and France had banned the sale of vodka and absinthe. The Bishop of Manchester wanted to know more about the effects of these prohibition measures and said that all was not well in England. He had heard, he said, a lot about 'drinking in houses and secret drinking' and was worried that if pubs were closed it would drive many people 'to other attractions.' What these attractions were he did not say.

The Lower House of Convocation discussed the interim report of the Committee on Moral Corruption in social life, which dealt with 'marriage problems and intemperance'. The birth rate was continuing to decline Archdeacon Mackarness reported, as it had done since 1876 and was now 'down to a remarkably low rate of 226 per 10,000 of the population per annum. Why ? The committee believed the decline 'was certainly due, to a large extent, to artificial family restriction' and they deplored this. They thought it 'nothing less than a national disaster and a serious blow to the moral life of the people in this time of terrible stress and strain ... that there should be so many grevious cases of selfish disregard of high obligations of the marriage tie.' Canon Lambert of Hull agreed, calling the restricting of families 'this great evil', and saying that practioners of the art of birth control were not only being unpatriotic and injuring the state but 'were bringing upon themselves a certain moral nemesis in the whole of their future life ... it would stunt their whole moral being and have serious effects on their whole spiritual development.' This sounds very much like the warnings of dire consequences young boys were given in the classrooms of the 1940s (and possibly later). Canon Rountree of Manchester blamed the medics and thought that an appeal to their patriotic feeling should be made. Presumably Rountree meant that participants in the delights of the flesh should be told to press on regardless, and fill their houses with kids they could not provide for, and wear the wife out by early middle age as so many were. The Dean of Carlisle thought that if 'the medical profession ... were encouraging' birth control it was 'a very terrible thing.' Reading the accounts of Convocation one is tempted to wonder where the church dignitaries had been all their lives. Had they not seen what unrestricted families led to; had they not read the famous Seebohm Rowntree reports (for example) ? Mackarness spoke of the 'high obligations of the marriage tie', but it is good to record that Canon Hughes of Chester, at least, spoke up for the sinners. People had 'to exercise a certain amount of self-denial to bring up families', he said, and told his colleagues of times, not long ago, when they had to be brought up on wages of 9s. or 10s. a week.

The Upper House of Convocation had made its support for the war apparent, and so did the Lower House. The Dean of Manchester moved a resolution saying it was 'the duty of all citizens to respond without question or delay to all demands which the King's Government may make upon them, as being necessary to ensure victory in the war.' Manchester, however, speaking to the resolution, drew attention to the inequalities of sacrifice, and told members that 'on the occasion of the Newbury race meeting' of 'last week' no less than '300 motor cars were counted on one road in two hours on the way to the races, expending 1,000 gallons of petrol - in the use of which economy was urgently needed'. He was right to do so and he might have reflected on the impression that such ostentation might have upon groups of workers who were labelled unpatriotic because of the wage demands they were putting in. Manchester then singled out three groups for criticism - those in the liquor trade, those members of the labour movement who thought like the ILP, and conchies. The latter were 'dupes of their own aims' and 'contemptible'. Manchester's resolution was passed and immediately below the report of this being done was an account of yet another court case involving someone he would certainly not have approved of. This was Lord Alfred Douglas who 'again appeared in person' in the Chancery Court 'as a respondent to an application by his father-in-law, Colonel Custance, for directions of the court as what should be done with Wymond Wilfrid Sholto Douglas, son of Lord Alfred.'

In addition to all the foregoing, the *Herald* of 4 May 1916 also carried an account of a lecture Seebohm Rowntree gave at the London School of Economics on 'Welfare Work among Women in Factories', and an extensive casualty list. In a separate column it was recorded that Lt Bryan Meredith Storey, the son of the secretary of the Yorkshire Liberal Federation had been wounded while serving with the Worcestershire Regiment. He was a 19 year old who had just left St Peter's School when the war started. There was also a three column report on an air raid which was incredibly coy in its style. It was headed 'THE ZEPP. RAID' and went as follows

> At about half past ten on Tuesday night [2 May 1916] a hostile airship visited a certain place in Yorkshire. A few moments before its arrival the detonation of the bombs could be heard in the distance, as though ten to fifteen miles away. The ominous thud of the bombs attracted a good many people into the streets, and very shortly the long-cigar-shaped form of a Zeppelin, flying at about

3,000 to 5,000 feet, came into sight. Over a great open space it remained stationary, with engines turned off, for fully three minutes. Not a bomb was dropped during this time, and it appeared to the onlookers as if the pilot was taking his bearings. When the engines were re-started the airship with its droning, humming accompaniment of sound, passed over the town. Great volumes of dense black smoke issued from the machine, and many who were too late to see the airship saw the waves and circles of smoke floating with marked contrast against the clear and star-bedecked sky.

Eighteen bombs, it is believed, were dropped in the district. Some dwellng houses were more or less shattered. One house entirely collapsed, leaving a hole in the ground, while another fell like a pack of cards about the ears of the occupants, a man and his wife, who were killed, and their bodies being extricated with much difficulty. The death toll totals nine, and approximately 40 people have been injured. ... The airship was over the locality altogether for about ten minutes and moved off in a north-easterly direction, as if for the coast. Three of the bombs fell in a field, leaving great cavities in the ground. Two or three minutes after the airship had gone out of sight sounds were heard as of the dropping of six bombs a good distance away.

The 'place in Yorkshire' was of course York, and a local reporter seized the opportunity to write about the raid at length. (1) '"It's a rotten shame," exclaimed a lady with a baby in her arms', he wrote. 'It was a rotten shame, madame,' he went on, 'It was the work of cads.' The executive committee of the York Conservative Association agreed with him, and the very next day they passed a resolution 'protesting against the uncivilised warfare of Zeppelins' and expressing their view that the prominent lights 'exhibited on an open place under Government control' might have been 'used as a guide' by the raiders. Edith Milner, it will be recalled, had protested about this some time earlier. Complaints about the NER also reached the *Herald* within a day of the attack. There were lights all round the station and up to a mile and a half away, it was alleged, and the carriage works 'were also lighted, and it is said the largest lights' on the workshops were not put out 'till after the danger was past.' Many of the lights other than those at the carriage works were signals, it was said later, and it was contended that it would have been unsafe to extinguish them. 'That, of course, would be so if the trains were running' the *Herald* said with devastating logic, 'but considering that all the trains were stopped there seemed no necessity for keeping the signal lights burning.' Had the offending lights been those belonging to Rowntree and

Company, no doubt there would have been allegations that they were guiding the Zeps in.

Inquests were held on the victims of the first air raid in York (with the local papers still referring simply to 'a Yorkshire town'). The first was on a young lady of 28 who was standing in the street with her mother, who lost an arm. Her father protested that a street lamp near his house had not been doused, and demanded that in future civilians should be empowered to put them out. Chief Constable Burrow said instructions to that end had already been drawn up and given to the public at large. The next two victims were a railway pensioner and his wife. They were in their home, in bed, when it was the recipient of a direct hit, and their bodies were not recovered by the police and the local VAD until 6 a.m. the following day. Other victims included a widow, a soldier on a month's leave, and a labourer. Nine people were killed in all; six men and three women. Some of the dead were buried by Saturday 6 May, with the *Herald*'s report still speaking of them coming from a 'Yorkshire town'. Two days later (9 May) it produced three photographs of a crater made by a Zep bomb, an incendiary bomb which did not go off, and 'A father whose two children had a narrow escape in last week's Zeppelin raid.' It still did not name York, though a letter from Fred Bradley attacking Edwin Gray would have made it clear even to a total stranger where the bombs had fallen. A collection started by 'A Soldier' for the distressed and bereaved families also made it abundantly clear that it was York that had been attacked. But while the *Herald* and the other York papers were trying to keep the target for 2 May unknown, other printers were not so cautious. The *Daily Mail* revealed that it was Old Ebor which had been clobbered that night and its revelations were repeated in *Le Temps*. Not only that, but a member of the government had let the cat out of the bag in the Commons - 'and a few seconds afterwards' the 'name of the town ... was exhibited in all the clubs in London.' (2) The culprit on this occasion was Henry Tennant who was asked by Theodore Taylor if he had 'anything to add about the Zeppelins that crossed Yorkshire during the night.' This was at question time on 3 May. *Hansard* records Tennant's reply thus: 'I have not full particulars, but I understand that the city of York was unfortunately injured in some respects.'

The Coroner's records enable the victims of York's first air raid to be identified. The records also identify where at least some of the bombs fell, and give some details of the unfortunate people who died.

The girl of 28 was Emily Beatrice Chapman and evidence was given at her inquest by her father Gerald. She was single and she lived with her parents in Nunthorpe Avenue. At 9.45 pm, it was said, she went to the front door 'to see the German Airship, and almost immediatly [sic] an explosive bomb was dropped in front of her parents house, and she was struck with a piece of shrapnel in the left shoulder and killed immediately.' The railway pensioner and his wife were George and Sarah Ann Avison, variously described in the Coroner's records as 70 and 74 (George) and 69 and 70 (Sarah Ann). These two lived at 3, Upper Price Street and both were in bed when the house was hit by a bomb which demolished the upper storey of the house. This was at 9.45 pm and their bodies were not found in the rubble that once was their kitchen until six o'clock next morning. Sarah, in the words of a summary of the incident, was found 'rolled up in the bed clothes dead with both her legs fractured and her scull'. She was removed to the police mortuary.

The rest of the victims of the May raid on York were killed in St Saviour's Place. The first was Susan Hannah Waudby, a 65 year old lady who ran a common lodging house (with its number given as both 13 and 8). She was inside the establishment when killed by a piece of shrapnel. Ernest Coultish was walking in the street when he too was hit in the stomach by shrapnel. He was taken to the County Hospital where he died at two o'clock the following morning. Coultish was a young man of 24 or 28 (both ages were given) who lived at 47, Volta Street, Selby, employed by Leetham of York as captain of the keel *Vera*. Benjamin Sharpe, a 21 year old labourer, of 1, Wilsons Row or Place worked at Leetham's mill and he had gone to work there that night, 'but owing to the lights in the City having to be extinguished owing to the raid he had to leave work about 9.30 p.m. and was on his way home when he was struck with [a] number of pieces of shrapnel in the back and was killed in St Saviours Gate.' William Chappelow (or Chapelow) was a carter who resided at 32, Garden Place, Hungate, and on the night of the raid he and his wife Sarah had been to a cinema. They were 'in St Saviour Place when he was struck with a bomb from a German Airship and killed, the lower parts of both his legs were blown off, and a fracture of his skull.' Sarah testified that her husband was 53 years of age, but later said she had been so distraught that she had made a mistaken. He was in fact 49.

A fifth person to be injured in St Saviour's Place was Pte Leslie Hinson, number 2194 of the 3/1st East Riding Yeomanry, an 18 year old soldier stationed in the camp on the Knavesmire. He was struck by shrapnel and was taken to the County Hospital where he died at 11 pm. This was also the fate of another serviceman. Cpl Edward Gordon Beckett, number 340, of the 1/1st West Riding Divisional Ammunition Column had gone home on 21 April on a months leave. He was staying with his mother at 4 John's Place, Hungate, and had spent most of the evening of 2 May there with her. He decided to go out into the city to see what was happening when a raid was threatened. '... when the Air craft was reported to be in the City he went out to see what was doing in the street, and whilst in St Saviours Place he was struck with a large piece of shrapnel in the right jaw which killed him instantly.'

The Chief Constable said that the populace behaved admirably on the night of the Zeppelin raid, that there was no panic, and that the air raid precautions worked well. The complaints that were made about lights, however, make one wonder whether that was absolutely correct. What were the arrangements for warning the populace that what the *Herald* called 'air-Huns' were out to send them to kingdom come ? They had been arranged by the end of 1915, it will be recalled, and in the event of a raid citizens were to be warned of the Zeps by the raising and lowering of the gas and electricity supplies. If the threatened raid was late at night, then the neighbourhood patrols would warn the sleeping citizens and knock them up. What they were to do then is not absolutely clear, but probably they were recommended to go out into an open space. The patrols were voluntary and if the experience of the Second World War is anything to go by, they would have become rather lax in carrying out their civic duties by May 1916. It would seem that the patrols might have been out each night during the 'season' for raids, but maybe not. Perhaps they only went out when they saw their own lights go down (a phenomenon in the Second World War which rumour had it denoted a raid), or were got out by their colleagues when they saw it. Anyway, whatever Chief Constable Burrow said, the system did not work well on 2 May, as was revealed when the Council discussed the matter on 5 June. (3) This was at a meeting at which Meyer revealed that women were only to be employed on the trams for the duration and were not to paid while being trained, and Horsman complained about them being employed anyway, 'on moral grounds.' Men would refuse to travel behind lady drivers Horsman said, before he and the rest of the the councillors stopped uttering such drivel and moved on to talk about the city's air raid warning system. The patrols, it was revealed, had had no means of knowing 'when warnings had been received.' This seems incredible, but that is what was said and a suggestion was made that a small red light should be suspended from gas standards giving a small glow, and when this went out 'the patrols would naturally take it as a warning.' Councillor Oscar Rowntree, moving the adoption of the Watch Committee's report said it had been decided that in the event of another raid 'the siren should not be brought into use again'. He also made the very reasonable observation that it was not possible to cut gas lighting off immediately - as 'a certain amount of gas [was always] left in the pipes after the supply had been cut off.'

There is no doubt that in the aftermath of York's first aid raid the patrols were more active - indeed they were too active according to complaints in the press which said they were trigger happy and got people out in the streets when there was no danger. What the citizens wanted, however, and this is not spelled out in the reports of those days, was anti aircraft protection as well as more efficient patrols, warnings and blackouts. The day after the raid the Lord Mayor visited the War Office to air York's grievances. It seems that he got nowhere, then went to the Horse Guards, where he was much more successful. It was quite clear that he had gone to criticise the military authorities in York for leaving their barracks illuminated like Edith Milner said they did, and he was promised that 'an enquiry' would be held 'by the Government on the lighting arrangements in the town on the occasion of the raid.' (4) It was also said that 'as a result of' the visit 'the town had been somewhat favoured as regarded the matter of protection, and in the event of the raiders paying a return visit they would probably meet with a hot reception.' This almost certainly meant that an anti aircraft gun or guns would be sent to protect York. (The paper which reported the Lord Mayor's visit, incidentally, was also the first to appear after the provisions of the Summertime Act of 1916 became effective. At 2 am on the night of Saturday/Sunday 20/21 May the nation's clocks were put forward by one hour. 'So far as can be ascertained', the *Herald* said, 'the matter of putting on the clock one hour ... caused no inconvenience'. Summer time ended in 1916 'at 3 a.m., summer time, or 2 a.m., Greenwich time, on October 1.')

The spirit of 'community' engendered by the war, though it did not go so far as contemporaries sometimes suggested it did, manifested itself in the collections organised for those hurt or dispossessed in the May bombings, and by 13 May over £375 had been sent to the *York Herald*. This was private enterprise, and private enterprise also set about developing efficient personal alarm systems that would make York safer (and their makers a profit). 'Zep alarms' began to be advertised that would make one just a little less dependant on those not too reliable patrols. The first, or one of the first, was mentioned by J.E.R. in a letter to the *Herald* published on 23 August. He described the appliance he had made and installed himself, and very impressive it looked too. It was connected to the gas supply, which was led from a central fitting into a U tube which was filled with water. Into this was put a floating stopper on which was a T shaped copper arm, which when the gas level was high, was kept above two terminals which were a part of the house's electric door bell circuits. When the gas pressure fell, as it would when an air raid alarm was being given, the T would fall across the two terminals, complete a circuit, the door bells would ring, and J.E.R. and his family would get up. A letter published the day after J.E.R. told York about his alarm said that the writer had had something similar in his house for months, but the trouble with it (them) was that the gas supply was often lowered around midnight as a matter of course, and this, of course, set the alarms ringing. Later local firms began manufacturing Zep alarms. How many had been sold and installed when the next attacks came is unknown. One of the producers of such things was the well-known firm of Barnitts of Colliergate who sold them at 7s. 6d. Their advertisement for them read (5) (it will be seen that their product is not a direct crib from JER).

A ZEPPALARM

will enable you to sleep in comfort
and Perfect Security.

This is a simple mechanical apparatus for attachment to an ordinary straight gas bracket and an ordinary alarm clock. There is no consumption of gas and no risk of gas escape. It can be easily fitted and adjusted by anyone. On three recent occasions it has proved most effective. It rings the alarm bell immediately the gas is lowered

It was ineviable that Barnitts would not be allowed to corner the market, and by the end of August they had at least one competitor, whose product really does look like an improvement. It worked from either the gas or electricity supply and was cheaper. (Though you had to have electric bells in your house for it to work.) The advertisement for it read, a little ambiguously

ZEPPELIN RAIDS.

BUY A RELIABLE DEVICE THAT WILL AWAKEN YOU
WHEN THE ALARM IS OFFICIALLY GIVEN.

EASILY FITTED TO EITHER ELECTRIC
LIGHT OR GAS.

A SPECIAL DEVICE THAT CAN BE FITTED BY ANY
AMATEUR FROM THE GAS TO THE EXISTING

ELECTRIC BELLS

5/6

ALEC W. HOUSE,

4, STONEGATE, YORK

Despite Chief Constable Burrow's remarks, and despite George Benson's loyal regurgitating of them, (6) York, at least in the opinion of its inhabitants, had not been well prepared for the May raid, and the emergency services had not worked as well as they should have. In the immediate aftermath of the raid a new organisation of street patrols was set up which would give the inhabitants warnings of impending raids. Someone signing himself 'Acomb' gave readers of the *Herald* an outline of how the Moorgate patrol worked. (7) Each householder in that area, he said, provided a member who would sit up until 3 am, presumably on a rota basis. If and when he saw the lights go up and down he would go to the houses whose occupants said they wanted warning and knock them up. When were the alarms given? It seems from a remark in a letter to the *Press* that they would be given when the Zeps were some 40 miles away. (8)

In the aftermath of the May raid the new street patrols began work, angry at whose who said they did not want knocking up. These people got up when they heard their neighbours being roused, they said. The patrols were enthusiastic, and a bit trigger happy it was alleged by Alderman Inglis and others, and on at least two occasions York was the scene of 'pandemonium'. Whether a watchman had misinterpreted a flicker in the gas supply for an alarm, or whether a Zep really had been 40 miles off and then went away from York is unknown, but on 31 July 'terrified women and children' flocked to spaces 'south of the River Ouse'. (9) This was the occasion when, Inglis said, the patrolmen ran around 'like maniacs'. (10) There was another panic on 4 August and this, again, led to criticisms of all and sundry, and to some serious consequences. Edith Milner said so. (11) She wrote that

> I was in a district yesterday where the panic has had very sad results. No less than three women were prematurely confined and three babes were lost. One woman being between life and death for 24 hours. Two women suffered from violent heart attacks, and nearly succumbed. Another woman ran out with bare feet and only a coat over her nightdress with her five days' old baby in her arms ... None of my servants could sleep with the tramping of an excited and agitated crowd all along Heworth Green largely composed of women and children. Some people were knocked up an hour before lights went out.

Angry letters began to appear in the local papers, ignoring what the writers had been told before, and demanding steam alarm buzzers. Ellen Rose, of George Street, was a typical correspondent. (12) How can people receive air raid warnings who turned off their lights at the mains each night, she asked, ignoring the fact that there was usually pandemonium in the streets from the patrols. They would not know of the raid until the bombs were dropping, when it would be too late 'to seek a place of safety.' Could there 'not be a "hooter" or "buzzer"', she went on, 'loud enough to be heard all over the town, blown as a warning and another safety buzzer sounded when the danger is over ... The sounding of the buzzer would obviate the necessity for patrols.'

The editor of the *Herald* commented on Ellen's letter in a 'where have you been all this time' tone, (13) and the York patrols' coordinator, E. Boyes, angrily replied to his critics, saying that silence was the keyword of the service they were providing, and that the banging on knockers and the subsequent panic had occurred in area where there were no patrols. W.A. Forster Todd, the Lord Mayor, issued a plea for calm and quietness during an alert and a letter writer urged the patrolmen to adopt the knockers up system of many towns and tap the windows with bamboo canes to which were attached twin wires with metal pellets attached to them. Forster Todd also urged people to keep indoors during a raid, and warned them that 'Calling out false information, or in any way spreading it is a most serious offence'; one which 'should be suppressed.'

There were any number of other suggestions about air raid precautions, and most of them advised people to stay indoors. There were few houses with cellars in the city, but places of (relative) safety were recommended. The Dringhouses Mothers' Meeting produced a pamphlet which is fairly typical, and W.P. Dott, of the Dringhouses Vicarage sent a copy of it to the *Herald* (which published it on 11 August) under the heading 'IN CASE OF RAID. AVOID PANIC. KEEP INDOORS.' Close all windows before going to bed, the ladies said, and take to the bedroom some clothes and 'some dissolved strong washing soda in a cup or basin.' When a warning came people were told to get dressed and check that all windows were closed. They were then to 'Put on pad (made of handkerchief, duster, or proper pad of wadding and gauze with ear tapes) dipped in strong soda water', then 'turn off gas meter, damp out fires.' There then followed some traditional advice

> (5) Sit quietly in lowest room away from windows, or under staircase, avoid alarm, and say your prayers to Almighty God asking for help and protection for yourselves and your neighbours.

Chief Constable Burrow issued a handbill a couple of weeks after that of the Dringhouses ladies, but which was remarkably similar to it (except in one important respect). (15) After a public warning was given, Burrow said, all lights had to be eliminated, and the striking of matches in the street was strictly prohibited. (This had been the subject of much discussion and the first person to be prosecuted for striking a match in the street was James Richardson of Dove Street. Jim was done under section 26 of the Defence of the Realm Act, 'the permission of the competent military authority having been obtained', and he committed his crime at 11.55 pm on 25 September in Scarcroft Road. He lit a fag, Jim said, 'and never gave a thought to the seriousness of the offence.' He was fined five shillings and told by the chairman of the bench that lights from matches were visible at a height of 2,000 feet.) People were told that they were not to congregate in streets or near windows, and to stay indoors and retire to the cellar (if they had one) or to shelter near the main walls of the house. They were told to keep a respirator handy - gauze saturated in washing soda - as a protection against leaks from broken gas mains (presumably), and the sounding of buzzers, bugles, bells or hooters was prohibited. It is quite clear from the foregoing that noise and lights were regarded as great dangers, and the authorities set about prosecuting offenders. In mid May, for example, there were no less than 25 prosecutions of this kind at one sitting at the York police court. (16) The 'defences' put up by some of the offencers are a delight to read. The Rev Patrick Shaw, for example, admitted that he had shown a light from his church but it was a 'dim religious light' and Arthur Brook of Walmgate was done on 4 September. The report on him said that he

> raised the novel defence that "he was not aware that he must shade lights at the rear of his house. He had had no notice to that effect."
>
> The Chairman: How old are you ?
>
> Defendant: Sixty-six.
>
> Whatever do you think is the object of shading lights at the front of houses if the rear is to be left illuminated ? - I don't know, sir.
>
> Defendant was fined £1.

With information thrown at them from the Dringhouses Mothers' Meeting, the Chief Constable, Edith Milner, the Lord Mayor and many others, the citizens of York must have been well aware of what to do if and when the Zeps visited York again. They did so on Monday 25 September, (17) two days after a huge raid (by the standards of those days) on London and elsewhere in which one airship was destroyed and another forced down. The latter came down in Essex and the *Press* told its readers on 26 September that 'The capture of the crew ... marks the first time that forces of an enemy country have landed in the United Kingdom, and [been] taken prisoners, since 1797.' (This was when a French force landed on the Pembrokeshire coast.)

The Zep raided 'a north eastern town' which had been visited before as the *Herald* put it. This time anti-aircraft guns fired at it and little damage was done by the four bombs the airship dropped. Initial reports on the raid said six sick horses were killed, and that one woman died of shock. She was a 58 year old painter's wife. The inquest on her heard that she and her husband went to bed, around 10.15 pm, and that three quarters of an hour before the attack the wife said they should get up '"as they were knocking".' This seems to indicate that the alarm system was working efficiently, and the husband revealed that in May 'we received no information until explosions were heard.' The coroner and the jury disputed about whether getting up was a good or bad thing ? (18) 'I don't know about this knocking up', the coroner said, 'it has always seemed to me a very doubtful thing as to whether it is a good plan or a bad one. ... whether it is better to get up and out or not, I think people are probably better in their houses than outside. ... I would much rather not be knocked up than be knocked up. It has become the fashionable thing to do so, but personally I am inclined to think it is not a good thing. It is a bad thing.'

Following the coroner's remarks the chairman of the York Patrols Committee issued instructions to householders which, in effect, reiterated what had been said by the coroner and Mr Burrow. (19) He, too, advised citizens to remain indoors during a raid - 'It is most undesirable that people should go into the streets: the experience of other places proves this.' A doctor from the the Retreat agreed, in a letter about 'Zeppelinophobia'. He pointed out the fantastic odds against an individual being hurt, and advised people to stay indoors, to 'keep calm ... and encourage everyone else to do the same.' (20) In the paper in which this letter was published the case of the Rev Patrick J. Shaw, vicar of All Saints, North street, a persistent offender who has been mentioned before, was reported. This time he had allowed 'a brilliant light' to shine from the windows of the church around 9 pm on 16 and 23 September. The Rev Gedge of St Denys, Walmgate, was also done, as was the caretaker of the Coop premises in Railway Street. (21) (Also done for being drunk and disorderly that day was Alice Gainley of Albert Street. She was employed at a York munitions factory and was making her fiftieth appearance before the beaks. No doubt Edith Milner would have made notes about her and concluded that high wages led to ladies behaving like Alice.)

On 9 October the York magistrates had a field day with lighting offenders, when no less than 64 persons were summoned. Sir Joseph Sykes Rymer presided that day and announced that henceforth fines would go up. He and his colleagues had met, Rymer declared, and had decided that 'the penalties hitherto inflicted were were not sufficient as so little notice had been taken of them. Greater penalties would have to be imposed, and unless there were some very special circumstances the fines could not be less than 10s.' The first to benefit seems to have been Alfred Jarvis of Belle Vue Terrace. He and his daughter, however, did not go down unprotesting and showed great spirit when they told PC Perkins that lights could be seen nightly 'from the War Office, as well as from a house not far away, but', she went on, because a magistrate lived there 'no notice had, apparently, been taken of it.' Dr Peter Schmidt, a resident of Heslington Lane, did not appear and he got clobbered with twice the going rate. This may have been because of that lapse of respect, or it may have been, as Sykes Rymer said, because 'the Bench had been informed that the defendant was not a British subject.' Very nasty.

It is usually almost impossible to trace daft, yet persistent stories to their origin, but it is just possible that the proceedings of 9 October might enable this to be done regarding a York one. That ludicrous story that Rowntrees had a light above the cocoa factory as a Zep guide, might just have originated in the case of Theodore Rowntree. He was summoned for an offence at the Cocoa Works on 27 September, two days after York's second air raid. Between 8.40 p.m. and 9.30 p.m. a light 'which had the appearance of a powerful bull's-eye' shone from the top of the building. It seemingly came from a ventilating shaft which was stopped up the following day. Leetham's Mill, Hungate, also allowed lights to shine out from a top storey window, and like Rowntrees the firm was fined. No 'help the Zep' stories started about the millers, however, and that is very revealing.

Noise and lights were still reckoned to be the chief Zep aids, according to general opinion in the autumn of 1916, and even more restrictions were imposed. Chief Constable Burrow urged residents not to bang doors, to stop their dogs barking, not to talk and laugh in the streets, and to move about quietly. (22) He was supported by a high ranking Army officer, and the threats they made were backed up by increased prosecutions for lighting offences. In October Burrow pleaded again for better blackouts and revealed that in the 20 months that lighting restrictions had been in force in York there had been no fewer than 461 prosecutions. (23) On that same day a film called 'The Strafer Strafed' (24) was showing at the Victoria Hall which does not seem to have been quite the thing to calm the nerves of those of Old Ebor, who were, well, a little nervous, though then again it might have, because it depicted the destruction of L21 over London. Section nine of the film showed 'how the observation car is lowered so that it may spy out the land beneath the clouds', a scene similar, perhaps, to that in Howard Hughes' famous epic 'Hell's Angels' (1930). The following week the Victoria Hall was showing what it described as 'Official War Film - THE TWO DESTROYED ZEPPS IN ESSEX' while the Electric had taken over 'THE WRECKED ZEPPELIN IN ESSEX', as a major support to 'Ultus and the Grey Lady.' The Zep film was regarded by the *Evening Press* reviewer as 'really excellent.' The 'detail given in the pictures is a revelation of the photographic art', he went on, 'and enables one to get an excellent idea of the construction of the monster baby-killers.' (25)

The prosecutions for lighting offences did not seem to diminish after the Chief Constable's latest instructions appeared and the papers continued to carry ideas about how the Zeps might be diverted (by lighting up an area in the country which was uninhabited, for example) and suggestions were made about 'safe' lighting which would cut down the number of accidents in the 'Stygian darkness that nightly envelops the city.' (26) Nevertheless, the citizens were still uneasy about the future, and in October a deputation from the City Council met the C in C Northern Command 'with regard to the protection of the city and its inhabitants in the event of a hostile air raid.' (27) They reassured the populace afterwards that 'very satisfactory action had been taken to minimise the danger which would arise if Zeppelins were to visit the neighbourhood' again. Two weeks later they did.

On the night of Monday 27 November 1916 the city of York was presented with what must have been the most spectacular event of its history until then. The *Press*'s reporter waxed lyrical, and his first paragraph went as follows (28)

AN EXCITING COMBAT
RAIDER HIT BY SHELLS OVER
A NORTH-EAST TOWN
BOMBS DROPPED BY TWO AIRSHIPS

"Go on! Go on!" were the full throated cries by hundreds of the inhabitants of a town in the North-Eastern Counties as they witnessed on Monday night a thrilling and exhilerating spectacle of the skies. It was a panorama which at one moment held the on-lookers spellbound, and a second later accounted for a whole-hearted outburst of delighted frenzy. Men's nerves tingled with the joy of battle as they saw a hostile invader held for four full minutes in the star-bedecked heavens by a powerful searchlight while the guns belched forth their message. They were minutes full not in the sense of time out of incident, and at last the climax came when a mighty cheer rent the air, followed by shouts of "She's Hit." It was a sound that was good to hear.

Quite clearly, if the *Press* is to be believed, many people in York did not heed the police's instructions to stay indoors, and according to that same source the airship came from the north. She was immediately picked up by searchlights and 'peppered' by AA guns, which scored a direct hit forcing the ship to take evasive action and a route eastward. She dropped a number of bombs in her retreat, both explosive and incendiary. A little later, about ten minutes later, 'there appeared in the starry firmament for just a moment a great fiery orb', and people thought the Zep had been brought down

in the vicinity, and cheer after cheer went up. Hosts of people rushed in the direction in which the airship was believed to have fallen, but it subsequently transpired that the flare was a considerable distance away, and was caused by the envelope of another Zeppelin igniting as a result of the welcome it received ... further north.

A second Zep visited York on the night of 27 November. It hovered over the city and was caught in the lights and shelled. It, too, dropped bombs, but like its predecessor did little damage and caused no casualties.

On that night of 27/28 November ten Zeppelins had set out to raid objectives in the north and the Midlands. Two of them turned back, and six failed to reach their objectives because of AA fire or mechanical troubles. Two were shot down, one off the coast of Durham and the second off Lowestoft. The former, commanded by Max Dietrich, dropped missiles on West Hartlepool and killed four people and injured eleven others. It was shot down by 2nd Lt I.V. Pyatt of 36 Squadron. (29) Within 12 hours of the destruction of LZ 34 - just before noon on 28 November - a German aeroplane dropped bombs on London, and a new phase of the war was ushered in, just as the British public thought (rightly) that the RNAS and the RFC had mastered the Zeps.

That the Zep threat was practically over was not immediately apparent, however, and the populace of York remained on tenterhooks for some time. Throughout 1916 there had been continual complaints (from Edith Milner among others it will be recalled) that the military authorities (and the railways) were not as conscientious about the blackout as they should have been. Numerous soldiers were prosecuted for showing lights on the Knavesmire and at various barracks and offices, and in December this dispute reached a head when L Cpl Clifford Blackburn was done for 'showing a light' at Northern Command HQ. He denied the offence, whoever was responsible was 'shielded', and the *Press* said there existed there a 'GILBERTIAN POSITION.' The case dragged on (30) and the War Office eventually produced a Colonel as the culprit. Poor old Clifford Blackburn had the case against him withdrawn, and quite right too.

The Lord Mayor had warned the city about scaremongers, and one caused a panic in York on the day after its last raid. On 28 November Thomas Braithwaite, of Cole Street, was (he said) in a shop when a post office girl came in who 'said that the Zeppelins were out and that the first warning had been received.' Maybe Tom should have checked, but he did not, and went off to the Bootham Row Mission, (31) where his mum was the caretaker. As a result of his warning, and no doubt thinking he was doing the right thing, Tom stopped two missionary meetings. A 'state of alarm' was created and eventually Braithwaite edged his way into York history by becoming the first citizen to be prosecuted 'for spreading by word of mouth a certain false report, contrary to Regulation 27 of the Defence of the Realm Act (Consolidation) Regulations.' (32) He appeared in the York magistrates court and got a right one from Alderman Norman Green, the chairman of the bench that day. He was just the kind of person the court had been waiting for Green told Braithwaite. 'He would be fined 20s., and they hoped it would be a warning to him and others that these false reports must not be spread about the city.' A little later Joseph Arthur Langham was also proceeded against - and he was a patrol man! (33) His actions had similar dire consequences to those of Tom Braithwaite. Joseph Arthur told people outside Rowntrees' gates 'that Zepps have been sighted', and as a result of this one woman went and took her child away from a choir practice at Clifton, in consequence of which 'the whole choir was dismissed' and some night shift workers stayed away from the cocoa works. For all this Langham got a fine of 10s., which seems little enough, with him a patrol man.

York, like many places, was in a state of continual tension while the Zeppelin threat existed, and that period coincided mainly with the time of the Battle of the Somme, which dragged on from July to November. Day after day reports of local casualties appeared in the papers and in November a third VAD hospital was added to those at Clifford Street and Nunthorpe Hall. In the summer of 1916 it was announced that St Johns, the Church of England training college for teachers, was to close for the duration (it was down to a handful of students) and it was turned into a hospital. Many of its patients would have been 'on the Somme', (34) and film of some of them had been the great cinema attraction of 1916. It caused as much interest in York as it did elsewhere.

Everyone knew that there was going to be a 'Big Push' sometime in the summer of 1916, and at 7.30 on the morning of 1 July (the middle day of the middle year of the war) troops went over the top on a combined British and French front of 23 miles. It was a terrible day, though the papers did their best to disguise the fact. *'In personnel'* wrote Winston Churchill, 'the results of the operation' were disastrous, in *'terrain* they were absolutely barren.' (35)

The French and the Germans had allowed cameramen at the front for a long time before the British decided to do so. Lord Kitchener was primarily reponsible for this, but eventually 'official' war films - called 'topicals' by the cinema proprietors - began to be issued. They were used as supplements to the usual cinema fare and were a regular part of the programmes at the Victoria Hall. Films from the fronts had been shown before the official ones arrived. These had been taken by freelance cameramen (before they were banned) and included such titles as 'Brilliant French Victory in the Vosges,' 'actually cinematographed by means of powerful lenses at some distance from the battlefield', (36) and records of Lord Kitchener visiting France. (37) At the end of January 1916 'By special arrangement with the War Office' the official British films began to appear at the Victoria Hall ('CAN ONLY BE SEEN AT THIS HALL'). (38) By the time 'the Somme' started a half a dozen official war films had been made and distributed.

The first official British films had their moments - one featured a mine explosion at St Eloi and another was filmed from a British aeroplane - but none were like 'The Battle of the Somme.' This was feature film length and depicted events (mainly) of 1 to 3 July and was photographed by Geoffrey Malins (39) and R.B. McDowell. Malins, a self publicist if ever there was one, took the shots of the mine blow mentioned above, and made the flying sequences. He was also responsible for some, if not all, of 'Brilliant French Victory in the Vosges.'

'The Battle of the Somme' was a sensation when it appeared (and at first its cameramen were anonymous). (40) This is 'the real thing at last' wrote the *Manchester Guardian* (41) singling out a mine explosion for special mention and telling its readers that it was 'in the region of Fricourt-Mametz.' It was actually near Beaumont Hamel and was filmed at 7.20 a.m. on 1 July by Geoffrey Malins. Ten minutes later Malins filmed men of the 29th Division going over the top. It was a dramatic sequence in which one man was shot and fell back into the trench. The film was shown for the first time in Manchester on 28 August. 'There were cheers when the men first went over the parapet', it was recorded 'but they died down to silence before the vision of the still, lifeless figure slipping back into the trench and the bodies just beyond the parapet.' (42) Everywhere that sequence was singled out for comment, and it was when the film finally arrived in York.

'The Battle of the Somme' was first shown privately in the second week of August 1916, then was released for public exhibition on the 21st, and the reviews in between these dates resulted in the largest demand ever 'for a long film' which was, the *Times* said, 'a drama which instead of being a mimicry is a fragment of history.' (43) Bert Rutter of the Victoria Hall, who was usually first with war films in York, was out manoeuvered on this occasion and the Somme film was shown to enthusiastic crowds at the Picture House just a week after its general release. The advertisement for it read

> The Greatest Picture in the history of the world
> THE BATTLE OF THE SOMME
> 5,000 feet of war as it really is. See what our
> boys are doing to the Boches.

The York reviewers were as enthusiastic as were those elsewhere. The *Press* said that (44)

Never before has such a production been filmed. The artillery are seen pounding at the German trenches, troops are observed going up to the firing line, and their last grim preparations - the fixing of bayonets and wire cutters - are eagerly watched. Then follows the signal for the attack, and the gallant soldiers are seen to swarm over the parapet. Two or three are seen to fall victims of the German fire within the first two or three yards. It is all so real that its very reality comes as a shock to the person who does not know the fearful toll which war demands.

During the first run of 'The Battle of the Somme' there were no other war films showing in York though the famous play 'Sealed Orders' was at the Theatre Royal. (45) It is frequently said, however, that 'The Somme' made war films popular, and that may well have been the case in York. Henceforth war films, which had certainly not been absent from shows at the Victoria Hall, were given more prominence. When the Malins/McDowell film returned to the Electric to be shown four times daily (and billed somewhat strongly under a heading '"STEREO" PICTURES') the Picture Palace was featuring 'The Defence of Verdun' as a main attraction, while Bert Rutter was offering the aforementioned 'The Strafer Strafed'. Henceforth 'real' war films were staple fare. 'The King Visits His Armies in the Great Advance' got great publicity, for example, though its subject matter was not all that exciting (surely). Official Belgian film appeared with 'The Bombardment of Neuport' [sic] and 'On the Way to Gorizia from the Italians got a lot of mileage. Bert Rutter obtained the official British naval films and in October 1916 the Electric announced that it had booked the 'Sequel to the Battle of the Somme'. The French 'Somme' film ('The French Offensive on the Somme') made its appearance while the German version got considerable publicity, and was knocked for including 'faked' sequences.

The Electric seems to have been a little premature with its announcement that it had a sequel to the Malins/McDowell epic, or it was gazzumped by the Victoria Hall. Anyway, in November, the latter was telling patrons to 'LOOK OUT FOR THE SEQUEL TO "THE BATTLE OF THE SOMME." We hold exclusive Rights for Exhibition in York.' When that sequel appeared it must have been as much of a let down as 'The King Visits His Armies'. It was called 'Wounded Somme Heroes' ('The Film that does not bore you') and was shown in the first week of 1917.

The scenes in 'The Battle of the Somme' which made it world famous (46) should have been the blowing of Hawthorn mine or that haunting sequence of men of the Lancashire Fusiliers in what is simply known as 'the Sunken Road' near Beaumont Hamel, half way across No Man's Land, filmed before 6.30 am, men who were nearly all dead a half an hour later. The second of these scenes went practically unnoticed, but the mine blow was always commented on. What really made the film, however, was the scene already referred to of men going over the top, a sequence which still has an immense dramatic impact. The 'leap' scene was the real thing, audiences thought, and it, more than anything, made war films popular. It therefore occupies an important place in film history, but it is a superb irony that the scene was faked, and about that there is absolutely no doubt whatsoever. (47) British journalists clobbered the Germans for allegedly faking scenes in their Somme film, but the British had done precisely the same thing in their own - to great effect. (48)

Shortly after the Somme film appeared in British cinemas the Allies (on 15 September) introduced a secret weapon into the fighting on the Western Front. This was the tank, and it will be recalled that a son of York's most famous family was in the most famous one used that day. (49) The tanks were not an unqualified success, but the nation waited eagerly for pictures of what they looked like, and its cartoonists had a field day speculating about their appearance. Official photographs of the tanks were not issued until December 1916, (50) but before then the Victoria Hall had shown a 'tank cartoon' which got some enthusiastic reviews. 'A film is to be shown at the Victoria Hall, York, which may be said to be a comedy of the "Tank"', the *Press* told readers on the 10 November,

> It is called the Kineto Tank, and until it starts playing the goat with its arms, the Kineto Tank is a convincing creature, and isolated sections of the film might well deceive the unknowing. But the trenches where it was photographed, the houses it wrecks, the trees it pulls up, are all in London at the headquarters of the film manufacturers.

The advertisement for the Kineto film was even more enthusiastic than usual.

> The man who invented the "Tank" is a Genius, but the man who conceived this film is more - he is a Genius, a Humourist, and an Artist rolled into one. We advise every MAN, WOMAN and CHILD to see the "TANK" CARTOONS.

Whether the Kineto tank bore any resemblance to the real thing is unknown. There was some film of Britain's most famous tank 'Creme de Menthe' (allegedly) returning from battle on 15 September, (51) but this was not shown for some time, it seems, and the first time the public saw film of tanks moving was in the second of Malins' and McDowell's trilogy. This was 'The Battle of the Ancre', which opened at both the Picture House and the Electric in late January 1917, and a huge number of people paid for admission to see it at the Picture House in one week. The tank most prominently featured in this epic was one called 'Oh I Say' which was involved in the attack on Beaumont Hamel towards the end of the Somme battles in November 1916. (52) The 'Ancre' is, in many ways, a better film than 'The Somme', but has nothing in it as dramatic as the famous leap from the trenches. The *Press* went to some length, however, to assure its readers that it was all genuine. It 'contains nothing in the nature of "fake" or "made-up" scenes', it said, 'having actually been taken on the battlefield.' (53) Could this be taken as evidence that the faked sequences in 'The Somme' had been spotted, as they surely should have been in an army city ? That men in winter clothing (sheepskin jackets) were supposed to be getting ready for a July battle must have looked odd even to the unsophisticated audiences of 1916, and the trenches from which the men allegedly left on 1 July would not have looked like Somme trenches to anyone who had served in Picardy. There were plenty of those, mutilated and shattered in York in late 1916.

1. There is a very slight account of the York Zeppelin raid(s) in a volume titled *Burdekin's Alamanack 1924-1930* (reference Y942 843) in the York local history library. The author was George Benson and he gave details of where the bombs fell. Benson was the author of scores of slight, antiquarian type articles on York history. He was also the author of a large 'history' which is a prime example of the scissors and paste 'method' of compiling history. The Archibishop of York at that time, Cosmo Gordon Lang, wrote of how he witnessed the Zeps in the first raid. As a direct result he immediately gave orders for the precious stained glass windows to be removed from the Minster and put into storage. J.G. Lockhart, *Cosmo Gordon Lang* (1949) p 253
2. *Herald* 10 May 1916. Letter signed 'ALL OR NOWT' dated 8 May 1916. Also letter from Edgar W. Dudding, *Ibid* 11 May 1916
3. Report in eg *Ibid* 6 June 1916
4. *Ibid* 22 May 1916
5. Eg *Press* 12 May 1916. A 'House' advertisement appeared in eg *Ibid* 26 August 1916. Of course there were bogus alarms and bogus alarm sellers. See the letter from H.E. Bloor, in *Ibid* 5 January 1917
6. *Burdekin's Almanack op.cit.*
7. *Herald* 4 August 1916. See letter in *Ibid* 7 August 1916 about the South Bank patrol
8. *Ibid* Later hooters were used as 'all clear' signals
9. *Ibid* 2 August letter from John Lane
10. *Ibid* 1 August 1916. Report of proceedings in the city council
11. *Ibid* 7 August 1916
12. *Ibid* 17 August 1916. See also *Ibid* 7 August 1916
13. 'Does it not occur to our correspondent that the sounding of a "buzzer" would be the very thing to attract a Zeppelin to the city if it were in this part of Yorkshire', he asked. It was also pointed out that a Home Office order prohibited sirens and buzzers in the Midlands
14. *Herald* 5 August 1916
15. *Ibid* 25 August 1916. The Jim Richardson case is reported eg in *Press* 19 October 1916
16. *Herald* 6 May 1916. See also *Ibid* 23 May 1916. There were many prosecutions of military personnel for showing lights, including officers stationed on the Knavesmire, one of the places people continually complained about.
17. *Ibid* 27 September 1916. *Press* 26 and 27 September 1916. Castle *op.cit.* pp 149-50
18. *Press* 27 September 1916
19. *Ibid* 4 October 1916

20. *Ibid* 5 October 1916. Pat Shaw's fifth offence (which cost him £1) reported in *Herald* 6 January 1917, supplement
21. The Rev Edward Bulmer of St Martin cum Gregory had a very narrow escape. He was staying at Sea View and left a light on. Private Robert Stead was on patrol duty at the cobble landing at Filey when he saw the light, thought it was a signal, and fired at it. The Rev Bulmer was fined £1 which he said he paid gladly as it might make other people more careful. *Press* 7 October 1916
22. *Ibid* 10 October 1916
23. *Ibid* 2 October 1916
24. Though in some advertisements it was called simply 'Destruction of L21 in London'
25. *Press* 10 October 1916
26. *Ibid* 21 November 1916
27. *Ibid* 11 November 1916
28. *Ibid* 28 November 1916. See also *Herald* 4 December 1916 for a letter which shows incendiaries were dropped
29. Castle *op.cit*. Mr Castle says that the airship shot down off Durham was L34 and that off Lowestoft L21, but it will be recalled that film of L21's destruction had been showing in cinemas in York for some time. L21 was in fact destroyed on 3 September. It might have come as something of a surprise to York Quaker knockers that one of the pilots who shot down the Zep off the Norfolk coast was Flight Lt Egbert Cadbury of the RNAS, a son of George Cadbury of Cadbury Bros Ltd. Egbert was awarded the DSC. Whitehouse *op.cit*. p 268. Whitehouse wrongly calls Cadbury 'Major'. He was flying a De Havilland DH4. Bodies from the Durham airship were washed ashore in January 1917 and buried with military honours 'In the corner of a village churchyard'. *Herald* 12 January 1917. Others were washed up later.
30. *Press* 7 and 14 December 1916
31. York's first war shrine was put up at the Mission. *Ibid* 6 November 1916. *Herald* 11 November 1916
32. *Press* 18 December 1916
33. *Ibid* 28 December 1916
34. A common description of the 1916 battles in Picardy, but a misleading one. The river Somme was in the French area of operations. On the closing of the college see eg *Ibid* 4 September 1916. Also G.P. McGregor, *A Church College for the 21st Century* ? chap 6 *passim* (York 1991)
35. W. Churchill, *The World Crisis* 1911-1918 (1939 Vol 2 p 1088
36. *Press* 3 April 1915. It was showing at both the Victoria Hall and the Electric. On the earlier war films shown in York see A.J. Peacock, 'Could Easily be Stock', *Gun Fire* No 2 (nd)
37. *Press* 17 May 1915
38. *Ibid* 21 February 1916. This advertisement actually related to No 4 in the series. Bert Rutter of the Victoria Hall would seem to have had exclusive rights only to first showings. The Picture House was showing some in March. *Ibid* 17 March 1916
39. He went to the French sector when banned from filming further north. Malins wrote an autobiographical book called *How I Filmed the War* which was banned by Lloyd George during the war. In it Malins does not even mention McDowell, gets place names appallingly wrong, yet manages to remember dialogues he had with soldiers in the most remarkable way
40. Conan Doyle and others campaigned to have their names put on the film
41. *Manchester Guardian* 11 August 1916
42. *Ibid* 29 August 1916
43. *Times* 9 and 22 August 1916
44. *Press* 29 August 1916
45. The Theatre Royal still sometimes functioned as a cinema pure and simple on occasion. In November 1916, for example, it showed D.W. Griffith's masterpiece *Birth of a Nation*. The Hippodrome seems to have closed
46. It was shown all over the world - in the USA, in China, Japan and Russia
47. For years there had been talk about 'the leap' sequence being faked. Malins, of course, said nothing about it, but Kevin Brownlow, *The War, the West, and the Wilderness* (1979) actually named someone who took part in the filming of it. There have been numerous notes about Malins' film in recent years, and some contentions put forward that 'the leap' was already in the can before the Somme battle started - that it was filmed for another production then taken off

the shelf and wound into 'The Somme'. On the film and its reliability as a true record of those days on the Western Front in 1916 (many 'stock' shots or library shots were used) see eg, R. Smither, 'A Wonderful Idea of the Fighting: The Question of Fakes in *The Battle of the Somme*', *Imperial War Museum* Review No 3, (1988). Also A.J. Peacock, 'The Somme Film - Some Notes', *Gun Fire* No 2 (nd), and 'The (1916) Somme Film', *Gun Fire* No 3 (nd)

48. The German film was extensively shown in neutral countries and was titled *Bei unseren Helden an der Somme*. It seems there is only one print of it in existence, but a handbook about it published in three languages is in the possession of the author
49. This was Lawrence Rowntree, and a biographical study of him has already been quoted
50. On the appearance of the first photographs and the speculation about what the tanks would look like see eg A.J. Peacock, 'Pleistocene Prodigies', *Gun Fire* No 6 (nd)
51. There is film of 'Creme de Menthe' returning on 15 September with one of its driving wheels smashed, but Mr David Fletcher of the Tank Museum, Bovington, is of the opinion that the return may have been redone a second time for the cameras
52. Beaumont Hamel was a first day objctive on 1 July. It was finally taken in early November. The last of the Malins/McDowell trilogy was 'The Battle of Arras ' (April 1917)
53. *Press* 30 January 1917

CHAPTER 15

ALLOTMENTS, PRICES, AND RATIONING

While York was concerned with air raids, while the conscientious objectors were annoying the intolerant, and while the tribunals were finding their feet, its citizens felt the effects of a continuous rise in prices and saw the first movements towards the rationing which was to become a fact of life in the not too distant future. There is plenty of evidence of the extent of the increase in the cost of living. In December 1916 tea prices went up, and two days before the rise was announced the cost of milk went up. (1) Between those two dates a report announced that there had been an overall price rise on foodstuffs of three per cent during November, and that prices were up by 84 per cent compared with August 1914 when the war started. The British housewife then, in December 1916, had to spend £1.16s.9d. to get what she could have bought for a sovereign on the eve of hostilities.

What could be done to stop inflation galloping away and causing immense problems for the authorities ? Already there had been some restrictions imposed on prices; in 1916 there were more. By November two food orders were promulgated that were complicated in the extreme, but by which milk prices were frozen at the levels prevailing on the 15th of that month and specifying that they should not exceed by more than a specified amount the pre-war price levels. (2) This proved to be immensely difficult, but the order was modified and prices duly went up in December. By the new regulations the price of milk was fixed at a maximum of 2d. a quart above pre-war prices. In York, where there had been a milk shortage, the result of a lack of profitability at prevailing prices it was said, (3) milk had been retailing at 5d. a quart, and in some parts 3d. a pint. It was reckoned that this would be the new price; the 'accommodation milk' could be more. This was what a customer bought over and above his or her normal regular daily supply.

Some of the price rises of 1916 were caused by shortages due to the crippling of overseas supplies, the rise in freight charges, or the inability of local producers to maximise production through labour shortages. The government reacted by introducing regulations about how much one could eat while dining out. The Regulation of Meals Order, 1916, issued by the Board of Trade in December, limited restaurant and hotel meals to either three courses (evenings) or two (other times). The *Press* reporting the order prophesised that a 'meatless' day per week was not far off, (4) a prophesy which was not all that clever as the Board of Trade had already issued an announcement saying it 'proposed shortly to make an order prohibiting the consumption of meat, poultry and game on certain days', and the King and the royal household had already set a trend by having two meatless days a week. George V's example regarding the giving up of booze had largely been ignored, but presumably it was hoped he would be followed this time. *The Daily Express* commented on these new regulations and others, which had come into force since the war started. (5)

> Prices of all commodities have risen to such an extent that the golden sovereign - or its paper substitute - has a purchasing power of 12s. 6d. or thereabouts. Milk threatens to become rarer and dearer and the same applies to eggs.
>
> The cause of all the changes of our daily life is the Defence of the Realm Act. Under its many regulations the free-born may not - among other things:-
>
>> Speak in a foreign language on the telephone.
>> Ring church bells after sundown.
>> Whistle for a taxi-cab after 10 p.m.
>> Treat a friend to a drink.
>> Travel alone in a railway carriage over the Forth Bridge.
>> Use a camera or make a sketch in a "prohibited area".
>> Post British newspapers to neutral countries except through approved agents.
>> Push a handcart without showing a white light to the front and a red one to the rear.
>> Row or sail in a pleasure boat further than a mile from the coast.
>> Keep a fragment from a Zeppelin bomb as a souvenir.
>
> ### NO MORE WHITE FLOUR
>
> These are some of the things we may not do. In a few days other additions will be made to our war-time commandments - for example, it will be criminal to use "white" flour.
>
> Prohibited imports make a very long list. Here are some of the items:-

Furniture.	Motor-cars.
China and crockery.	Matches.
Gold.	Bulbs.
Tobacco.	Toys.
Jewellery.	Soap.
Silver.	Preserved fruits.
Cutlery.	Musical instruments.
Playing-cards.	Beer.
Wearing apparel.	Diamonds.

    The *Express's* reference to white flour referred to the end of what the *Times* called the traditional 'porcelain white' loaf, an item of great importance to the working class. The Milling Order, 1916, gave the percentages of flour which had to extracted from wheat of various qualities. It came into force on 27 November and 'on and after January 1st, 1917, only flour milled in accordance with the schedule [could] be used for making bread or any other article of food'. (6) Henceforth Brits would only eat what was known as the 'national' or 'standard' loaf, and the schedule referred to ordered that 76 per cent of flour had to be extracted from English wheat and percentages from 73 to 78 per cent from others. Prior to the order the country had been addicted to a '70 per cent loaf', and in earlier times an attempt to dilute or change it could (did) lead to serious rioting.

    The U Boat menace was increasing towards the end of 1916, and was to get much worse, (7) and the new British government (8) set about increasing home production of foodstuffs. The Cultivation of Lands Order of January 1917 empowered county war committees to insist on the breaking up of suitable grassland (without the right of appeal). Under the Defence of the Realm Act powers were taken to set up allotments and there was a phenomenal increase in them with the number of plots rising to 1,400,000 in 1918 as against a pre-war figure of 530,000. (9) The benefits of having a small plot of land to a family are perfectly obvious, and in most towns and cities a movement began which was akin to the 'Dig for Victory' campaigns of the Second World War. In response to appeals from the authorities the NER, for example, made land available to add to the stock of allotments that already existed in York. (10) In many places like Filey and Leeds councils acted on the order of the Board of Agriculture and Fisheries and ordered that golf courses be turned into allotments, and in York the Parks and Small Holdings Committee set about creating allotments in several places in the city, including Heworth, Holgate and Hob Moor. (11) They aimed to create something like 417 units and by the beginning of 1917 had invited applications for them and had received well over 200. The holdings were to be let for ten shillings a year and a condition of a tenancy was to be that at least two-thirds of the holding had to be given over to the growing of potatoes.

The creating of allotments was a sensible way of helping the war effort and coming to terms with rising prices, but in themselves they could not have produced anywhere near enough to compensate for the rise in the cost of living. It was essential that wages went up, and they did so in the second part of 1916, without any industrial disputes of any consequence in York. Perhaps increased profits persuaded employers to give in readily to the demands that were put to them, or perhaps employers simply realised that wage increases were justified (and that refusing them could be dangerous and lead to allegations of profiteering and worse). Anyway in York wages went up in 1916. In August the railwaymen (nationally) put in a claim for an extra 10s. a week (12) and in September the famous Tom Mann was in York addressing them, supported by Farrar of the Railway Clerks' Association, H. Bagshaw, W. Hallaways and W. Powell of the various York branches of the NUR. Their greatest concern these men told their audience, was rising prices and profiteering, and they demanded regulation of food prices. With what looks like awful predictability the railwaymen got 5s. (13) Also in September Oscar Rowntree, chairman of the Watch Committee, moved a resolution in the city council increasing police pay by 3s. a week for those getting 30s. and under (excluding the war bonus) and 2s. a week for those getting more than 30s. (14) Wages at Leetham's were reported in October 1916 to have gone up by 5s. a week since the outbreak of war, (15) and Rowntree's workers got increases that meant that the minimum wage there for a married man was henceforth 30s. (16) In December wages for York tramway workers went up by 1/4d. an hour for a standard 53 hour week, (17) and during the year the minimum wage for women working on munitions had been advanced from £1 to £1. 5s. (18) The agricultural labourers, always at the bottom of the pile, would have regarded some of the wage rates quoted above as handsome. True they could 'obtain' a few extras without much fear of being caught, but their scarcity had not increased their lot by much if 'A WORKER'S WIFE' is to be believed. She wrote a letter which was published in the *Herald* on 5 January 1917, and in which she attacked the farmers and stated some obvious truths. The farmers, she wrote, 'wish to obtain the best possible prices for their foodstuffs', while their workers

> have the least possible wages. It is ... not surprising that so many men left the land in the early days of the war, as the farm workers are the very worst paid. What encouragement is there for a man with a family to work seven days per week for 21s. to 22s. Taking into account the increased cost of living since the commencement of the war, I think it is high time someone saw to the farm workers' wages as I consider them starvation wages.

(In February a scheme was produced which gave agricultural labourers a legal minimum wage of 25s.)

A group of people who received a wage increase, or an increase, around this time were the wives of servicemen. Now it is perfectly true that some firms - some have been mentioned in these pages - 'made up' servicemen's wages, and presumably some if not all of this went to their families. But many firms did not do this, and many men left (relatively) well paid jobs to join the services. Their wives were paid separation allowances, and these went up at the turn of the year, but left them badly off indeed compared with pre-war years. The new rates were given in (for instance) the *Herald* of 12 January 1917

	Old	New
Wife	12s. 6d.	Same
Wife and one child	17s. 6d.	19s. 6d.
Wife and two children	21s. 0d.	24s. 6d.
Wife and three children	23s. 0d.	28s. 0d.
Wife and four children	25s. 0d.	31s. 0d.

Many servicemen made allowances from their meagre wages to their wives and mothers, so for many that amount would have to be added to the figures given above. But presumably some did not, and some wives, unable to go out to work, must have been extremely hard put to make ends meet. Many wrote to the papers saying so. The *Herald* of 12 January contained many letters from soldiers' wives and on the 25th the same paper had another from a lady who said she had no children and received only 12s. 6d. a week. When her rent and gas bills had been paid, she said, she had 4s. left. She added that before he joined up her husband (who if she was telling the truth kept all his army pay) had been earning £2. 5s. a week. Another letter writer to the *Herald* (12 January), who was not a serviceman's wife, wrote of rents and included remarks which show how potentially dangerous the gulf emerging between those 'doing well out of the war' and those being left behind by inflation could be if it developed. She voiced the thoughts of many when, after saying she paid 9s. for a six roomed house, asked: 'What a curious thing it is - those who have plenty of money and businesses are saving money, whilst the poor are only existing.' That the situation was potentially dangerous might be illustrated by events in and near Maryport. There demonstrators forced down the price of potatoes by demonstrations in the Christmas market and at Dereham a crowd lifted a whole field of potatoes (the farmer having said he would let them rot rather than sell at the current rate). This behaviour smacked very much of the riotous working class behaviour of the past, a fact which would not have been lost on those in authority. The Maryport scenes were repeated in Whitehaven a short time later. There the local bellman went round the town on the instructions of the local miners' union telling people not to pay more than a shilling a stone for potatoes, and enormous crowds, 'chiefly the wives of soldiers serving at the front, flocked to the market' and forced the

farmers to sell at a 'fair' price just like the crowds did in East Anglia (and many other places) a century before. One man who refused to sell was mobbed.

In a period of rapidly rising prices it might have been expected that there would be a great increase in local trades unionism, but there was little, almost certainly the result of the wage rises which have been mentioned. Nevertheless, a York branch of the Workers' Union was formed sometime in the summer of 1916, and in October it held a public meeting addressed by a Labour MP at which concern about rising prices was expressed. Prominent at that meeting was F.T. Beney, the conscientious objector, and Miss G. Pearson a local organiser for women. (19) Early in 1917 the annual general meeting of the National Union of Gas Workers heard W. Shilleto report that it had enrolled 1,523 new members during the year and they had a membership of 3,550 (1,519 of whom were in the forces). (20) Clearly the government had to be very careful that prices did not rise in such a way that it could provoke industrial troubles. 1917 was to see many innovations that had that as at least a major motive behind them.

What was the standard of living like for families in York at the end of 1916? It is relatively easy to compare wage rates with prices and rents, but this does not tell the whole story as there was clearly overtime that would be and was worked - though with a basic week of something in excess of 50 hours the amount of overtime that could be worked was limited. There was now virtually full employment (21) for both men and women and for many workers from away there were living allowances. For many there seems little doubt that things were somewhat better than they had been before the war, but there were still many who were low paid and for whom there could have been few luxuries. Thirty shillings seems to have been the top wage for many (for a basic week) and prices were going up continually as has been said. The *Press* on Sunday 24 December gave a report on preparations for Christmas which leaves no doubt that belts were having to be tightened in many households, and in that report facts were given about what that third wartime Christmas was to be like. Shopkeepers unanimously agreed that 'sales were not up to the standard of previous years, owing, of course, to the increased cost of commodities', and for the third year 'the gorgeous' shop window 'displays ... of pre-war days [were nowhere] to be found.' Christmas cards, however, were greatly in demand, and the munition girls 'spent money somewhat freely'. Prices at the York provision market were given at some length (butter 2s. 4d. to 2s. 6d. a pound; chickens 3s. to 5s.; wild duck 2s. 6d.) and it seems that it was still possible to purchase items such as Almeira grapes, pineapples and Canary bananas, which seems rather odd.

In January 1917 the York Trades Council and the York Equitable Industrial

Society held a protest meeting in the city, which is worth mentioning because it was the first of its kind and shows again that inflation then, as now, was potential political dynamite. So far most of the labour movement had supported the war effort, but it looked as if rising prices might put a strain on that support and lead to questions about equality of sacrifice, fairness, profiteering and much more becoming important. J.H. Hartley told the meeting that he had attended a London conference of 'close on 900 delegates representing labour and Co-opration [sic].' He demanded the ploughing up and 'cultivation of hockey pitches, etc' and T.H. Gill wanted controlled prices and government purchase and retail 'of all imported foodstuffs' and much more. 'Mr. Gill said that if there was going to be a shortage of food ... the supplies should be distributed equally amongst all classes.' That seems reasonable.

The rising food prices, and the attempts to do something about shortages had an interesting side effect in York in that it brought Arnold Rowntree, once more, at least temporarily, back into the political life of the city. Since the war started Arnold had become an embarrassment to some of the Liberals because of his pacifist views, his stand against compulsion, and his support for the conchies. He was extremely unpopular for doing things he should have been given credit for, but in early January 1917 he got a platform which enabled him to make a speech which would not get him into trouble (a rare occurrence). Arnold spoke to 'A well attended meeting of the allotment holders connected with the Leeman-road and Acomb Adult Schools'. He extolled the virtues of allotments, said he hoped they would extend after the war, and revealed that the York Horticultural Association (23) had acquired more land in 'the Poppleton-road district, which was being laid out in 36 plots, all of which had already been applied for.'

The foregoing has concentrated on the workers of York and suggested that their condition was, well, precarious if they were on a basic week, or if they worked in a low paid job. But many businesses were booming and fortunes being made, a fact which would not have been lost on the likes of J.H. Hartley. Another indicator of prosperous times for some might be the number of bankruptcies in York. The Official Receiver in Bankruptcy's figures were revealed for 1916 early in the new year, and in one paper the headline under which they were given told all. 'EFFECT OF WAR ON THE TRADE. FEWER BANKRUPTCIES IN YORK' said the *Herald* of 6 January. A table showed the decline.

Year	No	Year	No
1909	34	1913	21
1910	25	1914	6
1911	19	1915	4
1912	19	1916	8

The early months of 1917 were taken up more and more by concerns about shortages and more and more government regulations were introduced to try to minimise wastage, increase food production and fix prices to stop trouble like that at Maryport and Whitehaven happening on an inceased scale. Early in the year there were rumours that the government was going to fix the price of potatoes, (24) and this led to wild fluctuations in price, some consumer resistance and nation-wide protests. In York the growers protested, but to no avail, and the Board of Agriculture duly pegged prices at between £8 and £9 a ton (depending on when they were sold). (25) The reason given for this by the President of the Board of Agriculture was that he wanted to stop gluts and encourage growers to produce other crops equally essential to the war effort. (The reason given to the York protest meeting was that the government wanted to supply cheap potatoes to munition workers earning high wages!) There were many other government moves into the market. The standard loaf of bread did not last very long, for example, and it was altered as early as the second week of January (and again at the end of February). Henceforth bakers had to add at least five per cent more of further milled wheat or something like barley flour. At the same time the price of chocolate and other sweet meats were regulated by price (3d. and 2d. an ounce), and it was forbidden to feed wheat to animals or game. Sugar was forbidden for covering the outside of cakes, pastry or similar articles and it was decided that chocolate manufacturers could use no more than 50 per cent of the sugar they used in 1915. (26) By the Brewers Sugar Act of 1917 it was ordered that all brewer's sugar had to be delivered into a warehouse, while the Dealings in Sugar (Restriction) Order restricted dealing outside the UK. In January and February the army requisitioned animal feed at various places in and around York - to the intense annoyance of the owners - and at about the same time 'drink' was clobbered again.

There had been a duty put on beer as early as November 1914, and its production was limited two years later. By the Output of Beer (Restriction) Act (27) breweries were ordered to restrict their output by 15 per cent compared with 1915 or, if they used a different datum line, 30 per cent. What would be the effect of this ? The secretary of the Licenced Victuallers' Protection Society of London was in no doubt. He reckoned that the prices would go up to 4d. a pint for mild (compared with 2d. in 1914), bitter would go up to 5d. (it was 3d. in pre war days), and old beer would be priced at between 6d. and 8d. (29)

Raising the price of beer (the restrictions would clearly have this effect) was done partly to raise revenue, and cutting down its quantity was done to release barley for other purposes. Raising the price, it was also hoped, would decrease drunkeness and the consequent absenteeism. What was York like in this respect in the third year of the war ? The Brewster Sessions were held in February (as they had to be) and after it was revealed there that there were now 36 clubs in the city and one pub to each 278 persons, (31) it was also recorded that York had dropped to seventh place in the national drunkeness league table (from second). During the year 115 persons had been convicted for drunkeness; that was 171 down on the previous year and 164 below the average for the last five years. The number of women in that total, however, had gone up. There were still those who wrote to the *Press* saying women married to soldiers spent their separation allowances in the boozers, and the figures given to the 1917 Brewster Sessions would have convinced them they were right.

The dissatisfaction with inflation, the concern about profiteering (real or imagined) and the unequal sacrifices being made for the war effort clearly indicate that war weariness was setting in. That process could not have been helped by a couple of incidents in York early in 1917. Col Meysey-Thompson could always be relied upon to fire off a blast at 'shirkers', 'conchies' or other favoured targets for the jingo merchants, but in February it was revealed that he had refused to give up some of his land for the war allotments which were considered so important. (31) Why ? Because the land was used for grazing for cows, he said, and his explanation satisfied Wilf Horsman, one of the few politicians who did his best to ignore the party truce on the council. (32) However Horsman made enquiries and found that the cows there supplied but one household (Meysey Thompson's presumably) and the owner was shown saying one thing, doing another. This could not have been good for morale, labour relations or anything else.

So discontent, albeit contained by wage increases and some price fixing, was kept in check. But what about hostility to the war as such - rather than hostility to the way it was being conducted ? The emergence of a new government at the end of 1916 which immediately set about organising affairs in a 'businesslike' way would have helped the authorities, but were the critics of the war *per se* still active ? They were. Were they active, still, in York ?

The York ILP was still implacably opposed to the war and it continued throughout 1916 to hold public meetings at which it said so, but its most prominent members were being picked off and appearing before the tribunals and in court as conchies. Much of its energy went into helping objectors, but its message was put before the York public on a regular basis through those meetings and letters to the *Press*. Few took any notice, it seems but the party carried on its activities in York unhampered by the police as far as one can tell. The Union of Democratic Control also remained as active as it had been. In July a public meeting was held which was addressed by Fred Jowett who denounced secret diplomacy (33) and later the well-known Edgerton Wake of Barrow was invited to York. (34) F.E. Pollard was still secretary and perhaps S.H. Davies was the UDC's most prominent local member. The latter took part in a peace meeting held at the New Year called by the NCF, the Fellowship of Reconciliation and the Young Friends. (35)

There had been numerous attempts to end the war by diplomatic methods, including some by President Wilson of the USA, but they had come to nothing. In December the Germans, in a vague document, proposed a peace conference, a move that was in part an attempt by the German Chancellor to stave off all-out submarine warfare. On 30 December the Allies rejected the German demands, but the situation was complicated by another intervention by Wilson, now re-elected to office, who wanted all the belligerents to state their war aims. Opinion in York was overwhelmingly on the side of the Allied governments. The Archbishop denounced the peace proposals in the Minster and the Rev William Watkinson denounced them from the pulpit of Centenary Chapel in a sermon from the text 'Be strong and of good courage; be not affrighted, neither be thou dismayed; for the Lord thy God is with thee withersoever thou goest.' (36) Watkinson opined that 'in the year that dawned our flag would be borne to victory', while the Archbishop spoke of there being a 'bad will' abroad 'a will to war, strong and unbroken. Peace arranged with that will unconquered', he went on, 'would not be peace but an armistice in the war, a breathing space to enable the bad old spirit to recover its strength and to watch for its chance.'

S.H. Davies took a very different view from that of the Archbishop, and many others. He was the main speaker at the peace meeting and told his listeners that the German overtures were 'a genuine cry for peace' and that 'A new Germany was coming, lean in body, but active in mind, prepared to question the policy of her leaders.' The German Chancellor's views were in the ascendant, he said, and we should react favourably to his approaches. He was wrong. The war lords, whatever he thought, still dominated Germany, and in the not very distant future they would prove that by unleashing unrestricted submarine warfare.

Davies was supported on his peace platform by Arthur Dearlove, a representative of the Leeds YMCA, F.L.P. Sturge and the Rev H. Brett. The latter said he had accepted the chair for religious motives, and he suffered for it. Can we wonder that our congregations are dwindling when they have ministers such as Henry Brett, one asked. (37) 'This man', he went on, who 'not so long ago was throwing out sneers and insinuations against the soldier in training in our city, (38) now turns his venom against politicians, and ... vows he will never have anything to do with politics again. Really this is a blessing for all political parties ...' (39) An idiot who wrote frequently to the papers as PHRENO (he refused many times to give his name) also attacked Brett in the usual jingoistic way, quoting scriptures and accusing people who did think as he did of being deluded. Just a month after his letter was published the most famous 'peace crank' of the 1914 war appeared in York. This was Bertrand Russell 'the notorious U.D.C. apostle and advocate of a "German peace"' who spoke at the Cooperative Hall under the auspices of the York ILP. Russell's lecture title was 'Individual Liberty and Public Control', and his chairman was S.H. Davies. (40) Later the famous J.A. Hobson appeared in York. Hobson shared a platform with Theodore Rowntree after the Allies had rejected the German peace overtures, and well after the commencement of unrestricted submarine warfare.

Davies, Dearlove and their colleagues put forward their peace ideas, but got nowhere, indeed they may well have had the opposite effect to starting a grass roots demand for a negotiated peace. They gave their opponents an opportunity to denounce them as cranks and traitors, and their opponents did so at every opportunity, usually on the abysmal level that Phreno did. When Davies and Russell both took their meetings, moreover, they did so during a campaign which brought patriotism to the fore again and was, it must be admitted, a great success. This was the period when the great war loan was raised and war savings committees were established in workshops, schools, indeed everywhere. Working class people were persuaded to buy (15s. 6d.) savings certificates on a 'coupon system' (41) and in February 1917 there were no less than 96 war savings associations in York. (42) How the very poorest managed to contribute it is impossible to imagine. Perhaps the kids of 1914 suffered the same as did some of their children in the Second World War. Classes in at least one village school began with 'national savings', when the kids from 'better off' homes would proudly go to the front to make their contributions to winning the war. The embarrassment of those who never took those steps to the front was dreadful.

It is strange to see the war savings movement prospering when shortages and high prices were beginning to cause concern, but run together they did. The intense campaign for war savings came to an end eventually, of course, but the price rises continued, and the shortages got worse. There was a world wide deficiency of potatoes as the result of poor crops, and frosts in Britain made matters worse. The city rates went by (by 5d.) (48) and every day the *Press* carried reports of more and more price hoiks. It must be said, though, that more and more prices were also fixed. In March, for example, Lord Derwent announced the pegging of retail figures for tea and coffee. (44) When announcing the increase in rates Sykes Rymer referred to the fact that it would be a 'great shock' as much council work was in abeyance and Alderman Walker spoke of the potential dangers that ever increasing prices could bring. '... the citizens were up in arms', Walker said, 'They were at the present time having to pay increased taxes, food prices had gone up, trade was bad in the city, and it was now proposed to increase the rates.'

One of the reasons put forward, quite reasonably, for the increased rates in York were the higher wage bills the Council (and the other rate levying authorities) had to meet. Police salaries had gone up, it will be recalled, and just after the 1917-18 rate was levied, Chief Constable Burrow's annual report for 1916 was published. What did it contain ? Had York changed much since his report for 1915 ? The authorised strength of the York force was '109 officers and men', and 41 had joined the Army and 39 attested under the Derby scheme. Constables Mason and T.C. Fineson had been killed in action. York had 82 'specials' and arrangements involving them when an emergency occurred had been perfected. The cost of the police department in the year ending 31 March 1916 was £13,771.15s.10d. (45)

Burrow spoke of York's darkened streets lending 'assistance to wrong doers' then went went on to give the city's crime figures (those for drunkeness have already been mentioned). In the year, he said, '351 crimes were reported to the police and 208 persons were proceeded against, which is 78 above the average for the past five years, while the number of persons proceeded against is 41 above the average.' Burrow detailed the offences which were committed for trial and tried summarily. 'Of the 194 tried summarily', he went on, 'nine were sentenced to various terms of imprisonment, 26 fined, eight committed to reformatory schools, seven whipped, and 24 discharged.' There were 1,287 persons proceeded against for non indictable crimes (965 males and 322 females). There had been an alarming increase in the amount of juvenile crime in the city.

The increase in juvenile crime had been the concern of a conference held in the Mansion House at which W.F.H. Thomson, a local magistrate presided, and which was attended by, among others, Mrs G.M. Trevelyan, the wife of the famous historian. She advocated the creation of 'Playing Centres' and told the conference of the success which had followed the setting up such places in London. ('When bigger boys were drawn into a centre ... "Black Hand" and "Clutching Hand" gangs disappeared with amazing rapidity, and the establishment of playing centres certainly imbued the world with a spirit of joy.') S.H. Davies and Mrs Edwin Gray wanted them set up in York immediately, but C.E. Heard of the Central YMCA spent his address talking about the causes of juvenile crime and said he thought it was the result of 'the removal of personal influence, whether in home, school, church or club.' What about the cinema which had received so much blame for juvenile misdeamenours ? It was 'a waste of breath to talk about cinemas doing so much harm', Heard concluded. 'Rightly used, the cinema was a most instructive' and useful instrument. Bert Rutter would have undoubtedly agreed.

Juvenile crime was the kind of issue that could once guarantee a letter or two from Edith Milner, but this time she did not give York the benefit of her views. She was now 72 years old, as active and reactionary as ever, and still a prolific writer to the *Press*. But now she stayed on safe ground. Perhaps the drubbing she got when she entered the fray over the conscientious objectors taught her a lesson. Anyway, Edith was then devoting her time to collecting eggs for the wounded soldiers in York - and then publishing her own efforts by writing to the papers about it again, and again, and again. There must have been more letters about egg collecting published in York than anywhere else in the country, perhaps more than everywhere else put together. And they were nearly all from Edith. Just occasionally, however, she still made a foray into other areas. The York magistrates were frequently criticised for being too lenient with their customers, and almost as frequently criticised for being too harsh. On one occasion they were considered to have been too heavy-handed when dealing with a lad who had swiped a banana (or some bananas), and his case became the subject of many letters to the papers, including one from Miss Milner. With awful inevitability the lad was nicknamed 'The Banana Boy' and it is hoped that he was able to look after himself, because his mates would not have let that go unnoticed. One wonders if he kept his nickname for the rest of his life, and if his experiences turned him to crime, or religion, maybe ? But speculation on such fascinating subjects is not rewarding, and in any case the rather less sophisticated boys of 1917 were uncorrupted by watered down Freudian psychology and pop sociology, as those of the 1990s are, and they may not have seen much wrong with being called 'The Banana Boy'.

The Banana Boy had a way of coming to terms with shortages, and one that was increasingly resorted to in York, as Chief Constable Burrow pointed out, but it was not one that could be used by all. What could be done to ensure that what there was to eat was equitably distributed ? The matter became more and more pressing as the U Boat sinkings went up and as Sod's Law came into play. There was already a potato shortage, as has been mentioned. Bad weather then made matters worse, there was some holding back of supplies, (46) and by Easter there was a complete shortage, with dreadful snow storms over the holiday period making matters even worse.

The first thing that people could do in situations like that of early 1917 - when prices were fortunately fixed - was to look for substitutes and this is what happened as far as potatoes were concerned. A minor if short-lived revolution took place in the nation's eating habits. In Germany, in one dreadful year of the war, shortages led people to look for substitutes for staple foods and there occurred what is, and was, known as the 'turnip winter'. In 1917 British people also looked for substitutes for the humble potato and took to eating swedes. In mid March it was not only recorded that the supply of potatoes would be non existent from May to June, but that swedes were being bought as an alternative food - and that they had already gone up in price. At that time they were selling at 7s. a bag (whatever that was) compared with 1s. 6d. a bag a year earlier, and a producer who had been selling half a ton each three weeks, a year earlier, was then selling two tons a day. (47) In York supplies of potatoes were exhausted around All Fool's Day. (48) (The issue of the *Herald* which reported that fact also recorded that, as was expected, the price of beer was going up in Northumberland and Durham - to 7d. a pint - and of course York followed suit very shortly.) (49)

Critics of 'the trade' would have had a ready answer to the toper who complained of price increases and possible shortages - they would have recommended abstinence - but the shortage of potatoes had an interesting, and alarming side effect. The shortage of potatoes led to an increase in the consumption of bread, just when Britain's grain ships were being sunk at an unprecedented rate. Figures released by the Food Controller made the point. According to him the pre-war consumption of bread per head per week had been 5 lbs 6 ozs.; in March 1917 it was 6 lbs. (50) He wanted it brought down to 4 lbs.

How could the consumption of food be reduced and made more equal? An obvious way was by instituting a system of rationing, but was this possible ? The answer is that, given the presence of many free trade Liberals in the government, given that rationing would take an enormous bureaucracy to make it effective, and given Britain's historical attitudes, it was not - at least not straight away. So there developed a situation which is in many ways analogous to the conscription controversy of 1916, with the Food Controller and others urging voluntary rationing, but threatening that if voluntaryism failed, compulsion (rationing) would be brought in. In many speeches at around this time, Lord Devonport made this threat, and it was made when the figures for bread consumption were issued. Unless consumption went down to 4 lbs a head, it was said, rationing would be brought in within six weeks.

Another way in which the problem of shortages could be tackled was to restrict more and more the production of 'luxuries' and this was done. A Food Order forbidding the making of muffins, crumpets and tea cakes for sale became effective from 21 April, for example. (51) Yet another way was to teach people to economise, and this was done too. The 'Eat Less Bread' campaign has been mentioned and it, if the figures are correct - and they seem to be - was remarkably successful. Nationally the consumption of bread went down dramatically, and it did so in York.

The Eat Less Bread campaign was taken over and run by the local national savings committees, fresh from their triumphs in the war loan campaign. W.A.

Forster Todd, the Lord Mayor, and the Archbishop of York made appeals for a voluntary curb on bread eating, and a York Food Control Committee was set up. (52) It leafleted the city with the appeal from Lord Devonport (53) and the Vicar of Heworth persuaded 90 per cent of the householders of Heworth to sign the King's Proclamation Pledge card. The powers that be in those days laid great store by 'pledges' and this one amounted to an undertaking that the signer would follow George V's example and cut down on bread. It was reported that for the week ending 2 June consumption in York had gone down to 3.01 lbs per head and that there had been no wastage of food. (54) A week later figures were produced which were equally impressive.

Persuading people to eat less bread was paramount in the campaign of 1917, but also important were attempts, first of all to provide meals cheaply, and secondly to teach people how to economize. In Leeds there had been set up what in the Second World War would have been called a British Restaurant, but was in 1917 called a Communal Kitchen. In May the Educational Settlement, (56) invited the Miss Lucas who was in control of such things in Leeds to lecture there. She had gained experience of communal kitchens as long back as 1870, when she worked in them during the Franco-Prussian war. (57) Miss Lucas' talk was well attended, and before she gave it, it had been decided to start a kitchen in York. (58) This was duly opened at 1a Clarence Street in May, and was an immediate success. (59 The speeches at its opening made it clear that it was a piece of wartime communal socialism, though its promoters would have alarmed to have been told so. The kitchen was to be efficient through the bulk purchase of produce, it was to use hardly any flour and provide no bread whatsoever. It was to be open from 11.45 to 2 pm and was to provide soups from 1d., fish and meat dishes from 2d., and puddings from 1d. A second 'British Restaurant' was opened by the Food Committee in July, housed at the Coffee House, Walmgate. It rapidly proved to be as popular as its predecessor.

The food campaign enabled Arnold Rowntree to make another appearance on a political platform in York. His wife had been present at Miss Lucas' lecture and shortly afterwards Arnold appeared on the same platform as J.G. Butcher. The latter gave a jingoistic speech full of information about the Huns and the U Boats, but Arnold dwelled on the events of the food campaign and drew attention to suffering in York and some of the consequences of recent decisions. Rising prices, he said, were making the plight of women relying solely on separation allowances, and the old, extremely difficult. He also revealed that the restrictions on the chocolate companies - denied their full sugar requirements - had led to people being paid off (presumably from Rowntree and Company). All had, fortunately, been able to get other employment. (60)

The communal kitchen was intended to demonstrate the merits of alternative or economical cooking, and hand in hand with that went instruction on how to economise. A splendid person called 'Miss Petty, the "Pudding Lady"' who deserves to be rescued from oblivion, gave lectures at the Girl's Patriotic Club beginning in March, (61) telling people how to 'make do' in those trying times and shortly afterwards the Food Control Committee began providing lessons and demonstrations in all of the York Education committee's ten cookery centres. At one of these the 'Hay Box' method of cooking was described in detail, evidence of the fact that a coal shortage was also expected. (62) At Dringhouses a Women's Institute came into existence with the avowed aim of eliminating waste (63) and a York Allotments Association was brought into being to get the ever increasing number of allotment holders the benefits of bulk purchase. Everywhere recommendations about alternative foods appeared. Swedes were sought after instead of potatoes, as has been mentioned, and imported beans and peas at pegged prices were recommended. A writer to the *Press* told readers how to make rice bread (though one would have thought this would have been in short supply) and sea gulls' eggs were highly recommended also. (64) War was declared on pests and both the Local Government Board and the Board of Agriculture suggested the setting up of rat and sparrow clubs with rewards to people taking in tails, heads and eggs from these enemies of the people (and recommending that they be destroyed immediately so that the enterprising could not resubmit them a second time). (65) In April a Food Control Order implemented both a meatless day and a potato less day. Henceforth customers in York pubs, hotels and inns were unable to get meals containing meat on Wednesdays and potatoes on any day except Wednesdays and Fridays. (66) To back up all these measures malefactors were taken to court and profiteers exposed. (67) The first prosecution for selling potatoes over the fixed price was reported in the middle of June. (68) The offender shall remain anonymous.

The Eat Less Bread campaign of the first half of 1917 was an incredible success. The nation had its back to the wall, the U Boats were at their deadliest and, although there were some British military successes, (69) it was obvious to all that the country was in dire straits. So 'the people' rallied round and displayed a fortitude and a determination to put up with inconvenience and shortages that is reminiscent of 1940. There were no anti German demonstrations in York, though Rhodes Brown still kept on about 'aliens' trading in the city, but one person, who undoubtedly ate less bread, wrote to papers saying that the name of a city street should be changed forthwith. He wanted Hungate (and some other places) renamed to avoid for all time the dreaded name Hun appearing in Old Ebor. (70)

The community efforts of 1917 were impressive, yet the picture of the nation solidly working together for victory and putting up with shortages is spoiled somewhat by the response it gave to another essential scheme of these months. More women had been set to work on the land, German prisoners of war had been set to work there also, and women, more and more, were taking over jobs in the towns. Yet still the Army needed more men. The calling up age was raised, there were innumerable 'comb outs', the medical standards were lowered, and the nation took a second look at men who had been rejected earlier. (71) In addition to all the foregoing the National Service scheme was started, presided over by a famous local politician who was eventually to become Prime Minister. This was Neville Chamberlain, and it is the response to this scheme which spoils that picture of 1917 somewhat.

Neville Chamberlain had been Lord Mayor of Birmingham and, in the words of one of his early biographers, as he was 'pitch forked into a position in which proper provision had not been made for fundamentals, his failure was inevitable.' (72) He became Director of National Service. His task was to persuade people to register for national service, then allow themselves to be sent to jobs to replace men who could be released for military duties. But, as with rationing, and military service, and for the same reasons, the government did not insist on compulsion, or 'industrial conscription' as it was always called. Conscription at one go would have been too much for many of Lloyd George's Liberal colleagues, and the labour movement was bitterly hostile to the idea. One of the York branches of the National Union of Railwaymen for example protested vehemently at any suggestion of conscription for industry. (73) Lloyd George said in his memoirs that labour's attitude was a main reason for not insisting on it - that and the volume of work that would have been involved in implementing it.

A huge advertising campaign was started on behalf of the national service campaign, conducted, incidentally, against a background of serious labour troubles amongst the engineers, though not in York. The York papers carried large advertisements appealing to people to register, and in March a 'National Service Week' was held to which the city's politicians - with the notable exception of Arnold Rowntree - contributed. In the cinemas a film called 'The Call to the Land' was shown at performances at which people like C.E. Elmhirst, the Tory party chairman, and C. Kirby, (74) the curator of the city art gallery spoke. Sir John Grant Lawson was another who took part. (75) J.G. Butcher was an enthusiast.

Chamberlain was not a success in his new job, and the national service scheme was reckoned to be a failure. The director went back to municipal politics and henceforth he and Lloyd George were bitter political enemies. No wonder. It is alleged that the Prime Minister called Chamberlain 'a pinhead', which is not very nice. The scheme called forth 3,000 emplacements at a cost of £60,000 spent publicising it, according to a statement of 17 April. An investigation showed that from its inauguration to 1 August 1917 the Department of National Service had spent £192,709, of which about £87,000 had gone on publicity. The return for this outlay was the placing in employment of 19,951 men and 14,256 women, the distribution of 68,595 soldiers and civilians for agricultural work, and the discharge of certain arrangements with regard to part-time work. (76) The scheme nationally was a failure, and it was a failure in York.

The National Service campaign failed in York and so did its football club; the club which had been opened with all those optimistic forecasts for the future such a short time ago. It was hit, of course, by the cessation of professional football (the situation in 1917 was bad enough for there to be a proposed total ban on horse racing) and in July the Official Receiver made a winding up order on the club. Published figures showed that it had regularly made a loss and that at the time of the order was made it had liabilities, apart from share capital, of £2,583. 13s. 10d. and assets of only £631. 14s. 2d. The receiver blamed the club's troubles on the extravagant payments it had made to players, and one of the petitioners (on behalf of the landlords) was that C.E. Elmhirst of the Tory party and the National Service campaign.

The day on which news of York City Football Club's demise was given to the inhabitants of York was the third anniversary of the outbreak of war, and this gave rise, naturally, to a resumé of the conflict so far and its impact on the city. The *Herald* said that estimates of enlistments for it, exclusive of garrison troops, many of whom had died at Mons, varied between 5,000 and 8,000. Much more exact were the figures of the fallen, and to date 591 had died. The *Herald* paid much attention to voluntary efforts and said that something like £25,000 had been raised for material comforts for the troops, by such organisations as the Comforts Fund run by the Lady Mayoress, the St John Ambulance Association, and the adult school movements. It also singled out the work of the YMCA which had a hut dispersing warmth and comfort on St George's Field and a bungalow at Fulford. This was all justified, and the efforts of the organisations singled out were impressive and laudable. The Girl's Patriotic Club might have merited a mention, however, and so too might the canteen run on the railway station, the scene of a very nasty incident at about this time. (79) The work of the Sphagnum Moss Collecting Depôt might also have been mentioned, and so too the establishment in Blossom Street whereat hospital supplies were made (the War Hospital Depôt). The VAD hospitals have been mentioned in these pages, and so too has the egg collecting by the redoubtable self-publicising Edith Milner. There were many activities of that kind carried on in streets, organisations, churches and chapels, which could also have been mentioned by the *Herald*, one of which was the York Stranded Soldiers Dormitories which put up stranded servicemen in the Assembly

Rooms and in 1917 provided bed and breakfast to no less than 28,322 persons. The *Herald*, too, might also have commented on that extraordinary allotments movement which, when it wrote, was just proving its worth and even having an effect on prices in the city. By the summer of 1917, there were 24 'groups' of allotments in York, with 2,300 allotment holders. It was calculated that 94 acres had been given over to the growing of potatoes, and that 1,000 tons of winter food would eventually be gathered in. (80)

When the *Herald* did its survey of three years of war home grown vegetables and fruit were available but, despite the optimism at the time of the Battle of Arras, and Third Ypres, the war did not look like ending and scarcely a paper was produced which did not contain details of yet another food order. These were invariably attacked by the sectional interests affected by them. The millers, for example, complained bitterly about the national loaf which, it was said, was causing severe stomach complaints, and the farmers were furious with a meat order. (They were annoyed at the price-level decided on, of course.) Protest meetings were held everywhere and the order was denounced in York, though not in quite such strong language as was used at Pocklington. There the meat order was referred to as the 'Greatest Scandal' of the war, which seems a bit of an exaggeration. (81)

Somewhat earlier in this text the various ways of combating the food crisis of 1917 were mentioned (economies, restraint, the abolition of waste, alternative foods, increased production) but there was another which was also mentioned - rationing. Continual threats were made that rationing 'might come', but that was regarded as unEnglish, undemocratic, indeed Russian, and Lord Devonport in the House of Lords went right over the top when he declared that 'Compulsion would be a national calamity without first giving trial to a voluntary system.' So instead of rationing the government had controlled consumption (in public places), controlled production, controlled prices and exhorted people to economise. It had also subsidised production, (82) but all this was still not enough, and in August it was announced by Lord Rhondda that a measure of real rationing was to be introduced. 'Sugar cards' would be issued in October, he announced, and people would have to register with a retailer of their choice. Rationing of sugar would start on 30 December. (82)

1. *Press* 18 and 20 December 1916. Potatoes went up in December. *Ibid* 16 December 1916
2. *Ibid* 21 November 1916
3. *Ibid* 15 and 18 December 1916. But see Coun Horsman's letter alleging price rigging in *Herald* 18 August 1916

4. *Press* 6 and 19 December 1916. The order came in force on 18 December
5. Quoted *Herald* 19 December 1916
6. *Press* 21 November 1916. *Times* 20 and 21 November 1916. When the standard loaf 'came in' the *Herald* contended that the changes were minimal (as they were then) and hardly noticeable. See issue of 2 January 1917
7. The Germans declared unrestricted submarine warfare in February 1917
8. The Lloyd George coalition government had replaced that of Asquith in December 1916
9. G. Walworth, *Feeding the Nation in Peace and War* (1940) p 36
10. Eg *Press* 16 December 1916. One of the existing allotment areas was in the Bishopthorpe Road area. See the report of the annual meeting of the Bishopthorpe Road Allotment Holders' Association in *Herald* 5 January 1917
11. *Herald* 1 and 2 January 1917. *Press* 27 December 1916. For a 'progress' report on the getting of allotments see eg *Herald* 3 February 1917. Report of a meeting addressed by Councillor Horsman, K.E.T. Wilkinson, and T. Hargrave. Also report of the Council meeting of February. *Ibid* 6 February 1917
12. *Ibid* 14 August 1916. Mann's meeting reported in *Ibid* 11 September 1916
13. *Ibid* 25 September 1916
14. *Press* 12 September 1916. *Herald* 12 September 1916
15. *Press* 30 October 1916
16. *Ibid*
17. *Ibid* 27 December 1916
18. *Ibid* 29 January 1917. Speech by Coun Woods of Leeds. There is a nice little clanger in a booklet published by the College of Ripon and York St John on the history of the Fulford Road area of York. It is not obviously clear about what the author is writing, but it is the First World War period when, he says, (my italics) 'More than one family was investigated by the governmental Means Test. To qualify for aid, the family was only allowed to keep the absolute minimum of possessions ... sofas, easy chairs, *and a wireless* were considesed unnecessary luxuries and had to be sold.' A wireless would indeed have been a luxury in 1914-18. Van C.M. Wilson, *The History of a Community* (York 1985) p 22
19. *Press* 13 October 1916. *Herald* 13 October 1916. The Labour MP was Charles Duncan
20. *Press* 29 January 1917
21. The *Herald* carried its usual survey of firms at the end of 1916 and the beginning of 1917. It is disappointing in its scope
22. *Ibid* 6 January 1917
23. '... established some years ago'. *Ibid*
24. Not seed potatoes
25. *Herald* 3 February 1917. Also eg *Ibid* 18 and 22 January 1917. On the growers' protest see *Ibid* 15 January 1917. The regulation was by the Potatoes, 1916, Main Crop (Prices) Order. It regulated prices to the grower, the wholesaler and the retailer
26. *Ibid* 12 and 20 January 1917. The February Flour and Bread Order made it 'compulsory on all millers to extract not less than 81 per cent of flour. Admixture with some other substance is compulsory to the extent of an additional 5 per cent.' Rice, barley, semolina, beans and other items could make up the mixture. Just a little later another order forbade: the making of currant, sultana or milk bread; the sale of bread less than 12 hours old; the use of sugar; the sale of loaves other than those weighing one pound or an even number of pounds; the sale of bread rolls weighing other than two ounces.
27. 6 and 7 Geo 5 Chap 6
28. The two datum lines were 31 March 1916, and 30 September 1914
29. *Herald* 26 January 1917
30. Figures based on the 1911 census figures. There were 296 outlets
31. Others did so too. A Miss Barstow for example. The freemen of Low Moor also refused. *Herald* 28 February 1917. Meysey Thompson's land was eventually commandeered. *Ibid* 20 March 1917
32. *Ibid* 6 February 1917
33. *Ibid* 18 July 1916
34. *Ibid* 28 September 1916
35. *Ibid* 1 January 1917

36. *Ibid*. Wakinshaw spent most of his time it should be said attacking 'drink'. He got clobbered for this in many letters in the *Press*. He made a comeback in a sermon in February. See eg *Ibid* 19 February 1917
37. *Ibid* 9 January 1917. Letter signed 'BRITON'
38. See earlier
39. *Herald* 15 January 1917
40. *Ibid* 15 February 1917. On J.A. Hobson's meeting see *Ibid* 24 March 1917
41. A stamp was purchased and stuck on a card until 15s. 6d. had been collected. It was then surrendered for a certificate
42. *Herald* 6 February 1917
43. Eg *Ibid* 3, 14, 20 and 22 March 1917. The increase put the York rates up to 8s. 4d. in the £, compared with 7s. 10d. in 1916-17
44. *Ibid* 17 March 1917
45. *Ibid* 28 March 1917
46. Under the price fixing arrangements the producers got more later in the selling year, and so had an incentive to hold back supplies into a 'better' selling period
47. *Herald* 16 March 1917
48. *Ibid* 2 April 1917
49. See the report of the LVA deciding to put prices up in *Ibid* 3 April 1917
50. *Ibid* 30 April 1917
51. *Ibid* 19 April 1917
52. *Ibid* 17 and 26 April 1917
53. He was replaced as Food Controller in June by Lord Rhondda
54. *Herald* 18 June 1917
55. *Ibid* 26 June 1917
56. In the 1980s
57. *Herald* 8 May 1917
58. *Ibid* 1 and 10 May 1917
59. *Ibid* 23 May 1917. On the second restaurant *Ibid* 21 and 26 July 1917. The Clarence Street 'communal' closed in December; at that time the place in Walmgate was profitable and serving 500 meals a day
60. *Ibid* 4 June 1917
61. *Ibid* 14 March 1917
62. *Ibid* 17 April, 12 and 18 May, 8 June 1917.
63. *Ibid* 3 May 1917
64. *Ibid* 12 and 17 May 1917. The national food companies rapidly latched on to the economy campaign in their advertising. See *Ibid*, for example, the advertisement in which Atora explains how to make dishes to take the place of potatoes, using rice, flaked maize, lentils and - of course - Atora block suet
65. *Ibid* 7 April 1917
66. *Ibid* 5 April 1917
67. A great deal of publicity was given to the activites of a dealer who was in the habit of going to Selby market, paying over the odds for eggs, taking as many as he could get, then flogging them to German prisoners of war
68. *Herald* 15 June 1917
69. In this period America came into the war and there took place the battles of Arras and Third Ypres. Both of these were hailed as breakthroughs, but achieved little. Third Ypres is better known as 'Passchendaele'
70. *Herald* 26 April 1917. There was a similar outcry in Pickering. See eg the letter signed, believe it or not, '(H)UNTROUBLED' in *Ibid* 13 July 1917
71. Through the Review of Exemptions Act
72. D. Walker-Smith, *Neville Chamberlain. Man of Peace* (nd) p 83
73. *Herald* 1 August 1917
74. Kirby had been having a lot to say about how the city should commemorate its dead
75. Eg *Herald* 24 March 1917
76. Walker-Smith *op.cit.* p 95
77. *Herald* 11 July and 4 August 1917

78. *Ibid* 4 August 1917
79. A major threw some hot tea or coffee over a private soldier, an incident which was reported in the papers and lead to a tremendous outcry. The matter was raised in the Commons, and was the subject of a letter by Edith Milner
80. *Herald* 23 July 1917. Report of the York and District Allotment Holders' Association prize giving. A good account of the work of the York Stranded Soldiers Dormitories can be found in an article and advertisements in *Ibid* 26 January 1918
81. *Ibid* 6 August 1917
82. The price of bread was kept stable by a subsidy when imports rose in price. It amounted to £60 million. A.J.P. Taylor, *English History 1914-1945* (Oxford 1965) p 78

CHAPTER 16

FOOD CONTROL AND THE END OF THE PARTY TRUCE

The party truce had held up well in York with only minor forays into forbidden territory. The ILP, of course, outside the city council, regularly and resolutely campaigned away and the UDC carried on its work, despite the bigots who demanded that it should be suppressed. On the council, however, there was little to disturb things, and in the autumn of 1917 the Lord Mayor (Forster Todd) and the Sheriff (C.W. Shipley) were elected yet again. These two, Tory Lord Mayor, and Labour sheriff (1) seemed to epitomise the fact that party politics were for the future - yet there had been signs of stress. Rhodes Brown had adopted the role of 'economiser' on the council and always opposed such things as wage rises, and this had given the likes of Will Horsman the opportunity to attack him as the party man he clearly was. There were also allegations that the Tories were packing committees, (2) and it was something like that which reactivated party politics in 1917.

In August 1917 the York Food Control committee was re-established under a new set of regulations, and from the very outset there was trouble, with the York Cooperative Society angry because it was not represented by a member. (3) This 'grievance' was aired at a meeting at which Shipley and the Lord Mayor were present, and in the three weeks or so before the next council meeting the labour movements held meetings to demand the Food committee's reconstitution, giving labour a majority representation - the argument being that it represented the majority of consumers in the city. The ILP raised its voice on the matter, and 16 organisations sent letters of protest to the council which was lobbied by a deputation from the Trades Council, (4) and from that moment on the committee was the centre of great political controversy.

The council rejected the attempt by J.F. Glew to substitute the names of C. Boyce, the tribunal member, J.H. Hartley and Mrs Jeannie Mercer for those of Rhodes Brown, Coun Bury and a Mrs Hope, who was a leading figure in the local SSFA. Labour maintained that the Food committee should be composed of consumers and not traders, while their opponents said that traders would be excellent administrators, but eventually agreed that no-one dealing in restricted goods should be a Controller. Rhodes Brown, as was his habit, was instrumental in turning the debate into a political one and protested vehemently that two of the petitioners were conscientious objectors and that Labour's lady nominee was the wife of one. (5) Jeannie Mercer's husband was indeed an objector and an NER employee who was also a councillor. He was also if not then, certainly a little later, the secretary of the York Labour party.

K.E.T. Wilkinson also tried to get York's Food Control committee reconstituted and three retailers were eliminated from it, including the York Cooperative Society's manager, and labour was offered five out of the 12 seats. This was not enough to placate the, by now reactivated, York labour movement, however. The Trades Council called on an existing labour member to resign and the Micklegate Ward Labour party protested against the composition of the committee. In October the matter came up again on the council. The three Labour men (Glew, Horsman and Boyce) had resigned, and it was revealed that no less than 13 protest meetings had been held during the previous week. The Corporation had flouted labour's legitimate demands, it was said, and Mercer said they would 'go to the people.' (6) His wife had been overlooked, with Rhodes Brown saying they did not want the wife of a conchie serving with them. (Shortly afterwards Rhodes Brown was elected as a York magistrate.) (7)

The Food Control committee began its work, but the row over its composition ran on. In a second meeting in October the matter was discussed in council again, when Sebastian Meyer called the committee 'middle class', which, then, it certainly was. (8) No agreement could be made, there was a heated 'debate' reminiscent of pre-war days, and it was decided that the Food Controller himself, no less, should arbitrate. In November he deliberated and Mrs Mercer, Glew, Boyce and A. Richardson joined the committee. A little later he agreed to enlarge the committee from 12 to 13 to allow a cooperator to join. (9)

It could be argued that labour's campaign had not been an overwhelming success as they ended up with five representatives on the Food Control committee out of 13, having been offered five out of 12 originally. Nevertheless, they had got Jeannie Mercer elected and had found an excuse, if they needed one, to become active again. From this point onwards, to the end of the war, the Labour party was a campaigning party, never questioning Britain's involvement in the war as the ILP did, but having a great deal to say about the conduct of it on the home front. There were other current issues which may in themselves have brought the party truce to an end as far as the Labour party is concerned, but it was the Food Control committee which in fact was the catalyst. That body, composed now of consumers, retailers who did not deal in regulated foodstuffs (with the exception of the Co-op representative) and local politicians, turned out to be an impressive body. It indulged in a bout of frenzied activity of 'war socialism', and seems to have been a force wholly for good. Rhodes Brown resigned from it as a protest against the membership of Mrs Mercer.

When the York Food Control committee had been reorganised, it had been as a part of a nationwide reorganisation. Regional directors had been created, with one at Leeds, and committees like that at York were set up under him. What powers had these local bodies ? They were empowered to organise supplies if necessary and could fix prices within their area, though they could not exceed the maximum figure fixed by the Food Controller himself - now Lord Rhondda.

There had never been anything like the York Food committee in York - but then there had never been a crisis situation like that of 1917/18. The papers kept telling their readers that the U Boats were becoming less effective, which they were, and that victory was just round the corner, which it was not, (10) but the food shortages got ever more acute. The York committee set about tackling them and in October fixed the price of meat in accordance with the Controller's instructions that retailers' profits should be limited to 20 per cent. (11) (The prices were regularly reviewed.) In late December Sir Arthur Yapp, the Director of Food Economy, visited York to help the work of the Food committee. He urged people to go out 'as "missionaries" of the potato' and urged the formation in York of a branch of the League of National Safety. He had earlier told the north of this organisation at a meeting at Keighley, and his reference to the potato indicates that the 1917 crop had been a good one and that a repetition of the shortages of earlier were not anticipated. (12) The Food Controller, in fact, started a campaign to persuade bakers to use potatoes in bread. (It became compulsory to do so in 1918.)

After Christmas the York Food Control committee became increasingly concerned about the inequalities of supply in the city. Margarine, in particular, was scarce. It was fixed by price but supplies were not getting round to all the shops, and there appeared in York a phenomenon hitherto unknown - the queue. People with time to spare were able to go round to various shops and get adequate supplies, while others, who perhaps relied on a slate with a shop which had no goods went without. What could be done ? The Food committee decided to appeal to the larger shops to distribute some of their margarine supplies to other shops in the city, but this met with great resistance, particularly from the Maypole Stores, which simply refused to cooperate. Given this situation the Food committee simply took over the city's supply of margarine, deposited it in the Guildhall, then redistributed it more equitably. (13) The Queue sub committee was reponsible.

The food situation deteriorated, and new restrictions were imposed daily. All breakfasts taken in public eating places were ordered to be meatless, and no glasses of milk were allowed to be sold with them. The York committee set about rationalising the transport of supplies and discouraged entertainments, then, at the end of January, it decided to set up a scheme of rationing. It had to receive the approval of the Food Controller, but what else could be done ? So far the poor had been protected by fixed prices, and regulations against hoarding, but there was nothing to stop those able to do so buying up to what reasonable limits were considered to be, and so depriving others. (14) Regulating what a person could purchase was the obvious answer - that and backing up the regulations by a vigorous persecution of wrong doers by taking them to court.

Sugar was being rationed nationally and consumers had to register with a supplier to whom they presented 'sugar cards', similar to the ration books of the Second World War. The process of registration for sugar had been going on in the last months of 1917, and the York Food Control committee decided to graft a scheme of further local rationing (15) on to what had already been brought into being. In February it decided that nobody should be allowed to have stored away more than a month's supply of tea, and that tea, butter, cheese, margarine, lard, bacon and ham but not meat (16) (which was about to be controlled nationally) should be rationed. How ? Each person would be entitled to, for example, one and a half ounces of tea for a week and four ounces of marge. (17) To get their rations consumers would be issued with five ration cards and would have to register with a retailer, but not necessarily the one they had signed up with for sugar, and they could in fact register with different suppliers for each of the restricted items. The legislation this was based on was the Food Control Committee's (Local Distribution) Order, 1917 and the registration was undertaken by York school teachers who did the work while their schools were closed. (18)

The York rationing scheme, which looks as if it could have been an administrator's nightmare, hit an early snag when Lord Rhondda refused to sanction it, saying that he preferred a 'one card' system to one involving five or six. (19) At the same time, it was viewed with some distrust by the York Labour party, the Cooperative Society and the Trades Council who demanded a system of compulsory, nationwide rationing. (20) Eventually the scheme was approved and got under way. The queues disappeared, it was said, and the Food Control committee undoubtedly did an impressive job in those early months of the last year of the war. It was a thankless task, yet the populace seemed to realise that it was a fair system which had been started. (21) Naturally there were continual complaints from traders, and complaints of anomalies as when, for example, Sheriff Shipley pointed out in March that German prisoners of war were getting twice the meat ration of an ordinary civilian. (22) It also decided to increase the number of communal kitchens in York, and an application was made to the council for a grant of £200 to help do so. (23)

As has been mentioned earlier the courts were to be used to back up the work of rationing, and quite frequently 'exemplary' sentences were passed on wrong doers. One of the first persons to be hammered was called John Thomas, who deserves a place in these pages for that fact alone. John Thomas was a metal refiner, not of York, who was given a sentence of £50 and six months in prison for hoarding. He appealed to the Walsall Quarter Sessions and had the prison part of his sentence quashed, but he probably had had his bag packed, given the climate of the time. (24) In York, at about the same time, David Keighley of Layerthorpe was done, the first person to get nicked under the Rabbit Prices Order. The maximum prices for rabbits had been fixed at 1s.9d. for a skinned creature and 2s. for an unskinned one. Keighley had charged a customer 2s.3d. and was fined 10s., and it served him right. (25) There were other prosecutions for overcharging, and yet more retailers or market traders were done for imposing conditions of sale. (26) In early January Liptons were prosecuted for selling coffee for 6d. a quarter, when the maximum permitted price was 4d., and for this a very heavy fine of £50 was levied. (27)

The very first prosecution by the York Food Control committee itself took place somewhat earlier, when Carl Wilfred Sorensen of the White Rose Dairy Farm of New Earswick was summonsed for selling milk above the fixed price. (28) The committee had pegged milk prices, at a level lower than that which prevailed at the time, on 1 October. This must have made the committee extremely popular and brought it public support (and it might also have drawn attention to 'profiteering'). On one day in November the York police court dealt with: Annie Bowness who had sold bread which had been baked less than 12 hours earlier; George Holmes of Micklegate, who had not displayed the prices of potatoes; and Robert West of Colliergate who had sold the same product over the odds. (29) Emma Knewshaw, a market trader who was very stroppy in court, was fined for selling a quantity of butter at above the permitted price (2s.5^{1}/2d. for what should have been 2s.5d.) (30) and in March the proprietor of the largest single shop in York was done for selling margarine to someone who was not registered with him. Laura Newton, a housekeeper at the York police station, went into William Banks' shop and purchased half a pound of margarine, though she was registered elsewhere. This looks a bit like a set up, and it could be argued that Laura was behaving something like an *agent provocateur*. However, as Percy J. Spalding who was prosecuting pointed out, rationing had only been in force two days. Banks, who said he was just off to France in some kind of advisory capacity, defended himself, saying the stuff Laura got was not marge for spreading on bread, but cooking marge, a 'cake compound' that was a substitute for lard of which he seemingly made and sold a quarter of a ton of a week. All to no avail. The beaks fined him £25. (32)

There were many other prosecutions by the Food Control committee for abusing the rationing system in some way or another. An almost random sample will give an indication of how complex it became before the war ended, with frequent price reductions, price rises, new additions to the ration lists, and trouble over substitutes. The whole system became even more complicated when it was decided that some groups within society qualified for increased rations with an appeal tribunal created to hear from dissatisfied persons. That started in April 1918 and a month later, on 10 May, the *Herald* reported the prosecution of Charles Frederick Crow, a butcher, for 'contravening the Meat Rationing Order of 1918 by selling a half pound of polony without the production of a meat card'. The local control committee had decided that polony could be sold at 1s. a pound and Crow had charged a customer the equivalent of 1s.4d. He was fined £10, and had to suffer an attack from the bench when J.H. Hartley said he would have clobbered him even harder had he had his way. Criticisms of the bench in York were never far away and it and Hartley were taken to task by many for this outburst. At the same sitting as Crow appeared, Jane Hubner of 50a Petergate was fined 5s. for selling tripe to someone without a ration card and John Heap was prosecuted for selling milk at $3^1/2$d. when the fixed price was 3d. Jane Hubner's offence, incidentally, would not have been an offence in York a week later, when the Food committee decided that offal meat (except tongue) was no longer part of the official ration, and that it could be sold without coupons. The *Herald* of 24 May received reports of profiteering in the sale of beef dripping and its price was fixed at a maximum of 2d. a pound. The issue of the same paper dated 6 June brought good news for some, when it announced that the six month ban on ice cream making had been lifted, and that henceforth merchants could make it out of sugar and milk substitutes, safe in the knowledge that they could not be hauled before the likes of J.H. Hartley .

The Food Control committee employed what seems to have been a husband and wife team of searchers, and these two would never have come top of any popularity poll conducted among the city's retailers. They were Mr and Mrs Pallister and the latter managed to get a warm loaf from Florence Wilson of Gillygate, for which she was fined 5s. A little later, as the *Herald* reported on 17 September, William Gray Whittaker of Clifford Street, chairman of the Bakers' Association was nicked and fined £20 and costs. There had been complaints in York about the national loaf and the Food committee had released extra white flour to improve it (it had been mixed with 'G.R.' flour). Whittaker had sold it on - an 'offence against the people.' Towards the end of the war A. Till of Hull Road was prosecuted for overcharging for four lots of blackberries. He was something of a persistent offender, having already been convicted of selling potatoes without displaying the official, fixed price and for unlawfully selling fruit. 'Till was obviously setting everyone at defiance' the chairman said when fining him £20 and costs. Till's offence was reported in the local papers on 27

September 1918, and Herbert Richardson's case was mentioned just three days before the war ended (8 November). Richardson was a market gardener and grocer of Baker Street, and he was fined £10 for using meal containing wheaten flour for feeding pigs, contrary to the Wheat, Rye, and Rice (Restriction) Order of 1917. Three weeks earlier (18 October) William and Mrs Harrison were fined £1 and costs for overcharging for damsons, in contravention of the Damson (Sales) Order, 1918. Their defence was that the fruit they sold were not damsons but bullaces, but expert opinion was produced to show they were Pinsen damsons, 'the best grown'. They had charged £2.17s.9d. for what should have been sold for 22s.6d. In November 1917 the Yorkshire Club had been fined. It had broken the conditions imposed on such places by the Public Meals Order, and the *Herald* (of 24 August 1917) told its readers that it had used too much sugar in catering for its members. The limit was two sevenths of an ounce per person per meal.

Just occasionally celebrities were prosecuted for offences against rationing when, of course, the papers went to town. Marie Corelli, as the *Press* reported on 2 January 1918, for example, was fined for using too much sugar and York's anti-Quaker factions must have rubbed their hands with delight when perhaps the most famous York Friend was prosecuted for using petrol contrary to the Motor Spirit (Consolidation and Gas Restriction) Order 1918 on 23 January of that year. The culprit was old Joseph Rowntree, no less, and he rendered himelf liable to a fine of £100, or six months, or both. He had been caught joy riding, an activity which had been banned on 31 October 1917, and the order under which he was prosecuted had 'come in' on 10 January. Joseph was lucky to get away with £5 and costs, and he really should have known better. Letters began to appear (for example in the *Herald* on 11 February 1918) asking why members of 'a certain family' were able to use their cars to take their children to school, when petrol was so scarce. It seems certain that this was a Rowntree family and using a car in this way (if they did) does have some semblance to a foot in the mouth action. Marie Corelli, incidentally, when she was done for getting too much sugar, somehow, engaged in a celebrated outburst in court which showed that she really rather over-estimated her importance. 'You are upsetting the country altogether with your Food Orders and what not', the author of *The Sorrows of Satan* told the Stratford on Avon bench, '"Lloyd George will be resigning to-morrow," [she added] ... "and there will be a revolution in less than a week."' She was wrong. (The thought that the English revolution could have started over Marie Corelli's sugar hoard is mind blowing.)

Prosecutions for hoarding were fairly common, though there were few in York to compare with that reported in the *Herald* of 10 March 1918, from Scalby. Mrs Margaret A. Thompson Pegge of the Laurels, a lady of 75, was prosecuted after a search of her house had revealed 60 pounds of sugar hidden away. She had not willingly cooperated with her persecutors and was fined £10, ordered to pay the costs, and made to forfeit the sugar. It served her right. The Rev Pearson, the vicar of Lockton, and his wife were also charged with hoarding, but they got off. This case is reported in the *Herald* of 14 May 1918 and they maintained that the hoard the investigators found at the vicarage had been left there by the previous tenants!

It was not always the purveyors of rationed goods who were prosecuted for selling over the odds, without coupons or for trying to impose conditions of sale. Just occasionally smart aleck purchasers were caught trying to buck the system. Thomas E. Chapman, for example, a locomotive driver, appeared in court on 27 May 1918, the first person charged with this particular offence. Chapman had 'unlawfully made a statement which was false in a material particular with a view to obtaining food under the arrangement for regulating its distribution or consumption contrary to the provisions of the Local Distribution (Misuse of Documents) Order, 1918.' Chapman had applied for his family's ration cards and had neglected to give the age of his child - with a view, the prosecution said, to getting it an adult ration. The case was proved and the defendant was fined £1.

Just as the Zep scares produced innumerable patent alarms, so the food shortages produced products which promised more than they could deliver. Proposals to add potatoes to the national loaf have been mentioned. There were other additives sold of a more dangerous kind. It was reported that the Health Committee of the local authority in November or December 1917 had caused the public analyst to examine a 'flour improver' which was on sale in the city, for example. The improver had been found to consist of ten parts ground rice and 90 parts Epsom salts, which seems like a pretty deadly mixture. (33) A 'bread improver' looked at at the same time was found to contain 'an excessive proportion of sulphate of lime.' These two concoctions look only slightly less dangerous than the quack medicines which still filled many of the advertisement columns of the papers. They look positively wholesome, however, when compared with what William Saxby sold to customers in the metropolis. Saxby was a milk roundsman who adulterated his milk with 'fouled water obtained from a public lavatory basin.' The following dialogue took place after the beak gave him two months with hard labour.

The prisoner: I will pay any fine you like. Can't you make it a fine ?

The magistrate: Certainly not. I only wish I could make it more.

The food shortages, and the composition of the York Food Control committee did much to reactivate the labour movement in York, but there were other factors doing so, and once the movement had found itself, as it were, it would not stop at one local issue. It say, much about the Labour party's attitude at that time that it chose a conchie as its secretary, and took up the case of the alleged maltreatment of another. Frank Higgins, a member of the Brotherhood Church, was, court martialled in December, then confined in the mental ward of the Fulford military hospital. He went on hunger strike and was forcibly fed for at least a fortnight. (34) The York Labour party protested against his treatment. In that same month it held a well publicised conference at which it demanded higher old age pensions (there were some modest increases), and earlier it had 'taken up' the case of Thomas Raftery (35) and had protested against the arrest of ex Private Charles James Simmons. He was a wounded soldier of the 3rd Worcestershire Regiment who was then regularly addressing 'peace meetings' and he had appeared in York at the invitation of the ILP. (36) He was causing great concern to the Home Office at that time, and was connected with an organisation whose title smacked of Bolshevism. This was the Council of Workers and Soldiers' Delegates. Simmons had been wounded in May 1916 and discharged in November 1917. In March of the following year, at York, he was charged with four counts of contravening the Defence of the Realm Act. He pleaded guilty and was sentenced to three months imprisonment and given a £25 fine. (37)

The York Labour party voiced concern about other matters, and there were yet more reasons for it becoming active again. One was that the end of the war did, genuinely, seem to be in sight and constitutional changes which were going on directed all the parties' sights on an election that might not be too far away. In these circumstances Labour chose a new candidate. Slesser had resigned as candidate in November 1916, 'owing to ill health' - a resignation which went practically unnoticed in the city. He was eventually replaced by T.H. Gill of the York Trades Council who was nominated by the Railway Clerks' Association. By this time the Labour party in York had become much more radical in its outlook and was more sympathetic to the objectors and, after the Russian revolution, much more willing to listen to and subscribe to the ideas of such bodies as the UDC. Only a week before he was elected Gill had presided at a meeting called by the Trades Council and the Labour party at which the aims and objectives of the Union of Democratic Control had been expounded. A Councillor Kneeshaw of Birmingham had denounced secret diplomacy, and was able to do so with much more effect than ever before. (38) (The two candidates Gill defeated to become York's Labour nominee were J.H. Hartley, who had been nominated by the ILP, and Walter Wood of Leeds, a nominee of the National Union of General Workers.)

The fact that a 'rival' organisation had made its appearance in York, was yet another reason for the Labour party becoming more active in 1917. The was the British Workers' League, an organisation which gets scant attention in labour histories, yet which was very important in its day. It was formed, with a different name, in 1916, and many politicians were associated with it - the most famous of whom were perhaps J. Havelock Wilson and James Seddon.(39) The BWL was set up to oppose what it said 'was the pacifist domination of the Labour party', was ultra patriotic, against a negotiated peace and for an economic boycott of Germany when the war ended. It became particularly active after the Labour party nationally adopted what was known as the Socialist War Aims Memorandum at a conference at Westminster. There Arthur Henderson, once a cabinet minister, sacked by Lloyd George, proposed the adoption of the memorandum, saying that war was 'the offspring of autocratic government and its issue - uncontrolled militarism and aggressive imperialism, working through the subterranean channels of secret diplomacy.' (40) The party, it said, should not necessarily support the prolongation of the war over, for example, Alsace and Lorraine. The memorialists wanted 'a settlement as soon as possible' and an approach to be made to the Germans. It was immaterial to the workers which set of capitalists owned the mines and industries of that area. (41) Henderson was bitterly attacked by Havelock Wilson who wanted to punish Germany. The ex cabinet minister was 'windy' Wilson claimed.

The adopting of the Socialist War Aims Memorandum and the condemnation of secret diplomacy brought the Labour party much closer at last to the ILP and the UDC and many rifts must have been healed at a local level. John Mercer as the York party secretary a few years ago would have been unthinkable; now there had been a coming together of the forces of the left, and the party truce was effectively over. At a conference of the national Labour party held in June it was officially ended. (42)

Faced with this swing towards considering a negotiated peace the British Workers' League became increasingly active, indeed Havelock Wilson seems to have become apoplectic. It appeared in York, representing itself as 'patriotic Labour's reply to pacifist attempts to use Labour's name.' (43) Early in February Havelock Wilson and the famous pre-war socialist, Victor Grayson, in the uniform of a private soldier in the New Zealand forces and carrying a wound stripe, addressed a 'patriotic meeting in York.' (44) Havelock Wilson was also accompanied on the platform by none other than J.G. Butcher and he laid about him with gusto attacking the Ramsay MacDonaldites, Arthur Henderson and the recent War Aims Memorandum, and the conchies and Russian and German Jews who had declared at a famous Leeds conference that they wanted the war to end with no annexations and no indemnities. 'Ending the war by negotiation with a murderer and burglar was a new principle altogether', said Wilson, 'and if we accepted such a principle we should stand condemned as a nation and the world would be doomed.'

By mid February there was a branch of the BWL in York, and, alarmed at the talk of peace, it and the Ligue Patriotique Des Alsaciens-Lorraine sponsored a lecture on the disputed provinces by O.P. Masterman-Smith. (45) John Lindsey, of Darlington, a former Labour candidate for Barkston Ash presided. He got very uptight about a resolution passed by the York No 1 branch of the NUR which had said, like Arthur Henderson, that it was not very concerned about whether German or French capitalists controlled Alsace and Lorraine. (46)

Little is known of the personnel and activities of the York BWL, though it seems certain that it did not do the Labour party there any good. That party and its associated organisations had, in fact, taken up an unpopular stance, and, perhaps influenced by events in Russia, was speaking in class war terms, in a way not heard in years. It did its long term prospects little good, for example, early in 1918. Great interest and enthusiasm had been shown throughout the country when 'Tank Weeks' were held to raise war savings. In these a tank visited the town and acted as a focal point and a bank, and a York Tank Week was held at which it was hoped a million pounds would be raised. Photographs of events during York's fund raising bonanza are some of the most frequent relics of the First World War to be found these days, but the Tank Week, was not supported by all sections of the community. The Trades Council, which had recently slated the government for its attacks on conscientious objectors, demanded 'proper' rationing, condemned birching, (47) and announced that it refused to be connected in any way with the Tank Week, believing 'that the wealth of the country, which is protected, should be conscripted to pay for the war.' (48) A couple of days later the Labour party passed a similar resolution - one which the *Herald* called contemptible. (49) John Mercer wrote to the *Press* about it, saying that he and his comrades believed 'that the conscription of wealth should have preceded the conscription of life, and not that those who possess wealth should risk nothing while the workers are called upon to risk the only thing they possess, namely, their lives.' Later the York Labour party objected to a proposal to confer the freedom of the city on Lloyd George. This, too, must have lost it votes among those who saw extremism everywhere, and a slight on the premier as good an indication of extremism as it was possible to find.

This was the language of the class war, redolent of what was coming out of Russia, and one would have thought that it was not likely to go down well in the early months of 1918. In March the Germans were to launch their last great offensive on the Western Front, yet here was the Labour party suggesting an approach to them and adopting attitudes which seemed to suggest, now, that it was less than totally enthusiastic about the war effort, and that it regretted having supported conscription. (50) Without any doubt the party's conversion was a genuine one, and led to unity on the left, but it has much of the appearance of it shooting itself in the foot. Perhaps the members considered that the nation was war weary and that the populace would support a radical left-wing programme. Perhaps they thought that events in Russia were the harbinger of a swing to the left. Perhaps they thought the nation was sick of bogus patriotism and would want a complete change from the parties and governments of pre-war days. If they did reason thus they were wrong. Their attitudes of 1918 helped their opponents who weighed in with charges that hurt. The *Yorkshire Herald's* editorial of 5 February showed that politics were once more 'on' in York. 'The Anti-Tank Bank resolution of the York Labour Party', it said

> following that of the York and District Trades and Labour Council, should be sufficient to make these Labour organisations stink in the nostrils of the general body of the citizens. It is not an enviable position for York to have had two such resolutions passed and trumpeted abroad by their authors as something to be proud of. In no other town or city which the Tanks have visited have such mean and contemptible resolutions been passed by any section of the several communities. Even on the Clyde, where there are acute labour difficulties, no such spiteful and wretched attempt was made to spoil the effort to raise money required for carrying on the war.

Alderman Rhodes Brown was not likely to miss an opportunity of knocking the Labour party for its refusal to take part in the Tank Week (and much more). He wrote to the *Press* attacking the 'un-English tactics of the York Labour party' and its secretary. John Mercer was pilloried for his pacifist views by Brown, one of the few members of the city council who wanted it to take part in a London demonstration which was to demand the interning of all aliens, (51) who also attacked Jeannie Mercer (again). Similar attacks were launched by others on the Trades Council. (52)

The return to political activity by the Labour party was accompanied by a more vociferous, and more left wing, attitude by the Trades Council, and several of the city's unions struck political attitudes which were similar to those of Arthur Henderson and the predominant sections of his movement. New organisations also came into existence in York, some of which, it must be admitted, had wage rises as their prime objective, though they undoubtedly capitalised on the new climate of labour opinion that was abroad. Prices were still rising and at the end of 1917 a York branch of the British Workers' Union was brought into existence which attracted some 350 members in its first three months of existence. General secretary of the BWU was Charles Duncan, MP, and the Union had the active support and encouragement in York of Arnold Rowntree. Its local secretary was a Mr Dawson, and its avowed objectives were to get better wages and conditions for civilian workers in government departments, particularly that of the Army Ordnance. A new womens' union also came into existence which decided to affiliate to the Labour party. (55)

The older unions also began to adopt a higher profile as the Labour party and the Trades Council set the pace. The NUR, or a branch of it, declared that it was prepared to support a negotiated peace, and that it too was not really concerned about Alsace and Lorraine. This has been mentioned. In March 1918 a joint deputation from the York Typographical Association, the National Union of Bookbinders and the National Union of Printing and Paper Workers lobbied the York city council, protesting against it getting printing work done outside the city. (56) The Amalgamated Society of Engineers protested against the constantly rising prices, and in April Tom Mann and Robert Smillie, two famous labour leaders attended a meeting at the Opera House where they were supported by Gill, J.H. Hartley, Jeannie Mercer and others. There Mann urged his listeners to prepare for the post war period, and demanded a 30 hour five day week and state control of industry; the full socialist programme. (57)

The Labour party and its constituent bodies were clearly putting everything into a campaign based on a belief that the nation was ready for a radical programme of socialist reform, and this must have been music to the ears of those in the ILP. They had never supported the war or conscription, and they, too, were against the Tank Week. They must have alienated potential Labour voters by saying so, and they might not have gained many converts as a result of what looks like an indiscreet move in the run up period to an election. In the summer of 1918 Forster Todd, the Lord Mayor, was knighted, and J.G. Butcher, the Tory MP, was made a baronet. At a council meeting labour members congratulated the recipients, to the intense annoyance of the ILP, which wrote to the papers saying it wanted to disassociate itself from the congratulations, 'believing that the conferring of titles makes an invidious distinction between one person and another, and is against the best interests of the community as a whole.' (58)

The likes of J.H. Hartley and W.H. Farrar were connected with both the ILP and the Labour party, and they were influential in the Cooperative movement also. It, too, was affected by the new enthusiasm and the fresh stance adopted by the labour movement in late 1917 and early '18 - and by the views of such as Hartley and Mercer - and in January it too was 'politicised'. The York Equitable Industrial Society had already taken part in protests about rationing and the composition of the Food Control committee. In late January it decided to set up an election fund to secure the election of MPs and JPs, donating to it one penny per member per year. (59)

The increased activity on the part of the labour movement in York was sure to have a knock on effect, and it did. The Conservatives had kept their central and ward organisations in existence throughout the war, and had honoured the party truce - though the likes of Charles Elmhirst, Rhodes Brown and Charles A. Thompson were continually criticising what they considered was, in latter day language, the loony left. In July, for example, Thompson was engaged in a vitriolic dispute in the letter columns of the *Press* with F.E. Pollard of the ILP who had maintained that 'the aggressive and dismembering policy of the Entente [had] stiffened the back of the German militarists.' Pollard had been lumped together with Richard Westrope of the Educational Settlement and Arnold Rowntree, and attacked as a German sympathiser (of course), and the coming together, at last, of the Labour party, the UDC and the Trades Council was referred to as 'an ominous combination'. (60) It was, but it was to promise more than it delivered.

The annual meeting of York's main Tory organisation was held in January, (61) where the annual report for 1917 thanked Butcher for his efforts on behalf of York and he responded, and in doing so welcomed women for the first time to the central executive committee and urged them to take part in the activities of the party at that and at ward level. (62) C.A. Thompson presided over the Micklegate Ward Conservative Association and he, too, reported that little or no party work had gone on during the year. Thompson, however, showed that the party truce was now under threat from the right as well as the left. He persuaded his group to pass a resolution to be sent to the central Tory organisation recommending that every council seat for which a conscientious objector was a candidate 'should be contested, as such action would be a breach of the political truce.' (63) What Thompson meant by this, apart from the fact that he did not like conchies, is not clear. Perhaps he reasoned that the war would end and municipal elections would be held in November 1918, and that he and his colleagues should be prepared to fight the likes of John Mercer. He was not far wrong.

The York Tories could not be seen to break the party truce, even if Labour had done that, in fact, but there was nothing to stop them taking part in the activities of organisations which effectively represented their views, and which *were* engaging in political activity. In the summer of 1918 a National War Aims Committee came into existence and a York branch of it was brought into being. Charles A. Thompson was prominent in its activities. A Mr A. Williams of York was another supporter, moving resolutions deploring, for example, the ILP's protests against the Allied expeditions to Russia. Hugh McGough, a local JP, was also prominent in the deliberations of the War Aims Committee, which held open-air meetings in Exhibition Square. (64) Speakers from Stockport, Manchester and Birmingham were brought to York to further the cause. (65)

The question of what exactly Great Britain was fighting for had become a burning political issue in 1917, one that was being continually raised by the left, particularly since the outbreak of the Russian revolution. For the right there was an easy answer - Great Britain was fighting for 'right against might', against 'Prussianism', for the rights of smaller nations and so on. Nevertheless it was felt that some kind of an organisation was needed 'to keep before the nation both the causes of the war and the necessity of continuing the struggle', and so the National War Aims Committee was started on the fourth anniversary of the outbreak of hostilities. (66) Its presidents were Bonar Law and Asquith, George Barnes and the Prime Minister, and the latter launched the committee at a meeting at the Queen's Hall in London. (67) Among the treasurers was Hamar Greenwood, (68) and the NWAC announced that it was intended to approach Liberal and Tory agents in the constituencies with a view to setting up local branches. Many famous figures gave their services as speakers.

Details of the history until then of the National War Aims Committee emerged during a rather bad tempered debate in the Commons on 13 November, 1917, the day Butcher launched an attack on pacifist MPs. It was introduced by Captain Guest, a Dorset Member, who revealed that the NWAC had been started when pacifist propaganda began to get a hearing in the summer of 1917. They must, Edward Carson said, fight 'the subterranean influence of a pernicious and pestilential character which [had] developed within the last few months ... beyond anything that has yet been described in this House,' and the NWAC was one way of doing so. Originally, it was said, it was hoped that the Tory and Liberal parties would pay for it, but this proposal had been met with little or no support and the government was now funding the committee's campaigns. To what extent? Ministers would not reveal to what extent, a fact which led a Labour Member to attack secret expenditure in the way others had attacked secret treaties. Some very nasty attacks were also made on the UDC, and on the quality of the vast amounts of literature being produced by the War Aims Committee. A quarter of a million pamphlets had been sent down to a certain constituency during a recent by election, Arthur Ponsonby said, and claims were made that the committee was set up to support the government. There was really no need for these, as that is exactly what the authorities said it was for. The Member for Burnley chose to believe the government acted as it did because it was losing the arguments about the continuation of the war, which is surely not true. The ideas of the UDC were gaining ground, of that there is no doubt, and the labour movement was adopting them, but overwhelmingly the country felt more sympathy for the ideas of Lloyd George than they did for those of Ramsay MacDonald, more sympathy for the ideas of J.G. Butcher than for those of Arnold Rowntree. Be that as it may, Burnley's MP said 'the reason why the Government was resorting to this method of corruption [financing pro government propaganda on a massive scale] was that the country had found them out in their disastrous conduct of the war.'

The Tories were clearly prepared, and well prepared, for an election which, it was confidentially predicted at one stage in the local papers, would be held in November. (69) They had a candidate whose record, if the election was to be one in which patriotism and 'who won the war' played a part, was impeccable. Butcher had never wavered from a wholehearted support for the war effort, had always denounced the peace moves and the peace cranks, and was 'hard' on the conscientious objectors. His current partner at Westminster, however, would clearly be a liability to the Liberals, if the election, whenever it came, was fought along the lines mentioned above. Arnold Rowntree was extremely unpopular among large sections of the community and was not helped by the indiscretions of Quakers like Joseph and Seebohm Rowntree who used petrol when they should not have, or asked for gardeners to be given exemption from military service. Arnold had resolutely believed that war would not come in 1914 and thereafter had frequently been missing from the Commons when crucial, and embarrassing issues came up. He never appeared on recruiting platforms (of course) and was opposed to the Military Service Acts. His appearances on political platforms in his constituency were limited to 'safe' occasions, and all this was repeatedly referred to in rather nasty letters to the *Press*. Would he be chosen to contest York if and when an election was called?

Liberal opinion in York had been stirred by what was going on in the political world generally and in the local labour movement in particular. The ideas of the Fellowship of Reconciliation, the UDC and for that matter the ILP were getting a much greater degree of acceptance in late 1917 and the winter and spring of 1918, than ever before, and these were the beliefs of many Liberals. They must have taken heart from that fact and the York party began to hold conferences at which pressing issues like should the war be prolonged over Alsace and Lorraine were aired. The first of these, at which Rowntree appeared, and at which J.B. Morrell was prominent, was held in March 1918, just before the German offensive on the Western Front, and the *Herald* recognised that this was in fact electioneering when it carried a headline saying 'THE PARTY GAME STARTED'. (70) The Educational Settlement had also played its part in preparing the party for its post war fights when it promoted a series of lectures titled 'After the War - What ?', the first of which was delivered by Arnold Rowntree. (71) The second Liberal conference was held late in March, (72) and it became obvious - after Gill was chosen by Labour - that the party would be left behind if it did not choose a candidate itself. Despite the fact that he was anything but a unanimous choice, Arnold Rowntree was selected again. (73)   On Armistice Day the choice was made known by the York papers, and the editorial in the *Herald* demonstrated - if a demonstration was needed - just how difficult it would be to sell him as a candidate. All during the war, the *Herald* said, Arnold had been mixed up 'with people of the Swanwick type - pacifists, conscientious objectors and other lose-the-war cranks.' (74) On the eve of the war, it went on, Arnold had said he would resign if hostilities started, but he had been persuaded to stay on. His record was as nothing compared to that of J.G. Butcher (except in one particular). He should be be thrown out at the first opportunity. He was. Arnold was not helped by the appearance in York not long before the election, of Helen Swanwick who had been invited there, like C.P.Trevelyan, Bertrand Russell, and many others, by the UDC. They had always been attacked by the *Herald*. This time, however, the attacks on a noted 'peace crank' were vastly more vindictive than before. An election was clearly on the way.

The one issue on which Arnold Rowntree and J.G. Butcher saw eye to eye related to York's representation in parliament. The city returned two Members, and the two representatives fought to keep them. They did so unsuccessfully, however.

A Speaker's Conference on Electoral Reform had resulted in a Representation of the People Bill which was introduced into parliament by H.A.L. Fisher in April 1917. This was far reaching in its ramifications, and it proposed to take away one of York's seats. Rowntree and Butcher (and others) tried to get a reprieve for Old Ebor, and Forster Todd and others went to the Commons to lobby Asquith, who does not seem to have been the very best choice, given that he was then out of office and the leader of only a section of the Liberals. Butcher put down an amendment which was debated on 7 November 1917. He and Rowntree banked everything on the hope that the government would allow a free vote on York's representation and they had a petition signed by no less than 146 MPs of all parties. When matters came to a vote, however, it was realised there was to be no free vote, and that the Whips had given out instructions to defeat Butcher's amendment to the redistribution schedule of the Bill. (75)

Butcher and Rowntree did their best for York, with Butcher treating Members to a historical resumé of the city's history, and Members treating him with more than a little levity. Rowntree made an appeal to tradition, saying that York had had two MPs since 1256, was the capital of the north, and so should continue to have two Members. These were poor arguments and they were shot down in flames by contributors to the debate who pointed to the size of York's population, the fact that Canterbury was going to lose its representation altogether and to many more facts which made York's claim look like the desperate last ditch measure it was. The amendment was lost by a majority of 94 (166:72). 'GRAVE INJUSTICE TO YORK' shouted a *Herald* headline when the result was reported.

The decision to take away one of York's MPs was yet another reason for the heightening of political activity and awareness in York after those years when only the ILP had raised contentious issues. From 7 November 1917 there was just one seat to fight for - the possibility of Arnold or Butcher sharing the spoils with maybe a Labour man or a dissident Liberal were gone. From now on the city's politicians had an eye on the next election and Butcher never missed an opportunity to display his patriotism, attack the conchies and their supporters, and remind his listeners that Arnold's 'war' record left much to be desired (in his eyes anyway). On 13 November the House debated a motion to prolong its life by another eight months, and during the debate Butcher spoke of 'a gross scandal and injustice to his constituents that a member holding opinions repulsive to the majority of his constituents should continue to sit in the House'. (76) He spoke here of a pacifist and clearly meant Arnold Rowntree, though he did not mention him by name. He did mention just about everybody else connected with the UDC, however, including C.P. Trevelyan, R.L. Outhwaite, Arthur Ponsonby and Whitehouse the Member for Stirling Burghs.

There were more debates to be held on the Representation of the People Bill before it became law, and Arnold Rowntree took an honourable part in one of them, but it was not seen that way then, and again it did his prospects no good whatsoever. Towards the end of November Sir George Younger said that he would move an amendment to the Bill which would take the vote away from conscientious objectors. (77) Bonar Law announced that this issue would be left to a free vote, but said that he would be for it. Other prominent politicians, like Austen Chamberlain, followed his lead, but Rowntree spoke out against Younger's move. He (and others) pointed out the unfairness of the House deciding to punish people for exercising a right which had been given them by Parliament and pointed out that people (like Lawrence Rowntree) who had been members of the Friends' Ambulance Unit (for example) had been in as much danger and had shown as much bravery as many front line soldiers. All to no avail, however. Younger's amendment was carried by a majority of 209 to 171. 'The resolution was received with loud cheers and a cry of "Prussianism triumphant"' a report of the debate said.

This was not the end of the question of the conscientious objectors' vote. Sir George Cave (78), like many other polticians, took on board Rowntree's points about the honourable and brave part that many conchies had taken in the war and wanted, in some way, for them to be differentiated from the others. He failed by 276 to 231 votes in a debate in which Lord Hugh Cecil said that 'every lawbreaker was to have the vote except the conscientious objector.' Arnold Rowntree, in an impassioned speech, chose to illustrate the unfairness of what was being proposed by telling the House of three objectors, one of whom, a relative, had twice been Lord Mayor of Harrogate and who would now not be able to vote (at either parliamentary or local elections) and who would be banned from serving his town as councillor. What was finally decided was that all objectors, except those who had joined the Non Combatant Corps, would be disqualified for five years from the end of the war, and 'As the state of war was not legally concluded until 31 August 1921, the disqualification lasted until 30 August 1926.' (79) The York Conservative Association would have welcomed these decisions. In June it had passed a resolution saying that both conchies and naturalised aliens should be disqualified from voting. (80) It looks as if the reactionary Rhodes Brown might have been behind that, certainly he would have approved of it. Somewhat earlier, in February 1917, after the conference on electoral reform had reported, (81) the York Conservative Association had declared itself against further reform (82) and the papers had carried letters from the likes of Edward A. Mitchell Innes, chairman of the National League for Opposing Women's Suffrage, saying that the nation should not - well - give votes to women. (83) This organisation eventually took advertising space in the *Herald* saying that the impending moves towards female suffrage violated the party truce. (84) The York Labour party at a delegate meeting opposed the moved to disenfranchise the COs, calling on 'the Government, ... whatever their views on the conscientious objectors may be, to ... amended the Bill on the third reading as to prevent such a blot on our constitutional history being recorded.' (85)

Arnold Rowntree's part in supporting the conchies over the vote - like all his other misdeamenours - would not be forgotten, but both he and Butcher were in favour of yet another of the monumental changes made by the Representation of the People Act - it gave votes to women, and this was yet another reason for the emergence of political activity in York (and elsewhere) in late 1917 and early '18. All the parties would now have to woo a much larger electorate, and just how much larger it would be, was given in an estimate made two days after the Lords finally passed the Bill. (86) Women, to qualify for the franchise, had to be over 30 years of age, ratepayers, wives of ratepayers, or graduates 'of one or other of the University constituencies'. Two fifths of the population, it was reckoned, would become voters and the size of the electorate would roughly double. In York, with a population of some 83,000 and 33,000 voters there would be 11,000 ladies voting. Little wonder that the party which had hitherto been hostile fell over itself to welcome women into its committees and deliberations as if it had always been in the forefront of the suffrage agitation. J.G. Butcher's words of welcome to them have been quoted; what Edith Milner thought about it all is unknown.

The moves towards female suffrage in 1917 and '18 reactivated the women's movement in York. The suffrage societies had honoured the party truce, but some women's organisations had kept in being and continually pressed demands for women's advancement. Mrs Edwin Gray and the National Union of Women Workers, for example, demanded the appointment of women police officers in York, (87) a demand which got a cold reception from the Watch Committee in July 1917. (88) The NUWW also wanted tighter film censorship measures. It is fact, also, that at about the time it became absolutely clear that women would get the vote, there was being held what was possibly the last great recruiting campaign of the First World War. It was directed specifically at women, and, at huge meetings like those held in York, they were urged to join the WAAC and other organisations.

In April 1917, just as the Representation of the People Act was beginning its passage through parliament a new, unashamedly left wing suffrage organisation was set up in York. It was the Workers' Suffrage Federation and its inaugural meeting was graced by the presence of local left wingers like Will Horsman, Mr and Mrs F.T. Beney, and Sylvia Pankhurst. She now linked her demands for the vote - which it must have been clear would be granted - with a demand for what would now be called child benefits, but which were then called 'Mothers' Pensions'. Sylvia described how such benefits were paid in 27 American states; suggested people did not register for national service; and joined in the singing of 'The Red Flag' which ended the meeting.

There is no evidence that the York Workers' Suffrage Federation was particularly active; it was just another organisation set up at a time when new organisations were being set up all over the place. Another women's group appearing at that time - illustrative of the same forces and attitudes which led to the appearance of the WSF - was a trades union. In December 1917 a York branch of the National Union of Uncertificated Teachers was brought into existence, declaring from its inception its political allegiances when it announced that it would affiliate to the local Trades Council and the York Labour party. (89)

There had been continual trouble during the middle years of the war over the teaching profession in York, with Rhodes Brown playing a star role in obstructing wage increases (for very good reasons he would have said) and resisting the employment of conscientious objectors as teachers. In March 1917 the teachers had made a wage demand to the Education Committee, when it was revealed that maximum salaries for men were £150 and for women £110, and that the average weekly salary of certificated male teachers was £2.8s, and of certificated females £1.17s.3d. (90) In May recommendations for a £20 increase were made, (91) but there were still wrecking attempts to be made by by 'economisers' in the council chamber. The teachers were clearly dissatisfied with the way their demands were being treated, and many of the ladies in the profession were equally dissatisfied with the way they were being treated 'unfairly'. Quite rightly so, and their disatisfaction was voiced by the Misses Byett and E.W. Child - the latter reading a paper to the York Teachers' Association titled 'The Future Remuneration of Women' in which she demanded equal pay for equal work. (92 A little later the famous Margaret Ashton appeared at the Educational Settlement. She was the sole representative of women on the Manchester City Council and she undoubtedly raised similar issues. (93)

It is a common place of histories of the First World War that, as the conflict went on, women took over more and more men's jobs, and some of them have been mentioned in these pages. In York and the surrounding districts there were women porters on the railway, women ambulance drivers and women working on the trams. In November 1917 there was another instance which showed that the trend was continuing, or even speeding up as the demand for men for the forces became desperate. In that month the North Eastern Railway began training railway policewomen, and in the following May 13 were sworn in. (94) It will be recalled that York City Council refused to have lady coppers.

No doubt, such were things in those days, the lady policewomen would have received a lower wage than their male counterparts, like the women teachers. There was still a long way to go before equality was achieved, and much work for such bodies as the Uncertificated Teachers Union. Despite the fact that they did not enjoy electoral equality with men, the ladies of the York Women's Suffrage Society decided to disband. They did so at a meeting at which F.H. Rowntree and E.P. Holmes were present - Holmes being the Tory working man who had been entirely out of line with his party over women's suffrage for years. Isabella Ford was also present and she did say they wanted equality, as well as women cops and women JPs and jurors. (95) The YWSS bowed out of existence recommending its members to join the York Women's Citizens Association.

Many speakers, in York and elsewhere, spoke almost with disbelief when they reflected on how easily the women's vote had finally been won, with the inevitable 'like a thief in the night' tag being regularly being pressed into use, and historians of the women's movement frequently pay scant attention to the events of the autumn of 1917. The passing of the Representation of the People Act had something of the air of an anti climax about it, but everywhere ex-suffragettes were determined that what they had worked for would be used. The York Women's Citizens Association was created in May 1918 - with Mrs D.S. Chrichton and Mrs Philip Newman its most prominent figures. (96) Mrs Edwin Gray became associated with the new committee and it set about creating ward organisations, with Mrs Gray saying, quaintly, that its aim was 'to bring "the maternal into public life."' (97) A week after she made this announcement the York overseers held their annual meeting and at that it was reported that the local electors lists had been prepared, (98) and that they showed there were 37,603 voters in the city including 15,393 women - 41 per cent of the total. (99) Naval and military voters amounted to 7,999 and 48 conscientious objectors had been disfranchised. Sheriff Shipley challenged this figure saying that it was almost certainly too few.

The York Women's Citizens Association's first aim was to help with the registration of women voters, and the ward organisations organised a canvass of people who had not applied for inclusion on the electoral register. With this work done, it held a meeting in October 1918 at which the Archbishop promised to attend and the announcement of it stated that the Committee's aims were (100)

> to bring together on non-party, non-sectarian and democratic lines all women's societies and individual women in order to:- (a) Foster a sense of citizenship in women, (b) encourage the study of political, social, and economic questions, (c) secure the adequate representation of the interests and experiences of women in the affairs of the community.

The programme the Women's Citizens Association had sketched out for itself, after its initial bout of registration activity, looks very similar to that of the Union of Women Workers and the Women's Institutes which were now appearing, and it might have been thought that its educational function was in competition with the evening schools in the city, the Educational Settlement and the recently reactivated York branch of the Workers' Educational Association. (101) There is little doubt that it would have been unattractive to the left and the working class, but its campaign had hardly got under way when the war finished.

1. Charles William Shipley was a train driver who was promoted to an inspector of locomotives on the NER. See biography of him in the *Herald* 8 September 1917
2. This was a complaint of Horsman's, which seems a little unfair as the Tories were in a majority on the council. See eg *Ibid* 1 August 1916
3. *Ibid* 17 August 1917
4. *Ibid* 11 September 1917
5. *Ibid*. There is some biographical material on the unpleasant Rhodes Brown in the account of his admission as a member of the City of London Feltmakers Company. *Ibid* 5 October
6. *Ibid* 15 and 20 September, 2 October 1917
7. Along with at least two political opponents. Forster Todd was also made a JP at the same time
8. *Herald* 16 October 1917
9. *Ibid* 13 and 29 November 1917
10. Third Ypres had come and gone, and so had the Battle of Cambrai. After the first day of Cambrai, when tanks were used *en masse*, it really did look as if the promised breakthrough had occurred and the Minster bells were rung in celebration. But the Germans counter attacked and regained their lines.

11. *Herald* 5 and 8 October 1917. On the question of food control on a national scale see eg W.H. Beveridge, *British Food Control* (1928), also E.M.H. Lloyd, *Experiments in State Control* (1924) and J. Williams, *The Other Battleground* (Chicago 1972)
12. *Herald* 5 November, 20 December 1917
13. *Ibid* 28 December 1917, 3 and 10 January 1918
14. The courts and the Food Control committees had to address themselves to the question of what amounted to hoarding
15. Neighbouring food control areas cooperated with the scheme. In York, by the end of September, 400 suppliers had been registered for the supply of sugar and 12,400 householders had applied for cards. *Herald* 28 September 1917
16. The meat ration (it varied from time to time) was fixed at ten ounces for adults and half that for children in late February. *Herald* 28 February 1918. National rationing started on 25 March. *Ibid* 21 February 1918
17. *Ibid* 28 February 1918
18. *Ibid* 29 January 1918
19. *Ibid* 11 February 1918
20. *Ibid* 25 January 1918
21. On the subject of food during the war, where this point is made, see eg J. Burnett, *Plenty and Want* (1952)
22. *Ibid* 19 March 1918. This was not, strictly speaking, anything the York Food Control committee could do anything about - meat was rationed nationally - but it was brought up by them, and the committee made representations on the matter
23. *Ibid*
24. *Ibid* 19 February 1918
25. *Ibid* 15 February 1918
26. Refusing to sell a rationed item unless something else was purchased. An early criticism was that some shops were only supplying margarine to customers who had registered for sugar. *Ibid* 10 January 1918
27. *Ibid* 11 January 1918
28. *Ibid* 26 October 1917. *Press* 25 October 1917
29. *Herald* 13 November 1917
30. *Ibid* 20 November 1917. *Press* 19 November 1917
31. The Town Clerk
32. *Herald* 1 March 1918
33. *Ibid* 4 December 1917.
34. *Ibid* 7 and 14 December 1917, *Press* 13 December 1917. The Labour party conference on old age pensions reported in eg *Herald* 3 December 1917
35. The case of Thomas Raftery caused a great furore in York, and quite rightly so. See later
36. *Herald* 27 February 1918
37. *Ibid* 28 March 1918
38. *Ibid* 14 March 1918. The Russian communists had revealed the secret treaties which had been entered into to get Italy into the war. Slessor's resignation is noted in the Labour party's minute books (26 November 1916) which are deposited in the York city archives
39. Havelock Wilson was first elected to parliament (for Middlesborough) in 1892 - along with Keir Hardie and John Burns
40. *Herald* 29 December 1917. *Times* 29 December 1917
41. The Henderson demands were: to get a settlement as soon as possible, as said in the text; territorial annexations not dictated by imperialist greed; and a post war trade policy which was not based on economic oppression
42. *Herald* 26 and 27 June 1918
43. This was said at a regional conference held in March. *Ibid* 14 March 1918
44. *Ibid* 2 February 1918. The meeting was said to have been sponsored by the Merchant Seaman's League
45. *Ibid* 13 February 1918
46. The iron areas of Briey in Lorraine had been (were) of vital importance to the German war effort, and during the war and afterwards persistent and persuasive arguments were put around that the

mines had been practically left alone by both sides. On the claims see, eg, F. Brockway and F. Mullaly, *Death Pays a Dividend* (1944), H.C. Engelbrecht and F.C. Hanighen, *Merchants of Death* (1934) and C.K. Street, 'Assassins of the People', *Foreign Affairs* (1920).For a more recent attempt to explain the situation see A.J. Peacock, 'Steel Has No Fatherland', *Gun Fire* No 4 (nd)

47. *Herald* 7 January 1918
48. *Ibid* 2 February 1918
49. *Ibid* 5 February 1918
50. Strictly speaking it did not oppose it
51. *Herald* 2 July 1918. The Council considered a letter from one Norah Dacre of London, asking for support for the demonstration. Sykes Rymer was another who supported the idea; Vernon Wragge, who seems to have become a little more tolerant than he once was, called the request 'absurd'. The Council voted against taking part.
52. *Ibid* 8 and 11 February 1918
53. *Ibid* 6 February 1918. Letter
54. *Ibid* 13 October 1917
55. See later
56. *Herald* 5 March 1918
57. *Ibid* 1 April 1918. The ASE complaint in *Ibid* 26 November 1917
58. *Ibid* 5 July 1918
59. *Ibid* 19 November 1917 and 23 January 1918
60. *Ibid* 30 July, 3 August 1918
61. *Ibid* 30 July 1918
62. *Ibid* 25 February 1918. The two pioneering Tory ladies were a Miss Percy and a Mrs Gardner. C.E. Elmhirst was re-elected Conservative president
63. *Ibid* 19 December 1917
64. *Ibid* 26 July and 2 and 9 August 1918
65. For example G.W. Worsey, variously described as from London or Birmingham, E.W. Pike of Leeds and P.J. Kelly of Manchester
66. *Times* 24 July 1917
67. *Ibid* 6 August 1917
68. *Ibid* 30 July 1917
69. The *Herald* announced confidently that it would be held on the 30th. *Herald* 1 November 1918
70. *Ibid* 11 March 1918
71. *Ibid* 26 January 1918. Earlier the Settlement had promoted an important series of lectures on 'The Governance of the City'. Burrow, for instance, had lectured on crime and policing and the city engineer on 'The Traffic of the City'. *Ibid* 10 November 1917
72. *Ibid* 25 March 1918
73. F.H. Rowntree died at about this time. *Ibid* 27 February 1918
74. A reference to Helena M. Swanwick, a UDC supporter. See later
75. On the debates on this part of the Bill, see eg *Press* 7 and 8 November 1917, *Herald* 8 November 1917
76. *Herald* 14 November 1917
77. *Ibid* 20 November 1917
78. Cave was the Home Secretary and in charge of the Bill. On him and his part on the passing of the Representation Act see eg C. Mallet, *Lord Cave. A Memoir* (1931) p 194 *et seq*
79. Rae *op.cit.* p 235
80. *Herald* 16 June 1917
81. See eg *Ibid* 31 January 1917
82. *Ibid* 17 and 26 February 1917
83. Eg *Ibid* 6 March 1917
84. *Ibid* 14 April 1917
85. *Ibid* 4 December 1917
86. The Lords passed it on Thursday 10 January 1918. See eg *Ibid* 12 January 1918
87. *Ibid* 6 June 1917
88. *Ibid* 31 July 1917. Oscar Rowntree was chairman of the Watch committee. It is a strange fact

that during the war - and just before it for that matter - the Tories did not take all the important chairmanships of committees. Some remained controlled by Liberals. Meyer was in such a position, for example, along with Rowntree

89. *Ibid* 14 December 1917, *Press* 14 December 1917. The inaugural meeting was addressed by Miss E.E. Walsh, the general secretary of the union, and a Miss Appelby was the first local secretary
90. *Herald* 30 March 1917
91. *Ibid* 18 and 19 May 1917
92. *Ibid* 10 and 29 September 1917
93. *Ibid* 2 March 1918
94. *Ibid* 24 May 1918. See *Ibid* 31 May 1918 for an article for women on the NER
95. *Ibid* 24 May 1918. There is an extended article on the York Women's Suffrage Society in one of the city's newspapers, written by 'A Lady'. She may well have merited that description, but she was also, almost certainly, Mrs K.E.T. Wilkinson. *Ibid* 14 June 1918. Perhaps to a later generation she would not have revealed the fact that the ladies were known as the 'Cocke-Hennies', or maybe this is why she chose a *nom de plume*. That the author was Mrs Wilkinson is made certain by an earlier reference to her reading such a paper. It is not very good
96. *Ibid* 10 May 1918
97. *Ibid* 10 July 1918
98. Up to 29 June 1918
99. *Herald* 20 July 1918
100. *Ibid* 29 October 1918
101. *Ibid* 21 May 1917

CHAPTER 17

THE NATIONAL FEDERATION, THE COMRADES, AND THOMAS RAFTERY

Many reasons have been given for the ending of the party truce in York and when it did end the old political organisations became active for the first time for four years and new ones came into existence. The city in 1918 had groups advocating a harsh peace (like the Dean, the Very Rev Foxley, who wanted a 'peace with punishment)', (1) and others a negotiated peace (claiming that Prussianism had disappeared in Germany). The newest women's organisation was involved in making sure that every woman who qualified got on to the electoral register and some of the unions, who got wage demands reasonably easily, were talking in the language of the Bolsheviks who had become supreme in Russia. In addition to this the Labour party and the Liberals were preparing for a general election, with the latter holding conferences at which post war problems and policies were discussed. Other organisations had also come into existence which were concerned with post war problems. They were certainly 'political', whatever they said, and they sometimes put forward some very unpleasant views and demands. They were ex-servicemen's groups.

The first of the important national ex-servicemen's organisations to come into existence was the National Association of Discharged and Demobilised Sailors and Soldiers which was created at Blackburn in 1916, and was linked to the TUC. (2) There were others, (3) but the Association seems to have been as ignored by historians as it was by the national press at the time, (4) but a branch was established in York. (5) It was formed in December 1917 and elected a committee under J.F. Lawson. (6) What did it stand for ? What views were aired at its inaugural meeting ? A major resolution said the organisation was 'in favour of the war being carried on to a successful conlusion', and another showed that members were understandably concerned about their job prospects when they said they were worried that employers might knock their wages down by an amount equalling their pension award. They were also concerned that they might be called up again, and demanded the repeal of the Review of Exemptions Act. They deplored the fact that men who had been discharged were being compulsorily re-enlisted while 'young men who have no intention of serving [in the forces], and who are sheltered while being in reserved occupations, and also conscientious objectors who are able and fit to serve' were left free.

One of the resolutions of the York DSSA (that on wages) suggests that it might indeed have had some connections with the labour movement, or that many of its members were of labour sympathies, but the other two (on continuing the war and conchies) shows that it was very out of sympathy with the Labour party and what it stood for in late 1917. Perhaps the likes of Lawson and C.H. Akers, the secretary, created the Association and only then realised that their members were not sympathetic to the 'new look' Labour party, its attitudes and its personnel. Anyway one Sunday in February 1918 the Association held a meeting at the Victoria Hall to decide which of two new organisations which had come into existence it should affiliate to. (7) They chose to align themselves with the National Federation of Discharged Sailors and Soldiers, and they underlined their alienation from Labour by passing a resolution condemning the fact that Jeannie Mercer, the wife of the Labour party's conchy secretary, was a member of the York War Pensions committee. In April the *Herald* (on the 3rd) reported that E. Worthington, the Federation's York secretary, had written to J. Hutchinson of the Trades Council protesting about Jeannie Mercer's membership of the Pensions Committee. Hutchinson told Worthington to get lost, and quite right too.

The National Federation of Discharged Sailors and Soldiers was created in July 1917 at a meeting addressed by J.M. Hogge at the London Palladium which was attended by delegates from three existing organisations representing a 100 branches 'with an aggregate membership of something like 100,000'. (8) Hogge became president and in January 1918 he went back to York where he addressed a meeting on licensed premises to the delight of the papers which had regularly clobbered him when he used to go on in Old Ebor about the dangers of Old Nick's Brew. The Federation had been started, Hogge said, to fight the Review of Exemptions Act, and he demanded that every man who had been discharged, who had not been abroad, yet was subject to recall, should be given work of national importance. Where, then, would the much needed manpower come from ? The shirkers and the conchies should be called up, Hogge said. (9)

Hogge's suggestion about an alternative to being called up looks remarkably like industrial conscription which he, as a good old fashioned liberal might have been expected to oppose, and some of his other attitudes at the time were not what might have been expected from a one-time associate of the Rowntrees. He was for pressing on with the war, and against conscientious objectors and was immensely proud of his son who had been awarded the Military Medal. He agitated for increased pensions for war widows, saying the prevailing levels were scandalous, and drew attention, as many others did, to the hundreds of discharged servicemen with tuberculosis who were not being treated. (10) But Hogge also associated himself with condemnations of striking munition workers, (11) which was perhaps fair enough, and demands for a 'fairer' application of the Military Service Acts (which meant call up the objectors) and others that all aliens should be interned. In July the Federation held a rally in Hyde Park at which Hogge and Pemberton Billing (12) appeared as speakers, and at which banners were carried saying 'Comb them out' and 'Intern them all.' Hogge also associated with some noted rabble rousers, and at a Federation gathering at the Albert Hall shared the platform with Horatio Bottomley, no less. (13) This was held just three days after the commencement of the March offensive on the Western Front, and there can be little doubt but that Bottomley would have risen to the occasion with hysterical denunciations of the hated 'Germ-Huns'.

There was something of a revival of 'King and Country' patriotism at the end of 1917. (14) The troubles over food had taken the labour movement's attention away from the profiteer and concern to get a fair system of rationing (and foreign developments) had led to its revival. This had had an effect on the other politcal bodies who had seen labour as 'pro-German' or German infiltrated and this in turn had been partly responsible for the ugly attacks on aliens by such people as Rhodes Brown starting again. The ex-servicemen's organisations both reflected this polarising of attitudes and did much to perpetuate those against objectors and foreigners which culminated in the 'Hang the Kaiser' election of December 1918. The banners at Hogge's Hyde Park demonstration have been mentioned.

No organisation with Jimmy Hogge heading it could possibly expect a trouble free existence, and in 1918 the Federation was in the courts. (15) This might have had some effect on a decision to start a rival organisation; certainly the fact that the Federation would only accept officers who had risen from the ranks did, but a third, and the predominant motivation in the creation of the Comrades of the Great War must have been a political one, pure and simple. The Association was 'Labour', the Federation was 'Liberal' and to some extent anti-government. There was a need, some said, for a third force, and that third force was the Comrades of the Great War.

Lt Col Sir John Norton Griffith, a service MP, and a very famous one indeed, (16) wrote to the papers just before Hogge's London Palladium meeting, suggesting the formation of an ex-servicemen's organisation which he tentatively called the Veterans of the Grand Army, and he was very fond of telling audiences of how the idea had originated in a discussion he had had with an NCO while under fire at the front. (17) Within a month a further letter appeared in the press, signed by Norton Griffiths and five other service MPs - among whom was Hamar Greenwood - saying that an organisation, to have county and borough organisations, had been set up. It was to be called The Comrade's of the Great War. (18) What was it to do ? A prime aim was to represent disabled men returned from the war in applying for their disability pensions. Would it interfere with the work of the Ministry of Pensions ? Officials of the Comrades were at pains to point out that it was intended to help the work of the Ministry. (19 What was the Comrades' attitude to the Review of Exemptions Act ? It was in favour of it (though it did not publicise the fact). No wonder. He had fought the Review of Exemptions Act tooth and nail, Hogge said, and had created the Federation to carry on the fight. The Comrades, however, had been started by MPs who, to a man, had voted for 'the conscription of married men.' (20)

The Comrades of the Great War was officially inaugurated at a noisy meeting at the Mansion House in London at which Federation members heckled the speakers - and were thrown out. A letter from General Smuts was read out, and gifts to the new organisation of £35,000 were announced. Those gifts (and the donors) did nothing to lessen the belief that the Comrades was a political organisation, and the unbiased observer would be hard put not to see it as analogous to the National War Aims Committee, a body that would support the government's determination to pursue the war to a successful conclusion, and which might, at the same time, do something to marshal support for the coalition if and when a general election came along. Pemberton Billing made repeated statements in the Commons (often in questions) maintaining that the Comrades was political in nature and surely he was right, though the government itself may not have been directly behind it. It had only recently created the National War Aims Committee; the Comrades had exactly the same ideas on the war.

The Comrades organisation spread rapidly and in December 1917 its first club opened at Addlestone, near Weybridge, (21) and by May 1918 it had 320 branches and posts (22) and 32 clubs. (23) A branch was set up in York in July, and that it was of a right wing political nature might be inferred from the presence at its creation of Sir Frederick Milner, the brother of Edith, who had been, according to his sister, 'exhausting himself' in the fight (24) for reasonable pensions for ex-servicemen. C.H. Akers, once secretary of the York branch of the York Discharged Sailors and Soldiers Association, had clearly made a mistake when joining that organisation, and did not join the Federation as his colleagues did. He was present when the Comrades branch was formed in York, and he became chairman. He had served in the West Yorkshire Regiment and his two leading colleagues were A.C. Smith, late of the 2nd Yorks and Lancs, and W.J. Bellerby, who had been in the Army Service Corps. (25)

The York Comrades immediately made their presence in the city felt. They represented their members before the pensions authorities, and they also added their voices to those who were indulging themselves in the last, disgraceful campaign of persecution of the First World War - and in doing so they behaved exactly like Hogge's Federation of course. In July they met and applauded Lloyd George's stand against striking munition workers (they had to in reality, as the

ASE was striking against a 'comb out' of workers). They also gave voice to some very unpleasant sentiments about aliens, seemingly oblivious of all the arguments which had gone on about some of these poor people having lived in this country for 40 years or so, with children who could only speak English serving in the forces and so on. The Comrades wanted committees of enquiry set up in various localities which would collect evidence on aliens which would be sent to central government agencies for them to use. This dreadful suggestion was prompted by what? By a belief 'that German influence' had 'penetrated deep into the heart of our constitution' (26) and that stringent measures should be taken to neutralise that influence. No unnaturalised aliens, the Comrades said, should be allowed to work in banks, shipping offices, government offices, or workshops, and no alien naturalised since the war began should be allowed to keep his or her certificate of naturalisation. (27) In August, the York secretary wrote to the local press telling readers that the Comrades nationally had 467 branches and 83 clubs, and that the organisation was 'Pressing' the aliens question and that of the objectors. (28) It would not have been exaggerating to have said that they were trying to get up a witch hunt; certainly they were making a contribution to the atmosphere in which the general election was to be fought in December.

Both the York Federation of Discharged Sailors and Soldiers and the local branch of the Comrades behaved in an appalling way over the 'aliens question' in 1918. There were no window breakings it is pleasant to record, but renewed demands for the renaming of streets with 'German' names might be an indication of the feeling got up in those last months of the war. (29) The two ex-servicemen's organisations were also concerned, of course, to get better treatment for discharged members of the forces, and in York a great deal was heard about how one sick veteran had been neglected. His was a tragic story. He was Thomas Raftery.

Thomas Raftery had enlisted in the Army in the first month of the war - on 27 August 1914 - and served in the Dardanelles campaign and later in France, where he was gassed. (30) He was discharged from the forces on 31 January 1916 and returned to live in York at 28, St Margaret's Terrace. In May 1917 he was 'notified' as a TB sufferer and in September admitted to the York Infirmary - the dreaded workhouse. He had refused hospital treatment before this, but by September he had become so ill that he could no longer be looked after by his aged parents and had been taken from home. The loathing of the workhouse, or the 'union' as it was called in some places, was never better demonstrated than by the way poor Thomas was taken there. A VAD ambulance called for him, so that the neighbours would not know his destination. He died six days after he was admitted on the 19th.

Raftery's brother was dissatisfied with the way Thomas had been treated, his complaints were supported by G.F. Glew and eventually a committee of enquiry was set up. (31) It showed that Raftery was in many ways responsible for the miserable situation he found himself in at the end, but perhaps helped to a successful conclusion a campaign for a local sanitorium to add to the existing inadequate facilities in York. A Miss Welsh, the secretary of the local War Pensions committee, said that Raftery's case first became known to her committee on 24 August and that five days later it was referred to the Tuberculosis Dispensary at Yearsley Bridge. The secretary of that institution, a Miss Coning, said that as an insured person Raftery was entitled to treatment, but he refused to go there. Some time later he changed his mind, but by this time there were no places at Yearsley (which was housing 100 wounded soldiers). Once more the Pensions Committee discussed Raftery's case, and in desperation made arrangements with the guardians to take him into the York Infirmary. Dr Sablis (32) told the enquiry that there was a long waiting list for admission to Yearsley, but that the very 'best accommodation had been made for him at the workhouse.' This was true, and Thomas's somewhat embarrassed relative accepted it was so.

There were many discharged soldiers and sailors suffering from TB in 1917, and the concern for them by the newly formed ex-servicemen's organisations has been mentioned. Concern about the scourge of consumption in York pre dated the Great War, by many years, and the work of some of the city's reformers in this respect - particularly those associated with the Health and Housing Reform Association - has been briefly mentioned. That work continued up to and during the war, to the everlasting credit of those responsible. In 1910 a travelling exhibition on TB was invited to York and conferences were held in connection with it at which public and philanthropic organisations were represented at some sessions, while members of the public were invited to others. (33) An average of over 4,500 people looked at the exhibition each day and the topics for the conferences were 'Public measures for the eradication of consumption' and 'How the working man can fight consumption.' At one the audience heard a description of what was being done in Leeds by the man primarily responsible - Dr de Carle Woodcock, who said he owed his inspiration to Dr Evelyn of York. He raised the question of whether there should be compulsory notification of TB, and contented himself by saying that there was in Scotland. There must be a crusade to stop spitting, he concluded, and Dr Smith, the York Medical Officer of Health, regretted that there was no legislation prohibiting that filthy and dangerous habit. Smith revealed that there had been voluntary notification of TB cases in York from 1902, and speaker after speaker attacked the existence of the appalling slums which were the breeding grounds of the disease.

A branch of the National Society for the Prevention of Consumption came into existence in York and a draft scheme for what S.H. Davies called 'a frontal attack upon this dreadful disease' was put before the Public Health Committee of the city corporation on 17 October 1912, and approved by the full council just a month later. (34) In June a decision had been made to set up the York Tuberculosis Dispensary (in premises at 11, Castlegate) and in September the city's first TB officer was appointed. This was Dr Bell Ferguson of Leicester who was paid a salary of £500. The council had originally advertised the post at £400 a year, a figure well below the official BMA rate. (35)

The Council applied to the Local Government Board for grant aid for sanatorium accommodation at Yearsley Bridge 'for treatment of insured persons and their dependants, under the National Health Insurance Act, 1911' and at the end of 1913 had a dozen beds there and a similar number on the balconies at the County Hospital. A more effective system of notification was set up, described at some length in the Medical Officer's report for 1913 and, although there were long waiting lists, considerable steps forward had clearly been taken. Government money (sanatorium benefit) was administered through the local Insurance Committee, and an impressive after-care and prevention agency was started. This was based on the Dispensary and a Tuberculosis Crusade Committee helped with it. This raised funds by holding annual 'Flower Crusades' which were simple street collections, held in 1911 on 14 and 15 June. (36) At that time, it was said, £3,000 a year was needed if effective measures were to be taken in 'this great campaign against the White Scourge'. It was recorded that the number of deaths from consumption during the previous year had been 69, compared with a deccenial average of 100. Deaths as a percentage of the population were given prominence in the city's annual health reports. For the first years of the 20th century they were

Cause of deaths at all ages				
Year Total	Tuberculosis of Meninges	Tuberculosis of Lungs	Other forms of TB	Total
1900	20	110	26	156
1901	11	109	27	147
1902	29	100	21	150
1903	17	98	18	133

The figures above were analysed as follows, with a note saying that almost half the cases of TB of the lungs occurred in York's worst area.

Phthisis. "Consumption" of the lungs. Yearly comparisons				
Year	Number of deaths	Death Rate per 1,000 living	% of total number of deaths from all diseases
1899	103	1.40	7.8
1900	110	1.48	7.0
1901	109	1.39	8.4
1902	100	1.26	8.2

48 (nearly 50 per cent) of the deaths in 1902 occurred in the Walmgate Sub-Registration District. Statistics compiled for the last few years of peace included the following.

Total deaths from TB in York per 1,000 of the population living at all ages	
1908	1.21
1909	1.32
1910	1.10
1911	1.22
1912	1.54
1913	1.15

The York crusade against TB went on into wartime, (37) with great emphasis being put on the stopping of spitting in the streets (no longer an offence in York as a bye law had been allowed to lapse), hygiene in the home, the need for fresh air and ventilation and some kind of sensible slum clearance programme to replace that 'system' whereby slum properties were pulled down and nothing affordable for those displaced put up. More and more, too, demands were made for sanatoria and a speaker at the TB conference of 1910 was C.H. Garland of the National Workers' Sanatoria Association. The ideas of such as Garland were put forward as not only sensible in themselves, but as being cost effective, (38) and they gained ground. With people like S.H. Davies and some of the Rowntrees in control in York the Corporation began to look for somewhere to start a sanatorium for consumptive patients. They did so in cooperation with the East Riding County Council, and eventually a property called Raywell House near Cottingham was found which was suitable. (39) The Local Government Board approved of the purchase, (40) but in September 1915 the project was killed off (at least for the duration of the war) (41) when a communication was received saying that the Treasury 'were of the opinion that the making of further Capital Grants in aid of the provision of residential institutions for the treatment of Tuberculosis cannot be justified under present conditions.' (42)

The problems of overcrowding, disease and consumption did not go away and the York Corporation, again to its everlasting credit, decided to go it alone and create a sanatorium of its own. In December 1917 Alderman Inglis told a full meeting of the Council that TB was on the increase in York and that the Health Committee recommended that Gate Helmsley House, some eight miles from York, should be purchased and turned into a sanatorium. The house, with four acres of arable and two acres of grassland could be obtained for £2,850, Inglis went on, and between 18 and 20 patients could be accommodated indoors and a similar number outdoors. The Council agreed to the plan, which also received the support of the York Insurance Committee and the York branch of the National Federation of Discharged Sailors and Soldiers. (43) The Thomas Raftery enquiry had been held less than a week before Inglis put his proposals to the Council.

Perhaps it was inevitable, even understandable, that there was local opposition to the Gate Helmsley House scheme, even although Thomas Raftery's recent death had demonstrated for all to see that such a place was desperately needed. In December the parishoners of Gate Helmsley publicly protested, with the Rev A. Whitaker prominent among the protestors. (44) A little later the Flaxton Rural District Council objected (45) and a deputation waited on the York City Council and attempted to get it to change its mind. It did not do so, but the objectors did not have to worry, as the Local Government Board refused to allow the scheme to go on. (46) At the City Council a disgruntled councillor said the Boards' decision had been influenced 'by certain influential residents at Gate Helmsley.' (47) He may well have been right, though the official reason given was expense.

Following the rejection of the Gate Helmsley scheme, the Corporation looked around for another site for a sanatorium. To begin with it considered trying to purchase Derwent Hall, Stamford Bridge, (48) which was a stone's throw away from Gate Helmsley, and a place which might well have angered the same people who had tried to stop their earlier plans. It then looked at Fairfield House and estate (some 16 and a half acres) and York's quest for a TB sanatorium was over. (49) By November 1918 plans for the new hospital were approved, (50) and in June 1920 it was officially opened. (51)

Reading the accounts of the attempts to combat TB in York is a depressing business and a reminder, if one was needed, that for many York had hardly improved since the beginning of the century. Then B.S. Rowntree was preparing his survey for the city which shocked the nation, and just a few years later Dr Smith was using Rowntree's findings in a report 'Upon the proposal for a a Housing Investigation in York.' (51) Smith had only recently recovered from typhoid, and there had been an epidemic of scarlet fever in York. The ease with which these diseases and TB spread was often due to overcrowded slum dwellings (in which 26 per cent of York's working class lived) Smith said. But why did people live in them? He gave some reasons.

> *Overcrowding is chiefly due to* inability to pay rent enough to secure adequate accommodation. It is also due to waste and slum contentment.
>
> *Overcrowding causes debility*, disease, reduction of stamina, and leads to drunkness, immorality, and thus to insanity, crime, &c.

Smith gave those dreadful figures for Walmgate and Hungate again, an area which

> contained 1642 families = 6803 persons (4.1 per family). Of these, 69.0 per. cent. were living in poverty. Birth-rate, nearly 40 per 1000; death rate, 27.7, 1613 persons, about one fourth, living overcrowded (over 2 per room). 584 houses, one third, are back to back.

Well over a decade after he wrote urging the City Council to use the Housing Act, which they never did wholeheartedly, Smith gave a public lecture at the Educational Settlement. (52) While admitting that sanitary reform had been held up by the war, and while pointing to some remarkable health improvements, he still had to complain about the slow rate of slum clearance in the city, and said the problems of overcrowding and the lack of houses for the working class to rent still remained and was probably worse than when he was first appointed. There was a scheme for council housing at Heworth, but much remained to be done and the disgraceful state of parts of York were highlighted in an article in the popular magazine *Tit Bits* just before the war ended. (An article which, it ought to be said, did not go unchallenged.) Dr Smith did applaud the government, however, for tackling another major health problem. That of VD.

In July 1916 there appeared the Public Health (Venereal Diseases) Regulations of the Local Government Board. These were intended to help prevent the spread of VD by: starting a system of free diagnosis; giving free treatment to sufferers; allowing doctors ample supplies of 'the present day costly specific remedy for syphilis, viz.: Salvarsan, or its substitutes'; and providing public information about the disease. The Local Government Board was authorised to provide 75 per cent of the funding for local schemes, and one was organised in York on 1 July 1917. (53) From the day it opened until the end of the year it was recorded that 85 people attended the York clinic as outpatients and that 66 cases were confirmed (36 males; 30 females). In addition to these there were eight inpatients, and nine cases of congenital syphilis were reported. In the whole of 1918 the total number of VD cases treated at York was 128 (67 males, 61 females). (54)

To help with the problem of fighting the ravages of VD a York branch of the National Council for Combating Venereal Disease came into existence, (55) comparable to the TB Crusade Committee, and nicely illustrating the combination of state provision supplemented by voluntary aid, that was being forced on the governments of the day. Perhaps today (well perhaps until fairly recent times) most people would think that education about and treatment of VD should be carried out by the state, but in 1917 the former was done by the local branches of the National Council. In York the indefatigible Mrs Edwin Gray was a member, and her committee distributed thousands of booklets, leaflets and posters which they displayed in public lavatories on the station and, presumably, throughout the city. They also held public meetings at places like the Girls' Patriotic Club, and, like the good liberal ladies and gentlemen most of them seem to have been, made their opinions known on a variety of related topics. They demanded women police officers, for example, and protested against the 'maisons de tolerance' established in France for the British troops. (56) The Council also declared its opposition to prophylaxis and demanded the rescinding of Regulation 40D of the Defence of the Realm Act. (57) Somewhat later the York Council for Combating Venereal Disease joined with the Durham organisation and appointed Mrs Mary Pendelbury as a paid lecturer. (58) Given all this activity it seems reasonable to assume that the patrons of such as Alice Pitts and Frances Noone, of Brompton Street, Leeman Road, some of whom were in hospital blue according to neighbours, were not totally ignorant of the risks there were running. (59)

The extent of VD in York might be inferred by the campaigning from mid-1916, but the figures of treatment given in the Medical Officer of Health's annual reports will not be a true indication of course. They do not include members of the forces stationed in the city, for example, who would have been treated by the army, and it is certain that many cases went unreported and therefore unchecked. They were also, surely, many who were untreated unless by the quack medicines which once filled the advertisement columns of the papers at the turn of the century, and were still available.

Mrs Gray and her colleagues would have been helped in their campaign by the immense amount of publicity given to a play which, a suffragette journal said, approvingly, was playing in no less than four London theatres at the same time in May 1917. (60) It was also played at the York Theatre Royal, was called Damaged Goods, and went on there during November 1917. (61) It was written by Eugene Brieux, and followed a production of Ibsen's 'Ghosts' which dealt with the same terrible problem. (62) 'Damaged Goods' was back in York in March 1918. (63) The advertisements for its first appearance ('FOR ADULTS ONLY') referred to it as 'The Great Play on the Social Evil' and said it had 'been approved by the highest Ecclesiastical and Medical Authorities' and a review of it in the *Herald* called it

> shortly, a scientific sermon and social study, which M. Brieux wrote purely as a piece of precise and passionate propaganda. ... [in which there was] just a savouring of psychological inter-play ... introduced simply to emphasise and ... reinforce the purpose M. Brieux had in view. It may be written, [the review went on] quite frankly and sincerely, that there is not a line in "Damaged Goods" to contaminate any normal mind or to incite one shady thought. Truthful portrayal there is throughout: of pornographic suggestiveness there is not so much as a whisper.

An earlier announcement of the appearance of 'Damaged Goods' had revealed that the play had been specially licensed 'by the Lord Chamberlain for propaganda purposes' and that 'all profits' would go to supporting 'the institutions engaged in combating the ravages' of VD. It was, the announcement said, 'A compelling lesson in moral pathology' which had 'won its way through the obstacles of old-time prudery and false shame to public performance ... at the most momentous period of the world's history.' (64)

Throughout the war the men of the Army Pay Corps had been clobbered in York as 'slackers', men who would have been better off at the front, who left lights on when Zeps were around, and much more. It was perhaps inevitable that they would come in for some hammer over the prevalence of VD in the city. One who signed himself or herself 'MENS SANA IN CORPORE SANO' wrote to the

Press to say that the Pay Corps men had too much time on their hands, which they sought to while away in a predictable fashion. They got leave, the writer said, 'from noon Saturday till Monday morning' yet 'the facilities that would enable them to visit their wives' were withheld. So they visited other men's wives instead, presumably, and 'whilst having the country's welfare at heart ... unwittingly' ran the 'risk of spreading a disease that is slowly but surely undermining the nation's strength'. (65)

Another disease that reached worldwide epidemic proportions in 1918 was influenza - 'Spanish flu' - and it hit York as it did everywhere. (66) There were two outbreaks, and the first lasted officially from 30 June to 27 July, (67) and at the height of it Old Ebor was *en fete* as it entertained the first (but by no means the last) American troops to visit it. (68) Once again a glance at the advertisement pages of the papers make one wonder how such things as the Spanish flu ever got a hold. Coverdales, for example, on 3 July inserted a large advertisement headed 'INFLUENZA! INFLUENZA!' in which they recommended various remedies - 'Influenza Mixture', a 'Camphor, Ammonia & Quinine Mixture', some 'Ammoniated Quinine tablets', aspirin tablets and 'Pynol "A sure preventative".' The Chairman of the Health Committee when commenting on preventative measures said 'he personally would recommend a little "Scotch".' (69)

Whether it was because the inhabitants of York did not take enough Pynol (or Scotch) the Spanish flu spread there with frightening rapidity. The Theatre Royal and the Opera House were put out of bounds to troops at the beginning of July and the paper which reported that said: an army clerk had died; that 12 out of 20 Minster choristers were infected; as were eight police officers; that many school children were ill; and that eight schools or departments of schools were closed. (70) Later, visits to the asylum were stopped. (71)

The second flu visitation at the end of the war went on for 14 weeks - from 13 October to 11 January 1919. The *Herald* of 29 October reported 28 deaths from influenza and eleven from pneumonia, bringing a York total of 61 deaths in a period of three weeks. At the end of October all places of amusement in the city were closed (72) and pressure on the staff at the York cemetery was so great that soldiers had to be drafted in to help dig graves. Over the last nine days, the *Herald* reported on 31 October, there had been 110 burials at the cemetery compared with a norm of about 30. Later all visits to the County Hospital were stopped, and all the York schools were closed. In Hungate, that most dreadful of areas, there were three deaths in one family in one week. (73) On 12 November 1918, on the day after the war ended, well over 10,000 people crowded into the Minster to give thanks for the ending of hostilities. They could not have known that the epidemic which was raging round them would, before it was finished, kill more people than had died during the Great War. For York the casualties were tabulated when it was all over - and once more they would not tell the whole story. Members of the armed services stationed in the city who succumbed to the Spanish lady would not be included.

	July epidemic		Autumn epidemic		Totals
	Influenza	Pneumonia	Influenza	Pneumonia	Total
Indoor workers	7	8	120	26	161
Outdoor workers	4	4	21	7	36
No occupation	1	1	3	4	9
School children	4	1	34	11	50
Children under 5	1	2	24	17	44
Totals	17	16	202	65	300

Between the two influenza outbreaks in York, when aliens, 'slackers', and conchies were regularly under attack, largely as a result of the activities of the ex-servicemen's organisations, and on the day which has come to be known as 'the blackest day of the German army' during the war - when the tide of war really turned in favour of the Allies - the *Yorkshire Herald* reported that Percy Rosewarne had been arrested. (75) He was a conscientious objector, and one of the best-known in York's history. What had been happening to the likes of him and to the tribunals since they were last mentioned ?

The story of York's conscientious objectors in the first months of compulsion ended when Andrews Britan was appearing before the tribunals - and before the bar of public opinion, with Edith Milner as one of his rather biased judges. That was in the summer of 1916. How had they fared since then ? How had the tribunals worked since then ?

1. *Herald* 1 November 1918
2. G. Wootan, *The Official History of the British Legion* (1956) p 2
3. For example the Veterans Association, registered under the War Charities Act and dedicated to setting up centres like the Veterans' Club in London (which it also wanted to revitalise). One of its most prominent members was Major Arthur Haggard, brother of Rider Haggard, and in 1917 it was trying to raise a quarter of a million pounds. See eg *Times*, 24 July, 3 September and 19 November 1917. The club had seemingly started sometime around 1911. And see the remark about Hogge's organisation being created out of 100 branches of presumably mostly autonomous groups later.
4. At least by the *Times*. There seems to be no references to it whatsoever from the time of its inception to the end of the war - at least according to *Palmer's Index*
5. It is possible that the York Association was not connected with the national body.
6. *Herald* 4 December 1917
7. *Ibid* 4 February 1918
8. *Times* 30 July 1917
9. *Herald* 26 January 1918. *Press* 26 January 1918. The pub Hogge spoke at was The Windmill
10. See the report of his speech to the City and Westminster branch of his organisation, for example. *Times* 20 November 1917
11. Eg *Ibid* 29 July 1918. The Union being criticised at the time was the ASE
12. Pemberton Billing was an extraordinary man. On him see eg A. Kettle's excellent book *Salome's Last Veil*
13. *Times* 25 March 1918
14. Dr B. Waites dated this from February 1918 and says that the onslaught on the Western Front in March completed it. See his brilliant essay B. Waites 'The Government of the Home Front and the "Moral Economy" of the Working Class' in P.H. Liddle (ed), *Home Fires and Foreign Fields* (1985)
15. See eg *Times* 5 November 1918. This was actually the date of an Appeal Court hearing in the case of Bloom v The National Federation. Bloom was suing it for an unpaid bill of £729.16.
16. Norton Griffith was closely involved in the underground war on the Western Front, and his exploits are mentioned in most of the books on the subject
17. *Times* 24 July 1917. *Herald* 21 July 1917
18. *Times* 23 August 1917
19. *Ibid* 28 and 29 August 1917. Letters
20. *Ibid* 20 March 1918. Letters between Hogge and Sir Edward Wood MP
21. *Ibid* 10 December 1917
22. A post was one of the groups the Comrades organised and it can cause confusion. When the York group was set up it was called by the *Herald* the 'Post Comrades of the Great War'.
23. *Times* 15 May 1918
24. *Herald* 1 July 1918 and 6 July 1918, supplement
25. *Ibid* 27 July 1918, supplement. Bellerby was treasurer; Smith was vice chairman; the secretary was F. George
26. It was at this time that stories of 'The Hidden Hand' and the 'mysteries' of Lord Kitchener's death were being aired. See eg *Ibid* 20 August 1918
27. *Ibid* 30 July 1918
28. *Ibid* 10 August 1918
29. Again there were demands to rename Hungate and, this time, Bismarck Street. See eg *Ibid* 2 August 1918
30. *Press* 1 December 1917

31. Its deliberations are reported in *Ibid* 30 November 1918 and *Gazette* and *Herald* of similar dates
32. This was Dr Ram Chundr Dutt Sabris, the temporary TB officer. The holder of that office had joined up. Dr Bell Ferguson had wanted to join the RAMC and the York City Council had objected (for what seems to be very good reasons). They were criticised for their action in *The Hospital* and eventually, as is obvious, relented. See eg *Herald* 25 January 1916
33. *Gazette* 19 November 1910, *Press* 12 and 14 November 1910
34. *Gazette* 30 November. *Press* 27 November 1912. The early history of the city's attempts to eradicate consumption are dealt with fairly extensively in the *First Annual Report of the Tuberculosis Officer. For the Year 1913* (York 1914)
35. *Gazette* 7 September 1912. *Press* 3 September 1912
36. *Press* 13, 14 and 15 June 1911
37. See eg the report of the annual general meeting in *Gazette* 6 May 1916
38. A great deal was said at the conference at which Garland spoke about the cost to Friendly Societies of TB patients among their members
39. There is a long report on it in the *York Corporation Minutes* 1913-14 pp 1041 and 1105-1113
40. *York Corporation Minutes* 1914-15 page 283
41. *York Corporation Minutes* 1915-16 page 332. Report that the East Riding had an option to purchase Raywell up to six months after the ending of hostilities
42. *York Corporation Minutes* 1914-15 p 978
43. *Press* 4 December 1917, 1 February 1918. *Herald* 18 March 1918 for the meeting at which the NFD and S supported the project, though by then it had been turned down. It also objected to the practice whereby servicemen with TB had to sign an agreement on entering Yearsley which released the Corporation from any responsibility for any other disease they might contract there.
44. *Gazette* 8 December 1917. *Press* 6 December 1917
45. *Gazette* 12 and 26 January 1918
46. *York Corporation Minutes* 1917-18 p 378. *Gazette* 23 February, 13 April 1918
47. *Press* 7 May 1918
48. *Ibid* 4 June 1918
49. *Herald* 3 August 1918. Half the cost was to be met by the Local Government Board and permission was given to the authority to purchase an extra 30 acres of land
50. *Ibid* 6 November 1918. On the opening see eg *Gazette* 5 June 1920
51. It is in the *Medical Officer of Health's report for 1904*
52. *Herald* 15 October 1917
53. *Medical Officer of Health's Report for 1917* (York 1918) *Herald* 8 June 1917. There was also passed (on 24 May 1917) the Venereal Disease Act of 1917, 7 and 8 Geo 5, chap 21. This was intended to ensure that treatment was only given by 'duly qualified persons', and it prohibited the advertising of 'remedies' which had been so common hitherto. The Act did not prohibit the sale over the counter of such concoctions, however.
54. *Medical Officer of Health's Report for 1918* (York 1919)
55. *Herald* 6 May 1918
56. These were attacked (through the government minister J.I. Macpherson particularly) by, among others, Lady Frances Balfour. See eg *Herald* 15 March 1918
57. *Medical Officer of Health's Report of 1917 op.cit.*
58. *Medical Officer of Health's Report of 1918 op.cit.* Its first annual meeting was held at the Tempest Anderson Hall in May
59. *Herald* 22 October 1918. Alice and Frances were done for running a brothel. They were either not very well paid for their services or were bad managers it seems. They were both fined £5, with a month in default. They went to gaol.
60. *The Vote* 11 May 1917
61. Eg *Herald* 28 November 12917
62. *Ibid* 24 July 1917. Brieux's play (with the same title) was made into a film which was released in 1919. Gifford *op.cit.* entry 06806 describes it thus: 'DRAMA Quack doctor "cures" victim of venereal disease, whose baby is later infected.'
63. Eg *Herald* 19 March 1918. 'Damaged Goods' was played throughout the world. The Hollywood star Joan Bennett made her stage debut in a production of it directed by her father in Chicago.
64. *Ibid* 24 November 1917

65. *Ibid* 29 November 1917. See also letter in *Ibid* 1 December 1917
66. On the epidemic in general see eg R. Collier, *The Plague of the Spanish Lady* (1974)
67. *Medical Officer of Health's Report for 1918 op.cit.*
68. *Herald* 11 July 1918. Four hundred other ranks and 8 officers were in the party and all of them were given copies of T.P. Cooper's guide to the Guildhall, the Corporation's guide to the city, and a post card 'showing some interesting bits of old York'.
69. *Ibid* 2 July 1918
70. *Ibid* 3 July 1918
71. *Ibid* 8 July 1918
72. *Ibid* 31 October 1918
73. *Ibid* 25 October 1918
74. A frequent misquotation from Von Ludendorff referring to 8 August 1918. Ludendorff actually said 'August 8th was the black day of the German Army', but he is frequently misquoted, as above. See *My War Memories 1914-1918 By General Ludendorff* (nd) Vol 2 p. 679
75. *Herald* 8 August 1918

CHAPTER 18

THE TRIBUNALS 1916-1918

Discussions about the tribunals set up to administer the Military Service Acts frequently tend, understandably, to centre around the way they dealt with the conscientious objectors to military service. This is understandable. Frequently when dealing with the conchies the tribunals showed themselves at their worst, bullying men, questioning their motives unreasonably, insulting them, and mocking them. But dealing with the objectors on conscientious grounds only formed a small, though annoying and newsworthy, part of their work. Most of the tribunals' customers were employers seeking exemption for an employee on various grounds, individuals asking for exemption on the grounds of hardship of various kinds, or parents saying their son was needed at home to support them and maybe their small business. People like that. How did the York tribunal deal with them ? By the standards of some other places, it would seem, reasonably well, and this may well have been because its membership was remarkably varied, with Quakers, Liberals and labour members sitting alongside such diehards as Rhodes Brown. There was some bullying, some has been mentioned, but by mid-summer 1916 the tribunal had settled down and was doing its work reasonably well, though occasionally rattled by the likes of Britan and others who will be mentioned. Then there were regrettable outbursts from 'the bench', but nothing like what had gone before, and nothing to compare with the occasion on the South Yorkshire Appeal Tribunal when the Earl of Wharncliffe, the chairman, went over the top and told one applicant for exemption on conscientious grounds 'Your appeal is disallowed. You are an absolute fraud' and another 'Your claim is disallowed. You are a regular, contemptible shirker, nothing else.' (1)

As a correspondent to the York papers who has been quoted said, it took a great deal of courage to appear before a tribunal as a conchy and, although some of those who did may well have been shirkers, as the Earl of Wharncliffe thought some were, the majority surely were not - and many of them had shown their courage in working as FAU personnel in the battle areas. The majority of shirkers had to be found not among the conchies, but among those who tried it on, who appeared before the likes of Rhodes Brown saying it was essential they stayed behind, and the vast majority of whom failed it must be said. Perhaps the workload of the tribunal in York can best be demonstrated by looking at its first two meetings in the second half of 1916. Its work was fairly typical, though the number of Derby ('attested') men it had before it would decline. The applications again tell much incidentally about the state of York's trade and, later on, much indeed about the desperate manpower shortage being experienced by the forces.

On 4 July 1916 the York tribunal sat and split into two courts as it usually did, the first under the chairmanship of C.W. Shipley, the labour Sheriff, the second under W.F.H. Thomson. Court one heard applications about 20 men. (2) The first was on behalf of a 31 year old single man who worked for a wholesale fruit merchant - the only employee left out of four. His claim was refused and his application was followed by another on behalf of five navvies. They worked for a sand and gravel contractor who contended they were indispensable. The firm, it was said, provided 1,000 tons of sand and gravel a week for admiralty and military purposes, and it had a Ministry of Munitions certificate, though no war service badges had yet been issued for its workers - in spite of numerous applications for them having been made. Only last week, tribunal members were told, the firm had supplied 1,093 tons of sand to douse a pit fire in Yorkshire, and before the war it had employed 24 men, but was now down to a dozen - with five youths having been substituted for horse drivers who were incapable of doing the heavy work the applicants did. The case was adjourned, and considered again in August when all the men were given conditional exemption from military service. (3) The condition, of course, was that they remained in their present work.

The foreman of the bottling plant at the Tadcaster Tower Brewery applied to the Military Service Tribunal for the exemption of the one man who remained out of the nine employed there before the war. The likes of Harry McGinty might have considered brewing and bottling as work of national importance, but it was unlikely, surely, that many tribunals would have agreed. The foreman did the best he could, and told the hearing that of the eight men who had joined up, two had been killed, and that one of them had been his son. His man simply had his call up deferred to 6 September. The landlady of a pub must have been a supreme optimist. She followed the Tadcaster foreman asking for her nephew, her barman, to be exempted to pull pints for the likes of the aforementioned Harry McGinty. He was deferred only to 6 August as was a coalman, who had only one eye and had been passed as fit for home service. (Applicants for exemption had to arrange to be medically examined before they appeared before the tribunal, a fact that was well publicised.) (4) The coalie's boss was adamant when questioned by the Military Representative, that heaving coal was not to everyone's liking, a contention that looks to be beyond dispute.

> Major Herbert: You have had men come to you for work, were they not suitable ?
> Appellant: I had one discharged soldier come to me, but he had a collar on, and was not at all suitable for the work. Men will not do work of this kind unless they are brought up to it.

A furniture remover appeared to plead for four of his skilled packers on 4 July, maintaining that they were indispensable to his business, and the result of his application might well have been something of a surprise to him. One of his packers was deferred to the same day as the one eyed coalie, a second to 20 August, and the remaining pair were given conditional exemptions. It could well be that some of York's populace thought that a removals man should not have been exempted. Three motor enginers who were employed exclusively on work for the Royal Naval Air Service, were also given conditional exemptions.

The first applicant to apply for exemption for himself on 4 July 1916 was a junior partner in a firm of seed merchants. He revealed that the other junior partner was involved in Red Cross work in Italy, and that the seniors were elderly. He contended that the work he was doing was of national importance and got conditional exemption. His business manager was not so lucky. He was deferred until 6 September, while a dealer in Irish cattle got conditional exemption. He attended five markets a week, it was said, and disposed of 250 cattle a week. Three of his brothers who had been drovers were serving in France it was revealed, and another was in the army stationed in Britain. The last firm to apply in Court One that day was represented by Norman Crombie, who did a great deal of work before the tribunals. He represented the firm of Messrs Oppenheim (sausage skin manufacturers) who wanted exemption for a gut cleaner. He did work that could not be done by a woman, Crombie said, anticipating an inevitable question from the bench, and scotched another (to no effect) by saying that the firm's branch in York would close if the gut cleaner was enlisted and that

> Messrs. Oppenheim were an American firm in 'which there was neither enemy blood or enemy money.'
> Major Herbert said he did not think Mr. Crombie would have appeared had this not been the case.
> Mr. Crombie replied that he would not.
> The application was refused.

What happened to Messrs Oppenheim's sausage skin making operation in York when their one remaining gut cleaner went is unknown, but Crombie, who had done much work in the field of licensing, it will be recalled, represented a firm of brewers in the second court on 4 July. Then he asked for exemption for their managing clerk, a traveller, and a foreman. Which brewery this was was not revealed, but Crombie said that in normal times it employed 20 men and boys and now had eleven male workers and eight females. The clerk was given conditional exemption, presumably on the grounds of indispensability, the foreman got deferred to 6 September, and the traveller's application was turned down flat. Crombie's next 'case' was representing 'the only comb manufacturer in the North of England' who 'conducted a special trade in tortoise shell combs and other varieties for large retail firms in London.' The manufacturer applied on behalf of a worker whose job description makes one wonder why he was not anxious to join up! (It would be interesting to know how many applications for exemption were made to the tribunals against the wishes of their workers. One can envisage a scenario in which a man was held back, against his own desires, then had to suffer from the slings and arrows of the white feather merchants and other ill-disposed persons.) The York man, it was said, was engaged in polishing the combs under cold water

> - warm water could not be used - and women could not constitutionally undertake the work, which was of a most technical character, different pressure being required in the polishing of the various qualities of the combs. In cold weather it was very arduous working in the cold water.

The comb-maker was refused conditional exemption and was deferred only to 1 November. A grocer then applied on behalf of a coffee roaster, saying it was dangerous work, unsuitable for women, and a job which needed some three to four months training. He got one month's exemption, a little less than a coat maker who was ordered to join up on 1 October. His boss, a tailor, told tribunal members that he had five city councillors among his customers, a piece of information which one would have thought of no consequence or even damaging to his cause. He, too, anticipated an inevitable question. That one about employing women instead of his man of military age. Women could not make coats, the tailor said, in what looks like a rather sweeping generalisation

> ... they could only make vests.
> The Military Representative: That must only apply to York, because in other places trousers are made by women.
> Applicant: Well, I am a high class tailor.

The York tribunal split into two as a general rule, but the full bench usually heard the applications from those troublesome people, the conscientious objectors. There were four on 4 July and the first was aged 25, had two brothers in the army, and worked for a large tailoring firm. He applied for exemption on the grounds of financial hardship and conscience. He was a member of the Church of England, he said, and thought war was contrary to the teachings of Christ. His application was refused and he was followed by a clerk in the Educational Department of the City Council. He had appeared before the tribunal earlier and had been exempted from combat service. He had refused that award and appealed for total exemption at the North Riding Appeal Tribunal. This had been refused and he went back to the York body asking to be allowed to go before the Pelham Committee to be given work of national importance. He achieved a hat trick when he was refused permission.

The third conchy dealt with by the full York tribunal submitted written replies to the questions the government said should concern tribunals. (They had issued leaflets incorporating them.) This man was a signwriter whose appeal was on the grounds of financial hardship and conscience. He was not a member of any religious body, he said, but he had religious objections to war. The 'taking of human life damned a man's soul for eternity', he said. He was given exemption from combatant service conditional upon him joining the RAMC. The fourth applicant appeared on crutches and objected on physical and conscientious grounds to military service. He was given absolute exemption. (5) Somewhat later the members of the York tribunal objected to the cavalier way they said the medical examinations for recruits were often carried out. No wonder.

A week later (11 July 1916) the York tribunal met again, and once more heard a mixture of what look like genuine and not so genuine applications for exemption. (6) Court One dealt, first, with J. Hutchinson, the secretary of the York Trades Council who represented 8,000 workers and was a member of the York Munitions court and the Court of Referees appointed under the National Insurance Act. Hutchinson applied for, and got, conditional exemption on the grounds that he was indispensable. Leethams then made an unusual application on behalf of a clerk who was also a conscientious objector, and one who had already appeared before a neighbouring tribunal and had not got what he wanted. The applicant was an 'absolutist', one who would accept nothing short of total exemption and moreover he had been a member of the Society of Friends since well before the war. Leethams, however, applied on his behalf, on the grounds that he was indispensable - and they laced up their comments with a liberal dash of anti-alien feeling.

> The baking trade had been monopolised to a great extent in London by the Germans, and the difficulty was to keep out the Germans who were behind the scenes in the businesses at present. The man applied for was a Quaker of ten years' standing, and held very extreme views. He would be a nuisance in the Army. He had applied for exemption but had been ordered by the Flaxton Rural tribunal to take up non-combatant service.

That the Leethams clerk would have been a nuisance in the army seems a certainty, but the York tribunal refused his employer's request and he was exempted 'till August 6th, this to be final.' Presumably this meant that he became liable to non combatant service that day, the Flaxton decision, and maybe an appeal decision, standing. The application must have been a very unusual one.

The case of a general secretary of a friendly society with about 30 members was adjourned, then a York doctor applied for an exemption for his chauffeur, a man five feet tall and weighing less than eight stones. He had to be satisfied with a month's deferment, and quite right too, then a fish and poultry dealer submitted a claim on behalf of a manager. He said that every man employed by him in four of his shops had enlisted, and that he had had to close two in Scarborough and Malton. In his York establishment, pre-war, he had employed five men, four of whom had joined up. He now employed women, girls and boys, and one wonders why he had not done this elsewhere. His application was unsuccessful and his man was simply deferred to 6 October, while the Medical Superintendent of Bootham Park Hospital had no more luck with one of his workers. This was a 25 year old attendant, who was let off military service only until early September.

An application was heard on 11 July 1916 from an insurance company which is of some interest. The company had had a pre-war staff of 15, it was revealed, of whom eleven had joined up, and another was about to go. The company had not appealed for any of these to be exempted and its policy then was to appeal only for branch managers, and they were successful at York. It was revealed that one person the company had let go was a man of 63 who was then serving as a colour sergeant in York.

A conscientious objector who was the manager of an upholstery business asked for total, but was given conditional exemption, and a warehouse assistant who worked for a firm of retailing and manufacturing chemists was also refused total exemption. He could well have gone on to be one of the great trouble makers in the army. The grounds on which he made his appeal were not reported, however, but those of a labourer in the York Cooperative Society's bakery were. He asked for total exemption and pointed out that he had been a member of the Thirsk Peace Society as long ago as 1905. He was given conditional exemption. Court One's list was completed on 11 July by the case of a NER station clerk. He had appeared before the tribunal before and had been given non combatant service, had appealed and had had his appeal dismissed. He now asked for a revision of his case on the grounds that 'fresh circumstances' had arisen, the Pelham Committee had been formed, and he asked for his case to go before it - saying that he would accept work of national importance. His application was refused and he became liable to non combatant service.

The second court on 11 July heard only two cases - one from 'a firm of confectioners', which was press shorthand for Rowntree and Company. It appealed on behalf of a 30 year old who was said to have been an amalgam of railway clerk, cashier and traffic clerk 'supervising the whole of the foreign trade.' He was given conditional exemption and recommended - told - to join the local Volunteer Training Corps, the 1914-1918 Home Guard. Towards the end of the year the York tribunal became concerned about people to whom they had given such instructions. In November the Town Clerk reported that of a total of 62 men who had been given conditional exemption and told to join the VTC, only 27 had done so. (7)

The final application of 11 July was presented by Dr Smith, the York Medical Officer for Health and he represented yet another time expired soldier who (understandably) was not too keen on going back to war. Smith appealed for exemption on behalf of an assistant sanitary inspector who, he said, 'had been discharged from the Territorial Force, having completed his time of service in France in the present war.' That he had done this means that the man had volunteered for overseas service, as recruitment to the TA was for home service only. Back in York he had commenced working for Smith in February and the MOH drew attention to the vital nature of the man's work, now that gross overcrowding was prevalent everywhere. 'War conditions', Smith said, 'necessitated a most vigilant surveillance on sanitary conditions in the city, especially in connection with the food supply and the diminished housing accommodation.' The case was adjourned *sine die* and the man left to do his work for the Corporation. In November Norman Crombie represented a canteen manager for a firm of army contractors who was, like Smith's man, an ex-serviceman. This person had been in the Boer War, and in the Battle of the Aisne, his solicitor revealed. He had been discharged and was then, presumably, one of those the authorities had decided to have a second look at.

Those two days (4 and 11 July 1916) are fairly typical of the work that the York tribunal did in its first year of existence. It is a great shame that its records no longer exist, but what can one say about it from what reports remain ? Some of its decisions, like those of modern day magistrates, look inconsistent, from the short press reports there are of them. The two packers for the furniture remover, who got conditional exemption, seem to have been rather lucky for example. But almost certainly the court was persuaded here by arguments that the firm would go out of existence without them - as it have every right to be. In cases like this tribunal members were certainly influenced by whether they thought the applicants could be replaced by women, and, if they could, exemption was seemingly refused. The number of men who objected on both conscientious and other grounds looks rather high and perhaps at this remove of time rather misguided. The number of employers who applied giving their workers' conscientious beliefs as a reason for exemption also looks rather high, and again perhaps misguided. It seems at least a possibility that tribunals would have been more sympathetic to a man who put his own case for conscientious objection than to one who let his employer do it. Rowntree and Company frequently appeared in this role. Some of those who were not well disposed to the company - and there were many in York - frequently alleged that it colluded with men to get them off military service. Appearing in this way would not have dispelled that impression in the eyes of the cynical.

What of the men who objected on conscientious grounds ? Did most of them get what they wanted ? Again it is impossible, from what reports remain, to sift out bogus claimants from genuine ones, but in York it does seem that men with conscientious objections were treated fairly liberally, at least after the first hectic months of the tribunal's existence. As has been mentioned above there were four applicants in this category on 4 July 1916; two were refused, one got conditional exemption and a third (the one on crutches) got absolute exemption. A week later two applicants (one a Quaker) had their applications turned down. In August Eustace Charles Henry Westley a 36 year old gardener who had given that up to work for Rowntree and Company, was turned down. (8) He was a member of the NCF, and perhaps his switching of jobs told against him. On the same day Westley appeared in York so did Tom Hayes of Heworth, an ILP member, whose objections to war service would almost certainly have been political. Tom was given exemption conditional upon him taking up work of national importance. Objectors on political grounds (like Arthur Hatfield earlier) frequently got short shift from tribunals. Perhaps the treatment of Tom Hayes is an indication that York's tribunal was not as harsh as many. Percy William Gill, a botanist, was another conchy who appeared that day. His case was adjourned, but A.H. Raine, the secretary of the Old Priory Adult School, a graduate of Leeds University and a trained chemist, got exemption conditional upon him taking up work of national importance. Francis Howard Knight, assistant headmaster at Bootham School from 1903, but then headmaster of Stranongate School, Kendal, a Quaker, was given conditional exemption. It was usual to give members of the Society of Friends exemption, though it was often made conditional, as was the case with F.H. Knight, but not always. In July (9) John Alexander Dow and Brian Sparkes, both masters at Bootham School were given conditional exemption, but then Arthur Rowntree appeared on behalf of two others - a classics master and a physics teacher. Both were turned down. (10)

As 1916 went on the work of the York tribunal did not diminish, and the number of what look like total try ons did not diminish either. On one day in August Norman Crombie appeared on behalf of a hotel proprietor on domestic and business grounds. He was a 35 year old, with the gout, who had nevertheless been called up for garrison duty. Crombie's second client was the son of an antique dealer who was said to have been indispensable to his father's business, and also that day a cinema manager appealed on the grounds of indispensability, which really does look like a bit much. (11) A little later the manager of the Theatre Royal applied for a 37 year old scene builder (12) and B.S. Rowntree appealed on behalf of his gardener, surely an indiscreet move. (13) On the same day as the Theatre Royal applied for exemption for the scene builder the York Opera House did so on behalf of its 35 year old electrician and stage manager. He was another of those soldiers who had not signed on again when his contract of service expired. The tribunal were told that he had spent seven years in the army and five in the reserve; that he had been called up; sent to France; and discharged in February 1916.

The military authorities, as will have become obvious, could take cases back to the tribunals on a number of grounds, and it happened frequently in York. O.G. Willey, a lecturer at the Educational Settlement and the Swarthmore Settlement at Leeds, for example, had earlier appeared and been given conditional exemption to carry out his teaching. He has been mentioned before. In November 1916 the military representative at York asked for Willey's certificate to be reviewed, contending that the kind of work he was doing had (in someone else's case) not been regarded as of national importance by the Pelham Committee. The application from the military representative was turned down. (14) This could, presumably, have lead to all kinds of complications, but Willey thereafter seems to have been left alone. (The authorities may have thought that two similar decisions by the York bench strengthened his case more than somewhat.) Something similar happened to a 'metal machinist and slotter' on the NER of 33 years of age. The railway company was largely on its honour as far as the tribunals were concerned in the York area, it seems, and if they categorised a man as 'indispensable' exemption followed almost as a matter of course. This man had been taken off the indispensable list; the military authorities had been notified; and an application was made to the tribunal to have his certificate withdrawn. (15) It was, and the power that this procedure gave to the management will be immediately obvious. The record of NER management was that of a harsh employer, and there was at least one case in York in 1916 which suggests that it used the threat of military service to get rid of a troublesome worker.

In September 1916 the military representative at the York tribunal applied for an NER railwayman's certificate of exemption to be withdrawn on the grounds that he was now no longer indispensable - that he was 'on the "spare list" of the company.' The man was represented by a solicitor who refrained from saying outright that his client was being victimised, but revealed that he had been 'something of a thorn in the side of the North Eastern Company.' (16) He had worked for the NER for 15 years, and for the last five had been on the North Eastern's Conciliation Board. He had seen the manager of the NER, A.K. Butterworth, and had requested him to come and give evidence. That powerful personage did not turn up, however, but a company solicitor revealed that it was indeed NER policy to notify the military if and when a worker was put on the spare list. The rulleyman's own lawyer also pointed out that the company would not release the man so that he could move to another protected occupation. The case was adjourned and was heard again in November. Then the 34 year old single man's certificate was duly cancelled. (17)

On another occasion the military representative asked the York tribunal to review the case of a coal merchant's son, claiming that he was no longer in a certified occupation. He had been granted conditional exemption before, presumably, and tribunal members were told that he carried coal from the barges - much of York's coal still came up the river - delivered it, looked after the firm's horses and kept the books. The business employed three men, it was said, but there ought to have been eight, and the father spent most of his time on or with the barges. The military's application was refused, and no one could ever have accused the York tribunal of simply carrying out the army's wishes. On this occasion 'Councillor Wilkinson said they must not "jigger up" the retail coal trade in York.'

The York tribunal usually began its sittings with a business session and on 1 August 1916 Major Herbert announced that things were to be tightened up. He had reviewed official instructions, Herbert said, (18)

> to do everything he could to secure men immediately for the Army, and to use his utmost endeavours and every argument to prevent conditional or temporary exemptions being granted to men under the age of 30. With reference to agriculturists, it might in a few cases be wise to suggest temporary exemption till October 1st, but this should be final. It was recognised [that] ... serious difficulties would have to be encountered, but they wanted the men now, and every man who was now even temporarily exempted was a very serious loss to the nation. Major Herbert added: "If we are to win we must have the men immediately."

A little later, in September, it was announced that all cases of exemption granted to men who were single, resident in York and aged under 30, were to be reviewed 'by a specially constituted committee'.(19)

Major Herbert in his statement above, recognised that agriculture might be, perhaps should be, regarded as a special case, but in November another of the military representatives had criticisms of the agricultural community. (20) It was in many cases, he said, paying wages of about 2s.6d. a day that were insufficient 'to encourage labourers to come forward and offer their services.' What did he mean by this rather puzzling statement? Perhaps he meant that the wages were so low that farmers could not get replacement workers, and that this would strengthen a claim for conditional exemption on behalf of their men! If this is so, and it seems to be the only logical explanation of the remark above, it shows that employers here were working (or trying to work) the system to their advantage.

As the year drew to a close, it was decided that apprenticeships did not automatically entitle a person to exemption, (21) and the York tribunal became highly critical of, first local medical boards, then the Pelham Committee. No wonder. The man who attended the tribunal on crutches has been mentioned. In September a man appeared at York who was a 27 year old cycle mechanic who worked for the Army Ordnance Corps. He appealed against military service on medical grounds and revealed that he had chronic neurasthenia and suffered from fits, sometimes three times a day. He had two brothers who had both been discharged from the army in a similar state, and he had been rejected by a medical board, but then re-examined and passed fit for general service on 1 August! He was exempted on medical grounds. (22) On another occasion W. Shilleto of the National Union of General Workers appeared on behalf of a man who could never have been accused of being a shirker, yet whom the state seemed to be mocking. He had been in the Army Service Corps and had been discharged with heart trouble. He then joined the Life Guards and was thrown out after only two days. He tried to attest under the Derby scheme, but was rejected, then, at the beginning of November, was called for a medical and passed fit for general service! At the time of his appeal he was at home, in bed, with appendicitis. (23) Sometime before this, and on a day when 70 cases were to be heard in York, the case of an ex NER fireman was brought up. He had been ill since 1914, and had had five serious operations, the last in early 1916. After that he had been sent home as incurable, and, of course, he was unable to work. Despite this he had been called for an army medical, and had been passed as fit for garrison duty abroad. This was referred to by C. Boyce, one of the labour members of the York tribunal, as a scandal. He entered a protest against 'the capricious nature of [the] medical examinations of late'. They had had before them, recently, he said, a lunatic who suffered from St Vitus dance, who could scarcely walk into the room, and men who fell down in fits in the street five or six times a week, all of whom had been passed for general service.' (24) There is a slight air of unreality about this protest, however, as Boyce should have known. Although men were still being passed who were not fit, a Central Medical Board had been set up by the end of September 'for the purpose of considering the cases of applicants in which the local Tribunal are dissatisfied with the decisions given by the local Medical Board.' (25) This clearly did not lessen the enormity of errors the examiners sometimes made, but it did give the tribunals a means of exposing them. Travelling expenses and subsistence payments were available for the men to be re-examined.

The York tribunal protested formally about the passing of men who were clearly unfit (and there were many, many more who they never saw who simply enlisted as instructed) and it received a prevaricating reply from a Major General M'Grigor. (26) The tribunal also made its feelings known on other matters during 1916. In October, for example, it publicly criticised the Pelham Committee for getting one conscientious objector work of national importance as a helper at the London YMCA where he got ten shillings a week, full board, and a khaki uniform. On the same day it criticised the same commitee for getting another conchy a post as an assistant chemist at Leeds University at a salary of £100 a year. (27) This looks as if it might have been A.H. Raine of the Old Priory Adult School. Somewhat earlier the members of the tribunal had had a row with the military authorities who had, they said, not fulfilled their part of the process laid down by parliament for them. The row revolved around the case of a Dr Coghlan. (28) His case, it seems, had caused great resentment in the city.

Dr Coghlan was in practice with Dr J.P. Wightman in East Mount Road, and he had applied to York for exemption. This had been refused and he had then exercised his right of appeal and gone to the North Riding tribunal where his appeal had been turned down. Some three months elapsed and Coghlan had still not been called up, and this began to agitate members of the York tribunal - and particularly vocal on the matter were two labour members. Coghlan had a certificate saying he was available for service in the RAMC, but 'The Sheriff [Shipley] characterised it as a crying disgrace that Mr. Coghlan, who was a single man should be walking about the city, when all the other doctors who were eligible had been taken. There was a very strong feeling current about it. He was very much in favour of some action being taken at once.' W.H. Farrar agreed. He said there was a feeling in York 'that there were men evading service in spite of the justice of the Tribunal.' He went on to attack the military for not taking Coghlan, who had a reputation as a boxer of some note. 'The best way to bring the military authorities to their senses', Farrar went on, 'was to adjourn the tribunal until they got the man into the army.' Tribunal members decided to write to the military representative with their complaints. (29)

It looks as if the York tribunal was set for a confrontation with the army authorities, but the situation did not develop. Whether or not action had been prompted by the protests of Shipley or Farrar, is unknown, but only two days after they had been made, Wightman wrote to the *Press* about his partner. Coghlan had been awaiting orders from the Central Medical War Committee, he said, and they had arrived. Coghlan was to report for military service on 29 August. (30) In the following year a not dissimilar dispute was to result in the York tribunal going on strike.

Towards the end of 1916 a well-known York personality appeared before the tribunals and the courts as a conscientious objector of 'absolutist' beliefs. This was James Wardropper of New Earswick, someone who was prominent in the activities of both the Labour party (31) and the ILP. Wardropper, who had a BSc degree, often lectured for the ILP (32) and in August he had taken part in that press controversy when Arthur C. Taylor demanded that the city council should stop the ILP's Sunday meetings in Exhibition Square where its 'pernicious views' were aired with impunity. Weak-minded people, Taylor said, needed to be protected against 'purblind pacifists' like Wardropper, (33) whose case would have been going through the system then. Wardropper, an ex York Rugby Club player, worked for Rowntree and Company, and had applied for exemption before the York tribunal. This had been refused and his appeal had been turned down. Wardropper had ignored his call up and in October was arrested and taken before the magistrates of the Bulmer East Petty Sessions. He was fined £2 and handed over to the army as an absentee. (34) Before being sent off Wardropper had addressed the court and used what looked like unanswerable arguments. He said that no-one, at either the York or the Appeal tribunal had ever questioned his sincerity, yet he got nowhere. He was reported as saying that

> I went before the local tribunal and the Appeal tribunal and asked for absolute exemption on conscientious grounds, and according to the Military Service Act if the Tribunals were convinced of the sincerity of the man they ought to grant absolute exemption if nothing less would meet the case. I asked both Tribunols [sic] if they had any doubts as to the sincerity of the views I hold but there was no denial and I claim that I am entitled to absolute exemption under the Military Service Act.

There were many others like Wardropper who ignored the findings of the tribunals - some had appealed, some had not. Frederick Charles Watkinson was perhaps not typical, but ended up the same way as did Wardropper. (35) He was a shoemaker's apprentice, a conchy, who had been given absolute exemption by the York tribunal. The military authorities had appealed against this decision and Watkinson had then been ordered to undertake non-combatant service. He ignored his call up, was arrested as an absentee, fined £2 and duly handed over. Leonard Heaton, a 20 year old of Lower Darnborough Street, another conscientious objector, should have reported for non-combatant military service on 24 May. He did not do so, and in July he was duly arrested, taken before the beaks, and handed over. George Broadley, a 25 year old tailor, of 41 Russell Street, had been before two tribunals and refused to join up. He was fined £2 and handed over to the army in August, (36) and William Varley of New Earswick, an employee of De Little and Fenwick appeared in the same court as Wardropper. He had been given non-combatant service and had not answered the draft. Fairly frequently objectors who had been given conditional exemption were arrested for not conforming with those conditions, and sometimes they, too, were handed over to the military authorities. This happened to William Fox, 31, a confectioner of 28, St Olave's Road. Fox had been given exemption on the condition that he took up work of national importance, and he had simply not done so. He was arrested and handed over in the same way that Broadley and Wardropper were. (37)

No court is complete without its members of the awkward squad, and the York tribunal had its share of bother with a client in 1916. He was a bolshy chimney sweep who appeared for the second time in August. (38) He breezed into the court and 'explained that he had nothing to say himself, but had rather come to hear "what you chaps have to say." He had no objection to serving his King and country, but ... Had they satisfied themselves that he was beyond 41 years of age? That was what he wanted to know.' The Sheriff pointed out that they had had difficulty in tracing his birth, to which he replied that that was because they 'had not gone properly about their business, for he had distinctly informed them that he was baptised at the Church of St. Denys', while they had gone searching in the records of St Margarets. His case was adjourned for him to discover proof of his age. 'It is for you to satisfy us as to your age, not for us to accommodate you', said Shipley. (39) 'We are going to adjourn this case for a fortnight, and in the meantime we shall expect you to find out how old you really are.' What happened to him then is not known, but his attitude suggests that he really knew he was above military age. (As was James Melrose, a 'genial York veteran' Justice of the Peace in the *Herald's* words, who got his calling up papers in May 1917 when he was 89! His worship said that, unlike the chimney sweep - seemingly - he was 'ready to report for service when his group is called up.')

Throughout 1917, as the need for servicemen got greater and greater, the government continued to 'comb out' men by reclassifying many groups and occupations, and adding to the workload of the tribunals as the military authorities applied for the withdrawal of the certificates which had certainly led to many men thinking they were safe. On 9 January, for example, the York tribunal received a letter from R. Newbald Kay, the chairman of the local advisory committee about changes as far as apprentices were concerned, an issue raised in 1916, (40) and a couple of weeks later the situation regarding some apprentices was clarified in a letter which a later generation might have said created something like a Catch 22 situation. Employers, like parents with under-age soldier sons, (41) could claim their apprentices back if they were still under 21 and they would be released. But, if the lad had not told the authorities he was an apprentice when he joined up, and it is almost a certainty that most would not have done this, then he had committed an offence and could be charged. In this situation, it was said, 'The effect of the cancellation of an apprentice's attestation' would make him 'liable under the Military Service Acts.' (42) A short while after this was made clear it was declared that all teachers who were exempt and in medical category A would become liable to call up, as would men in category B1 who were under the age of 31. (43) A little earlier the tribunals had been told to take part in the big 'comb out' and use their powers more stringently. 'Tribunals must not on the grounds of "national interest" exempt' men who are 'fit and under 31' beyond the end of January, it was decreed, 'unless they clearly come within certain specified exceptions.' Not only that but they were told they must 'not be less strict' with older men, and it was stated that as a general rule the government considered that men were more useful in the services than at home it said. The *Press* summed up. (44)The instructions are interpreted as equivalent, it said

> to an order that all conditional exemptions shall be revised as quickly as possible. Military representatives will be busy forthwith in giving notice to terminate the exemptions, and when the conditionally exempted man comes up the tribunal will have no alternative but to send him to the colours.

The military authorities had asked for certificates to be reviewed in 1916, when they took local initiatives, but in 1917 men appeared before the York tribunal as a result of the government's new instructions. In February, for example, the certificates of three employees at the Gas Company were reviewed. (45) Two of these were fitters and, as always, the employers gave evidence of the numbers of their men who had already gone. (One department which had employed 94 men in pre war days now employed 35; in 1914 there had been 38 fitters, and now there were only 17.) All to no avail, however, as the men were ordered to join up. On the same day, at the same tribunal, J.B. Morrell appeared on behalf of Rowntree and Company to plead for 23 men whose exemptions the military was challenging, while a lorry driver employed by a York alderman had his certificate withdrawn. It was revealed that he had already been in the army and had been discharged with rheumatic fever. A little earlier a tramway motorman and an agricultural implement iron moulder had had their certificates withdrawn, (46) and in the summer the York Council's Tramway and Electricity Committee found that the certificates of 20 of its employees were reconsidered. A half of the men were called up, (47) as were 13 out of 22 of Leetham's employees in July. (48) In September the York tribunal heard that before the war the York Cooperative Society employed 193 men of military age and then had 87. The military wanted the certificates taken away from 22 of those remaining. (49)

As 1917 went on the need for more and more men increased, as has been said. Early in the year the call up age was dropped to 18 and in November the military representative announced to the York tribunal that all men in medical grade C were then needed. (50) Before this, however, discharged men had been called back for medical re-examinatons under the Review of Exemptions Act and the medical examiners were often doing their jobs as badly as they had in 1916 when Boyce criticised them publicly. Many of the men re-examined, of course, appeared before the tribunal seeking exemption on medical grounds. One, a 'caramel roller' of 32 years of age who had been passed B2 told York members that 'he had scarcely "any inside left at all"' and was dyspeptic as well. How had to got through his medical? He said the doctors had simply measured him, which seems a bit much even given the dire straits the country was in in 1917. (51) Another man of 35, a baker with three children, had been passed for general service by the military doctor, though private medics said he had pulmonary tuberculosis. (52) At the end of the year new instructions were issued regarding medicals and an appeal procedure set up whereby the victims of some of the travesties the tribunals heard about could challenge their gradings. This came after a much publicised sitting of a Select Committee before which people like Surgeon General Hathaway, the ex Deputy Director of Medical Services, Western Command, gave evidence. A letter describing his experiences was read to the committee from a doctor who had served on the Liverpool medical board, and much was heard about dreadful incidents like that involving a shoemaker who had been drafted into the Army 'who could not put on his puttees because he had to wear leg-irons.' (53) This man, presumably, had simply gone through his sham of an examination, got his calling up papers and reported. He had not gone to a tribunal, as he had every right. The Liverpool doctor's letter showed how the shoemaker could have been treated.

> We examined in all just over 750 cases, and the other three doctors did not get to know the result of any case. I made it my business to find out by asking certain men to show their cards before they left the premises.
>
> I collected 100 results and analysed them. One man who served in the Boer War, and since had suffered delusions and depression, and has twice been in an asylum, was, after bringing a certificate from the asylum, put in Class B1.
>
> Two cases of epilepsy, in one of which I assisted in the production of the history sheet showing he had previously been rejected for epilepsy, were both accepted.
>
> A member of the Select Committee said he had another case which

is verified by an alderman of Colwyn Bay. Two civilian doctors put a man into Class C, and then a military doctor put him in Class A. His heart was so weak that after the least exercise he was of no use. Then there appear to have been epileptics in the Oswestry labour camp. Men were apparently transferred from C2 or C3 to B1 after a week. One man with a double rupture lay dead in hospital within three weeks of being recruited.

The stupidity of some of the medical examinations and re-examinations annoyed members of the York tribunal, and so did a number of other things. Rhodes Brown objected to the fact that the York tribunal had refused exemption to a local Cooperative Society manager, but that he had not been called up for military service, but sent to work for Raimes, a local wholesale chemists. (54) This led to numerous allegations about men 'being able to escape military service behind the back' of the York local tribunal at a specially convened meeting to discuss the matter. (55) There Farrar told his colleagues that a councillor's son was still walking the streets of York, though refused exemption, and they decided to report matters to the War Office. But how could this happen? In the case of the councillor's son he had probably had his application for exemption turned down but given a deferment, and had then applied to Newbald Kay's advisory committee, which had extended it - something it could do, without notifying or getting the approval of the tribunal. The Lord Mayor and his colleagues in York were appalled that such things could happen, and they won their 'case' with the military authorities. From that time onwards, the military representative told that special meeting, he would not consent to the recommendations of the advisory committee, but would send them before the tribunal.

The case of the councillor's son annoyed York tribunal members, but this was nothing compared with their anger at the doings of Colonel Meysey-Thompson of Nunthorpe Court - he who, it will be recalled, had written to the papers suggesting that conscientious objectors should be put into the front lines on the Western Front. Meysey-Thompson had, in the words of C.W. Shipley, completely 'flouted' a decision by the York tribunal. How?

Meysey-Thompson employed a cowman called Walter Porter who had been exempted when things were easier, but had then been caught up in the comb out of early 1917. He had had his certificate of exemption withdrawn, and was given a deferment to 20 February. The Colonel had appealed on Porter's behalf; the appeal had failed; and Porter had been ordered to join up on 1 April. But he was still working for Meysey-Thompson in May. What had happened? The Colonel had gone 'behind the back ' of the York tribunal and obtained 'conditional exemption' for his man from the Board of Agriculture and Fisheries 'so long as he remained a cowman'. Was this fair ? It certainly was not according to Shipley, and he was right. Meysey-Thompson had nine beasts, only three of them were in milk, and all the milk this trio produced was used in the Meysey-Thompson household. Not only that. Meysey-Thompson had no arable land whatsoever and so his holding should not have been classified as agricultural, and the Board of Agriculture and Fisheries should therefore not have been able to exempt Porter. Colonel Boothroyd told the York tribunal that he was definitely of the opinion that the Board has exceeded its powers. And there was another thing, too, that the patriotic colonel had done, which certainly suggests his patriotism was of the nimby variety. He had been allowed the services of a soldier he had tried to keep out of the army whose job was simply 'to cultivate' the Meysey-Thompson garden.

The Meysey-Thompson case led to a crisis on the York tribunal. Not long ago, Shipley said, they had sent into the army a man who supplied 200 people with milk, yet here was a person keeping a man at home to supply one family. '... it was monstrous for Colonel Meysey-Thompson to be allowed to keep this man to supply his own family', the Sheriff concluded. What should they do ? The tribunal considered a proposition that they should go on strike until they got satisfaction. The result ? The York tribunal duly went on strike.

The York tribunal's dispute lasted three weeks, during which there was frantic activity. Poor old Porter's case went to the West Riding War Agricultural Committee, which was asked to decide whether he was on work of national importance or not. It seems a perfectly simple question at this remove of time, but the committee members decided it was beyond their powers to make a decision - so the army took an obvious step. They sacrificed Porter, and quite rightly so. Acting on instructions from Northern Command HQ, Boothroyd told Shipley and his colleagues, Porter was sent his draft papers. But what about the man who was doing Meysey-Thompson's garden when he should have been bayonetting sandbags on the Knavesmire prior to bayonetting Germans on the Western Front ? 'The man is there yet' Shipley said on 2 July, (56) and he was right. There followed the kind of hedging that occurs on these occasions, with the officer commanding on the Knavesmire saying that the man did not come from his lot, but from the North Riding Agricultural Company, which had its HQ at Richmond.

The way Meysey-Thompson had flouted the wishes of the tribunals, was also discussed at the North Riding Appeal body, which heard a report of the attitude adopted in York. (57) Vernon Wragge objected to outside bodies having the power to override their decisions, and the military representative said that he thought Porter should be called up. J.F. Glew said 'There is a good deal of dissatisfaction in this matter', and it was revealed that the Board of Agriculture had not notified either the York or the North Riding Appeal tribunal of its decision regarding Porter. Here, as on the York body, the labour representatives were prominent in exposing the Meysey-Thompson 'scandal'.

What happened to Meysey-Thompson's soldier gardener is unknown, but the episode demonstrated one of York's leading and most influential citizens behaving in an appallingly selfish way. Old Joseph Rowntree using petrol for pleasure, and Seebohm Rowntree wanting to keep his gardener out of the forces were bad enough, but this showed a person who wrote hate letters to the papers berating men of conscience for not joining up, deliberately flouting the intention of the state and using his influence to maintain his own standards. There must have been slackers with consciences in easy jobs that were not really as important as their employers said they were, who felt a little easier when they read about the way the Colonel had used his influence for selfish ends.

The Meysey-Thompson case could not have come at a worse time, in fact, because when he was getting Porter off, and getting his garden done by a member of the North Riding Agricultural Company, the York tribunal and huge sections of the community at large, were worried about the effects that the new, more stringent call up could have on one-man businesses. Should a man running a concern on his own be automatically exempted ? Clearly not, as such a blanket decision could lead to all kinds of problems. What then could be done ? What should be done ? Farrar wanted a policy decision. 'The Army's demand for more and more men was so great', he said, 'that he failed to see how the local Tribunal could any longer feel justified in allowing single and other able men between 20 and 30 years of age to remain immune from the exigencies' of military service on 'the ground that they are the sole proprietors or managers of a business, which, without them could have to be closed, while at the same time married men of 35 and 36 years of age, with families of five or six children, were being sent to the Army.' Clearly Farrar did not have too much sympathy with the small businessman and the York Traders' Association tried to come up with a scheme which would be both fair and protect the little trader. But it failed, (57) and the one-man businesses went under. One of the first men of this kind to go, after Farrar's remarks were made, was a saddler in Walmgate, a man of 36. He had once been a soldier but was invalided out in pre-war days. When war broke out he volunteered but was rejected. Now, with medical grades lower, and needs greater, he was needed and was called up. His claim for exemption was rejected, and his business, it was said, would have to close. (58)

Late on in 1917 an editorial in the *Yorkshire Evening Press* said that York was getting a reputation 'as a seat of pacifism'. (59) This was something of an understatement, because York already had (or at least should have had) a considerable reputation in that respect. The *Press* was alarmed about the number of public meetings being held 'at which statements are made' which it would not be 'permissible for a newspaper to publish.' These were meetings usually held by the ILP and the UDC which had increased in importance and credibility since events in Russia had proved that many of their contentions (about secret diplomacy for example) were correct. The *Press* was also angered, however, at the leniency it said was shown to some absolutists who appeared before the city magistrates. George Broadley, for example.

George Broadley was a 26 year old tailor of Russell Street, York, who had been rejected as medically unfit on 3 August 1916. He was called for re-examination under the Review of Exemptions Act, did not comply with his instructions, and was called up on 15 September 1917. Broadley had had claims for exemption on conscientious grounds turned down by both the York tribunal and the Appeal tribunal, and was posted as an absentee when he did not report for service on the 5th. He was taken before the York magistrates where Robert Kay, not for the first time, expressed sympathy with one of his customers.

The *Herald* and the *Press* were furious with Kay, perhaps more than they might have been because similar expressions of sympathy for an objector had been made by two other members of the York bench less than a fortnight earlier. Then Charles Whettan Whitfield aged 38, of Spen Lane, had been arrested and charged in court as an absentee. Whitfield was an absolutist who contended that he had a right to exemption. He had appeared before the York tribunal asking for exemption on grounds of conscience, but this had been refused and he had been offered farm work instead. His appeal failed and he refused to work on the land, saying that he regarded his work at the Cocoa Factory as 'of sufficient national importance to warrant him' remaining there. On 8 September he was arrested and taken before the magistrates where he heard words of considerable sympathy from the chairman J.W. Proctor. 'I am myself a conscientious objector in so far as the logical aspect of taking part in military service is concerned, whether it is combatant or non-combatant' Procter said. However, he went on, whatever his personal feelings were, he and his colleague had to carry out the provisions of the law. Here he was mistaken. His colleague that day was J.H. Hartley, and he refused to take any part in the proceedings. Proctor was unwilling to override Hartley and the case was adjourned for two more 'sympathetic' magistrates to be found. (60) Once more one is forced to wonder at the stupid arrangement whereby benches consisting of only two magistrates met to deliberate on contentious issues in those days. Whitfield appeared again the following day, and was duly handed over.

On the second occasion Whitfield appeared in court as an absentee it was revealed that his first claim for exemption from military service had been on business grounds - that he was on work of national importance or that he was indispensable to his firm (Rowntree and Company). That claim had been withdrawn and Whitfield had only then claimed on grounds of conscience. If that was done at his instigation, it was to his credit, but many objectors, as has already been mentioned, applied on dual grounds, or substituted 'conscience' when 'business' failed. One cannot help thinking that this was a strange, not say somewhat hypocritical way of carrying on. If objections to war were held which were a matter of conscience, then they, surely, should have been the main, perhaps the sole grounds for a claim. Submitting conscience as a second string to an appeal, or substituting it for another which had failed, might have caused even the very well-disposed to wonder about the applicant's motives. Nevertheless even when this was done tribunals frequently granted exemption, if not the total exemption that was asked for. They did this in Whitfield's case, of course, but he, as an absolutist, was not satisfied with anything short of absolutism.

People like Kay, Proctor and Hartley, of course, were concerned that genuine pacifists (of whom they considered Broadley and Whitfield to be two) were being denied their rights as prescribed by statute. Another who had certainly had his rights denied was Arthur Hatfield, the socialist member of the ILP, who reappeared in York in 1917. He has been mentioned before.

Arthur Hatfield was arrested on 1 July 1916, the day of the commencement of the Battle of the Somme. He was taken to Richmond where he was sentenced to four months in Durham gaol, 'but during that time his case was taken before the Central tribunal' where he was 'adjudged to be a genuine conscientious objector' and put on work of national importance. Arthur worked at Warwick, then Weston super Mare, then Hull, then was given his discharge from the Army - 'being handed over to the civil authorities to work under the Home Office committee.' He said he had heard nothing more, then was arrested and charged with being an absentee from the forces. (61)

Hatfield reappeared in court where he was described as being in No 4 Northern Company of the Non Combatant Corps. A Captain Groves said that he had indeed been transferred from the Non-Combatant Corps to 'the Army Reserve (Class W) to do work of national importance under the Home Office', but that he remained liable to recall at any time. He was duly recalled because he had broken the conditions under which he was released. This was only to be expected of Arthur, but Robert Kay wanted to know what the conditions of his release were that had been broken. This seems very reasonable, but Groves was unable to say, and a week later Arthur was handed back to the military authorities. (62)

Arthur Hatfield was recognised as a genuine conscientious objector, yet was another man who was refused the absolute exemption which he surely deserved. In his case, once again, it is a little puzzling to realise that he was prepared to compromise with authority - to accept work of national importance, in his case. One would have thought that Arthur, of all the York conchies, would have been resolute in his determination to demand his rights and refuse any compromise - as others did. No doubt he had his reasons, and perhaps his refusal to cooperate while on the Home Office scheme was the result of a realisation that he had to some extent sold out, and was an attempt (a successful attempt) to get back into the only logical position for one such as he to occupy. Anyway Arthur survived the war and returned to York to play a notable part in local politics in the inter-war years. (63) One who paid a far greater penalty for his beliefs was Alfred Martlew. (64)

Alfred Martlew, who was 24 years of age when he died in July 1917, had worked as a clerk for Rowntree and Company. He had applied to the local tribunal for exemption on the grounds of conscience, but had been 'awarded' non combatant service instead. He was an absolutist and resolutely refused to obey orders and was eventually one of a number of conchies who were ordered to France where, they were told, refusal to obey orders rendered them liable to the death pealty, as indeed it did. An early historian of the 1916-18 'peace' movement (65) presented this as a deliberate attempt by the military authorities to first of all defy the politicians, and secondly to obtain some victims 'for the sake of example.' (66) If it was that it nearly worked and some men including Martlew, were court martialled and sentenced to death. His award was commuted to ten years penal servitude and he was sent back to England where he served some time in Winchester Gaol and some in Wormwood Scrubs. While at the latter he went before the Central tribunal where, like Arthur Hatfield, he was adjudged to be a genuine conscientious objector and 'The Tribunal ordered him to take up work under the Home Office scheme.' Whether he first agreed, and so compromised himself is unknown, and whether doing so played on his mind and finally unhinged him is not clear, but he went back to York where he told Frank North that the Home Office had broken pledges to him. He had gone missing then made his way to his home town. (67) 'He ... had come to York', he told North, 'for the purpose of giving himself up to the police authorities in order to serve the remainder of his sentence rather than trust the Home Office.' What he meant by this is unclear, but the remark would seem to add to the foregoing contention that he felt he had shown weakness when compromising with the authorities. He went missing again, and on Wednesday 11 July 1917 his body was found in the river at Bishopthorpe. It was taken to the Woodman Inn and at the ensuing inquest it was said that it had been in the river about ten days. Annie Leeman, Martlew's fiancee, with whom he had been keeping company for some five years, gave evidence that showed he was in a disturbed state . The verdict was 'Found

Drowned'. (68)

Martlew and Arthur Hatfield were not the only York objectors from the early days of conscription to reappear in the city in 1917. One of the Couplands made some appearances (69) and so did Herbert Toes (sometimes rendered Tose). His case is of interest in that it had an unusual feature. Toes was 21 in 1917, and was one of the first of the York conchies. He had gone before the York tribunal in March 1916 and later before the Appeal tribunal, and both had refused to give him exemption on the grounds of 'insufficient evidence concerning the genuineness of [his] conscientious objection.' He had ignored his call up papers, and was arrested in August 1916. The military authorities then agreed to a rehearing of Toes' case and he was re-examined and was 'totally rejected' medically. Toes went back to work for the Post Office and sometime in the early summer of 1917 his employers put him on the 'spare list'. He was then recalled for a medical re-examination under the Review of Exemptions Act and was reclassified B2. In July Toes' case appeared before the North Riding Appeal tribunal sitting at York, and there he was represented by the first lady to appear before one of the local bodies. She was Mrs Horner Thompson of Acomb, a Quaker, and she made an impassioned plea on behalf of Toes, quoting the opinions of Brigadier General Childs, (70) and telling tribunal members of Toes' connection with one of the city's adult schools. All to no avail. Her client, who refused to join the FAU but said he would accept work from the Pelham Committee, had his appeal dismissed.

Once more Toes is one of those objectors whose attitude it is difficult to assess. He presented himself as an absolutist, even to the extent of refusing to work with the FAU, (71) yet would have taken work from the Pelham Committee! Someone who had rather more convoluted arguments to put before the tribunals was Richard Hawkin, chairman of the Sheffield branch of the No Conscription Fellowship, once 'a prominent participant in' public affairs in York, and the holder of 'advanced Socialist views.' Hawkin had gone to Sheffield where he carried out his trade as a journalist and he told a bench there that he had traced his ancestry back to 1517, when one of his forebears had been made a freeman of York. This was hereditary, Hawkin went on, and one of the advantages was that he, 'as [a] descendant, could not be pressed into the King's service.' Their worships would have none of this. Hawkin had been arrested as an absentee and he was duly fined the usual £2 and handed over for military service. (72) Hawkin's real grounds for claiming exemption would have undoubtedly been political. His work with and for the York ILP will be recalled.

The York tribunal, throughout 1917, had functioned, by the standards of such bodies, humanely and bravely. It had not flinched from a controversy with the military authorities and although its strike was not unique, it was significant. It had shown great concern for many of the claimants who came before it, and it seems to have been generous with many of its deferments. Its dealing with conscientious objectors seems to have been fair, with most of them accepting its decisions. Of course it was no more successful dealing with the determined absolutists than any other body, but it showed great concern for the effects its decisions could have on small businesses and family life. What to do about one man businesses (which it described as a business which would collapse if one man was taken into the services) concerned it early in 1918, as it had in 1917.

The 'fairness' of the York tribunal would seem to have had a great deal to do with the labour members of it. People like Rhodes Brown and Sykes Rymer were still inclined to have a go at the people before them, but W.H. Farrar, Boyce and Shipley were those who took the initiative in criticising the military, over unfair medicals for example, and the selfish, like Meysey-Thompson. They continued to do so in 1918. Why was this? Well, as the years went by, they must have been impressed more and more by the inequality of sacrifice for the war effort, and they grew in confidence and were undoubtedly affected by the revitalisation of the labour movement. They must also have been impressed by the way some of the larger employers (the Post Office and the NER for example) were capable of seemingly using the system that was in existence to get rid of troublesome unionists and politicians like themselves. Cases like that involving James E. Ellis, a conchy Post Office worker and union official for example. On 21 October 1916 he had been given conditional exemption on conscientious grounds - the condition being that he continued to work at the Post Office. Now - at the end of 1917 - he found that there was great pressure on him to leave, the result of a government decision covering such people as him. His case was brought up in the business session which always preceded the hearings at the York tribunal (when there was any business to discuss) by an indignant Farrar who said that 'as a labour representative' he was furious. York's acting Post Master (G.S. Shipley) described what it was all about in a letter read out to members. After 31 December 1917, it had been decided, Post Office employees given conditional exemption on the grounds that they remained with their existing employers, were to receive 'either the actual rate of remuneration drawn by them at the time of exemption ... or the rate which would be paid to a temporary substitute ... which ever is less; and their service will not count for pension increment.' (73)

Cases like that of Ellis raised all kinds of emotive issues like 'should a conchy left at home be allowed to earn more than the boys at the front' and should he be allowed to carry on in his existing job or move to another. It would have seemed eminently sensible from almost any point of view to have left him where he was, but it is a fact that the general practice seems to have been to move them. (74) Most of the Rowntree workers, for example, who got conditional exemption on conscientious grounds, seem to have been ordered to work elsewhere. Farrar, (75) Boyce and Shipley however were always on the *qui vive* for any evidence of victimisation, and there was more than a little of that. It kept tensions high, and was evident in the case of Edward Brown.

Brown was an employee of the North Eastern Railway, a conscientious objector who had presumably been given exemption conditional upon him remaining with the NER. That company had an agreement with the military authorities, it will be recalled, whereby if they could make a man 'spare' they did so, by taking him off their 'indispensable' list. They did this with Brown, in March 1917, and he took his case before the Munro committee on the Release of Railwaymen. This was a body set up after a dispute at Hull, and Brown argued that there were nine men on 'his' list and as he was at the bottom of it he should not go until all the others had been called up. He was represented in York by G.H. Mennell, a solicitor, and a representative of ASLEF, but they got nowhere and it was decided that Brown should go for a soldier. An attempt to re-open the case a short time later failed. (76) Later the National Union of Railwaymen condemned the railway companies for victimising conscientious objectors.

Very early in 1918 the York tribunal addressed itself to the problem of one man businesses again, and it would perhaps be correct to say that the issue became more pressing as the years went by and the age of the draft went up. On 8 January a sub committee was formed and it was decided to hold a public meeting to discuss the issues involved. As a result of it the various trades in the city created committees to help the tribunal by discovering what men of enlistment age could be released. (77) Whether they worked well, and whether the tribunal took much note of them it is difficult to say. In 1918 the press reports of tribunal proceedings came to be very sparse, too sparse in fact to form an opinion beyond that the one man businessman was treated in 1918 more or less in the way he had been treated in 1917, though he may have had just a slightly longer deferment and rather more words of condolence than in the past.

The manpower shortages of 1918, and the fact that the home front had been denuded of men, presented problems in an even more acute form in the later months of the last year of the war. Applicants (employers) were still asked if they could employ women instead of men, and on one occasion an aristocratic lady addressed the York tribunal on precisely that, but there were clearly depleted professions where such instant or near instant substitutions were impossible. This was so with the legal profession, for example, and in April York members were told that henceforth lawyers and solicitors' clerks were to be generally exempted (and figures were given about how the profession had been depleted). (78) On the same day Boothroyd announced that he would engage in yet another 'comb out' and would review the cases of all York men with exemptions who were in the higher medical categories. This led to a discussion about whether the certificates given to conscientious objectors should also be reviewed. W.F.H. Thomson thought they should, but the tribunal decided against such action.

Another adiministrative matter concerned York tribunal members in 1918, and once again Farrar and his labour colleagues were prominent in raising it and pursuing it. As the government moved the goal posts by taking certain jobs out of certified categories, men were being served with 'Decertification orders' which were tantamount to their calling up papers, and errors were being made, it was said. Farrar and his colleagues argued that many men were getting papers that were in fact erroneous, and were simply reporting for service. They went on to demand that with a decertification order should go adequate notice of how to appeal against it, which was before a bench of magistrates. The York tribunal members were opposed to this, saying that appeals should go before them. They enlisted the aid of J.G. Butcher, and in May received an invitation to discuss the matter with Sir Auckland Geddes. (79) 'Reforms' were made, but the York tribunal went on record in July as saying that it was still not satisfied with the arrangements. (80) Farrar repeatedly said that their main concern was to get men for the forces, but here they were acting on behalf of men who they had given exemption to. It did them credit.

Throughout their lives the Military Service tribunals in many places had in reality arrived at some kind of a *modus vivendi* as far as conchies were concerned by the beginning of 1918. The majority of them were prepared to accept conditional exemption, with many staying at their jobs and perhaps the majority of them going off to work elsewhere where they would certainly be less efficient. This seemed to satisfy tribunal members that they were doing their job, and maybe the fact that the alternative work would be less congenial, away from home as often as not, and almost certainly badly paid, invested the 'award' with a punative element which, whether they acknowledged the fact or not, the members found attractive. Anyway, that was what was frequently resorted to. But were there no absolutists in 1918, still unwilling to accept anything other than total exemption ? There were, and one of them has already been mentioned. He was in fact the last man to make the 'pure pacifist stand' in the 1914 war, though his attitudes do not seem to be totally consistent. He was Percy Rosewarne, a 23 year old locomotive fireman.

Percy Rosewarne was a member of the York branch of the No Conscription Fellowship, which was still in existence in 1918, but which, of necessity, kept a low profile. It helped young men prepare their cases for the tribunals, but whether it had any great effect it is almost impossible to say. Undoubtedly its members, or the people it instructed, put their cases better than they might have done, but the workloads of the tribunals were frequently so large, and the time given to individual cases so little, that they went through almost according to a formula. Members would listen carefully to arguments about means and prospects when deciding about a man with a small business or an aged or sick dependent, but with the conchies it was often very different. If you were a Quaker, Wilfrid Crosland said, you usually got exemption almost automatically. (81) If you were a Christadelphian, a Wesleyan or a member of the Church of England the going was much harder, and the prospects of success were slim. No coaching by the NCF could alter this, and there is no reason to believe that York's tribunal was very different in its attitude to religious objectors than any other.

Percy Rosewarne (who was also called Rosewall and Rosewaine by the press) was a member of the Society of Friends after the war, and he may have been when he objected in 1918, but he did so, almost certainly, purely on political grounds. He demanded total exemption, and revealed that he would not work overtime because he refused to be dictated to. He was awarded a certificate of exemption on condition that he undertook work of national importance, presumably away from the NER. This was in March 1918 and Percy told the tribunal that he would not accept its award. He appealed unsuccessfully and in April, when it was revealed that he was an Army Ordnance depôt employee, (82) a job which some may have thought he could not do and square his conscience, it was decided to call him up. In June a formal application was made to cancel Percy's certificate, when again much was made of where he worked. On this occasion the young man did not bother to appear, and eventually his calling up papers went out. These were ignored (of course) and he was arrested. In August he was fined £2 for being an absentee, and handed over to the military authorities. (83)

The newspapers which reported Percy Rosewarne's appearance in court also recorded that the tide of war had changed in the Allies' favour. The Germans were retreating, the *Press* told its readers, and in the not too distant future the retreat would turn into a rout. The war was nearly over.

1. *Herald* 27 May 1918. On tribunals behaving in the way Wharncliffe's did see J.W. Graham, *Conscription and Conscience. A History 1916-1919* (1922)
2. *Herald* 5 July 1916
3. *Ibid* 16 August 1916
4. See eg *Ibid* 29 November 1916
5. Mack *op.cit.* p 167 says that the York tribunal only awarded absolute exemption on 14 occasions, but this looks to be on the low side
6. *Press* 11 July 1916. *Herald* 12 July 1916
7. *Herald* 1 November, 1916
8. *Ibid* 9 August 1916
9. *Press* 25 July 1916. *Herald* 26 July 1916
10. Given a deferment until 6 August

11. *Herald* 2 August 1916. The gouty hotel proprietor was deferred to 6 October; the indispensable antique dealer to 20 September; and the picture house manager to 6 November
12. *Ibid* 23 August 1916
13. *Ibid* 25 July 1916. *Herald* 26 July, 18 October 1916
14. *Ibid* 15 November 1916
15. *Ibid* 29 November 1916
16. *Ibid* 6 September 1916
17. *Ibid* 15 November 1916
18. *Ibid* 2 August 1916
19. *Ibid* 20 September 1916
20. *Ibid* 29 November 1916
21. *Ibid* 20 December 1916
22. *Ibid* 6 September 1916
23. *Ibid* 29 November 1916
24. *Ibid* 18 October 1916
25. *Ibid* 20 September 1916
26. *Ibid* 1 November 1916. M'Grigor pointed out that men's physical states often changed rapidly, inferred that the medical boards were better able to assess what a man's capabilities were, and asked for specific cases to be brought to his attention
27. *Ibid* 18 October 1916
28. *Ibid* 9 August 1916. *Press* 8 August 1916
29. *Press* 8 August 1916. *Herald* 9 August 1916
30. *Press* 10 August 1916
31. This is clear from the Labour party records, not from press reports
32. See eg *Press* 2 September 1916
33. *Ibid* 18 and 21 August 1916
34. *Ibid* 20 October 1916
35. *Ibid* 10 July 1916
36. *Ibid* 2 August 1916
37. *Ibid* 16 February 1917
38. *Ibid* 8 August 1916
39. Shipley had a son (J.W. Shipley) who was a member of the Machine Gun Corps. See note of a letter from him in *Ibid* 5 September 1916. He was wounded in September 1916
40. *Herald* 10 January 1917
41. Parents could claim their under-age children out of the forces, and there were many examples of this happening. Vernon Wakefield's parents did this, and, so did those of a much more famous personage, Victor Silvester. On these two see A.J. Peacock, 'A Rendezvous with Death', *Gun Fire* No 5 (nd) and V. Silvester *Dancing is My Life* (1958)
42. *Press* 23 January 1917
43. *Herald* 20 February 1917
44. *Press* 22 January 1917
45. *Ibid* 20 February 1917
46. *Ibid* 23 January 1917
47. *Ibid* 3 July 1917
48. *Ibid* 24 July 1917
49. *Ibid* 4 September 1917. The tribunal agreed to 21 going
50. *Ibid* 27 November 1917. The lowering of the call up age occurred in January, after when the only exemptions to military service were to be for apprentices 'on urgent war work'. Hitherto youths had had to report on reaching the age of 18, when they were registered and put on the reserve. They could then return to civilian life for seven months or go into the army if special arrangements were made.
51. *Ibid* 20 March 1917
52. *Ibid* 10 May 1917. It was ordered that the man should be seen by the York TB officer, then that he should go to the Central Medical Board
53. *Ibid* 12 July, 1917
54. *Ibid* 3 April 1917
55. *Ibid* 2 May 1917

56. *Ibid* 3 July 1917. There is a 'biography' of Meysey-Thompson in *Yorkshire Who's Who* (1912)
57. *Herald* 8 May 1917
58. *Ibid* 10 May 1917. *Herald* 11 May 1917
59. *Ibid* 26 September 1917. See also the editorial in the *Herald* 27 September 1917
60. *Press* 14 and 15 Septembr 1917
61. *Ibid* 19 March 1917
62. *Ibid* 23 and 30 March 1917
63. He became a prominent member of the York Council eventually
64. No record of Alfred Martlew remains in the 1917 files of the York City coroner. This is strange as those records seem to be complete, and indeed appear to have been unused until consulted by me.
65. Graham *op.cit*.
66. 'For the sake of example' was an expression frequently used to justify capital punishment within the British Army, a controversial issue then and now. On it see, eg, A. Babington, *For the Sake of Example* (1983), and J. Sykes and J. Putkowski, *Shot at Dawn* (1992)
67. At his inquest his address was given as The Lodge, Morton, Gainsborough
68. *Press* 13 July 1917. *Herald* 13 July 1917. *Tribunal* 15 and 29 June, 19 July 1917
69. See eg *Ibid* 23 March 1917
70. This was Wyndham Childs, who wrote a well-known volume of autobiography
71. Though there were arguments for not doing this, used notably by Corder Catchpool. The arguments being that by joining the FAU other men were released for fighting
72. *Press* 23 and 25 June 1917
73. *Ibid* 8 January 1918. *Postal and Telegraph Record* 3 January 1918, quoted *Tribunal* 17 January 1918
74. Graham *op.cit*.
75. The rule with tribunals was that men of military age should not sit on them, for obvious reasons, and when the age went up Farrar fell into this category. He was over 50, and grade 3, and offered to resign, but his resignation was not accepted. See eg *Press* 14 May 1918. The Act increasing the call up age was the Military Service Act (No 2) 1918
76. *Press* 8 and 22 January 1918
77. *Ibid* 22 and 29 Janury 1918
78. *Ibid* 16 April 1918
79. *Ibid* eg 30 April 1918.
80. *Ibid* 31 July 1918
81. On one of his documents in the York NCF archives
82. Presumably he worked for the NER at the depot
83. On the Rosewarne case see, eg *Press* 5 March, 14 May, 11 June and 8 August 1918

ERRATA

Page 196 Oppenheimer should be Oppenheim. Pages 111 and 118 should read W.F.H. Thomson. Last word, page 135, should be Mysto. Broderick, page 139, should be Brodrick.

INDEX

Acomb Working Mens Club 24
Adams Hydraulics 406-7
Adams Lt JB 195
Admiral Hawke, The 367
Adult School Union 61
Agar J 113-14,194,256,262,278
Aged and Poor Peoples Christmas Dinner Fund 60
Ahearne Young 264
Air raid warnings 361-62,428-33
Airey Miss 267-69
Akers CH 189,201,494,496
Albert Inn, The 65
Albion Brewery, The 65
Alden Percy 58
Aldridge Mr, passive resister 112
Alexander Lt. Guy Bedan 316
Alexandra Concert Rooms The 68
Alexandra Hotel, The 138
Allen Edward 129
Allotments 447-48,457,463
Amalgamated Society of Engineers 479,497
Amalgamated Society of Railway Servants 16-17,41,57,78,87-88,125-28,208
Amalgamated Society of Tramway Workers 212
Amery LS 139
Anchor Inn, The 114-15
Anderson Miss Annie MS 41
Anderson GP 14
Anderson George Richard 16
Anderson HF 115
Anderson Thomas 7-10,12,20,29,71,116-17, 160-61,237
Anderson Walter 59
Andrews Mr, solicitor of Doncaster 367
Anfield Alfred 360
Angell Norman 270
Ankers J 33
Appleton H 221
Argles Canon 21-23,32,66,70-71,91, 111,114,155,219,235,253-54, 259,261,273,308,368
Argyle, Duke of 181
Armstrong, Whitworth and Company 346,405-6
Army Temperance Society, The 33
Arnold-Foster HO 139
Ashton Margaret 487
ASLEF, York branch of 345,535
Asquith HH 110,134,142,157,160,167, 177,185,194,214,217,226-27,334,337-39, 341,368,379,422,481
Assinder GF 229
Atha JH 314-15
Atherley John 117
Avery Dan 134
Avison George 427
Avison Sarah Ann 427
Backhouse James 118
Baden Powell Robert 192

Bagenall Mrs 58
Bagshaw H 448
Baker George 95
Bakers, York 353-54
Bakewell John Robert 317-18
Bakewells London Tea and Drapery Stores, Goldthorpe 317-18
Baldock Major General 295
Balfour AJ 4,48-50,61-62,71,84-85,103,107
Banks and Company Ltd 289
Banks Stoker Petty Officer GF 298
Banks W 7,289,471
Barber Mrs 332-33
Barclay Albert George 282,295
Barnes Charles E 399
Barnes MP George 481
Barnett Mr 224
Barnitts of Colliergate 429-30
Barnwell William 212
Barrett George 366
Barrett Samuel 270
Barry Emily Eupotoria 259
Bartley W 357
Basing Colonel Lord 360
Bassett HG 309
Battle of the Somme film, The 439-41
Bay Horse Walmgate, The 65
Bayton Mr 209
Beck Capt 266
Beck Miss, suffragette 226
Beckert August 300
Beckett Corporal Edward Gordon 427
Beehive, The 155-56
Beerhouse Act of 1834 26
Beerhouse Act of 1869 156
Behan Brendan 88
Bell Canon CC 187,191,361
Bell Clive 335
Bell Colin 264
Bell Richard 125-26
Bellerby John 84
Bellerby Nathan 70
Bellerby WJ 496
Beney FT 308,335,379,413-14,450,486
Beney Mrs FT 486
Bennington Miss 152
Benson Coun Charles 260
Benson George 430
Benson John 212
Bentley Ald William 89-90,97,113-14,119
Beresford Lord Charles 1,2
Bermingham J 163-64,198-99,208,213-15
Betchetti T J 234,314-15,366
Betchetti Wilfred 243
Betting Act of 1865 30
Beveridge William Henry 195
Bewicke-Copley Col R 140
Billing Pemberton 495-96
Billington-Greig Mrs Theresa 144
Bilton Robert Cecil 389

540

Birch Frederick William 117
Birch Ald James 7,10,117,164-65,167,245, 255-56
Birch Ald WH 95-96,165,216,245,295,305,404
Birell Augustine 110-11
Biscomb Mr 222
Bisset Joe 264
Black Bull, The 68,92
Black Horse, The 66
Blackburn Clifford 437
Blackburn Inspector 32
Blackburn John 265
Blakey Coun 115
Blakey Walter 389
Bleasdales Ltd 309
Bluebell Fossgate, The 63,65,366
Blundy Messrs 210
Boaler Fred 228
Board of Guardians, York 13,275,297
Boddy Coun W 70,94,96,107,114,156,158,366
Bodgener Robert 416
Bolderson William Frederick 410
Booth James 299
Booth T Allison 196
Bootham Park Hospital 516
Bootham School 389
Boothroyd Col 528,535
Border Ald S 6,113
Bosanquet Helen 121
Boscawen Griffith 105
Bostock Frank C 192
Bottomley Horatio 311,367,495
Bower Miss HM 12
Bowling Green Hotel, The 22
Bowman GH 354
Bowness Annie 471
Boy Scouts movement 192-93,207,303,315
Boyce C 382,467-68,534-35
Boyes E 432
Boyle Peter 222
Bradley Fred 379,393,401-2,407-8,410,412,426
Brain FA 168
Braithwaite Thomas 437-38
Brett Rev Henry 314-15,454
Brewers Arms, The 92
Bricklayers Arms, The 138
Brieux Eugene 504
Briggs George 7
Brighouse Robert 241,243-44
Brightling Rev James 155,254,280
Brinton Police Constable 364
Britan Andrews 399-402,410-11,506
Britannia, The 22
British Tar, The 114-15
British Workers League, York branch of the 475-77
British Workers Union, York branch of the 478-79
Broadhurst Henry 6,29
Broadley George 409-10,523-24,530-31
Brockway Fenner 335
Brodrick William St John 139
Brogden, Sons and Company, Robert 64
Bromley J 257-58

Brook Arthur 433
Brough Henry 303
Broughton Urban H 227-29,279
Brown Arthur 119,122,175,182
Brown Brothers and Taylor Ltd 95
Brown Cow, The 366
Brown Edward 535
Brown George 105
Brown Coun Henry Rhodes 165-66,175, 195,197,215,231-36,245,254,258-60, 262,277,280,283-84,299, 301,305,308,327,361,363,381-82,386,403-4, 412,460, 467,478,480,485-86,495,511,527,534
Brown Mr, Leetham's employee 209
Broxup J 113
Bryce Commission, The 15
Budget Protest League, The 180
Burgess. Procurator Fiscal of Haddington. William Murray 333
Burley Bennett 48
Burnett Sergeant 363
Burritt Joseph 186
Burrow Chief Constable J 23-24,32,92,114, 205-6,240-41,246,273,359-60,363,368-69, 371-72,416,426,428,430,432-35,456-57
Burton Stone Working Mens Club 24-25
Burtt Philip 328
Bury Coun Charles Arthur 260-61,386,467
Bushell and Sons. Messrs H 369-70
Business Government League 367
Bussey Miss Alwyn 141
Butcher JG 4-5,11,25,27,34,49,53,61,67,70, 83-84,98,103,105-7,109, 111,123,132,161-62,179-80,183,185, 187-90,200,224-26,228-29,258, 295-96,308,336,345,459,461,476,479-81, 433-85,536
Butterworth A Kaye 125,198,519
Byett Miss 487
Cabbies, York 57-58
Cadbury Brothers of Birmingham 186-87
Cadbury versus *The Standard* 187
Cadbury William 186
Cammidge FA 89
Campbell Bannerman Sir Henry 4,84,103, 111-12,134
Campbell Inspector, NSPCC 152-53
Campbell J 401
Camps Mr DE, guardian 238
Cantley Rev JB 164,168
Cargill Mrs Winifred 366-67
Carl Rosa Opera Company 421-22
Carlisle Dean of 423
Carpentier Georges 264
Carrall JW 280
Carrett Mrs May 12
Carson Sir Edward 187
Carter Alderman T 205,279,404
Carter Edward Sardison Dashwood 14,22,26,32
Castlegate TB Clinic 275,499
Cattle Timothy 63
Cavalry Barracks, York 290
Cave Sir George 484
Chadwick Edwin 7

541

Cecil Lord Hugh 484
Central Control Board (Liquor Traffic) 366-68
Chalker Adjutant Oliver 224
Chamberlain Austin 484
Chamberlain Joseph 48,80,82-84,161,177
Chamberlain Neville 461
Chapman AC 24-25
Chapman Arthur 163
Chapman CW 24-25
Chapman Emily Beatrice 426
Chapman Gerald 426
Chapman JE 24-25
Chapman Lily 163
Chapman Mrs, shopkeeper 240
Chapman Thomas E 474
Chappelow William 427
Charity Organisation Society, York branch of the 35,41,121
Charlesworth Mrs 346-47
Charrington FN 303
Chester Bishop of 423
Chichester Constable Lt Col Raleigh 332
Child Miss EW 487
Child Messenger Act 26-28,62
Childrens Order of Chivalry, York 42
Childs Brigadier General 533
Chinese Slavery 77-78,105-6
Chrichton Mrs DS 487
Christadelphians 391-92
Christian Social Union, York branch of the 282
Church Club Marygate 62
Church League for Womens Suffrage 270
Churchill Lord Randolph 26,82
Churchill Winston 110,134-35,142,159, 185,195,228-29,438
City Arms, The 65
City Picture Palace 263-64,294
City Picture Palace, York Ltd 263
City Roller Skating Palace 192,221,263
City Roller Skating Palace Ltd 192,221
Clack CW 54,93,144,155
Clarence Working Mens Club 24-25
Clark Mr HA 267-68
Clark TF 307
Clarke G Wilson 211-13
Clarke James Botterill 215-16,223
Clarke Coun John Thomas 117,132,197, 255-56,258,260-61
Clarkson PC 163
Clayton JW 244
Clifford Dr John 53
Clifton bridge, proposed 254,263
Clifton Cycling Club 137
Clifton Methodist Church 194
Close John 86
Close Major 86-87,96,99
Clynes JR 270
Cockerton Judgements, The 62
Cocoa Tree Walmgate, The 62
Coghlan Dr 522
Colley Robert William 302
Collins Gladys Annie 407
Committee for Promoting the Commercial and Industrial Development of York 132

Communal Kitchens 459-60,470
Comrades of the Great War, York branch of the 495-97
Coning Ald 31
Connelly James, prospective Labour candidate 79,81
Convocation of York 422-24
Cook Will Marion 134
Cooke and Sons T 310
Cooper Ernest 30-31
Corelli Marie 473
Cotsworth Mr 127
Cotton Sir Henry JS 81-82
Coultish Ernest 427
Council for the Study of International Relations, York branch of the 327-28
Coupland Frank 409
Coupland Herbert 408-9,411
Coupland Thomas 30
Court of Referees, The 515
Coverdale George 242,244,292
Coverdale and Sons, Chemists, George 292-93, 421,505
Creyke Ralph 5
Crichton Mr 14
Crockatt J 55-56
Crombie Norman T 66,68,91,114,155-56,158, 212,246,265,291,414,513,517-18
Crooks Will 104,108
Crosland R Wilfrid 237,328,380-81,388, 392-93,396,411,537
Cross Keys, The 32
Crossthwaite Ponsonby Moore 167
Crow Charles Frederick 472
Crown Brewery Inn, The 367
Crown and Cushion, The 64,66
Cunningham Thomas 163
Curran Pete 80,104
Cuss Henry Gladin 12
Cutcliffe-Hyne CT 140
D'Abernon Lord 364
Dalby Sarah 364
Dale AP 263
Davies BN Langdon 327
Davies DM 394
Davies Rev JJ 27,67
Davies R Harrogate 381
Davies Samuel Henry 115,117,131,159,168, 175,183-84,206,233-34,236,238, 261-62,336-37,378-81,388,400-1,454-56,498-99
Davis Allen 155
Davison James 230
Dawes Capt 266
Dawnay Lady 144
Dawnay Lord 144
Dawson, British Workers Union Secretary Mr 478
Dawson Rev Provost 15
Day Frank 242
De Bear School 363
Dean Frank 408
Dearlove A 253
Dearlove Arthur 54-55,93,110,112, 144,155,193,337-38,366,379,397,401,411,454
Debenhams store 358

542

Dees Robert O Irwin 291
Deighton Harold 397-99
Denman, MP, RD 327
Deramore Lord 133,140
Derby Lord 331,334,338-39,342,375,377
Derby Scheme 338-43,375,382-83,386
Derwent Lord 45
Despard Mrs Charlotte 144,155,187,312-13
Devonport Lord 458-59,463
Dick,Kerr and Company 181-82
Dickenson G 355
Dickinson Coun D 215
Dickman Miss 268
Dietrich Max. Zeppelin commander 437
Dilke Sir Charles 18
Dixon JW 196
Dixon Willie 422
Dobbie Will 124,128-29,182,200,209,211, 213,215-16,223-24,228-29, 238-39,242,245,262,267-69,273,279-82,304, 306,308,311,344
Dodsworth Benjamin 259-60
Dott WP 432
Douglas Lord Alfred 424
Douglas Wymond Wilfrid Sholto 424
Dow John Alexander 518
Dringhouses Mothers Meeting 432-33
Dringhouses Womens Institute 460
Dugdale Una 142
Dukes Head, The 66
Dunbar Arthur 275
Duncan MP Charles 478
Dunningham Jonathan 360
Duxbury JW 222
Dyson Arthur Scott 399
Dyson Will 158
Eat Less Bread Campaign 458-60
Ebor Floor Mills 209
Ebor Hotel Vaults, The 243
Edgar Albert 282
Edmundson of Thirsk, JW 381
Education Act of 1904, The 82
Education Bill, Augustine Birrell's 110-11
Education Bill of 1902, The 48-53
Education Bill of 1907, The 111-12
Education (Provision of Meals) Act 132
Educational Settlement (see St Marys)
Electric Theatre, York 220,263,294,421,441
Ellis James E 534
Ellis William 360
Ellison Mr Goldthorpe solicitor 318-19
Elmhirst Charles E 132-33,136,139,189,227, 279,298,461-62,480
Emerson G 299
Emerson James 97
Empire The. See Opera House and Empire
Empson Henry W 84
Enfield Police Constable of Doncaster 367
Engine Drivers Rest, The 155-56
Ensor RCK 11,49,112
Evelyn Dr WA 41-42,153,298,421,498
Exhibition Buildings York 300
Exhibition Hall 39-40,134,136
Extensions Order of 1912 277

Faber George Denison 2,4,10-11,25,27,34,49,63, 71,78,83-84,103,105-7, 109,132-33,161-62
Fades John (or Jack) 318
Fairfield House Sanatorium 502
Farnham Judgement, The 65,69-70
Farrar WH 356,382,448,479,522,527, 529,534-36
Fawcett Mrs 356
Fawcett Mrs Millicent 313,413
Federated Builders Labourers Society 17
Fellowship of Reconciliation 379,454,482
Fels Joseph 88
Fenwick John T 119,175
Ferguson Dr Bell 499
Ferguson Sir J 28
Festival Concert Rooms 40,134,136
Feversham Earl of 331,344
Fineson Police Constable TC 456
Fisher HAL 483
Fisher JM 59
Fisher John 129
Fisher Sir John 2
Fielden Mary 188
Fields WC 33
Fleming Canon 135
Flint Glass Makers Union, York branch of the 17
Flynn Peter 241,244
Ford Dr 41
Foster Ald L 30,245
Foster John 63
Foster Lancelot J 306
Foster Thomas 31-32
Fowler James of Bentham 412
Fowler John of Bentham 412
Fowler Stephen of Bentham 412
Fowler WA 168
Fowler William of Bentham 412
Fox Arthur Richmond 129
Fox William 524
Foxley Rev 493
Frankie Louis 246
Frankle Mrs 316
Franks Mrs 267,270
Free Trade Union 180
French Sir John 187,312
Friends Guild of Teachers 380
Friends Social Services Committee 61
Fry of Bristol, Messrs 186
Fryatt Captain 404
Furness Christopher 1
Furness Sir Kit 108
Gainley Alice 434
Garden Gate, The 32,114
Gardener JM 53
Gardiner James M 92
Garland CH 501
Garrowby Hill Climb, The 138
Gascoigne of Malton, Tom 408
Gate Helmsley House TB Scheme 501-2
Geddes Sir Auckland 536
Gedge Rev 434
General Railway Workers Union, The 88,126-27,163
Gent Mr, headmaster 212-13

George Henry 88
George Lloyd 53,71,82,110,126,144,
177-79,185,191,214,217,303,313-14,
338-39,345,364,368,379,461,473,476-77,481,496
Gibb Sir George 87-88
Gibbs and Company motor traders 309,369
Gibbs George 71
Gibbs Coun JE 234,260
Gibson Sir James 217-18
Gilbertson CW 265
Gill Percy William 518
Gill TH 335,451,475,479,482
Gilman FJ 328
Ginnett Fred 192
Girls Friendly Society, York branch of the 35
Gladstone Herbert 110
Gladstone WE 26,61
Glasier Mrs Bruce 80,141
Glasier J Bruce 81
Glass Makers Arms, The 274
Glassworkers and General Labourers Union, York branch of the 17
Glew Coun John Francis 207-8,214-17,223,225,
228-29,236,239,246,253,
255-56,262,264,270,273,278-79,306,
403,412,467-68,498,528
Goldthorpe riots, The 317-19
Goodchild 'Shunter' 198,213
Gorst Sir John 16,48
Grace Capt 242,244
Grainger Charles 268-69
Grand Stand, The 23
Grapes Beer House, The 92
Gray Alderman Edwin 35,65-66,68-90,168,426
Gray Mrs Edwin (Almyra) 35,67,122,141-42,188,225,315,346,456,486-87,503-4
Gray and Dodsworth, solicitors 35
Gray and Sons John 369
Grayson Victor 476
Greaves Rev PH 127
Green Miss, racing cyclist 138
Green Mrs Lycett 347
Green Ald Norman 129,165,182,261,
278,363,409,438
Greenwood Arthur 327
Greenwood Hamar 81-82,103,105-10,123-26,141,159,167-68,180,185,188-90,200-1,481,495
Greenwood William 221
Greer A 60
Gregg Rev 254
Grey Sir Edward 84,187
Griffith DW 315
Griffith Lt Col Sir John Norton 495
Griffiths David, Goldthorpe rioter 318
Grigg John 143,177
Grimthorpe Lord 2
Grove Thomas 391
Groves Capt 531
Groves Wesleyan Chapel 194,314,411-12
Groves Working Mens Club 24
Guest MP Capt 481
Guild of Loyal Women of South Africa 194
Gulland John 137,342
Haggard Rider 61

Haldane RB 84,160
Halèvy E 48
Hall Marshall 28
Hallaways J William 126,128-29,411,448
Halliday GW 245,284,308-9
Hamilton Lord George 2
Hancock Mr, ILP lecturer 413
Hand and Heart, The 66
Hannah Ian 331
Hardacre James 56
Hardgrave Coun Joseph 260,409
Hardie James Keir 18,79-80,108
Harding John Robinson 410
Harewood Earl of 333
Hargrave H 59
Hargrove W 41
Harling Cooper 25
Harrison Alfred 68-69
Harrison T 304,306
Hart Charles 134
Hartley JH 11-12,80,97-98,106,116,123-25,
127-31,165,176-77,181-82,184,
193,195-96,201,209,214-15,223-24,229,
233-40,242,245-46,255-58,261-62, 267,
279-81,283,304-5,311,344,356,
380,451,467,472,475,530,531
Hatch JJ 71
Hatfield Arthur 395-96,407-8,410-13,518,
531-32
Hathaway Surgeon General 526
Haverfield Honourable Evelyn 346
Hawkin Richard 60,80-81,85,533
Hawkins Walter 241,245-46
Hawksby Tom 316
Haxby Road Auxiliary Military Hospital 404
Hayes Harry 63-64
Hayes Tom 518
Headley Mrs 56
Heap John 472
Heard CE 456
Heaton Leonard 523
Hebden PC 32
Helmsley Lord 105
Henderson Arthur 476-78
Henderson James Ritchie 397-99,408,411
Henderson WJ 253
Hepworth Henry, Goldthorpe rioter 318
Herbert Lt 266
Herbert Major 512-13,520
Hewitt AE 306-7
Hewitt of Croydon, Miss Amelia Elizabeth 338
Hewison Rev GH 14
Heys RG 15,55,95,112
Hibbert Coun 130,132,231,234-35,245,254
Higgins Frank 475
Hills Brothers 309
Hills Rodney 130
Hilton John 270
Hind Rev 53,61-62,71,93,155
Hinson Pte Leslie 427
Hippodrome, The 294
Hirst Rev 112
Hobhouse Miss Emily 47-48
Hobson JA 455

Hodge MP John 334
Hodgson Charles T 389
Hodgson Mr 129
Hodgson William 332
Hogge JM 58,88-89,94-95,115,120-21,129, 131,162,164,168,175-77,180-81, 183-84,194-97,199,201,207,209,217-19,222, 226,232,236,258,273,281,311-12,494-96
Hogge Mrs JM 219
Holgate and District Cycling Club 137
Holgate Gardens Estate Society Ltd 259,277
Holgate railway bridge 207
Hollesley Bay 88
Hollowell Rev J Hirst 16,48,53
Holmes EP 188-89,225,285
Holmes George 471
Holmes S 354
Hope Mrs SSFA member 467
Hope Street Adult School 122
Hopkins WHR 93,284
Hora Col Manoel Herrera de 140
Hore Rev ES 270
Horner Thomas 30
Horsley and Sons Ltd, Thomas 421
Horsman Enos Thompson 332
Horsman Will 233-34,238,246,283,311-12, 356,363,413,428,453,467-68,486
Houldsworthy Sir W 28
House Alec W 430
Housing of the Working Classes Acts 35-36,276
Howard J 331
Howard John 239,254
Hubner Jane 472
Hucks BC 265-66
Hudson Charles 63-64
Hudson George, The 'Railway King' 6,9,24, 56,86,193,201,242,257,305
Hudson George 24
Hudson Thomas 32
Hughes Canon 424
Hughes Rev F 68
Hughes Howard 435
Humanitarian League 31
Hummel Abe 136
Humphries Mrs Florence 406
Humphreys Arthur 165
Hungate Mission 120
Hunt HC 329
Hunt JJ 242-43,416
Hunt John J Ltd 23-24,64-65
Hutchinson Charles 253
Hutchinson J Trades Council Secretary 356, 494,515
Hutchison Sergeant A 298
Hutson Mr 176
Hutty Annie Wren, suffragette 338
Hyndman Henry Myers 356
Influenza epidemic 505-6
Inglis Coun JB 122,176,255,258-61,278, 283,363,404,431,501
Ingmanthorpe Hall 2
Innes Edward A Mitchel 485
Iredale Alfred Verrell 260,413
Irish National League Club 24

Isaacs Rufus 187
Ison Thomas, oculist 292
Jackson Christopher Swales 29
Jackson Trooper 140
Jacobs Well 66
Jameson J Gordon 217-18
Jane Fred T 357
Jannings Emil 47
Jarvis Alfred 434
Jarvis Thomas William 282
Jennings Ernest 30
John Bull, The 64
Johnson Jack 264
Johnson Rev R Harrington 333-34
Jones Ald A 113
Jones Coun G Fowler 133
Jones Dr Helena 225-26
Jones Miss Violet Key 225-27,233,242-43, 270,283
Joplin Scott 264
Jordan Joe 134
Jowett Fred 413,453
Joynson-Hicks William 134-35,380
Judson William 399,411-12
Juvenile crime 456-57
Kaiser Mr, watchmaker 393-94,396
Karkeek Wilmot 264
Karno Fred 357
Kay and Backhouse Ltd 370
Kay Robert 14-15,33,65
Kay Robert JP 398,408-9,411,530-31
Kay Robert Newbald 56,92-93,110,115, 155,159,295,337,524,527
Kay WA 328,413
Keighley David 471
Kelly J 128
Kelly Lt, Airman 266
Kemp (or Kempe) Dr Arthur 197,217-18
Kendal Miss May 58
Kennedy Justice 29
Kerr Kenelm 386
Kessack J O'Connor 201
Kilmartin William 275
King Nosmo 34
Kirby C 461
Kitchener Lord 313,315,338-39,368,399,403,438
Kitchener Miss 339-40
Kitching Miss MO 12
Kitching W 316
Knapton and Company 86
Kneeshaw of Birmingham Coun 475
Knewshaw Emma 471
Knight Arthur 31
Knight Francis Howard 518
Knight George 31
Knight RA 129
Knight Reginald 367
Knocker Miss 39
Koch Julius 300,315
Labour Protest Committee 367
Lady Mayoress's Comforts Fund 462
Lamb Albert 79
Lamb James 264
Lambert Canon of Hull 423

Lambert Coun RB 52,119,130,134,158,165-67, 175-76
Lambert TS 270
Langcroft Capt CAH 266
Langham Joseph Arthur 438
Langstaff Walter 241,244
Langwell WW 211-12
Lansbury George 88
Lansdowne Lord 159
Larkin Jim 279
Lasker B 168-69
Lassetter Mrs 317
Lauder Harry 331
Laundry Workers Strike 267-70
Law Bonar 217,337,481,484
Lawrence Mrs Pethick 225
Lawson Arthur 52
Lawson Grant 5,70
Lawson Major General HM 332
Lawson JF 493-94
Lawson Sir John Grant 461
Lawson Lady Wilma 346
Layerthorpe and District Cycling Club 137-38
Layerthorpe Wesley Mission 275
Leadbetter James 389
Leaf John 152-53
League of Honour for Women and Girls of the British Empire 315
League of National Safety, York branch of the 469
Leak and Thorp 363,405
Leake Miss 230
Leason WR 245
Leavis WP 245
Lee Sing 363
Leeds Arms, The 66
Leeman Annie 532
Leeman George 9
Leeman Road Concentration Camp 300,315-16
Leeman Road Working Mens Club 24-25
Leetham Henry Ernest 84,118,302-3
Leetham Ltd Henry 209-11,266,296,435,448,525
Leetham Mrs 12
Leetham Sidney 66,84
Legion of Frontiersmen, York 140-41
Lendal Literary Society 328
Lenton Lilian 283
Leopard Inn, The 92,115
Leven and Melville, Lt The Earl of 298
Levitt Railway Guard 198
Licensing Act 1872 66,72,155
Licensing Act 1902 62-63
Licensing Act 1904 70-72
Licensing Act 1921 25-26
Licensing Bill of 1908 156-59
Licensing Law Compensation for Non-Renewal Bill 67
Light Railway Act of 1896 277
Lighting regulations 359-60,362-64
Lincoln Trebitch 320
Lindenburg Herbert 300
Lindsey John, of Darlington 477
Linnet singing competitions 138-39
Loch Charles 121

Lockwood Frank 1,2
Locomotive Act of 1898 167
Locomotive Inn, The 314
London and York Steamship Company 166
Londonderry Lady 347
Long Dr Sanderson 165,167,175
Long Walter 356,376-77
Lord Nelson, The 139
Lord Walter 85
Louise Princess 181
Lowther William 212
Lucas Coun Clarence Cecil 260,263
Lucas food lecturer, Miss 459
Lumb J 7
Lumley Police Constable 367
Lusitania, The 317,328,393
Luty Frank 40
Lyon Henry 22
Lytellton Mrs Edward 301
MacDonald J Ramsay 80,110,327,481
MacDonald Dr Peter 196-97
Macgregor Prof 328
Machen Arthur 347
Mackarness Archdeacon 423
Mackay Donald S 409
Maclaren Andrew 378
Majuba Hill 4,42
Malins Geoffrey 439-41
Malt Shovel, The 66,302
Manchester, Bishop of 423
Manchester Clinical Hospital for Women and Children 41
Manchester, Dean of 424
Manderfield Joseph Foster 316
Mann Tom 448,479
Mansbridge Albert 137
Mansfield Coun G 124,129,131,196
Marris WM 80,96,108
Martel Mrs, suffragette 142
Martin William 114-15
Martlew Alfred 532-33
Martyn Mrs Edith How 143-44,149,155
Masefield John 401
Mason Rev Joshua 89,91
Mason Police Constable 456
Masons Arms 314
Masterman Lucy 159
Mawson AP 14-15,52,79-80,93,96,120,131,159, 165,197,219,237,259,260,282,299, 308,408,411
May Olive Mabel 151-54
Maypole Stores 469
McClelland Rachel 328-29
McDowell RB 439-41
McGargle Hugh 260
McGinty Harry 63,65-67,72,97,114,512
McGrigor Major General 522
McGough Hugh 480
McKay Ald 278,279
McKenna Reginald 111,355-56
McKinley President W 40
Medical Inspection of Schoolchildren Act 196
Melbourne Terrace Soldiers Club 347
Melrose James 82,364,524
Mennell Brothers, woodturners 370

546

Mennell Coun GH 231,255,261,307-8,535
Mercer Jeannie 467-68,478-79,494
Mercer Coun John Noble 259-60,467-68,476-80
Mercer Capt SM 336
Metcalfe Ald Robert 408
Meyer Sebastian 52,67,95,97,104,120,124, 129,138,175,181,231-32,234-36,308,327, 377,428,468
Meyer Mrs Sebastian 225
Meysey-Thompson Col RF 389,397,453,527-29,534
Micklegate Labour Association 228
Middleton T 331
Miles Harry 115,117-18,159,180,237,253,254
Military Service Acts of 1916 376-77,380-81,413, 422,494
Mills Kerry 134
Milner Edith Harriet 3,12-13,33-34,41-42,49,120-21,132,134,137,140,143-44, 162,167,191,207-8,211,226,270,283,300-2,304,308,310,312,314-16,329-30, 334,346-48,357,359-60,378,380,400-2,413,425,429,431,433-34,437,457,485, 506
Milner Sir Frederick 49-50,312,330,334,496
Milner George Edward, Goldthorpe rioter 318-19
Milner Lord 78,333
Mirrlees William J 201
Mitchell Mr, prospective Labour candidate 79
Money Leo Chiozza 200
Montagu Andrew 2
Moody Andrew 12,16,18,59,71,117
Moore John 282
Moore Tot 223,265
Morant Robert 15
Morel ED 327
Moret Neil 134
Morison-Cumming Rev R 93
Morley William 282
Morrell Coun Cuthbert 258-60,299,408-9
Morrell J Bowes 58,60,71,79,81,122,128,304-7, 336,339-40,342,382,525
Morris Israel 403
Morris Lewis 403
Morris Solomon 403
Morris Coun Tom 234,247,258,278,306
Mosley Capt EN 282
Moss George 10
Mothers Union, York branch of the 35
Mount Hotel, The 23
Munby FJ 29,140
Muncaster House Scheme,The 119-20,122
Municipal Employe's Association 303-4
Municipal School for Girls 162
Murray Alexander 3-6
Murray Hugh 117,119,130
Music Hall Artistes Association 68
Musicians Union, York 197
Myers and Burnett, Davygate 294
Mysto Carl 40,135-36
Naburn Asylum 89
National Amalgamated Sheet Metal Workers and Braziers Society 282
National Amalgamated Society of Operative Housebuilders and Ship Painters 282
National Amalgamated Union of Shop Assistants,Warehousemen and Clerks,
York branch of the 17,309
National Anti-Gambling League 94
National Association of Discharged and Demobilised Sailors and Soldiers, York branch of the 493-94,496
National Association for the Prevention of Consumption 41
National British Womens Temperance Association 347
National Council for Combating Venereal Disease, York branch of 503
National Federation of Discharged Sailors and Soldiers 494-97,501
National Federation of Laundry Associations 267
National Federation of Laundry Workers Associations 267
National Federation of Licence Holders 73
National Federation of Women Workers 267
National Free Labour Association 127-28
National Insurance Act 218,273
National League for Opposing Womens Suffrage 226,485
National Passive Resistance Committee 53
National Right to Work Council, York branch of the 162
National Service campaign 461-62
National Service League, York 139-40,270,333-36,338
National Society for the Prevention of Consumption, York branch of the 498-99
National Union of Bookbinders 479
National Union of Gasworkers and General Labourers, York 209-10,267-68,282,345,450
National Union of Printing and Paperworkers 479
National Union of Railwaymen 355,461,479,535
National Union of Uncertificated Teachers, York branch of the 486-87
National Union of Women Workers, York 36,67,315,346,359,360,486
National Union of Womens Suffrage Societies 34,142
National Union of Womens Suffrage Societies, York branch of the 225
National War Aims Committee 480-81,496
National Womens Social and Political Union, York branch of the 142
National Womens Social and Political Union 142,144
National Workers Sanatoria Association 501
Neave Basil 388-89,392
Neptune, The 66
Nevinson HW 187
New Earswick Village Guild 327
New Hippodrome, The 191
New Inn, Askham Richard, The 297-98
New Street Palace of Varieties, The 191
Newcastle Inn, The 114-15
Newman Sir George 404
Newman Mrs Philip 487
Newsholme Dr 61
Newton Laura 471
Newton Corp W 298
Nicholson Miss Mary 243
Nickalls Brigadier General NT 332
No Conscription Fellowship 378-80,393-

94,396,398,407-8,454
No Treating Order 365-66
Noone Frances 503
Norris Mrs Harold 226
North Eastern Railway Company 41,60-61, 87-88,124-27,163-64,172,197-99,213-15,266, 270,281,296,344,347,353,386,407,425,487, 519-20
North Eastern Railway League of Riflemen 139
North Eastern Railway Temperance Union 33,70
Norton Cecil 18
Nottingham Rev EE 111
Nutbrown Mr JM 39-40,67,125
Oakley Olly 135
Offer Avner 415
Old Age Pensions 18
Old Age Pensions Bill 160-62
Old George Hotel, The 113
Old Number Five, The 155
Oldfield John E 118
Oliver Thomas 22
Oliver Whitby C 235
Opera House and Empire, York 39,134-36, 191,264,293-94,505,519
Operative Bakers Organisation 354
Oppenheim Messrs 196,513
Osborne WV 208
Outhwaite RL 484
Owen Rev EC 111,184
Page Coun William 197,245,255-56,258,260
Palliser C 302
Pallister Mr and Mrs 472
Palmer Sir Charles 140
Palmer Capt Lionel 140
Pankhurst Adela 188,206
Pankhurst Christabel 142
Pankhurst Emmeline 142,242
Pankhurst Sylvia 345,486
Parker John Glasby 116-17
Parker Police Constable 363
Parker RS 331
Parker Rev Stanley 253-54,261,264
Parker Thomas 54,92-93
Passive Resisters Anti-Martyrdom League, The Bradford 93
Pates Rev C 23
Peacock Florence 422
Pearson Miss G 450
Pearson Mrs, imprisoned suffragette 242
Pearson of Lockton, Rev 474
Pearson Ald (Capt) WA 119,123,153-54, 167,306-7
Peat Edwin 363
Peckett Mrs, Linnet singing champ 139
Peel Lord 3
Pegge of Scalby, Margaret A Thompson 473-74
Pendlebury Mrs Mary 503
Penny Rev EC 54
Peoples Budget, The 177,187-88
Perkins Police Constable 434
Peters Joseph 6-7
Petty Elizabeth Richardson 259
Petty Miss, food lecturer 460

Petty Coun R 159,262
Pickard Miss E 413
Picture House, The 370,421,439,441-42
Pierce Beresford 411-12
Piercy Edwin 307
Pinder Coun 130
Pinkney Police Inspector 240
Pitts Alice 503
Plumer Sir H 290,301
Plumer Lt General 266
Pocock Roger 140-41
Pollard FE, of Clifton Dale 378,454,480
Pollard Coun Francis Edward 256,258
Pollard GH Sir 229
Pollard GS 29
Ponsonby AW 327,481,484
Poor Childrens Free Dinner Fund, York 89
Pope-Hennesey Una 329-30,336
Porter Walter 527-29
Poverty, A Study of Town Life 19-21,25-26,39
Powell Thomas 207-08
Powell W 448
Pressly DL 105
Preston, Col D'Arcy B 296
Preston Mrs 192
Preston William 399
Price Crawford 357
Price George 7-8
Primrose League, The Ebor Habitation of the 34
Primrose League, The Milner Habitation of the 12,34,49,137,144,304
Prince of Wales Inn, The 274
Priory Street Socialist and Political Questions Guild 13
Proctor Alfred 9,10
Proctor JW 14,23,530-31
Promenade Working Mens Club 24
Provision of School Meals Act 123
Pub opening times 364
Pugmire of Heywood, Harold 338
Punch Bowl, The 22
Purey Cust Arthur P 91,167,183-84,187,189
Purnell Ald 29,31,207,398
Pyatt Lt IV 437
Queens Head, The 65
Queux William le 294
Raftery Thomas 475,497-98,501
Railway Clerks Association 127,354
Railway Institute, The York 137,327
Railway Womens Guild 327-28
Raimes Chemists 527
Raine AH 518,522
Rainer Miss Amelia 422
Randall Frederick 366,368
Raphael JE 270
Rason Sir Cornthwaite Hector 224-27,229
Restrictions on meals in restaurants 445-46, 460,469
Rationing 463,469-70
Raven Vincent 270,281
Rawdon Canon 192
Rawdon Miss Edith 192
Red Lion, The 65,332-33
Redmond John 226

548

Refreshment Houses Act 1860 26
Reilly Francis 209,211
Reissman Rev AT 53-54,68,92,110,144
Relton Coun Edward 247,259-60,276-77
Reynolds Frank 22
Reynolds W 125
Rhondda Lord 463,469
Ricard Pte Walter 298-99
Richards F, prospective Labour candidate 79
Richardson A 468
Richardson Mrs Emma 193
Richardson Rev GF 347
Richardson GP 211
Richardson Herbert 473
Richardson James 432
Richardson Coun R 96,130,165,210
Rickaby Frank 165
Ridges J Rendel 401
Riley-Smith HH 27-28,66,71,103,133-34, 139,155-59,179-81,185,187-90,200-1,205,224
Ripon Bishop of 66
Ripon Lord 3,40
Ritchie CT 83
Roberts Miss Adeline M 41
Roberts Lord 15,47,139-40,300,377
Robertson Theresa 364
Robinson Charles 241,246
Robinson of Malton, George 408
Robinson Coun W Robie 7,262
Robson William J 30
Roller skating craze, The 191-92,220-22,263
Rose Ellen 431-32
Rose EB 108-9,111,116
Rose Susan 363-64
Rosebery Lord 50,84
Rosewarne Percy 506,536-37
Rountree Canon 423
Rowlands Agnes 367
Rowntree Arnold 3,5,9,13,58-59,61-62, 82,104,107-10,118,175,185,188-90,200,209, 226-27,231,256,320-21,327,329, 336-37,347,377,380,451,459, 461,478, 480,482-84
Rowntree Mrs Arnold 328-29
Rowntree Arthur 518
Rowntree B Seebohm 5,17,19-21,25,57-59, 61,66,94,125,168-69,182,223-24,237, 270,292,379,415-16,423-24,482,519,529
Rowntree Mrs BS 66
Rowntree and Co Ltd 36,59,84,89,94, 128,137,162,186,207,218,238,296,309, 321,368,370,377,383-85,387-88,391,405, 415-16,435,448,459,518,525,530-31
Rowntree Joseph 14,29,50,71,94,103-4, 116,473,482,529
Rowntree Lawrence 329-30,336,388,484
Rowntree Oscar F 94-95,116,131,262, 306-7,336,358,428,448
Rowntree Theodore H 158,233,239, 255,262,404,435,455
Royal Military Hospital, Fulford Road 298
Royal Mr, solicitor 332
RSPCA York 139
Rushworth Case, The 151-54

Rushworth Charles George Golden 151-54
Rushworth Mr 120
Rushworth Sarah Catherine 151-54
Russell Bertrand 455,483
Russell Rev FA 58,71,84
Rutter Bert 190-91,220,222-23,263-65,294, 439-40
Rymer Ald Sir J Sykes 6,90,130-32,175,194, 206-7,211,213,215,232,256,261,277, 279,308,381,389,393,412,434-35,455,534
Rymer Matthew 12
Sabris Dr Ram Chundr Dutt 498
Sadler Dr ME 330-31
Salisbury Lord 11-12,27
Salmet M 266
Salvation Army, York 224
Samuel Herbert 367
Sand catchers, York 210-11
Sanderson Thomas Henry 169
Saxby William 474
Scannon WB 64
Scarborough, shelling of 316
Schloesser HH (also Slesser) 257-58,268,319-20
Schmidt Dr Peter 434-35
School meals 132
Schoolchildren's strike of 1911 212-13
Schumacher Mr 299
Scott Dennis Vivian 217,306-7,381
Scott HV 52,111,302,342,388-89
Scott-Galter Sir AS 90
Screampoke 27,30,62
Scrivener Kate 363-64
Scruton S 304
Scrymgeour Edwin 229
Seddon James 476
Seely Jack 377
Segler Clifford 134
Sellar John 16
Sellers Enid 264
Sessions WH 129,165,177,180,217,262, 306-8,382
Severs Edwin 193
Sexton James 311,334
Shaftoe JA 7,239,245,253-54,261
Shannon John Strangman 197,334
Sharp Elizabeth 259
Sharp Fred 212
Sharp Coun George 167,184,189,232-34
Sharp John William 116-17,125-26,128
Sharpe Benjamin 427
Shaw Rev Patrick 433-34
Shaw Thomas 78
Shaw WH 8-10,12,14,16,20
Shaw William 73
Shepherd Henry 410
Shilleto W 123,268,345,405-7,450,521
Shipley CW 233-34,237,247,336,342, 381,396,414,467,470,488,512,522,524, 527-28,534-35
Shipley GS 534
Shonut Mr of Goldthorpe (sometimes Sconut) 317-19
Sibthorpe Col 28

Sigsworth Professor Eric 276
Simmons Charles James 475
Simon Sir John 187
Simpson of Terrington, Mrs 344
Skeldergate Bridge tolls 278,280
Skeldergate Hall, The 265
Skelton Lydia 259
Slesser HH. See Schloesser
Slip Inn, The 22
Smiles Samuel 31
Smillie Robert 335,479
Smith AC 496
Smith E 10
Smith Mrs Edith 406-7
Smith Dr EM 138,310,384,387,498,502-3,517
Smith G Albert 220
Smith Gunboat 264
Smith Henry Wilkinson Riley 133
Smith Joseph, Goldthorpe rioter 318
Smith Mark Herbert 31
Smith Rev Russell 253-54,258,264
Smith William Henry 224
Smithson of Doncaster, Thomas R 367
Smuts General 496
Snowden Mrs Philip 142
Snowden Philip 79-80
Soldiers and Sailors Canteen, York 347
Soldiers and Sailors Family Association 467
Sorensen Carl Wilfred 471
South Bank District Citizens Association 115,155
South Bank Working Mens Club 23,25
Southgate F 87
Spread Eagle, The 65
Square and Compass, The 66,92
St Clements Temperance Society 70
St Cuthbert's Band of Hope 422
St John Voluntary Aid Association 298
St Johns Ambulance Association 347,462
St Johns College 394-95,438
St Lawrence Working Mens Club 24-25
St Marys Educational Settlement 55,95,184-85, 226,237,270,328-29,380-81,393-94,459, 480,482,488,502
St Peters School 424
Stamp Ralph 364
Stanton MP CB 414
Stark JW 267
Steigmann G 319,329
Stephens Leslie 222
Stokes Robert 242
Storey Lt Bryan Meredith 424
Storey Cuthbert 299
Storey T 159
Stott Mr 113
Spalding Percy J 471
Sparkes Brian 518
Sphagnum Moss Collecting Depôt 462
Streicher Charles Augustus 216
Stuart GH 71,79,81,103,105-9,143,228-29,257
Stuart FD 415
Stuart Mrs KHR 48
Sturge FLP 78,381,454
Suggitt J 30
Summary Jurisdiction Act of 1879 30

Summertime Act of 1915 429
Sunday Trams 194
Swales John Richard 65
Swales Meat Stores 293
Swanson Mary G 259
Swanwick Helen 483
Swarthmore Educational Centre, Leeds 394
Swayne Sir Eric 334
Swetenham Major 299
Sycamore Skating Rink, The 192,221
Tadcaster Tower Brewery Company 65,512
Taff Vale Judgement 18,110,127
Tank Week, The York 477-78
Tanks 441-42
Tapley Mark 401-2
Tariff Reform League 224
Taylor Archie 303
Taylor Arthur C 414,523
Taylor Mrs Denis 35
Taylor MP, Theodore 426
Taylor W 240
TB Dispensary, Yearsley Bridge 498
Tee Charles E 167,184
Temple Jonathan 138
Temple Mary Emma 63
Tennant Henry 2,14-15,33,70-71,82
Tennant Henry, Secretary of State 412,426
Terrett Joe 367
Terry and Co Ltd 36
Terry Sir Joseph 225
Terry Mary Evelina 225
Thaw Case, The Harry 136-37
Theatre Royal York 39-40,133-34,136,283, 293,421,504-5,519
Thirsk Peace Society 516
Thomas JH 126,128
Thomas John 471
Thompson Charles A 110,139,165,168,207, 246,378-80,386,403,480
Thompson Mrs Horner 533
Thompson Joe 264
Thompson John E 29
Thompson Mrs M 412
Thomson WFH 83,111,118,342,381,384,456,512
Thornton, Board of Trade, Miss 345
Thorpe William 280
Three Cups, The 92,115
Till A 472
Till Albert 260
Tillett Ben 104,229,311
Todd WA Forster 8,134,222,242-43,256, 258,336,342,358,381,383-84,387,428-29, 432-33,458-59,467,479,483
Toes Herbert 533
Trades Disputes Bill of 1906 110
Trafalgar Bay, Nunnery Lane.The 64
Tramway Workers Dispute 266
Tramways Act of 1870 96
Tredale Mr 297
Trevelyan CP 483-84
Trevelyan Mrs GM 456
Trinity House Hotel, The 64
Trod Harry Robert 64
Trumpet Inn, The 155-56

Tuberculosis 275-76,421,494,498-503
Tuby Coun G 137
Tudor Rear Admiral FLT 313
Tupper-Carey Canon 346
Tupper-Carey Mrs 315
Turks Head, The 114-15
Turner of Batley, Coun Ben 335
Turner JH 21-23
Turner JM 65
Twyman TA 58-59
Unemployed Workmen Act of 1905 85
Union of Democratic Control 327,378,453-54, 475,481-84
United Kingdom Society of Amalgamated Smiths and Strikers, York branch of the 17
United Labour Committee 18,79
United Suffragists 304
Unwin Mrs Jane Cobden 313
Urban Charles 220
Vaccination Act 1867 28-29
Varey Coun Robert 255,258,260
Varley William 524
Venereal Disease 503-5
Victoria Hall, The 126,134,190-92,220, 263-64,294,439-41,494
Victoria Inn, The 22
Voluntary Aid Detachment, York 347,362,462
Volunteer Training Corps, York 362,517
Waddington and Sons Ltd 369-70
Waddington William Henry 265
Wagoners Special Reserve 294
Wailes-Fairburn WF 296-97
Wake Edgerton 453
Waldron Capt 266
Wales Benjamin Stoker 116,182,242,244
Wales and Son Motor Traders 369
Walker Ald 215,256,279
Walker Alfred 86
Walker Ald Charles 87,455
Walker Messrs JH 210
Walker Joseph 86
Walker Samuel 31
Walker Syd 357
Wallhead RC 228
Walsh James 408,412
Walter Ald CC 113
Walton and Company, Isaac 291-92
Wanted Laundry, The 268
War Emergency Rent Committee 356
War Hospital Depôt, Blossom Street 462
Ward George 245
Ward Mrs 332-33
Wardropper James 413-14,523-24
Ware William 30
Warren Mr 22
Warriner Mr 228
Wasling Frank 244
Waters Ethel 134
Watkinson Frederick Charles 408,410,523
Watkinson SC 402
Watkinson Rev William 454
Watson Canon 111
Watson James 410
Waudby Susan Hannah 427

Weigall MP, Major 363
Wellington Duke of 139
Wellington Inn, The 68,274
Wells Bombardier Billy 264
Wells Justice 29
Welsh, War Pensions Committee Secretary, Miss 498
Wenlock Laundry, The 268
Wenlock Lord 66,78,139
Wesley Mission Mens Class 194
Westcott Bishop 184
Western Counties Electric Railways and Tramways Company 118-19
Westley Eustace Charles Henry 518
Westrope Richard 54-56,58,72,77-78,91,93, 104-7,109,141-42,144,184,226
Wharncliffe, Earl of 511
Wharram Mrs 332-33
Wheatsheaf, The 22
Wheeler Rev W 54
Whitaker Rev A 501
Whitaker Herbert 221
Whitby Strafford B 180
White Horse, The 63
White Stanford 136
Whitehouse MP, Mr 484
Whiteman Dr JP 522
Whitfield Charles Whettan 530-31
Whiting George 66
Whittaker Thomas 67
Whittaker TP 67
Whittaker TT 61
Whittaker William Gray 472
Wickenden FH 319
Wilcock Pte Henry 299
Wilkinson Miss AM 13-15,34
Wilkinson Coun Arthur 207,256,258,260,336
Wilkinson ET 95
Wilkinson Miss ET 34
Wilkinson KET 3,14,23,95-96,104-5,116-17, 130-31,159,177,184,188-89 217,226,230,232-34,236,238,246-47,255, 261,276,278,304,308,327-28,342,381, 394, 411-12,468,520
Wilkinson Mrs KET 225
Wilkinson William 95
Willey OG 379,394,396,519
Williams A 480
Williams Miss Annie 225
Williams Eric, actor 358
Williams JE 335
Wilson F 223
Wilson Florence 472
Wilson J Havelock 476
Wilson John J 378
Wilson Mrs 151-52
Winchester Bishop of 27
Wine and Beerhouses Act 1869 26
Winnifrith Rev DP 380
Winspear Fred 116-17
Winterburn Pte J 299
Wiseman Coun Alfred 260,278
Womens Freedom League 144
Womens Freedom League, York branch of 143

Womens Labour League 378
Womens Local Government Society 313
Womens Relief Corps 346
Womens Social and Political Union, York 225, 242,283
Womens Suffrage Society, York 304,487
Womens Volunteer Reserve, York 346-47
Wood EJ, chemist 293
Wood FD 78,311
Wood Mr, trades unionist 209
Wood Walter 475
Woodall JR 18
Woodcock Dr de Carle 498
Woodcock Edward 422
Woodhouse Florence, of Doncaster 367
Woodward Police Constable, of Doncaster 367
Woolford George 106,158
Workers Educational Association, York 137,488
Workers Suffrage Federation, York branch of 486
Workers Union, York branch of 450
Working Mens Clubs, York 23-25,91,205
Workman Emma 259
Workmens Compensation Act 4
Worsley Sir William 408
Wragge RH Vernon 12,22-24,26,33-34,53,56-57,60,62-64,68-69,72,89-93,98,112-14,117-18, 137,154,165,182,189,229,231,233,235.246, 254-55,258,274-75,277, 279,285,320-21,327,380,392,405,409,412,528
Wrigglesworth W 29
Wright Ginger 27
Wynne AE 221
Yapp Sir Arthur 469
York Adult School Temperance Society 33
York Allotments Association 460
York Amateur Swimming Club and Humane Society 33
York Anti Vivisection Society 155
York Benevolent Society 60
York Board of Guardians 12-13
York Bye Election Peace Committee 5
York charities 278
York Church of England Mens Society 328
York Cinderella Club 42
York Citizens Association for Dealing with the Unemployed 55,58-60
York Citizens Committee 309
York Citizens Council 159
York Citizens League 53
York City Association Football Club 222-23, 265,303,358,463
York City Brass Band Club and Institute 302
York City Hairdressers Association 57
York City Mission 89
York City and Suburban Bicycle Club 138
York Cooperative Society 7,13-14,16,353, 450-51,470,479,516,525,527
York Cooperative Womens Guild 35,328
York Corporation Bill 1914 284-85,310
York Corporation Light Railways Order of 1908 175
York County Hospital 41
York County Hygienic Laundries Limited 267,269

York Diocesan Board of Education 49
York Distress Committee 88-89,119-21, 129,162,164,177,181,195
York and District Anti-conscription Council 380
York and District Band of Hope Union 27,32-33, 95,422
York District Citizens League 67
York District and East Riding Public House Trust 65
York and District Retail Licence Holders Protection Association 302,314,365-66
York Dispensary 41,275
York Emergency Kitchen 89,120
York Engineering Company 59,86,118,300
York Equitable Industrial Society. See York Cooperative Society.
York Evangelical Free Church Council 155
York Extension and Improvement Act 1884 67
York Fabian Society 279,328
York Food Control Committee 459-60,467-73
York Free Church Council 95,158
York Gas Bill 234-37
York Girl Guides 315
York Girls Patriotic Club 346,462
York Glass Company 211-12,219,267
York Grocers Association 355
York Harriers Cycling Club 137-38
York Health and Housing Reform Association 35-36,94,122,168-69,172,180,216, 275,498
York Historic Pageant 181,191
York Horticultural Association 451
York Junior Imperial and Constitutional League 158-59
York Labour Bureau 80-81,85-86
York Labour Exchange 196,224
York Labour Representation Committee 79-81
York Liberal Club 328
York Liberal League 84
York Liberal Unionist Association 82-83
York Licenced Victuallers Association 27,70-73, 94,155,157,201,314,365-66
York Light Railways Order of 1908 277
York Lying-In Society 41
York Master Builders Association 167
York Master Printers 283
York Mens Committee for Womens Suffrage 225
York Miniature Rifle Club 139
York Munitions Bureau 344
York Munitions Committee 345-46
York Munitions Tribunal 406,515
York Mystery Plays 191
York Naval Vegetable Depôt 347
York Off Licence Holders Protection Association 72,113
York Operative Bricklayers Society 17
York Out-Relief Union 188
York Painters Strike of 1911 282
York Parliamentary Bill 18-19
York Passive Resisters League 93
York Pensions Committee 498
York Picture House Limited 265,358
York Ratepayers Association 284
York Recruiting Committee 298,308,331,337
York Relief Committee 308

552

York Right to Work Committee 89
York Roller Skating Pavilion 192
York Roller Skating Rink Company 191,221
York Rugby League Club 223,265
York School Board 13-15,22,27,51-52
York Small Traders Association 253-54,277
York Soup Kitchen 57,89
York Steamship Company, City of 166
York Stranded Soldiers Dormitories 462-63
York Temperance Society 39
York Traders Association 529
York Trades Council 13,16-18,51,123,132, 195,197,328,335,344-45,381,450-51,467, 470,475, 477-78,515
York Tramways Company 96
York Typographical Association 12,479
York Union Workhouse 63
York United Gas Company 219,231,237,355,363
York University Extension Society 137,331
York War Pensions Committee 494
York White Cross Temperance Society 33
York Womens Citizens Association 487-88
York Womens Federation 356
York Womens Liberal Federation 84
York Womens Suffrage Society 55,141,188
York YMCA 270,328,462
Yorkshire Bone Products Company 196
Yorkshire Club 473
Yorkshire Council of Womens Liberal Associations 141
Yorkshire Farm Workers Union 294
Yorkshire Federation of Trades Council 335
Yorkshire Insurance Company 360,393
Yorkshire Laundry 268
Yorkshire Licenced Victuallers Association 27
Yorkshire School for the Blind 421
Young Frederick 118
Young Friends The 454
Younger Sir George 484
Youthful Offenders (Whipping) Bill 31
Zep Alarms 429-430
Zeppelin raids 361-362,424-428